BAYREUTH
African Studies Series

Publisher/Editor

Pia Thielmann & Eckhard Breitinger
Bayreuth University
D 95440 BAYREUTH
Germany / R.F.A.
www.breitinger.org

A catalogue record for this book is available from the British Library.

Bibliographic information published by Die Deutsche Bibliothek

Die Deutschen Bibliothek lists this publication in the Deutsche Nationalbibliografie; detailed bibliographic data is available in the Internet at http://dnb.ddb.de

Price per copy: EUR 29.95 (plus postage)

ISBN 3-927510-83-1
ISSN 0178-0034

Printed by Rosch Buch, D 96110 Scheßlitz

Haike Frank

ROLE-PLAY IN SOUTH AFRICAN THEATRE

Bayreuth African Studies 70

D 25

Dissertation der Philologischen Fakultät
Universität Freiburg

Table of Contents

Acknowledgements

This thesis represents a contribution to the Freiburg University research project "Identities and Alterities" (SFB 541). It was written under the auspices of Prof. Dr. Paul Goetsch to whom I am very grateful for giving me this opportunity and for introducing me to a fascinating chapter of 20th-century theatre. I would like to thank him for his strong support of my ideas and plans and for his continual guidance throughout the course of this large project. My thanks also go to my co-supervisor Prof. Dr. Monika Fludernik for her insightful comments and support.

I would like to thank Prof. Dr. Eckhard Breitinger for editing and publishing this thesis and providing the title photograph as well as for his support throughout the creation process of this dissertation, especially during my stay in South Africa.

I would further like to express my gratitude to several organisations whose financial support strongly facilitated the completion of this project. I worked as a research assistant in the frame of the Freiburg University research project "Identities and Alterities." My studies and research were also supported by a generous grant from the German National Merit Foundation (Studienstiftung des Deutschen Volkes). I spent the academic year 2000/2001 as a visiting graduate student at Indiana University in Bloomington, USA, an exchange organised by Freiburg University's International Office. My thanks go to IU for sponsoring my research and studies with a full-time grant and to the Fulbright Commission for providing me with a travel grant. During my stay at IU I had many fruitful discussions with one of the leading American Fugard scholars, the late Albert Wertheim. I owe him the opportunity to meet Athol Fugard whom I would also like to thank for taking the time to tell me about his plays and his work in the theatre.

During my trip to South Africa in 2001 I met many artists and scholars who readily discussed with me their involvement in South African theatre. My thanks go to Mike van Graan, Sindiwe Magona, Phyllis Klotz and Smal Ndeba for their willingness to talk about their work. I am also grateful to Malcolm Purkey (Witwatersrand University), Temple Hauptfleisch, Johan Esterhuizen (Stellenbosch University) and Ari Sitas (University of Natal). I would like to thank Malcolm Hacksely and his team from the National English Literary Museum at Grahamstown where I did research. I would especially like to thank my friends Jill Gallimore and Mike Nicol for making my stay in South Africa unforgettable. I owe the end version of this thesis to Jill's proof-reading expertise.

A thank you als goes to Geoffrey V. Davis (Technical University of Aachen) for generously lending me his material on South African theatre.

I would like to thank my friends and colleagues whose unexhaustable willingness to discuss my work was a source of motivation: Dorothee Birke, Nicole Cujai, Traute Finn, Greta Olson, Natascha Pesch, Jochen Petzold, Julia Simon, Susanne Wagner, Ulrike Zimmermann. A thank you also goes to Frederick Rose for his support.

A special thanks goes to my parents for supporting me in every way. This work is dedicated to them.

Introduction

MORRIS. [...] what's your job at the gate?

ZACHARIAH [*pause*]. They put me there to chase the black kids away.

[*Morris hesitates.*]

MORRIS. Are you sure we should play this?

ZACHARIAH. It's only a game. Walk past.

MORRIS. Just a game. No harm done.

[*He flourishes his umbrella and then saunters slowly towards Zachariah.*]

Shame! Look at that poor old boy. John? What are you doing...?

ZACHARIAH [*cutting him*]. No, Morrie. [...] They never talk to me, man. Try it again.[1]

In this scene from Athol Fugard's play *The Blood Knot* (1961) the two coloured[2] protagonists, light-skinned Morris and dark-skinned Zachariah, are playing a role game. Although the brothers act in the privacy of their own home and declare their exercise "only a game," the roles they are embodying are not merely based on their imagination but are derived from the social reality of life in apartheid South Africa. Zach wishes to teach Morrie, who wants to pass as a white man in apartheid society, how to 'act white.' Therefore Zach bases his own role in this game on the degrading experience in his daily working life and transforms himself into the black[3] gate keeper of a whites-only park. At the same time he defines his sibling as a white man strolling around the park grounds. Zach coaches Morrie on how to present himself in public so that he is recognised as someone who, according to apartheid ideology, is considered a white 'master.'

In this role game Zach clearly demonstrates that he knows how he is perceived and judged by racist apartheid society. As George Herbert Mead would say, he is able to regard himself with the eyes of the "generalized other" and thus develops an identity based on the social expectations of his environment (cf. 1967: 156). The apartheid state classifies human beings according to racial origin and then uses the

[1] Athol Fugard, *Blood Knot*, 115. This quotation comes from the revised edition (1985).

[2] In the South African context 'coloured' means 'of mixed racial descent.'

[3] In a general sense, the term 'black' comprises all non-white groups in South African society, i.e. 'coloureds,' 'Indians' and 'Africans' (see Chapter 1.1).

criterion 'race' to define and control their social positioning. Zach is aware of what behaviour is expected of him and members of the other racial groups in everyday life. In his case apartheid has reduced him to a black servant who must obey orders and demonstrate a servile attitude towards the white members of society. The problems raised in this example will be expanded upon in the present study.

This study examines anti-apartheid South African plays in English created between 1961 and 1989 which focus on protagonists from different racial groups of society under apartheid. These characters are generally forced to accept state-prescribed role identities and are thus hindered from developing a sense of self-respect and self-worth. According to sociologist Hans-Peter Dreitzel's understanding of role theory, all of these individuals 'suffer' *from* and *in* the social roles they are expected to play in a pathological society that prevents people from constructing healthy role identities (cf. 1980[3]). Several of the selected plays feature one particular character who can be described as having a fairly strong sense of self. This protagonist then acts as a teacher and attempts to influence the other characters in a positive way, allowing others to develop their own identity and thus flout the state-prescribed definition. In several cases the individuals are successful in opposing state ideology and constructing new, positive role identities which assert their humanity and reveal the inhumanity of the state representatives. However, sometimes the characters are defeated by the all-powerful regime and cannot prevent their personality from disintegrating. It is in these instances that the individuals' continued imprisonment in the given role system of the pathological society is especially apparent.

The central ideas of role theory are presented in Chapter 1. This chapter also surveys the major tenets of apartheid ideology and politics as well as important landmarks in the historical development of South Africa under apartheid rule that formed the background of the plays under review. This is supported by an overview of the development of a distinctly 'South African' theatre/performance tradition which emerged during the second half of the twentieth century. This overview is based on Temple Hauptfleisch's model of performance forms created in South Africa by the combination of indigenous, communal, imported and/or Western performance elements or styles (cf. 1997). Hauptfleisch's emphasis on the increasing hybridisation of South African performance genres shows that these new theatrical forms cannot be described using traditional indigenous or Western categories but require a new terminology.

Because culture, including theatre, was considered to be an important element in the political struggle against apartheid, the evolution of theatrical genres is depicted in relation to the political developments in the country. An attempt is made to cover different types of plays from three decades of apartheid rule so that both the development of the representation of life under apartheid as well as the evolving concept of theatre can be illuminated. The plays are discussed as comments on the effects that apartheid had on the social role behaviour of its individuals. This is why the focus lies predominantly on the ideas of role theory and the notion that individual identity is influenced by the social roles people play in daily life.

Critics researching South African theatre have introduced various sets of terms to designate specific new types or genres of regime-critical theatre that developed during apartheid. While Hauptfleisch's model, which has been mentioned above, is based on formal stylistic criteria, by contrast, these other sets of terms are, when seen as a whole, more eclectic. They are neither exclusively derived from the formal, methodological characteristics of the plays nor solely based on the plays' thematic orientation. Instead, they emphasise aspects as different as the plays' intentions, aims or methods, the groups' political opinions and/or 'racial' composition or describe the target audience in 'racial' or social/class terms.[4]

The terms chosen to designate the types of theatre discussed in this study are 'protest theatre,' 'resistance' and 'Black Consciousness theatre,' 'workshop theatre' and 'theatre by women.' Although this combination of terms may appear methodologically eclectic, it is effective because it can be used to describe and reflect the historical evolution of the relationship between theatre and politics/society throughout the whole apartheid era, not just during specific phases of this time (cf. Chapter 1.3.2). In accordance with the sets of terms that have already been suggested by critics, these four categories follow neither formal nor thematic criteria but highlight intentions and aims (protest, resistance, Black

[4] To give some examples, Peter Larlham looks at the plays' political intentions and distinguishes between 'protest theatre' and 'committed theatre' (1987), which resembles the terms 'protest' and 'resistance theatre' used by Zakes Mda (1996; 1998); Kavanagh differentiates between 'town theatre,' 'Black Consciousness theatre' and 'township theatre' (1981: xiv) to describe the popular (black) theatre of the 1970s in geographical, class and political terms; Anne Fuchs prefers terms that reflect the system of racial oppression and suggests 'theatre of the oppressor,' 'theatre of the oppressed' and 'non-racial theatre' (1990). Temple Hauptfleisch and Ian Steadman propose 'Afrikaans theatre,' 'English theatre,' 'Black theatre' and 'Alternative theatre' (racially-mixed), which reflect ethnic and linguistic criteria (1984).

Consciousness) or racial conscience and group composition (Black Consciousness, workshop, women).

The first pair of terms emphasises the intentions of the dramatists and actors, captures the mood of the plays and reveals the tenor of the messages conveyed to the audience: 'protest theatre' and 'resistance theatre' (cf. Mda 1998: 257).[5] 'Protest theatre' refers to the historical groups of anti-apartheid performers who first emerged in the 1960s and 70s. Its aim was to protest against apartheid by voicing "disapproval or disagreement" (*ibid.*) These plays were primarily addressed to the oppressors and appealed to their conscience. They were created by members of both the black and white middle classes and mostly performed in towns and cities. Chapter 2 discusses three plays by Athol Fugard (including *Blood Knot*) which belong to this category of 'protest plays.' The works created by actors John Kani and Winston Ntshona in collaboration with Fugard, which are explored in Chapter 3, appear to fall under the category of 'protest theatre' as well. However, as they also aimed at raising the consciousness of the oppressed and used agitprop techniques common to more radical theatre, they clearly went one step further than Fugard's self-authored plays.

A new form of theatre developed in parallel with the radicalisation of black resistance politics by the Black Consciousness Movement in the 1970s. This militant 'resistance theatre' was based on the ideology of Black Consciousness and was therefore also called the 'theatre of Black Consciousness' (cf. Brink 1997: 168; Kavanagh 1981: xiv; Larlham 1992: 46; Mda 1998: 257; Steadman 1991: 84). In agitprop fashion it aimed to mobilise the oppressed to reflect on and rebel against their oppression. It was created in workshop and performed in various places from funerals to political rallies, from church halls in the townships to multi-racial theatre venues in the cities (cf. Mda 1996: 201f.; 1998: 258). The plays analysed in Chapter 4, such as *Bopha!* by Percy Mtwa, illustrate this development.

---

[5] Mda's distinction between 'protest' plays and 'resistance' plays presented here has, *inter alia*, also been made by Steadman (cf. 1991: 84). Other critics employ these terms more freely. For example, Peter Larlham refers to a single play using the terms "Black Theatre," a play that "conscientise[s] black audiences" and "'protest'" play (cf. 1992). Bhekizizwe Peterson calls all anti-apartheid theatre "theatre of power" (1995: 574). Terminology has also changed during post-apartheid times due to new theatrical developments such as 'community theatre' and 'theatre for development.' See also, for example, Hutchison (1996; 1999), Kruger (1995a) and Steadman (1990a; 1991).

Another term that was developed to designate a new genre of anti-apartheid plays is 'multi-racial theatre.'[6] It is often also referred to as 'workshop theatre.' Discussed in Chapter 5, this type of theatre is named after the multi-racial composition of the groups and their democratic approach in workshop sessions. Although 'workshop theatre' can generally comprise any theatrical activity created by a group of practitioners, the term often refers specifically to plays by practitioners from different racial groups who worked together in an institutionalised setting such as the Market Theatre in Johannesburg or the Space Theatre in Cape Town in the late 1970s and 1980s. These plays usually staged black and white actors and characters. Their focus was an exploration of the problems of and possibilities for multi-racial co-existence during apartheid. They ideally addressed black and white audiences simultaneously (cf. Fleishman 1990). The play *Sophiatown* by Junction Avenue Theatre Company is an example of this type of theatre.

The final group of plays examined in Chapter 6 have been created exclusively by women and can thus be referred to as 'women's theatre.' It was not until the late 1980s that the male-dominated anti-apartheid theatre was challenged by black and white women who addressed the sexism prevalent in both apartheid and the 'struggle' against apartheid. The play *You Strike the Woman, You Strike the Rock* by the Vusisizwe Players is an example for this development. For the first time playwrights also focused on the private lives of women under apartheid.

The plays included in this study represent a selection from the works belonging to the extensive list of South Africa's performing arts and literature. It is axiomatic that the inclusion of a play necessarily implies the exclusion of others that could equally have been chosen as representatives of the same specific development. My selection was made on the basis of the presentation of character identity and interaction, the drama group's intention, the plays' political mood and its artistic features. A common feature of all the plays is that they emphasise their own theatricality and make abundant use of overt role-play. It is in such plays that social role-play and role games in the theatre can be compared and used to explain the behaviour of actors and characters.

Plays that have been influential in the development of anti-apartheid drama as a whole, but do not reflect the general mood of resistance prevalent at the time, have

---

[6] It has also been called "'non-racial theatre'" (cf. Fuchs 1992: 171). The terms 'multi-racial' and 'non-racial' are often used synonymously. However, 'multi-racial' foregrounds the coming together of different races while 'non-racial' emphasises the deliberate lack of focus on race.

been excluded. The South African musical, despite its popularity among the black population, is an example of this exclusion.[7] Movements such as 'theatre for development' (for instance worker or trade union theatre[8]) had to be left unconsidered because the texts were not available. Indian theatre was excluded for reasons of scope.[9] Only plays in English were examined. Those in any of the other ten official South African languages were not considered due to a lack of language competence.

[7] The South African musical industry began with the economic support of black performances by white liberals. However, this developed into the control and exploitation of blacks by white-owned recording and entertainment industries as the story of the jazz opera King Kong (1959; cf. Glasser 1960) exemplifies. It also represented the patronising attitude of whites wanting to protect blacks from falling into crime or radical politics. King Kong's commercial success ignited a tradition of musicals financed, written and directed by whites in the 1960s and 1970s. These musicals not only exploited black talent and workforce, but also disseminated the stereotype of the happy, singing and dancing rural native and were thus heavily criticised by apartheid-critical practitioners (cf. Akerman 1977/78; Horn 1986; Mda 1996; creating musical drama as the career of Gibson Kente exemplifies. Kente's work is characterised by artistic dynamism and social authenticity as well as political deficits. Black township musicals by Kente and others in the late 1960s were fairly uncritical of apartheid. In the mid-70s ideological pressure from the Black Consciousness Movement and audience demand for politicisation pushed township dramatists in a more radical direction. The musicals How Long (1974), I Believe (1974) and Too Late (1975) put Kente into continuous trouble with the state. After his arrest in 1976 his work clearly moved away from politics once again (cf. Kerr 1995: 216-20; Coplan 1985: 207-9).

Mbongeni Ngema's musicals of the 1980s and 1990s, *Sarafina*, *Sarafina II* and *Township Fever*, won international acclaim (cf. Jones 1994). Their acceptance in South Africa (especially of *Sarafina II*) is debatable.

[8] Worker or trade union theatre was initiated in the late 1970s and early 1980s. It addressed economic exploitation and helped African workers both as audience and participants in theatre to acquire agency. It was often led and sponsored by white activists such as Ari Sitas and Astrid von Kotze. Kelwyn Sole and Keyan Tomaselli have widely written on the class aspect of South African theatre (cf. Gready 1994; Sitas 1996b; Sole 1984, 1987a, 1987b; Tomaselli 1980, 1982; Tomaselli & Muller 1987; and von Kotze 1984, 1988). Zakes Mda, among others, is active in theatre for development (cf. 1993, 1994, n.d.).

[9] The main representatives of so-called 'Indian' theatre are the cousins Kessie and Ronnie Govender, operating in Durban (cf. Solberg 1999). In the 1970s the Black Consciousness Movement's attempt to unify all black groups in a common anti-apartheid struggle led to plays such as Shanti by Mthuli Shezi which depicts a love affair between an Indian and an African (cf. Kavanagh 1981, 1985).

1. Interaction and Identity in Anti-apartheid South African Theatre

> [Apartheid] is a system which since the coming to power of the Nationalist government in 1948 has denied, in the name of 'separate development', the mutuality which is the normal social basis for the open-ended expressiveness constituting social theatricality.
>
> Brian Crow[1]

This study of anti-apartheid theatre discusses thirteen English-language plays created in South Africa between 1961 and 1989. Methodically it departs from the contributions of sociological role theory to theories of human interaction and identity construction. These results are then linked to performance theory. The presentation of the theoretical foundations for this study is preceded by reflections on the history of apartheid and the classification of anti-apartheid South African drama and theatre.

1.1. Apartheid as ideology and policy of oppression

In 1948 South Africa's system of apartheid became the "national institution [...] of racism" (Tiffin & Lawson 1994: 8).[2] With its victory in the elections the National Party was able to pursue its aims of consolidating state control in the hands of Afrikaner nationalists. By promoting Afrikaner interests, the state could implement racial segregation[3] and 'separate development' as a means of protection against black groups. "Apartheid," in the words of James Barber, "was both a creed and a set of policies" (1999: 140). On the one hand, apartheid must be seen as an

---

[1] 1992: 151.

[2] For a discussion of the terms 'racism' and 'race' see Miles (1989).

[3] The policy of racial segregation was implemented in the early twentieth century under English rule. Segregation has many historical roots. Elements can be traced back to both Dutch and British colonial rule in South Africa, older traditions of slavery, agrarian paternalism, the frontier conflict as well as the modernising dynamics of a newly industrialising society after the discovery of gold in Johannesburg and diamonds in Kimberley in the second half of the nineteenth century. See the collection of essays edited by Beinart & Dubow (1995) for an overview of the different sources of segregation in South African history, especially the articles by Beinart, Dubow, Giliomee, Legassik, Marks, Posel, Swanson and Wolpe. See also Dubow (1987) and Wolpe (1970).

ideological program that allowed the Afrikaners to establish a Christian-nationalist identity as an exclusive *volk* or an 'elect people' with a sacred history (cf. Giliomee 1995).[4] On the other hand, it was also a system of political, economic and social oppression of the black population. Its aim was to secure the economic prosperity of the traditionally poor Boers vis-à-vis both the large black population and the more affluent group of English descent.[5] From both a psychological as well as a pragmatic perspective it was necessary for the Afrikaners to define and thus to delimit each racial group's scope of action and interaction. To the extent that "[...] ruling elites structure relations between states and civil society, shaping norms and reinforcing social and political identities accordingly" (A. Marx 1998: 4), a system of social roles and expectations of behaviour in South African society was developed to shape the identities of whites and blacks.[6] This was done with the help of apartheid laws and promoted through apartheid discourse that defined identity according to racial ideology. Apartheid ideology was based on binary oppositions and a Manichean world view, differentiating between the 'white' ruling class and the 'black' or dispossessed and oppressed class.[7] This is reflected in the racist language of apartheid, the medium through which the "hierarchical structure of power" was perpetuated (Ashcroft, Griffiths & Tiffin 1989: 7). In apartheid discourse 'white' equals 'good, human and civilised' and 'non-white' equals 'bad, inhuman and savage.' Robbed of its 'scientific basis' after World War II,[8]

---

[4] The term '*volk*' connotes both an ethnicity and organic unity, elements not conveyed in the English translation 'people' or 'nation' (cf. O'Meara 1983: xv).

[5] Giliomee (1995) describes the growth of an ethnic Afrikaner identity as a result of several (for the Afrikaners) devastating historical, social and economic events in the course of the first half of the twentieth century. See also Marks & Trapido (1987) for an overview of the interplay of race, class and nationalism. Further representations of Afrikaner nationalism are offered by Du Toit (1976), Moodie (1975), O'Meara (1983), Van Zyl Slabbert (1976) and Worrall (1972).

[6] Role theory is discussed in Chapter 2. Apartheid can also be described as a discursive strategy of power in Foucault's sense. In order to make a Foucauldian reading of apartheid useful for literary analysis, the subject must be seen as produced by dominant state discourses while possessing the possibility and faculty to oppose these discourses by constructing counter-discourses (cf. 1981a). Such a reading of Foucault is implied by Martin Orkin in his examination of South African drama (cf. 1991) and Lliane Roots in her analysis of the gender aspect in South African drama (cf. 1997).

[7] Post-colonial theorist Homi Bhabha calls this process of colonial discourse the "ideological construction of racial otherness" (1994: 66), a concept that will be exemplified in an analysis of the manipulation of spectator identification in *Sizwe Bansi is Dead* (cf. Chapter 3.4).

[8] The idea of racial inferiority of blacks was historically based on nineteenth century 'scientific' evolutionist and social Darwinist thought and was reflected in the language of eugenics. It fed general white fears with regard to black urbanisation and proletarisation in early twentieth century South Africa. Dubow argues that the political debates of the 1910s and 1920s focused on

apartheid's white-black dichotomy must be seen as a conscious effort in "race making" or the "construction [...] of race" to maintain social order by "Selective exclusion" (A. Marx 1998: 2, 3).[9] Apartheid society was, however, also based on gradation, dividing the population and its accorded roles into a racial hierarchy. 'Whites' belonged to the superior race whereas racial inferiority was attested for all 'black' groups: 'Indians' (or 'Asians,' 'Asiatics') were considered superior to 'coloureds' who were defined as superior to 'Africans' (or 'Natives,' 'Bantus,' 'blacks').[10] The hierarchy was supposed to prevent alliances between the black groups and make a common anti-apartheid identity construction difficult.

In the following some events of the apartheid era will be highlighted in as far as they are relevant for the analysis of the plays under review.[11] In general, as Nigel Worden summarises, "[...] apartheid has not been static or monolithic. Each decade,

---

three domains with regard to the topic of 'race': "speculation about the relative intelligence of blacks and whites, the almost universally expressed horror of 'miscegenation,' and fear of racial 'degeneration' following upon the uncontrolled development of a black and white proletariat in the cities." Africans were widely regarded as being "a natural part of the land where they should stay for their own protection from the alien environment of vice and immorality in urban areas" (1995: 155; cf. 1987).

A. Marx states that after World War II the scientific community proclaimed that categorical distinctions of race were "artificial and inconsistent with the continuum of skin color evident in the world's increasingly mixed population" (1998: 3).

[9] A. Marx's general interest lies in the analysis of nation building on the basis of racism. He rejects the concept of apartheid South Africa as an 'imagined community' (Anderson) based on a "spontaneous and inclusive process of nation building," foregrounding instead the state's methods of "exclusion" and institutionalisation of cleavages (1998: 5, 25).

The idea that apartheid South Africa is either essential, biologically justified or God-given is also refuted in formulations such as "*The Making of Modern South Africa*" and "*The Making of Apartheid*," the titles of historical accounts by Deborah Posel (1991) and Nigel Worden (1994). The concept of 'race as construct' has already been suggested by W.E.B. Du Bois: "Turning to real history, there can be no doubt, first, as to the widespread, nay, universal, prevalence of the race idea, the race spirit, the race ideal, and as to its efficiency as the vastest and most ingenious *invention* for human progress" (1996: 40, emphasis added). The idea of construction is also conveyed in Valentine Mudimbe's concept of "*The Invention of Africa*" (thus the title of her 1988 monograph) which emphasises the creation of Africa in Western discourse. Similar ideas are brought forward by Edward Said (1979) who ascribes the creation of 'the Oriental' to Western discourse.

[10] The use of these terms in this study is not an attempt to support or justify apartheid ideology and language usage. However, their application makes it easier to explain how apartheid functioned and to show how the oppressed group appropriated the same terminology and strategies to subvert the system. See also Girvin (1987) for an overview of 'race classification' in South Africa.

[11] Histories of South Africa are offered, amongst many others, by Barber (1999), Thompson (1995) and Worden (1994).

broadly speaking, was marked by differences in both the content and the implementation of the policy, as well as in ways of resistance" (1994: 95).

In the early 1950s a number of laws were passed that led to apartheid's infiltration into everyday life: the Population Registration Act officially categorised individuals by race; the Group Areas Act delimited living areas and removed black communities from urban centres to the surrounding land where they were relocated in new 'group areas' or 'townships'; the Bantu Authorities Act reinforced traditional African tribal structures; and the Bantu Education Act defined African education in a way that blacks could not acquire access to the white educational system.[12] Various other acts prohibited mixed marriages, interracial sex and social mixing in public places such as cinemas, restaurants, beaches, busses and park benches (cf. Barber 1999: 141, cf. Chapman 1996: 221).[13] Athol Fugard's plays *Blood Knot* and *Statements after an Arrest under the Immorality Act* focus on the effects of some of these laws on individuals. So do, for example, *Egoli* by Matsemela Manaka, *Sophiatown* by Junction Avenue Theatre Company and *Have You Seen Zandile?* by Gcina Mhlophe.

Historically it soon became evident that the economic interdependence of whites and blacks (i.e. blacks supplying whites with cheap labour) made apartheid's concept of separation impossible to realise (cf. Barber 1999: 141). Thus "practical apartheid," the strict control of labour (Worden 1994: 93), was executed with the help of 'influx control.' This policy regulated and limited the entry of blacks from the townships and rural regions into white areas by issuing only temporary work permits. In order for whites to control blacks, the latter were required to carry passes that gave information about their temporary residential and work permits.[14]

---

[12] Richard Lapchick describes the Bantu educational system as "one that was intended to inculcate a servile attitude in the African people." Girls were taught to perform domestic duties and boys were "trained not to expect more from the regime than the little it was prepared to give to African men." In addition, a lack of adequate facilities led to overcrowding in the classroom and the exploitation of often underqualified teachers (1985: 236).

[13] Laws that promoted segregation had already been passed during British rule after the foundation of the Union of South Africa in 1910. They include, among others, the 1911 Mines and Works Act (employment segregation), the 1913 Natives Land Act (forcing segregation in the rural areas and prohibiting blacks to purchase land outside of reserved areas), the 1923 Natives Urban Areas Acts (urban residential segregation), the 1936 Natives Representation Act (removal of all Africans from the common roll) and the 1936 Native Trust and Land Act (which was an expansion of the 1913 Act). See Beinart & Dubow (1995: 3f.).

[14] The pass laws for various groups were first introduced as early as the nineteenth century under colonial rule (cf. Cameron 1987: 96, 101).

Although the 1950s saw apartheid's legal implementation and consolidation, there was also strong and persistent public political protest against these laws. The African National Congress (ANC)[15] and the white Congress of Democrats initiated a series of defiance campaigns in 1952 which criticised the pass laws and the segregation of public amenities. The bus boycotts of the 1950s, for example, are evoked in Athol Fugard's play *A Lesson from Aloes*. This decade also witnessed the rise of protest by women of all races against the implementation of pass laws specifically for African women, a subject addressed in *You Strike the Woman, You Strike the Rock* by the Vusisizwe Players. The proclamation of the Freedom Charter in 1955 by the National Congress of the People, an alliance of the ANC, the Congress of Democrats, the Indian Congress and the South African Coloured People's Organisation, stressed the wish for a democratic and multi-racial South Africa.[16] The general series of public protests countered by state repression culminated in the Sharpeville massacre of 1960, in which the police brutally broke up a non-violent demonstration against the pass laws. Sharpeville became a symbol for the struggle against apartheid as many contemporary works show (cf. Barber 1999: 146-48, 165). The government reacted to the decade of protest by imposing a state of emergency, banning anti-apartheid political organisations and imprisoning their leaders for life (cf. Chapman 1996: 222; cf. Worden 1994: 99-108).

During the 1960s black protest turned to violent resistance and defiance to a liberation struggle. Armed groups such as Umkhonto we Sizwe ('Spear of the Nation') from the ANC and Poqo ('only,' 'pure') from the Pan Africanist Congress (PAC)[17] emerged (cf. Barber 1999: 166). This development led the government to replace the multi-racial state with a so-called 'multi-national' or 'multi-ethnic' state in the 1970s. The government then propagated the idea of separate African or 'Bantu' nations as well as separate coloured and Indian national groups. While 87

---

[15] The ANC supported a multi-racial development of South Africa and fought for black liberation to establish a system of democratic racial co-existence. Founded in 1912 as the South African Native Congress and later called African National Congress, the organisation attempted to establish a united forum for the representation of African interests after the exclusion from any effective representation in the new political structure of the Boer-British alliance in the 1910 Act of Union (cf. Snail 1993: 133). For a detailed overview of the history and ideological beliefs of the ANC and its political rivals, see Fatton (1986), Meli (1998) and Snail (1993).

[16] Worden points out that ANC ideology became founded on charterism (cf. 1994: 105f.).

[17] In 1959 the PAC emerged from the ANC's Youth League (CYL), an organisation that strictly rejected alliance with whites and other ethnic groups in South Africa in favour of African nationalism. The PAC supported race-conscious nationalism as a strategy to arouse Africans to political awareness and action (cf. Fatton 1986: 4f.).

percent of South African land had been reserved for whites under the 1913 Land Act, the remaining territory was transformed into 'Bantustans' or 'homelands' where the large majority of the (often forcefully) resettled population was to live. This meant that the poverty-stricken former African reserves became homelands where the Bantu peoples, who the state considered essentially unlike Europeans, would 'develop separately.' The African population was grouped into various Bantustans by tribal origin, a state measure to break down African alliances. At first self-government was given to the homelands. Later they received nominal independence, a process by which the citizens of the homelands lost their South African nationality and became 'foreigners' (cf. Barber 1999: 173-78, Worden 1994: 111).[18] Poverty in the Bantustans was increased by the infertility of the soil and the state's exploitative tax system. The continuing need for cheap manual labour in the white cities led to predominantly male labour migrancy to the urban centres. The migrant labour system resulted in broken families in the homelands where the women and children were forced to survive by subsistence farming, often impossible in the infertile and drought-stricken areas.[19] The complexity of problems for blacks resulting from this policy is depicted in plays such as *Sizwe Bansi is Dead* by Athol Fugard, John Kani and Winston Ntshona, *Egoli – City of Gold* by Matsemela Manaka, *Bopha!* by Percy Mtwa and *You Strike the Woman, You Strike the Rock* by the Vusisizwe Players.

After a decade of strong oppression and increasing numbers of arrests, detentions and bannings, a new political movement appeared in the 1970s. The Black Consciousness Movement stood for black rights in the name of black pride and self-awareness (see Chapter 4.1). An important event in this decade was the Soweto uprising. In 1976 students in Soweto protested against the role of Afrikaans as the language of education and were violently dispersed by the police. Clashes with the police and increasing rioting spread throughout the country and led to a general militant atmosphere in the following years (cf. Barber 1999: 211-14). This is a central theme in Mtwa's play *Bopha!*.

---

[18] By 1978 the Transkei and Bophuthatswana gained political independence and six other Bantustans had self-governing status (the Ciskei, Gazankulu, KwaZulu, Lebowa, QwaQwa and Venda). The homelands were not recognised internationally as independent (cf. Barber 1999: 184; Worden 1994: 111). They all are located in the eastern part of South Africa. See the maps offered by Barber (1999: 174) and Worden (1994: 110).

[19] Geoffrey Davis (1989) gives a detailed presentation of the migrant labour system, its origins and its effects on the population.

By the 1980s opposition to the state had grown to unprecedented levels. In 1983 a new popular alliance of hundreds of different interest groups was formed under the banner of the United Democratic Front (UDF). The UDF – with its aims echoing those of the ANC – maintained a public profile as a resistance movement despite constant police harassment. The government deemed reforms necessary to secure the survival of white South Africa. The recognition of strong interracial economic dependence led to the Labour Relations Act, which abolished job reservation in the manufacturing industry, improved training facilities and legalised African trade unions. Pass laws and influx control were relaxed with the result that the African population was divided into permanent urban and rural dwellers. In the new constitution of 1983 the Immorality and Mixed Marriage Acts were repealed. After a redefinition of the white-black dichotomy a new coalition was formed between sections of the white, Indian and coloured population to strengthen the state's power over the Africans. Still deprived of political representation in South Africa, anti-apartheid organisations met the new constitution with protest. The unrest started in the townships and spread to the Bantustans. There were mass boycotts and strikes as well as attacks on policemen, homeland leaders and suspected informers. Massive state repression and declarations of several states of emergency only seemed to ignite further resistance. Some of the violence also resulted from continuing black rivalry such as between the Inkatha Freedom Party and the ANC (cf. Barber 1999: 224-27, 231-33, 243-46; Worden 1994: 121-41).[20]

This reading of apartheid history has implied to some extent that black action was a reaction to white policies. In his study of racial domination in South Africa, the United States and Brazil, Anthony Marx suggests that this kind of view of black protest is rather one-sided: "Indeed, racial identity, movement, and protest cannot be understood simply as a response to actions from above. Blacks have pursued their own ideas and actions, often forcing a reconfiguration of rule imposed upon them" (1998: 18). Tommy Lott argues in a similar fashion when he states that American "black cultural traditions [...] developed *partly* in response to a dominant racist culture" (1999: 1, emphasis added). A. Marx believes that it is insufficient to regard relative deprivation as the trigger for opposition, to consider reforms and repression as political opportunities for mobilisation and to regard sufficient

---

[20] The Inkatha Freedom Party fought for the rights of the Zulus under Chief Mangosuthu Buthulezi, who revived the movement in 1975, moving it away from the aims of the Zulu aristocracy to address broader issues of discrimination (cf. Barber 1999: 189-92). Maré and Hamilton (1987) offer a presentation of Inkatha under Buthelezi.

resources as a requirement for resistance. In addition, he also focuses on "identity formation as a prerequisite" for protest: "In the absence of a self-conscious group, there is no collectivity that can interpret and act upon its situation" (1998: 19, cf. 17-23). This thesis is supported by the plays analysed in this study, for many suggest that a clear notion of collective identity must precede successful protest against apartheid. Or, to appropriate Karl Marx's class-based argument, a group must be conscious of existing "in itself" before it can act "for itself" (A. Marx 1998: 20; cf. K. Marx 1977: 214).[21]

The plays in question work within apartheid discourse and employ the polarisation of 'black' versus 'white' in their denunciation of apartheid and their deconstruction of the apartheid role set. They avoid reflecting historical differences between the various black political formations in a general and all-comprising reversal of the 'good versus bad' dichotomy. Working with this fixed opposition, they rarely attempt to depict hybrid developments that Homi Bhabha detects in the colonial encounter (cf. 1994). It is interesting to note that the plays, insofar as they do not voice the hope of multi-racial co-existence in South Africa, do not question the validity or the constructed character of the concept of 'race.' Many dramatic texts reveal the humanity of the black population at the expense of the inhumanity of whites. Thus they work within the same (but reversed) discursive strategy as apartheid ideology and reproduce 'race' in terms of Gayatri Spivak's "strategic essentialism" (cf. 1988). The plays emphasise the effects of the racial system on the daily life of individuals, their interaction and self-definition within the prescribed role set.

In summary, during the apartheid era free interaction between the races and the possibility of creating relations outside of the 'master/servant' pattern were strictly curtailed by the state's ideological laws and regulations. Outside of the prescriptive and narrowly determined 'madam/maid' or '*baas*/boy'[22] relationship the African became invisible in the eyes of racist whites. However, as critics such as Frantz Fanon (cf. 1963; 1967) and Homi Bhabha (cf. 1994) have shown, the repressed black group did not accept the strict and hierarchical regulation of the relationship

---

[21] Karl Marx explains: "In the bourgeoisie we have two phases to distinguish: that in which it constituted itself as a class under the regime of feudalism and absolute monarchy, and that in which, already constituted as a class, it overthrew feudalism and monarchy to make society into a bourgeois society. The first of these phases was the longer and necessitated the greater efforts" (1977: 214).

[22] '*Baas*' is an Afrikaans term with which black South Africans addressed their white 'superiors.'

between whites and blacks (or colonisers and colonised) without resistance. Anti-apartheid South African theatre celebrated the resistance of the oppressed to their subjugation by the system. Lliane Loots asserts that "[...] ideologies of racist victimhood within an all powerful racist system were being counter-pointed by the fact that these discourses could (and did) find a voice in terms of performance spaces and audiences" (1997: 143).

In the introductory quotation to this chapter Brian Crow emphasises that in the name of separate development South Africa's apartheid regime denied the black and white populations "the mutuality which is the normal social basis for the open-ended expressiveness constituting social theatricality." He adds, "Such existentialist concerns as the intrinsic theatricality of being cannot be divorced, in the context of South Africa, from the economic, political and ideological realities of *apartheid*." This statement functions as a basis for the interpretations presented in this study (1992: 151; cf. Crow 1992: 150f.; 1996: 14f.; Crow with Banfield 1996: 102f.).

1.2. 'Apartheid' and 'post-apartheid': Some thoughts on terminology

This study examines South African plays written in English during the last three decades of the political period of apartheid. In recent literary and cultural criticism apartheid has been seen as a specific epoch of South African history which was succeeded by the post-apartheid era. Such a temporal distinction has also been made between the terms 'colonial' (as the historical stage of, for example, British imperialism) and 'post-colonial' (as the period after the breakdown of the British Empire). However, 'colonial' and 'post-colonial' are, analogous to the pair 'modern'/'post-modern,' more often seen in a cause-and-effect relationship as terms that can refer to the same situation. In this sense post(-)colonialism[23] "addresses *reactions to* colonialism in a context that is not necessarily determined by temporal constraints." Its political agenda aims to "dismantle the hegemonic boundaries and the determinants that create unequal relations of power based on binary oppositions" such as 'first world and third world' or 'white and black'

[23] Vijay Mishra and Bob Hodge distinguish between post-colonialism and postcolonialism. The former refers to the historical phase of post-independent countries whereas the latter signifies "an always present tendency in any literature of subjugation marked by a systematic process of cultural domination through the imposition of imperial structures of power" (1994 [1991]: 284). See also Ashcroft (1996), who argues that many historically oriented critics prefer the hyphenated form to signify post-colonial studies as a field and distinguish it from colonial discourse theory, one of the prominent approaches subsumed under the term 'post-colonial.'

(Gilbert & Tompkins 1996: 2f.). Graham Pechey speaks of the "postcolonial condition" as a "dispersal, a moving field of possibilities which everywhere carry within them the mutually entailing, intimately cohabiting negative and positive charges of both power and resistance" (1994: 153). Bill Ashcroft, Gareth Griffiths and Helen Tiffin define all culture influenced by imperialism as 'post-colonial.' They describe apartheid South Africa as a post-colonial state whose post-colonial political development has begun long before the country's independence (cf. 1989: 2, 83). For them South Africa is a society "caught between two phases, manifesting the dynamic of colonial domination but producing both white and Black writers whose engagement with the processes of abrogation and appropriation is part of a continuing struggle for survival" (1989: 83). Pechey views the post-apartheid situation as analogous to the postcolonial condition and offers the following reading of the 'apartheid'/'post-apartheid' complex:

> 'Post-apartheid' [...] is similarly open to different uses. South Africa's ruling party today would regard the post-apartheid condition as something already empirically in place, on the ground that segregationist ideology had been officially discarded and that some of the forms of legal exclusion and separation legitimated by it were being 'dismantled'. [...] Against this banality of usage, the sense of 'post-apartheid' I am invoking here defines a condition that has contradictorily always existed and yet is impossible of full realisation: always existed, because apartheid as a politics of permanent and institutionalised crises has from the beginning been shadowed by its own transgression or supersession; impossible of realisation, because the proliferating binaries of apartheid discourse will long outlive any merely political winning of freedom. (1994: 153)

Depending on one's historical, political and economic point of view, apartheid South Africa can be referred to as either 'colonial,' 'post(-)colonial,' 'neo-colonial,' 'modern,' 'pre(-)modern' or 'post(-)modern.'[24] This list of terms serves to highlight the complexity of apartheid as a system as well as the many already existing

---

[24] From a Boer perspective South Africa can be called 'post-colonial' as of the foundation of the Union of South Africa in 1910 which marked the country's formal political independence from British rule. From a different perspective "[...] South Africa might be called the first neocolonial state in Africa" since, as Pechey points out, 'postcolonial' is a euphemism for countries whose population was still economically and culturally dominated by an élite group after independence. Apartheid South Africa has also been described with the term "'internal colonialism'" by the Communist Party and the ANC. This term refers to the geographical co-existence of centre and periphery (Pechey 1994: 152, 154). Pechey also argues that apartheid "modernises by imposing premodern cultural identities upon those it dominates" (1994: 155). Many critics discuss the relationship between 'post(-)colonialism' and 'postmodernism' (see for example Hutcheon 1989, McClintock 1994, Mishra & Hodge 1994 [1991], Slemon 1989). With regard to South African literature see Carusi (1989).

perspectives on how to approach it as an object of analysis. This notwithstanding, the plays in question here are all characterised by a 'post-apartheid'/'anti-apartheid' thrust. Given the parallels of the concepts 'post-apartheid' and 'post-colonial,' it is interesting occasionally to examine ideas propagated by colonial discourse theory and post-colonial theory in this study. They can be used to challenge the notion of apartheid as a monolithic system of power.

1.3. What is anti-apartheid South African theatre?

1.3.1. Drama, theatre, performance

This study is based on written forms of performed plays, which performance theorist Richard Schechner calls 'drama' in contradistinction to 'script,' 'theatre' and 'performance.' Schechner defines 'drama' as a "written text, score, scenario, instruction, plan, or map. The drama can be taken from place to place or time to time independent of the person or people who carry it." The 'script' can be transmitted in time and space. It is "the basic code of the events. [...] The transmitter of the script must know the script and be able to teach it to others." 'Theatre' refers to the event that a specific group of performers enact. It is the "manifestation or representation" of the drama- and/or script-version. Finally, 'performance' signifies the "whole constellation of events, most of them passing unnoticed, that take place in/among both performers and audience from the time the first spectator enters the field of the performance [...] to the time the last spectator leaves" (all 1988b: 72). It must be stated that many South African plays existed in several versions ('theatre') as performances were often adapted to changing political circumstances on a daily basis. Nonetheless, usually only one version was published ('drama'), often many years after the first performance.[25]

Temple Hauptfleisch states that the field of theatre history "cannot simply rely on the printed word as source (e.g. the [printed] text and the reception document [the printed review, etc]), or as a means of conveying its own findings (i.e. as history)" (1997: 11). This observation is even more crucial for a study in theatre criticism which aims to analyse and evaluate. I follow Hauptfleisch in his view of 'theatre as system' which leads him to emphasise that theatre is

[25] In this study 'drama' and 'text' explicitly refer to the printed version while 'performance' or 'theatre' are used to signify the enactment of the written text. 'Play' is used as a stylistic variant for either text or performance.

> a team event, to which all the players contribute something of value: the author, the performer, the audience – and inevitably the company and its venue. It is the power and celebrity generated by that particular combination of elements which is the driving force behind the true impact of theatre as a socio-political instrument. (1997: 114)

Thus an attempt will be made to consider elements that shaped actual performances of the plays. As far as possible, multiple written versions of one play, videotapes of performances or personal interviews with actors and dramatists have also been consulted.

1.3.2. A classification of anti-apartheid South African theatre

To speak of 'anti-apartheid South African theatre' as if it were a precisely defined category is inadequate and misleading. Firstly, the appellation 'South African' suggests that a clear idea existed of what was South African. In fact, 'South Africa' represented one thing to the supporters of apartheid and something else entirely to its opponents (who amongst themselves also had differing opinions as to how South Africa should develop). This difference is apparent in the statement of (white) theatre director Mshengu (Robert McLaren Kavanagh) in 1977. Asked if the play *Survival* by Workshop '71, a racially mixed theatre group which he directed, was South African theatre, he replied:

> I would say it's South African theatre. I don't mean the present wishy-washy definition of what people assume is South African. South African only has meaning for me not in the way in which it relates to the rugby team. That is not a South African rugby team, that is a white rugby team. South African is a term which applies to something which doesn't exist at the moment. When we can really talk about things being South African, according to that definition, we will have a country where the major impulse in everything is black but the rest of the population which makes up that South Africa will also have its own important part. (Workshop '71 1977: 127)

During the time of apartheid the term 'South Africa' had strong political and ideological connotations. This must be kept in mind throughout this study.[26]

---

[26] A collection of articles that problematises historiographical classification with regard to South African literature has been published by Smit, van Wyk & Wade (1996). Erhard Reckwitz (1996 [1995]) emphasises the plurality of literary creation in South Africa and reminds us that literature in English only represents one part of South African literary production. Dennis Walder also reflects on the question "What is South African Literature?" (cf. 1998: 156).

Secondly, Zakes Mda emphasises that South African drama or theatre is "not a homogenous monolith" (1996: 197). Similarly, Temple Hauptfleisch and Ian Steadman point out that due to South Africa's multicultural situation, "There just has never been any *one* theatre tradition in the country." They identify several traditions which can be characterised by "such opposing classifications as African/Western, Afrikaans/English, indigenous/ imported, Black/White, literary/theatrical and popular/political theatre" (1984: 3).[27] Hauptfleisch expands these ideas to develop a "complex and interrelated polysystem of performance" (1987: 176) that comprises all performance events found in South Africa and its history (for example, initiation ceremonies, gumboot dances, Voortrekker ceremonies, plays imported from Europe, township musicals and performance poetry [cf. 1987: 177]). With this "polysystem" he fulfils Steadman's call in the early 1980s for an extension of the concept of 'theatre' from "a tradition rooted in a Hellenistic-Renaissance cultural continuum" to a "concept in terms broad enough to embrace virtually all aspects of performance" such as "work activities, dance forms, harmonies and hymns of southern Africa" (1981: 1).

Despite the fact that taxonomic exercises always remain problematic, classification is a useful tool for analysis because it allows the critic to narrow down and define the field of research according to their point of interest. It goes without saying that such categorisation is never final and remains subjective, reflecting the user's political, cultural, social, ideological and also temporal point of view. For example, whereas in 1984 Ian Steadman and others referred to revolutionary theatre by African artists as "alternative," Zakes Mda suggested in 1996 that in the course of the 1980s these kinds of plays became "representative of [...] mainstream South African theatre" (1996: 198).[28]

Hauptfleisch identifies a general tendency in the development of South African performance forms: an evolution away from "certain separate and distinctive forms

[27] Hauptfleisch and Steadman developed a system of classification in which they differentiate between 'Afrikaans theatre,' 'English theatre,' 'Black theatre' and 'Alternative theatre.' The first three genres "constitute different theatrical systems" based on exclusivity (Hauptfleisch 1992: 407). Only 'Alternative theatre' is influenced by various theatrical traditions and "does not define itself in terms of ethnic or linguistic factors" (Hauptfleisch & Steadman 1984: 166, cf. 7; see also Steadman 1984a).

[28] That categorisation and classification are always subjective and political exercises is shown in Mshengu's characterisation in 1977 of the play *Survival* (1976) as "not fringe theatre" but "mainstream." His definition of 'mainstream' is implied in his statement that theatre which does not educate the population about the reality of apartheid is "relatively unconnected to what really matters" (Workshop '71 1977: 125).

[...] towards a set of more integrated forms" which he calls "'hybrid'" and David Coplan terms "'syncretic'" (Hauptfleisch 1987: 176; 1997: 49f.; cf. Coplan 1985: 236f.).[29] Apart from being a general post-modern manifestation of eclecticism, 'hybridisation' and 'syncretism' signify the "blending of resources from different cultures in order to produce qualitatively new forms in adaptation to changing conditions" (Coplan 1985: 270; cf. Hauptfleisch 1987: 176; 1997: 50).[30] In the end the new works take on their own "*gestalt*," "not quite African, not quite Western, but somewhere in the middle" (Hauptfleisch 1987: 185, 181). They constitute a "distinctive new tradition" (Hauptfleisch 1997: 32).

The plays in this study can - with the help of Hauptfleisch's terminology - be described as "indigenous." They include the well-written play which follows Western traditions of realism, naturalism and the theatre of the absurd. Parts of Athol Fugard's work fall into this category of "indigenous, Western." New developments of "alternative" theatre created in experimental workshops challenged the existing forms as far back as the late 1950s, a trend that became prominent in the 1970s. These new forms generally incorporated pantomime as well as pre-colonial, African forms of dance, song and storytelling (orality) into the performances, techniques that "served a wide range of functions, including the teaching of social roles and behaviour, explaining the history of ethnic groups, social criticism, celebration and the fulfilment of religious rituals" (Banham & Plastow 1999: viif.). These artistic elements were generally characteristic of post-independence English-language theatre in Western and Eastern Africa as early as

---

[29] Christopher Balme uses the terms 'theatrical syncretism' and 'syncretic theatre' (1999: 25) to refer to forms of theatre created in countries that were being colonised or decolonised. In Africa 'theatre' as a specific form of (Western) art and entertainment was introduced to cultures that were not aware of this cultural-aesthetic system. 'Theatre' as a system was implemented in colonised countries and enriched with indigenous elements. In Balme's reading an art form only constitutes 'syncretic theatre' if the programmatic intention to modify the imported theatre-aesthetic system by imposing indigenous elements on it is apparent. This means that at least one of the indigenous elements takes on a dominant function in the sign system without threatening the theatre-aesthetic orientation of the production. Balme's aesthetic-theatrical approach differs methodically from Hauptfleisch and Coplan's anthropological performance-based approach (cf. Balme 1995: 16-35, esp. 32-35; 1999: 13-15).

[30] Monika Fludernik traces the use and development of the meaning of the term 'hybridity' in the (post)colonial context and distinguishes it from related terms such as 'syncretism' or 'creolisation' (cf. 1998a; 1998b: 9-14). In contrast to Hauptfleisch and Coplan's use of 'hybrid' and 'syncretic' to refer to the mixing of performance elements to create a new category of theatre that eventually became mainstream, 'hybridity' in the (post)colonial sense has come to "function as a key concept of cultural diversity in which racist 'impurity' has been reinscribed as subversive multiplicity and as progressive (but not unidirectional) agency" (Fludernik 1998a: 21).

the 1960s and can be found, for example, in the plays by the Nigerian writer Wole Soyinka, the Ghanaian author Ama Ata Aidoo, and the Kenyan writer Ngũgĩ wa Thiong'o (cf. Amankulor 1993).

In South Africa in the 1970s, influenced by the growth of radical political thinking, "provocative" and political "anti-establishment" theatre emerged. The main aim of the (often) multi-racial casts was the transcendence and breakdown of apartheid's colour-coded barriers. Plays by Athol Fugard, John Kani and Winston Ntshona, Workshop '71 or Barney Simon and the cast exemplify this. As they became decreasingly propagandistic, these works acquired a central position in the theatre system of the 1980s: a "hybrid" and "uniquely South African" tradition had emerged. In the attempt to incorporate different concepts of society and theatre into one performance, improvisation and workshop techniques were employed to combine non-theatrical elements of indigenous, communal performance with forms from Western conventions. This category of "cross-over theatre"[31] includes plays by Matsemela Manaka, Mbongeni Ngema and Percy Mtwa (cf. Hauptfleisch 1987: 177, 181-86; 1997: 49, 57-62).[32]

The choice of plays in this study is influenced by a specific social and political interest. In the light of the political development from 1960 to 1990, and to the extent that the theatre activities of the time reflected and also influenced these changes,[33] one central question of this study is: How does the presentation of South African individuals, society and the image of apartheid develop in South African plays over the course of three decades?

It must be kept in mind that the play as a socio-political mirror of its time remains, as Hauptfleisch puts it, "necessarily fractured, its glimpse of reality partial and skewed" (1997: 168). He argues, "No single artist can 'reflect' or represent more

---

[31] Hauptfleisch appropriated this term from American popular music: "crossover music" refers to music which can be categorised in more ways than one. By analogy, South African play-makers use "the form of one tradition or art form, to enhance, alter, give weight to another – and, in the process, possibly creat[e] a new form, or at least a work which would have a wider potential acceptance and impact – whether in box-office and sales terms, or in terms of social, political or educational aims" (1997: 69).

[32] For a more detailed rendition of the development of South African theatre see Hauptfleisch (1987; 1990; 1997: 29-65) and Hauptfleisch & Steadman (1984, esp. 3-7 and the individual introductions to the plays).

[33] Mda maintains that South African theatre can "never be abstracted" from its "particular context" (1996: 195). Theatre did not only reflect the liberation struggle but played a "catalytic" role in it (1996: 257).

than a few selected aspects of life about him or her at any given time, particularly not in a single artefact [...]." This is because "[...] it is the theatrical system and the sum of artefacts in any given period and given context which may be said to 'reflect' that context, and which, in the longer term, may be able to 'influence' or 'change' that specific context" (1997: 2f.).[34]

1.4. Reflections on role theory

As suggested above, apartheid can be defined as a system in which the group in power structured the relationship between the state and its subjects on the basis of race, introducing norms and defining social and political identities. A system of social roles with strictly defined behavioural expectations in South African society shaped the identities of whites and blacks. The concept of sociological role theory, on which this study is based, is introduced in the following section.

1.4.1. Role theory: Identity and role at the intersection of sociology and psychology

The increasing prevalence of the discussion on social roles in modern industrial societies in the first half of the twentieth century shows, as Thomas Luckmann argues, that modern woman and man are no longer born into their roles. Compared to pre-industrial times the modern individual is confronted with a large number of roles that are anonymous and determined by their institutional functions.[35] These roles often do not easily fit into the individual's subjective perception of their life. This means that individuals become more and more conscious of the fact that they are playing roles (cf. 1979: 305f.).[36]

In the twentieth century, parallel to debates on social roles, the topic of personal identity was also introduced into scholarly discussions in the social sciences. Luckmann asserts that personal identity developed from a social condition or a

---

[34] Richard Schechner and Victor Turner's model of the relationship between stage drama and social drama is presented in Chapter 1.5.2.

[35] Luckmann argues that in archaic societies economic, political, religious and family functions were merely aspects of fairly standardised actions while in modern societies society, politics, religion and family are structures that form institutions (cf. 1979: 305).

[36] Kurt Müller argues that Luckmann's assertion of a qualitative difference between modern industrial society and pre-industrial society is a construct that functions as a typologic outline (cf. 1991: 32).

given quality of human beings in archaic times to a subjective problem for the mass of modern individuals. Modern identity depends on the specific historical social structures of industrial society. The increasing division of labour and the reduction of direct social interaction forces the individual to accept a growing number of anonymous social relationships. Luckmann suggests that an examination of social and cultural history in combination with a sociological (role theory) and socio-psychological (symbolic interactionism) analysis of modern social structure is useful for explaining the concept of personal identity as a social problem (cf. 1979: 294f.).

The question of personal identity and social action/interaction is much older than the existence of social sciences. In philosophy the relationship between being and (re-)
presentation has influenced the discussion on the identity of man since antiquity. Odo Marquard gives a brief overview of this development and shows that up to the nineteenth century one recurring theme was the idea of the difference of and distance between being and (re-)presentation. Marquard concludes that in this tradition the self is worth more than an individual's self-representation in the opinion of others (1979: 347-49).

Modern social sciences abolished the idea of absolute distance between the self and its appearance in society but emphasised the connection between the two. In this way Kurt Müller follows Luckmann's approach when he characterises the modern categories of 'role' and 'individual' as complementary (cf. 1991: 34). Several theories have been developed in the field of socio-psychology that take into account both social frames as well as individual interaction and manifestation of identity in these social frames. There are, however, also approaches that either exclusively examine the concept of 'role' without looking at the individual's relationship to their roles (pure sociological role theory) or that analyse 'identity' while placing the individual outside of all social contexts (pure psychology). This latter category of psychological theories, which operate outside of social frames, is not useful for an analysis of personal identity in specific social settings such as South Africa's apartheid society. By contrast, a look at abstract sociological theories is helpful towards establishing a terminological apparatus for dealing with the concept of 'role.'[37] This overview is followed by a presentation of socio-psychological theories that focus on 'identity' and 'role.'

1.4.2. Dahrendorf's concept of the *homo sociologicus*

In his analysis of the Anglo-American discussion of social roles Lord Ralf Dahrendorf introduced the *homo sociologicus* to sociological discussion.[38] This concept identifies the individual as the carrier of social roles. It is based on the idea that there is a fundamental difference between the individual as a role player and the actual 'role-less' or 'pre-societal' individual. Dahrendorf asserts that many similar, identical or even etymologically related terms have been used to define the point of intersection of individual and society: 'mask,' 'persona,' 'character' and 'role.' These words all belong to the domain of theatre and have several aspects in common: they signify something that, for the actor, is given and that exists independently of that actor, namely a complex of expectations of behaviour. This behaviour has to be learnt by the actor. No role is all-encompassing, but the actor can learn to play a multitude of different roles. At the same time the player remains an individual behind the roles performed on stage (cf. 1974[14]: 20-22).

Dahrendorf is not the first scholar to take up the famous quotation from William Shakespeare's comedy *As You Like It*: "All the world's a stage,/And all the men and women merely players;/They have their exits, and their entrances;/And one man in his time plays many parts;" (II,7, ll. 139-42). Here Shakespeare develops an idea that anticipates the characteristics and possibilities of the modern category of 'social role.' He focuses predominantly on one type of social role, namely age roles ("infant," "schoolboy," adult, old man), but also mentions socially developed forms of behaviour (professional roles: "soldier," "justice"). The world is a stage that individuals enter and exit wearing different masks (cf. II, 7, ll. 139-66). After their deaths other individuals appear on the world's stage succeeding them in exactly the same roles (cf. Dahrendorf 1974[14]: 25f.).

---

37 Luckmann asserts that the term 'role' is part of sociology's taxonomic equipment and that by contrast, the term 'social role' carries theoretical importance in philosophic-anthropologic reflections on human nature. See for example Helmuth Plessner: "Immer ist der Mensch in seiner Verdopplung zu einer erfahrbaren Rollenfigur erst er selbst" which states that human beings, in their doubling in a role figure that can be experienced by others, are first and foremost themselves (1966: 33).

38 Dahrendorf's reception has predominantly taken place in the German field of sociology.

Dahrendorf maintains that Shakespeare's metaphor "all the world's a stage" has been adopted as the basic principle of sociology. The individual as carrier of socially formed attributes and patterns of behaviour mediates between the individual and society. Society tears the individual out of their individuality by giving them a certain profile. Society defines every existing 'position' that an individual can occupy, i.e. a place in a field of social relations, with the help of attributes and behaviour patterns. These positions range from gender to age positions, family to professional positions, national to class positions (and in the South African context, predominantly race positions). The carrier of a specific position is confronted by these demands and must cope with them. If an individual adopts and accepts these demands completely, they may give up their individuality but receive society's approval. If, by contrast, the individual refuses to conform to society's demands, then they may succeed in preserving a certain independence but will also be sanctioned by society (cf. 1974[14]: 26f.).

Every social position places the individual in a field of positions that are related. For instance, the positions of mother, father and child belong to a specific field (cf. Dahrendorf 1974[14]: 30). Every position that an individual occupies is linked to certain patterns of behaviour that are socially expected. These expectations are comprised in social roles. Consequently, 'social roles' are defined as a complex of *expectations* of behaviour, not actual behaviour as it takes place. Uri Rapp characterises roles as the embodiment of human potentialities (cf. 1973: 94). As a participant in society the individual is required to occupy many different positions and roles. Every position can include a plurality of different relationships. For instance, a teacher (position) interacts with students, parents and the headmaster ("counter positions"). Each of these dyadic relations is called a "*positional sector*." A "*role sector*" is defined as a "set of expectations applied to the relationship" of a position to its counter position (Gross, Mason & McEachern 1964[2]: 52, 62; cf. Dahrendorf 1974[14]: 31-33).

Dahrendorf highlights those aspects of the social role which make it an element of sociological analysis. Social roles (as well as positions) are quasi-objective complexes of expectations of behaviour which are independent of the individual. The conduct of a role is defined and changed by society, not by an individual. The expectations of behaviour associated with a role are obligatory: an individual cannot ignore these expectations without being sanctioned by society (cf. 1974[14]: 30-35).

With these definitions of 'position' and 'role' Dahrendorf follows the tradition of scholars such as Talcot Parsons and Robert Merton, a tradition that is sociologically, not psychologically, oriented.[39] Merton maintains that there are "structurally defined expectations assigned to each role" (1949: 110). Similarly, Walter Coutu defines 'role' as the "socially prescribed duties or functions to be performed, and rights to be enjoyed" with every social position (1951: 180). Gross et al. understand 'position' to be the "*location of an actor or class of actors in a system of social relationships*" (1964²: 48).[40]

Dahrendorf focuses on the power of sanctions that influence role behaviour. He maintains that individuals learn to meet the expectations associated with their roles. Society has at its disposal sanctions with which it can enforce its rules. These sanctions can be positive or negative. But it is the threat of negative sanctions that puts the individual under pressure to behave correctly. Dahrendorf differentiates between different kinds of expectations: mandatory, preferential or permissive expectations.[41] Depending on the expectations, sanctions may range from juridical persecution to social exclusion to general antipathy. Social roles and sanctions change with time and reflect a shift in social norms, values and laws (cf. 1974¹⁴: 37-40). Role expectations and sanctions are determined by those norms and sanctions that are valid in an individual's reference group[42] and that refer to the positions and roles associated with the reference groups (cf. 1974¹⁴: 48).[43]

---

[39] Cf. Merton (1949) and Parsons (1967).

[40] Gross, Mason and McEachern give an overview of the various definitions of 'role' (cf. 1964²: 11-20).

Dahrendorf explicitly distances himself from another tradition which follows the ideas of Ralph Linton. Linton uses the term 'status' instead of 'position' to signify "a collection of rights and duties." Furthermore, when an individual "puts the rights and duties which constitute the status into effect, he [*sic*] is performing a role" (1936: 113f.). Dahrendorf questions this definition because it sees roles as actual behaviour and thus as a socio-psychological phenomenon, not a sociological one. Linton's approach suggests that roles do not exist objectively and independently from the individual but that they are subjective and individual aspects which belong to the individual (cf. 1974¹⁴: 60-64, esp. 62).

[41] Dahrendorf adopts these terms from Gross, Mason and McEachern: there are expectations that the individual "*absolutely must*," "*preferably should*" or "*may or may not*" fulfil (1964²: 60).

[42] Dahrendorf uses the term 'reference group' to signify the group which an individual's position brings them in relation to (cf. 1974¹⁴: 45)

[43] See Spittler (1967) on the relation between norms and sanctions. Wiswede looks at the relation between roles and power, focusing also on role sanctions (cf. 1977: esp. ch. 4).

Dahrendorf's reflections initiated an interdisciplinary discussion during which his premise, his image of man and his method have been criticised.[44] Because this study of South African drama is concerned with the staging of human behaviour, it is useful to examine what Dahrendorf's approach contributes to the interpretation of performance. Kurt Müller, who approaches the genre 'novel' with the help of role terminology, offers criticism which is also relevant for drama. Müller maintains that Dahrendorf's approach is characterised by its abstraction from reality. Society is composed of a strict order and hierarchy which are threatened to be disrupted by the individuality of every person. By contrast, the individual perceives society as an "*ärgerliche Tatsache*" (unpleasant or annoying fact), a recurring term in Dahrendorf's essay. His theory is useful as an analytical tool in understanding the relationship of forms of social interaction and in constructing an abstract presentation of social structures. However, it looks neither at individual interpretations of self nor at the relationship of the individual to their own roles or those of others. Furthermore, because roles are defined as expectations of behaviour, Dahrendorf's theory cannot take into account actual behaviour in concrete interaction in daily life (cf. Müller 1991: 37).[45]

1.4.3. Socio-psychological theories of identity

Dietrich Schwanitz maintains that in contrast to Dahrendorf's 'role-less' individual, it is possible to develop the notion of an empirically identifiable personal identity that is complementary to the notion of role. Such an approach was introduced by George Herbert Mead and the school of symbolic interactionism (cf. Schwanitz 1977: 16). Mead argues in *Mind, Self and Society: From the Standpoint of a Social Behaviourist* that the identity of individuals results from their self-presentation. By acquiring the ability to see themselves with the eyes of their environment – Mead calls this "taking the attitude of the generalized other" (1967: 156) – and by internalising the expectations of others and behaving according to them, the individuals develop their own identity.[46] Mead differentiates between the "I" or

---

[44] For a summary and comment on this criticism see Dahrendorf's 1963 essay "Soziologie und menschliche Natur," which is included as an appendix in the later editions of *Homo Sociologicus* (cf. 1974[14]: 97-118). He also provides a list of critical reflections on his work (cf. 1974[14]: 119).

[45] Müller gives a concise overview of Dahrendorf's role concept and argues that it is only useful as an instrument of literary hermeneutics in a limited way (cf. 1991: 34-37).

[46] Walter Coutu traces the difference between 'role-playing' (the act of playing a social role, "overt behaviour") and 'role-taking,' a term coined by Mead. 'Role-taking' as a "strictly mental

agent of this internalisation and the resulting identity, the "me": "Through taking those attitudes [of others] we have introduced the 'me' and we react to it as an 'I'" (1967: 174, cf. 173-78). This identity is not only defined in a general social setting but also in relation to specific groups, situations and routines. Consequently, individuals do not have only one identity, but many different identities. The "I" and the "me" are two separate categories, yet they are intrinsically linked. Role theory reflects this in the concept of 'role distance' which was introduced by Erving Goffman in 1961 (cf. Goffman 1961b: 105-10; Marquard 1979: 349).[47]

In his monograph *Identity and Life Cycle* (1959) Erik Erikson examines the development of human behaviour from a psychological and psychoanalytic perspective. He analyses the unity of the human life cycle and the specific dynamics of every phase in this cycle that result from the characteristics of personal development and social organisation (cf. 1979[5]: 7). He introduces the term 'ego identity' to signify the maturation of the personality which the individual has developed by the end of adolescence with the help of their childhood experiences. Ego identity is both a psychoanalytic and a psycho-social concept: identity develops through the reciprocity of human desires and society's expectations (cf. 1973: 123). After a phase of introjection and projection during early childhood in which the concepts of 'self' and 'object' are learnt, the child then gradually internalises social norms through identification with parental role behaviour. Identity[48] develops after the phase of identification and experimental role-play is completed. By that stage the adolescent has adopted socially accepted role behaviour and methods of conflict resolution to regulate the interplay of personal desires and social norms. Society recognises this person as an individual whose behaviour, in turn, shows that she or he recognises society and its norms (cf. 1979[5]: 139-42). Erikson calls the failure of the ego to develop an identity 'identity diffusion' (cf. 1979[5]: 153-88).

---

or cognitive or empathic activity" or "psychological process" signifies a "phase of the symbolic process by which a person momentarily pretends to himself that he is another person, projects himself into the perceptual field of the other person [...]. The purpose of this is to enable him to get the other person's 'point of view' so that he can anticipate the other's behaviour and then act accordingly" (1951: 180f.).

47 Goffman writes: "a wedge between the individual and his role, between doing and being. This 'effectively' expressed pointed separateness between the individual and his putative role I shall call *role distance*. A shorthand is involved here: the individual is actually denying not the role but the virtual self that is implied in the role for all accepting performers" (1961b: 108).

48 Erikson's term 'identity' resembles Mead's concept of 'self' (cf. 1979[5]: 188).

Later theories developed in the light of the sociological reception of Mead and Erikson depart from the theoretical juxtaposition of identity and role to analyse this relation in actual role behaviour. For example, Hans-Peter Dreitzel's monograph *Die gesellschaftlichen Leiden und das Leiden an der Gesellschaft* examines the individual's difficulties in striking a compromise between their individual needs and social obligations. Lothar Krappmann takes a similar approach in his study *Soziologische Dimensionen der Identität.*

1.4.3.1. Krappmann and the inconsistency of personal needs and society's expectations

In his 1969 study *Soziologische Dimensionen der Identität: Strukturelle Bedingungen für die Teilnahme an Interaktionsprozessen*,[49] Lothar Krappmann examines how identity is made possible in a system of social interaction. He connects the individual and society by analysing the structure of the psyche as the inner representation of the social system (cf. 1982^6: 20-23).

Krappmann's theory revolves around the notion of 'identity.' An individual must arrive at an identity in order to communicate and interact with others. This step is required by the structure of interaction. To interact with others, individuals must present themselves in their identity. At the same time they must respect the exigencies of the current situation as well as expectations of others. Identity also links present expectations to former interactions and thus creates continuity. The more individuals introduce elements of earlier situations into their construction of identity, the more consistent their biography will be. It is identity that makes the individual unique (cf. 1982^6: 8f.).

Individuals are constantly confronted by society's contradictory expectations. The inconsistency of the norm system and the contradictions between the frames of action in social systems are socio-structural elements that allow individuals to develop a unique identity. They need this identity to cope with these inconsistencies and to engage in social interaction where they balance out their own needs against demands by others. Krappmann's approach recognises society as dynamic: conflicting norms and inconsistent expectations constantly lead to a new interpretation and change of present conditions (cf. 1982^6: 8-11).

---

[49] This translates as "sociological dimensions of identity: structural conditions for the participation in processes of interaction" (trans. H.F.).

In contrast to Mead's assertion that the individual internalises society's expectations, Krappmann argues that the individual's existence relies on their ability to *negotiate* the definitions of identity suggested by society. He states that individuals cannot interact successfully by merely adopting society's expectations and interpretations as these do not fully express the individual's unique behaviour (contrary to society's expectations) and social biography (cf. 1982[6]: 34-42).[50]

Individuals who come to terms with society's contradictions have developed an identity that successfully strikes a balance. Krappmann calls this 'balancing identity' ("balancierende Identität"). This concept of identity defines the individual as spontaneous and creative. These attributes result from the structural necessity to rebel against a generally present social pressure to conform. The idea of a 'balancing identity' does not oppose the self to social conditions but describes the function of the self as a part of these conditions. In other words spontaneity and creativity are not challenges to social determinism but a personal contribution to interaction required by the social process (cf. 1982[6]: 68f.).

Krappmann regards personal identity as the precondition for successful *role behaviour*. Individuals will never achieve total consensus over the definition of the situation or fully agree on the content of roles.[51] Therefore identity is necessary to guarantee the subjective interpretation of role norms which makes role behaviour successful (cf. 1982[6]: 97f., 122). Consequently, successful role behaviour indicates that society's expectations do not meet the needs of a balancing identity and that the individual must transcend the frame of reference of the interaction (cf. 1982[6]: 128).

Krappmann argues that individuals need several abilities to *maintain* their identity. One such ability is role distance, the capacity to exceed the requirements of roles in order to choose, negate and modify. Like Erving Goffman, Krappmann also argues that role distance exists because every role is interpreted through other roles that are

---

[50] To successfully participate in an interaction, the individual must learn to cope with the following: (1) consideration of divergent expectations while demonstrating consistency and continuity; (2) acceptance of a working consensus of the definition of the situation while showing reservations; (3) presentation of their behaviour in the light of their own expectations in full awareness of the fact that full congruency is never possible; (4) participation not only in the interaction but also with regard to others; (5) demonstration of being a reliable partner of interaction while showing that one can also act differently (cf. Krappmann 1982[6]: 56).

[51] Like Dahrendorf, Krappmann regards roles as socially defined and institutionally promoted expectations of behaviour that make complementary interaction of individuals possible (cf. 1982[6]: 97-102).

themselves subject to constant re-interpretation. A second ability is empathy or role-taking, which Mead defines as the cognitive capacity to take over expectations from partners of interaction. A third ability is the acceptance of ambiguity. This allows individuals to maintain their identity while accepting both their own and others' contradictory role behaviour and inconsistent motivational structures (cf. 1982[6]: 136f., 143, 155).

To conclude, Krappmann combines psychological with sociological reflections on human interaction. His focus on the individual's biography and on the fact that individuals never fully agree on how to interpret a specific interaction, emphasises the personal element of role behaviour and the individual's capacity to invest themselves.

1.4.3.2. Dreitzel and the conflict between individuality and role identification

The sociologist Hans-Peter Dreitzel also reflects on the connection between the individual and society. In his approach role theory occupies a more central position than in Krappmann's. In his 1969 (1980[3]) monograph *Das gesellschaftliche Leiden und das Leiden an der Gesellschaft: Eine Pathologie des Alltagslebens*[52] Dreitzel begins with the general observation that people encounter problems in daily life with which they are unable to cope. To the extent that these problems are of a social nature, disruptions of behaviour are thus social in origin. His study is based on the idea that people are social beings who are created through social relations and that their identity is also shaped by these relations. This means the individual can never escape social reality. Dreitzel concludes that psychic disruptions have social causes and that pathological aspects of society are mirrored in disrupted or pathological behaviour. He claims that it is possible to deduce the structure of society by analysing individual behaviour. And vice versa, by looking at the social structure, it should be possible to name social aspects which have a pathological influence on the members of society (cf. 1980[3]: 14-17).

Dreitzel analyses socio-pathological phenomena in society by examining human interaction. Human behaviour follows certain aims and rules imposed by society which are institutionalised in social roles. As problems seem to arise when these rules cannot be followed, Dreitzel concludes that the sources of these disruptions

---

[52] This translates as "society's sufferings and the suffering from society: a pathology of daily life" (trans. H.F.).

reside in the social norms and socially institutionalised aims of behaviour. This means that individuals are confronted with socio-pathological phenomena in their social roles. Their reactions to these phenomena become manifest in their disrupted role behaviour which is an indicator for disruptions in the normative structure of behaviour. Dreitzel concludes that the deficient constitution of social roles mirrors the deficient constitution of social organisations and institutions. Thus he calls for a role-analytical examination of socio-pathological phenomena in society (cf. 1980[3]: 32f., 256f.).

A concept central to the understanding of Dreitzel's theory is that of 'identity.' Dreitzel argues that the individual is *per se* a product of society ("vergesellschaftet" [1980[3]: 52]) because an individual only exists as the representation of a specific character in a specific environment. On this social level human subjectivity is not pure interiority but must embody itself in role identities which existed before the individual. Individual and role are never identical yet remain connected. Individuals are identified by others through their roles and also identify themselves through their roles. This means that the individual always acts as a role player. Dreitzel asserts that the theatre metaphor for describing interaction foregrounds the theatrical character of social roles (cf. 1980[3]: 51-53). Individuals do not react to role expectations directly but perform inside the frame of these expectations. It is the individual's personal identity - Dreitzel uses the term *Ich-Identität* ('I-identity') - that allows them to develop their performance creatively to play roles and to interpret the role behaviour of others. At the same time social roles help the individual's personal identity to orient and stabilise itself (cf. 1980[3]: 55f.).

Dreitzel demands that role theory should recognise the importance of personal contributions (*Ich-Leistung*) to role behaviour as well as the individual's identification with the role. Roles and role expectations normatively and unconsciously require both of these elements (cf. 1980[3]: 83). He emphasises that people individually adapt their behaviour to certain roles and situations. In so doing they develop a mechanism of defence against the expectations connected with social roles. Every role puts pressure on the individual by dictating norms of behaviour. Even a strong personal contribution is limited because the domains of action in which it is exercised are structured according to power relations and status hierarchies (cf. 1980[3]: 225f.). Dreitzel's theory is largely dominated by the idea that the individual must move within those given power structures and hierarchies. That is why role-playing may be frustrating and have negative effects on the role player.

The accessibility of individual role behaviour varies according to the degree of both identification and personal contribution. Personal contribution depends on the nature of the norms. Dreitzel distinguishes three kinds of norms: the requirement to conform to strict rules of behaviour, the need to accomplish tasks and the aim of realising social values with personal style. Each kind of norm determines personal contribution. For instance, to be a convincing politician one must personally contribute to one's own role much more than a soldier who is required to obey orders. By contrast, the degree of identification with norms depends on their origin. Ranked in order of decreasing identification, norms may have originated in the cultural milieu, result from the power structure of organisations or can arise spontaneously in the respective situation of interaction. To give an example, roles such as those of child or parent require more identification than roles that are linked to specific situations such as driving in traffic or hosting a party. The lower the degree of identification with the role and the higher the degree of personal contribution, the more the individual can shape, change or even acquire distance to their role (cf. 1980[3]: 83-85).

Dreitzel emphasises the fact that after the significance of personal contribution and identification has been recognised, deviations from normal role behaviour become manifest in the actual disruption of social action. He discusses two different categories of disruptions. The first is an expression of external friction between the individual and the groups they interact with (friction in the social structure itself). Here contact with others is disrupted. The second category represents the internal disruptions between a player and their role which can arise either in the form of a loss of orientation or of distance in role behaviour (cf. 1980[3]: 265f).

With regard to the first category, disruptions of contact, Dreitzel argues that even in an open and socially mobile society access to most positions in society is limited. Additionally, if an individual is prevented from acquiring knowledge in the milieus of learning which bear relevance to their life, then a decisive basis for discovering and practising role-play is lost. In this way the individual becomes 'underprivileged' due to a lack or loss of contact with people in a certain milieu. Dreitzel calls this 'relative deprivation.' This concept refers to how role players judge themselves in relation to the status of other members of the same role system. The individual in question may feel that their possibilities are limited because they do not have access to certain roles. This disadvantage manifests itself in disruptions of the process of interaction. If an individual loses contact with the members of their own group or milieu, the common basis for role-play will disappear, and role behaviour becomes disrupted. Stigmatisation also influences role-play. When role partners discredit an individual's physical or social attributes, they refuse to recognise their full value as a role player and disrupt the common basis of interaction. Following Erving Goffman (cf. 1963), Dreitzel points out that successful stigma management is a way to avoid becoming a victim of relative deprivation. Striking disruptions of role behaviour arise in situations of discrimination: an outside group appropriates the power to interpret an individual's place in society by externally imposing domains of relevance and behaviour patterns on them. Thus group membership is forced and leads to absolute deprivation from the individual's original milieu (cf. 1980[3]: 231-34).

Dreitzel sees the second category of disruptions, internal disruptions between player and role, as a failure of the player's personal contribution to role behaviour. The individual cannot maintain a healthy balance between the two components of personal contribution: engagement and distance. Engagement signifies the personal intensification of the role game and gives expression to the intentionality of behaviour in the context of social roles. It is always oriented to role norms and therefore respects the other player's expectations of behaviour (cf. 1980[3]: 83, 240f.). Furthermore, a player must maintain distance from the expectations of behaviour of the role sender in order to explore the full range of possibilities of role behaviour. Distance is necessary not only to guarantee the continuing development of identity but also to cope with ambivalent situations and external influences which threaten to weaken one's personal identity (cf. 1980[3]: 133, 182, 240). It is only via role distance that an individual can avoid being absorbed by the role and thereby actively engage in role behaviour. A reduction or loss of role distance leads to a reduction or loss of personal contribution and finally to self-estrangement and loss of identity. The reduction of role distance is a consequence of the totality of expectations of behaviour in a certain field of action. This means that an individual can no longer design their role repertoire flexibly because role behaviour is repressed. When external pressure grows and norms become too dominant ("überprägnant"), as is the case in total institutions,[53] it ultimately becomes impossible to stage any form of individual behaviour. Personal identity is then no longer intact. Since the individual can no longer defend themself, disruptions in

[53] Total institutions must by all means prevent the growth of role distance to keep their subjects from critically inspecting the legitimacy of the role expectations. Such institutions will strive to reduce the individual's relative autonomy and their will to resist by making norms too dominant (cf. 1980[3]: 241-49).

role behaviour will arise. Consequently, social roles lose their function as mediator between the individual and the environment when the normative regulation of fulfilling individual needs is no longer secured. Individuals will either try to reorient themselves or create new roles better suited to their identity. This means engagement loses all distance, and the individual defines themself on a purely subjective basis, losing all control over reality (cf. 1980³: 240-49).

The other consequence of internal disruption between player and role is loss of orientation. In this case norms become so vague and blurred that it is no longer possible for the individual to recognise the intentionality of the role. Situations arise that cannot be connected to a certain domain of relevance because they are ambivalent and poorly defined or, in the extreme case, not defined at all. This ambivalence can result from an unclear temporal and local segmentation of the field of action as well as from insecurity about role norms because the external factors of the role game are no longer fixed and thus fail to provide the action with the required support. A state is ultimately created in which personal contribution to role behaviour is not possible. Loss of orientation can have two sources: isolation due to relative deprivation or dissolution of the normative profile of certain social roles. Loss of orientation can lead to forms of role-play that Dreitzel describes as unengaged distance or forced definitions of the situation. In the first case of unengaged distance, the individual does not sincerely take part in the action and maintains an artificial distance; in the second case of forced definitions of the situation, the situation and its norms are defined by the authority prior to action so that personal contribution is no longer possible. In extreme cases loss of orientation can induce the individual to completely break out of and negate the role (cf. 1980³: 252-61).

It has become clear that role behaviour is not only characterised by conformity to expectations and norms imposed from the outside but that it relies strongly on the individual's capacity to adapt to new situations. Personal contribution is important because it mediates between role regulations and intentionality as well as between the various role expectations predominant in the many role sectors. Furthermore, it is vital that the role player is able to interact and communicate with their partners because social roles are not only versatile but will also develop and change in time.[54]

---

[54] Krappman also emphasises the importance of language for the manifestation of identity (cf. 1982⁶: 12, 44-46).

Dreitzel's theory paints the picture of an individual as a social being caught in society's rules, norms and customs. The title of his monograph, which emphasises the suffering of humans in their roles and in society, also points to the general pressure emanating from society. The possibility of adapting behaviour for individual need remains restricted in scope. Thus his concept can help to analyse the desolate conditions and constraints to which the oppressed population in the anti-apartheid plays is subjected, in addition to identifying the devastating effects apartheid also has on its executors. What Dreitzel's concept does not offer, however, are ways out of the suffering caused by role-playing in society.

1.4.4. Apartheid, roles and the individual

According to Lothar Krappmann, the more powerful ruling interests are, the less norms are accessible to interpretation by the individual and the more likely it is that expectations of interacting individuals will be taken into consideration (1982^{6}: 28). He defines an absolute system of power as a society which as a whole can be considered a total institution. The totalitarian state described in George Orwell's dystopia *Nineteen Eighty-Four* is an example of such an absolute system. In a totalitarian society it is impossible to develop and maintain a personal identity because everyone is forced to follow the same norms and interpretations. Individuals living under repressive social circumstances are subjected to the given definition and interpretation of social norms by threat of severe sanctions (cf. 1982^{6}: 31, 126).

As apartheid ideology is based on the role definition of whites as masters and blacks as servants and forbids resistance to this, it can be regarded as the basis of a total society. However, apartheid society was never able to silence all voices of opposition or, in sociological terms, those voices that acknowledged and questioned discrepancies between social norms and individual needs. Apartheid did not succeed in developing into a total institution where self-defence against the system of repression was impossible. The fact that individuals suffered from apartheid's pathological role repertoire points to the failure of the state to totally control its subjects' thoughts, feelings and needs (cf. 1982^{6}: 31). Goffman points out in *Asylums* that individuals in total institutions resist being deprived of their identity by developing an underlife which lies outside the reach of the institution: "The practice of reserving something of oneself from the clutch of an institution [...] is not an incidental mechanism of defense but rather an essential constituent of the self" (1961a: 319). The South African plays under review all show how the oppressed subjects use role-play to manifest personal identities which the state does not allow, but ultimately, cannot control. Thus these characters are still able to personally contribute to role behaviour, maintain role distance and successfully execute resistance to prescribed roles and expectations.

1.4.5. Goffman and the idea of behaviour as theatrical performance

The metaphor of the theatre, be it "all the world's a stage" or *theatrum mundi,*[55] is appropriated by many scholars writing on role identity.[56] Erving Goffman adopted the concept of the theatricality of everyday behaviour in his monograph *The Presentation of Self in Everyday Life* (1959). In contrast to the other sociologists presented here, his version of role theory looks at actual individual role behaviour in daily life. In his heuristic model (cf. Müller 1991: 37) he presents an analysis of the interaction between individuals. He claims that behaviour in interaction resembles the role-play of actors in front of an audience. The individuals become performers who attempt to stage characters. Goffman examines in detail the techniques of impression management that individuals employ to present an idealised image of themselves and to control their audience. He also looks at contingencies associated with the employment of such techniques. This allows him to identify the dramaturgical problems that individuals encounter when they present their activities in front of others. He also discusses how they can avoid disruptions that would discredit their behaviour and threaten their definition of the situation (cf. 1959: 15).

According to Goffman, performances are never completely individual and unique presentations but are social events in social institutions that are formed to fit the expectations of society. Performances often attempt to incorporate society's officially accredited values and can be seen as an "expressive rejuvenation and reaffirmation" of communal moral values (cf. 1959: 35). Thus when individuals act in established social roles, parts of the performances will function in general and

---

[55] The idea of *theatrum mundi* was developed in the Middle Ages. People were seen as puppets that God moved across the stage of the world. For a discussion of the *theatrum mundi* metaphor see Jauss (1979).

[56] Uri Rapp (1973; 1993) analyses the sociology of the theatre in combination with social communication. See also Bruce Wishire (1982), who takes a phenomenological approach to the complex of role-playing and identity.

fixed fashions using established expressive equipment that Goffman calls "fronts" (1959: 22). "Personal front" therefore refers to the "appearance" and "manner" by which a certain individual is identified (1959: 24). Often social interactions underpin restraints established by values and norms that force individuals to suppress their impulses and moods. Audiences, for their part, process the information conveyed by the performer by referring to past experiences and stereotypical thinking and thus develop abstract stereotyped expectations in order to manage information more efficiently (cf. 1959: 20-26).

Goffman, who deals with the mid-twentieth century Anglo-American societies, views society as a fairly fixed class hierarchy. Nonetheless, he gives many examples which demonstrate that individuals do not only interact as members of their class, but they also play roles which transgress class boundaries. Goffman shows that by observing how society functions, an individual can slip into many different social roles. In order to foster a certain impression, a performer must identify the elements that make up the relevant role identity and use these to lead the audience into accepting the created definition of the situation. It is also vital to avoid disruptions that could discredit a presentation. Such "inadvertent acts" are, for example, all "unmeant gestures" such as a loss of muscle control or remarks that give away the secret (1959: 208, 51). A presentation may also be discredited by "too much or too little concern [...] with the interaction" such as forgetting one's lines or showing too much interest in a topic, or "inadequate dramaturgical direction" such as an improper setting or wrong timing (1959: 52, cf. 52f.).

Because individuals are able to take on roles, the construction of the accepted, over-all definition of the situation does not primarily involve agreement on what objectively constitutes reality or truth. Instead, the situation is defined by agreement on subjective reality in the sense of "agreement as to whose claims concerning what issues will be temporarily honored" (1959: 9f, cf. 1-76).

The individual is not only concerned with the presentation of self, but "[...] the definition of the situation projected by a particular participant is an integral part of a projection that is fostered and sustained by the intimate co-operation of more than one participant" (1959: 77f.). Goffman calls the group of individuals who stage a single routine together in front of an audience a "team" (1959: 79). Ideally, team members should agree on the impression they wish to convey and possess an equal degree of information about the routine that will be staged. Thus "back region" or "backstage" preparations serve to give a consistent presentation in the "front region" where the action takes place (1959: 112, 107). Although backstage behaviour is related to the performance, it can be "inconsistent with the appearance fostered by the performance" (1959: 134). Dramaturgical loyalty and discipline are necessary to control the information that is spread behind the scenes and to keep secrets from seeping through to the audience (cf. 1959: 85-91). The team's director plays a dominant role in that she or he is usually responsible for controlling the performance (cf. 1959: 98-101). If team presentations involve a larger number of characters, the chances are that behaviour will be disrupted and the fostered impression will be inconsistent.

Müller suggests that Goffman's terminology is suitable for the analysis of both characters and action in literary texts that present social reality through personal interaction and emphasise the theatrical artificiality of interpersonal relations and actions (cf. 1991: 38). Ewald Mengel argues that this concept is especially useful for the analysis of drama because this is where human interaction takes place in its purest form (cf. 1978: 17).

1.5. Performance theory: The relationship of performance and society

Erving Goffman's sociological approach to human interaction makes use of the language and concepts of theatrical performances. It has been called a "scenographic approach" (Schechner 1977: 120). By direct contrast, performance theorists such as Richard Schechner and Victor Turner analyse theatre or 'stage drama'/'aesthetic drama' by examining actual social behaviour. Both of these approaches emphasise the dialectic relationship of society and theatre. However, it is important to keep in mind that theatre and society are not congruent or identical domains. Theatre undoubtedly mirrors society to a certain degree while social behaviour has a certain theatrical quality. Nonetheless, the idea that 'life is art and art is life' remains a loosely metaphoric equation in this perspective. An examination of the ideas by Schechner and Turner on the relationship between performance and society helps to identify social expression in performance art and theatre's contribution to social analysis and change.

1.5.1. Performance art and social behaviour

Richard Schechner names seven public performance activities of human beings: play, games, sports, theatre, music, dance and ritual (cf. 1988a: 6). In his analysis of these activities Schechner leaves all evolutionary approaches behind. He focuses instead on the horizontal relation of the performance types - that is, "what each autonomous genre shares with the others" (1988a: 6). Looking at the formal relations among these performance activities, he identifies a "definitive break" between games, sports and theatre on the one hand and play and ritual on the other. This break is "indicated by the different quality and use of the rules that govern these activities" (1988a: 13). Schechner categorises these performance forms into three groups. In the first group he classifies 'play' as self-assertive "'free activity'" where the players create their own rules. 'Ritual,' the second group, follows rules decreed by the authority and expresses "the individual's submission to forces larger or at least other than oneself" (1988a: 13). 'Ritual' is an example of "the reality principle, the agreement to obey rules that are *given*." The third group, 'games,' 'sports' and 'theatre' (including dance and music), allows people to "express their *social* behaviour." Schechner argues that in this third group, which mediates between 'play' and 'ritual,' "rules exist as frames." Rules demarcate what "must be done" and what "must not be done." However, the space between the frames is characterised by freedom. Schechner claims that "the better the player, the more s/he will be able to exploit this freedom" to pursue personal goals (all 1988a: 14).

From this perspective theatre is closely related to sports and games. Schechner suggests that one way of approaching theatre could be via game theory or transactional analysis because dramas represent what these theories analyse: "interpersonal relationships usually pivoting on a conflict situation" (1988a: 16). Although it is not the aim of this study to further examine the relationship between these various fields, it is, however, interesting to note the compatibility of these theories with theatre. This highlights once again the idea that plays give expression to social behaviour by mirroring, critiquing, developing and inspiring it.

1.5.2. Stage drama and social drama

Victor Turner and Richard Schechner consider the similarity between social crisis situations ('social dramas') and conflicts presented on stage ('stage dramas') and then examine how these two domains affect each other.[57] Schechner addresses the

[57] A. Paul Hare (1985) offers an approach for analysing human interaction by combining the fields of social psychology and conflict resolution.

use of the "theatrical paradigm" (1988c: 166) in Turner and Goffman's analysis of social interaction:

> For both Turner and Goffman the basic human plot is the same: someone or some group begins to move to a new place in the social order; this move is acceded to or blocked; in either case a crisis occurs because any change in status involves a readjustment of the entire scheme; this readjustment is effected performatively - that is, by means of theatre and ritual. (1988c: 166)

In addition, Schechner further qualifies Turner's approach:

> Turner [...] analyzes "social dramas" using theatrical terminology to describe how disharmonic or crisis situations are dealt with. These situations - arguments, combats, rites of passage - are inherently dramatic because participants not only do things, they *show themselves and others what they are doing or have done*; actions take on a reflexive and performed-for-an-audience aspect. (1988c: 166)

Turner uses the term 'social dramas' to refer to "units of aharmonic or disharmonic process, arising in conflict situations" (1974: 37). They are composed of four main phases of observable action in public: breach, crisis, redressive action and reintegration. 'Breach' refers to an action that disrupts a social unit. 'Crisis' signifies the conflicts between different parties that succeed the breach and reveal opposing "characters, interests and ambitions" (1990: 8). The crisis must be overcome by 'redressive public action,' executed by the group's leaders, to guarantee social unity and continuity. 'Reintegration' refers to the solution of the social drama - either the restoration of the pre-breach situation or the recognition of a schism which cannot be overcome (cf. 1974: 38-42; 1986: 74f.; 1990: 8f.).

In Turner's opinion, Goffman considers the world of social interaction a stage which is composed of ritual or "standardized unit act[s]" (Turner 1986: 75). By contrast, Turner speaks only of a "dramaturgical phase" when "*crises* arise in the daily flow of social interaction." He argues, "[...] if daily living is a kind of theatre, social drama is a kind of metatheatre, that is, a dramaturgical language about the language of ordinary role-playing and status-maintenance which constitutes communication in the quotidian social process." This includes an element of reflexivity or the "ability to communicate about the communication system itself" (1986: 76). The phases of crisis and redress both rely on reflexivity. In the mostly unconscious phase of crisis, reflexivity succeeds manifestation, while in the conscious phase of redress, reflexivity is present in its machinery, from legal to ritual (cf. 1986: 76). Schechner departs from this idea to assess the relationship between social and aesthetic drama. He suggests that the "visible drama is in the crisis and redressive action. With hindsight, from beyond reintegration, the whole sequence can be easily reconstructed. The elegance of the whole pattern as reconstructed is where social drama and aesthetic drama coincide" (1988d: 188). This reconstruction is possible because, as Turner points out, "Social dramas and social enterprises - as well as other kinds of processual units - represent sequences of social events, which, seen retrospectively by an observer, can be shown to have structure" (1974: 35).

Schechner emphasises the idiosyncrasies and specific cultural characteristics of both stage/aesthetic and social dramas. He argues that Turner's breach/crisis/redress/reintegration-scheme is modelled on European notions of theatre (cf. 1988d: 190f.). Turner, however, believes that his model can be used to describe the social dramas of many different societies - societies whose various cultures give the style and tempo of the social dramas their characteristic touch. What these social dramas seem to have in common in many societies are some elements of "*public reflexivity*" in their redressive phases. Turner asserts that "[...] by their activation groups take stock of their own current situation: the nature and strength of their social ties, the power of their symbols, the effectiveness of their legal and moral controls, the sacredness and soundness of their religious traditions, and so forth." A controversy compels the conflicting parties to "diagnose its source, and in doing so, to become fully aware of the principles that bond them beyond and above the issues that have temporarily divided them" (all 1990: 9). This leads to the creation of what Turner calls a "communitas" or "social anti-structure" because it unites people beyond their formal social bonds (1974: 45), allowing them to recognise and critique social and political reality. This *communitas* is temporary and liminal.[58] It exists in the "'subjunctive mood' of culture, the mood of maybe, might-be, as-if, hypothesis, conjecture, desire [...]" in contrast to the "indicative mood [...] of cause-and-effect, of rationality and commonsense" in normal daily life (1990: 11, 12).

---

[58] Turner derives the concept of liminality from ritual and rites of passage. Theatre as one of the successors of ritual is striving to rediscover its hidden, liminal power sources. Ritual and the performance arts stem from the subjunctive and liminal redressive phase of social drama "where the contents of group experiences [...] are replicated, dismembered, remembered, refashioned, and mutely or vocally made meaningful" (1990: 13).

Figure 1:

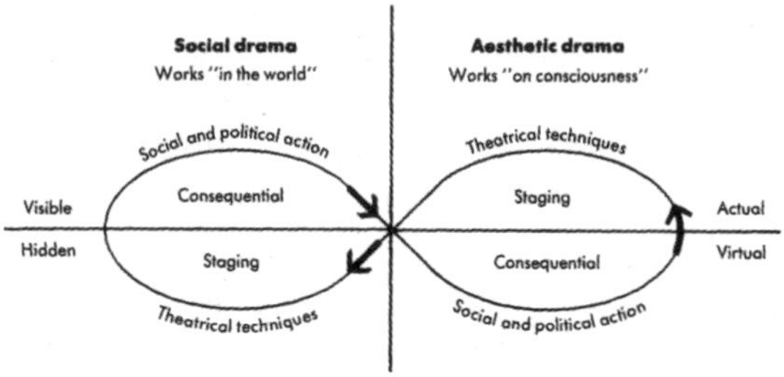

(Schechner 1988d: 190)

A successful performance which offers a heightened experience will lead to a general feeling of *communitas*.[1]

Turner and Schechner have represented the interrelationship of social drama and stage or aesthetic drama in a horizontal figure of eight (see Figure 1).

The two half circles above the dividing line signify the manifest, visible public realm. The half circles below the line represent the hidden, virtual sphere. The circle on the left represents the social drama (breach, crisis, redress, integration) and the one on the right stands for the sum of a society's performance art (cf. Turner 1990: 16). The crucial idea behind this figure of eight is that social and stage dramas affect each other: the figure of eight represents an "'infinity loop'" (Schechner 1988d: 190). Turner emphasises that the manifest or overt social drama influences the latent realm of stage drama. Its unique cultural form "unconsciously, or perhaps preconsciously" shapes form and content of the stage drama of which it is the "active or 'magic' mirror." The stage drama has the function of supplying entertainment and "metacommentary, explicit or implicit, […] on the major social dramas of its social context (wars, revolutions, scandals, institutional changes)" (1990: 16). At the same time the stage drama's message and rhetoric influence the social drama's "*latent* processual structure" and promote its "ready ritualization" (1990: 16, 17). This means that life takes the role of a mirror held up to art and that

[1] Schechner makes an interesting point: "One of the beautiful ironies of theatre is that it is a *communitas* infiltrated by structure, a liminal event refracting the tensions of social order and disorder. The conventions of performance are a latticework supporting the liberties of theatrical *communitas*" (1988d: 193).

the “living now *perform* their lives,” having adopted some of their opinions and ideologies from stage drama (1990: 17). In Schechner’s words the action of a social drama is “informed” or “shaped, conditioned, guided” by hidden theatrical and rhetorical techniques as well as aesthetic principles. Reciprocally, a culture’s performed aesthetic drama is “informed,” “shaped, conditioned, guided” by hidden processes of social interaction (1990: 190). In other words Schechner believes that the sequences of events of “probably all [aesthetic] dramas” are influenced and guided by “deep social sub-structures” (1988d: 192). He gives an example: “The politician, activist, militant, terrorist all use techniques of the theatre (staging) to support social action - events that are consequential, that is, designed to change the social order or to maintain it.” In a comparative fashion the “theatre artist uses the consequential actions of social life as the underlying themes, frames, and/or rhythms of her/his art. The theatre is designed to entertain and sometimes to effect changes in perception, viewpoint, attitude [...]” (1988d: 190). Turner concludes:

> Neither mutual mirroring, life by art, art by life, is exact, for each is not a planar mirror but matricial mirror; at each exchange something new is added and something old is lost or discarded. Human beings learn through experience, though all too often they repress painful experience, and perhaps the deepest experience is through drama; not through social drama, or stage drama [...] alone, but in the circulatory or oscillatory process of their mutual and incessant modification. (1990: 17)

Turner asserts that the aesthetic form of theatre is “inherent in” social drama or socio-cultural life. By contrast, the reflexive and therapeutic character of theatre, which he sees as “essentially a child of the redressive phase of social drama, has to draw on power sources often inhibited or at least constrained in the cultural life of society’s ‘indicative’ mood.” He concludes that the “deliberate creation of a detached, still almost-sacred liminal space, allows a search for such sources” (all 1990: 12). One such source of power is the “liberated and disciplined body itself,” central to experimental theatre theories of, among many others, Jerzy Grotowski. The body with its “many untapped resources for pleasure, pain, and expression” (Turner 1990: 12) is one of, if not, *the* essential dramatic element in the work of many South African playwrights and actors from Athol Fugard to Percy Mtwa.

The “indicative mood” of apartheid South African society was largely dominated by racial oppression based on a hypocritical “rationality” and “commonsense” that catered to pro-apartheid society’s aims of political and economic dominance. In a situation such as this anti-apartheid protest culture can be said to exist in a liminal position. It represents the “subjunctive mood” of culture - the mood of desire for the abolition of apartheid. Protest culture attempts to comment on and critique social conflict situations of the apartheid era such as daily instances of racial discrimination, be they on a political, economic, social, cultural or psychological level. By presenting these conflicts on stage, playwrights and actors aim to initiate the audience's self-reflexivity which, ideally, leads to the spectators' heightened consciousness. They are united in a "*communitas*," recognising their common plight. During the time of apartheid performance culture and literature had a highly political character. They were influenced by political thinking and also strove to influence politics with their ideas, engaging in the process of reflection, comment and modification. Dennis Walder emphasises that there has been a "uniquely close relationship between the 'event on the stage' and 'the social and political reality on the streets'" in South Africa in general (1992: 344). One period in which the "oscillatory" mutuality between society and the stage was especially dominant was, for example, during the 1970s with the emergence of the Black Consciousness Movement. It is not until apartheid is recognised as an evil system by the pro-apartheid group that South African society as a whole can form a "*communitas*" which abolishes racial oppression.

This study examines the plays under review as "expressions of social behaviour" - not only in Schechner's sense as working with, in and around society's rules but also in Turner's sense of social reflection and influence on society. The plays' direct statements and action as well as their omissions and silences are regarded as reflecting the 'do's and don'ts' of the society in which they are set.

2. "A man's scenery is other men":[1] Identity and Transgression in Athol Fugard's Plays

> Without consciousness we become victims instead of actors – even if it is only a question of acting victims. And in this make-believe of our lives the audience is self.
>
> Athol Fugard[2]

2.1. Athol Fugard's approach to drama

In his plays Athol Fugard responds to life under extreme circumstances in apartheid South Africa. Living in a society that was based on institutionalised, systematic racial segregation and oppression for over four decades, he thematises the effects of brutality and degradation on the people in his country. He foregrounds the distinct quality of humiliation, suffering and despair that pervades the lives and controls the identities of millions of South Africans. He also focuses on the effects that apartheid has on personal relationships and interaction.

Influenced by twentieth-century theatre practitioners such as Antonin Artaud, Bertolt Brecht, Peter Brook and Jerzy Grotowski,[3] Fugard believes in the actuality of performance and relies on the power of live actors to move a live audience. He does not place his audience in the role of passive theatre viewers who observe stage action through the proscenium arch. Reflecting on his first published play, *The Blood Knot* (1961),[4] he defines what he calls the audience's "pure theatre experience." Its main ingredients are "the actor and the stage, the actor *on* stage," "'[...] the actor in space and silence [...]'" (1986: n.p.; cf. Chapter 3.1.). He believes, "Only a fraction of my truth is in the words" (1983: 171). Dennis Walder defines this theatre experience as a "living moment" and concludes that it generates a

[1] Fugard (1983: 141), stated in 1966.

[2] Fugard (1983: 107), stated in 1963.

[3] Fugard often refers to Brecht's theatre practice and the impact of Grotowski's *Towards the Poor Theatre* (1967) on his work (cf. Fugard 1973b: 64-7; 1977/78: 81; 1983; 1984: 23; Walder 1984: 4). Walder describes Fugard's incorporation of Brecht and Grotowski into South African dramaturgic discourse as "crucial, innovatory, and influential" (1992: 346).

[4] Fugard wrote two plays before *The Blood Knot*, namely *No-Good Friday* (1958) and *Nongogo* (1959) about life in the township Sophiatown, but he refers to them as his "apprenticeship plays." Both plays were published after *The Blood Knot*.

"characteristic intensity of effect gained by his work, an effect of painful, shared awareness, which it is perhaps uniquely possible to create in the theatre" (1984: 3).

Fugard has been able to contribute to the creation of this awareness by living in South Africa with his eyes open to the world around him: "[...] my plays come from life and from encounters with actual people" (1983: 8), especially in the Eastern Cape region where he was born and has spent many years of his life.[5] He has been making notes on his observations of and interactions with fellow South Africans in his journals, parts of which have been edited and published as *Notebooks 1960-1977* by his friend Mary Benson. Fugard says of his notebooks that they represent a continuous literary exercise. He adds that they also "reflect a certain reality in terms of the South African experience but although I have lived through very major political crises, these are not reflected" (1983: 8). Instead, he explores the effects that politics has on the psyche of the country's inhabitants. For example, when he attended the trial of three black men who were arrested for sabotage in 1962, he witnessed what he called the "terror of the Law: of the legal machine" and justice without "dignity, or the respect for human dignity." He was greatly affected by the "violation of the personal, private image" in the courtroom and the fact that "[...] all the time the accused is present, hearing his movement, gestures, very words, talked about without any reference to the innermost realities of his being" (1983: 49f.). He concluded that this arrest for sabotage was "the spectacle of society with its hands on the outsider (Camus)."[6] In 1958 Fugard had his first "traumatic" experience of apartheid's institutions after accepting a job as clerk in the Pass Laws Court which dealt with offences against the pass laws: "I knew that the society was evil before I had that experience, but seeing the machinery in operation taught me how it works and in fact what it does to people" (1973b: 72).

In contrast to these public situations directly under institutional control, Fugard also records many public and more private encounters between members of the different ethnic groups that exhibit an analogous hostility and humanity-denying brutality. These anecdotes show to what extent all levels of society have appropriated apartheid ideology and used it to victimise each other, both in situations of which

[5] Fugard's biography is offered, for example, by Seidenspinner (cf. 1986: 98-162), Vandenbroucke (cf. 1985: 1-16) and Walder (cf. 1984: 19-32).

[6] Fugard uses Camus's term 'outsider' which refers to a man who does not give the authority of his consent to social sanction (cf. Fugard 1983: 48f.).

Fugard was merely a distant observer and in cases when he was affected directly. For instance, he made the following journal entry in 1960:

> Two coloured men came to the door. Trying to get to flat No. 4. 'That way,' I said. 'Thank you, baas. Thank you, my baas. We were frightened, you see. We just couldn't walk in there, could we baas? It's not our place.' This was for my benefit. They were collecting 'empties' to be resold to bottle stores. (1983: 21)

This reveals both his and the men's awareness of the theatricality and hypocrisy of the role behaviour that apartheid ideology prescribes. The next anecdote shows that apartheid does not only affect interaction between whites and blacks[7] but also creates cleavage among the different groups of the black population:

> Dice game in the light of a lamp in the Donkin Reserve, About [*sic*] six young coloureds ten-fifteen years. An African man had joined them – about thirty. Either he was losing or they were cheating but he said something [...]. He got angry, started swearing. They laughed and called him names, 'Kaffer! Swartgat!'[8] Once he tried to chase them but they were too quick. He had a tremendous battle with his pride and tried consciously, very obviously, just to walk away. (1983: 22)

Fugard often tries to put himself into the mind of the downgraded and abused party in order to understand their responses, be they peaceful as in this case or violent due to a deep frustration and helplessness. The incidents he writes down demonstrate that in the end all sides are victims of apartheid and that even members of the same group may sometimes have no way out other than to become violent with each other. Petty apartheid and daily racism infuse the co-existence and interaction of the people with prejudice, mistrust and hostility. This being the reality of life, Fugard is led to examine the effect of racial discrimination on the blacks' concept of self. He reproaches the apartheid state for destroying their sense of self, identity and dignity and explores the state-defined "facelessness" (1983: 49) of these individuals. When he witnesses how a coloured boy is chased out of a whites-only swimming pool, he speculates, "A nice, clear example of sheer unconscious brutality of the South Africa I know. Just one question: What? What did that little kid say, or ask, or reply to himself? How did he fit that rejection into

---

7 'Black' is a generic term which referred to members of the coloured, Indian and African population in apartheid South Africa (see Chapter 1.1).

8 Extremely derogatory names for black South Africans. 'Kaffer' is comparable to the American derogatory term 'nigger'; 'swartgat' translates as 'black arse.'

the tentative pattern of living?" (1983: 46). It is this question of the construction of identity and alterity that Fugard explores in his work.[9]

The dramatist repeatedly refers to his need for a powerful image to create a play, an image which he acquires by closely observing the world around him.[10] He looks into the reality of the lives of his fellow South Africans, focusing mainly on poor white Afrikaners, coloureds and the most suppressed group, the African majority.[11] His reliance on the stories of ordinary people's lives and circumstances represents his attempt to "'witness as truthfully as I can the nameless and destitute of one little corner of the world'" (Benson 1973: 55; cf. Fugard 1993: 386; Walder 1992: 350-61; 1994: 126-33). Jeyifo Biodun concludes that Fugard presents the audience with situations in which the social background goes beyond the "usual 'setting' of the drama." Instead, the "'social background' is the very stuff and texture of the dramaturgy, a kind of background-as-structured-content." This close dialectic between society and art demonstrates, as Schechner and Turner have also suggested, the "dynamic interplay of 'theatre in society and society in the theatre'" (Biodun 1985: 100; cf. Chapter 1.5.2).

Fugard usually focuses his plays on two or three characters. Their lives are connected either by ties of blood, love and friendship or by the common suffering from social, cultural, political, racial and religious forces. Yet these public forces recede into the background and give way to the examination of human relationships and identity construction. Fugard develops individual identities that are affected by apartheid's definition and fixation of social intercourse in both the public and private sphere. He shows the great strain that this situation exercises on personal relationships, integrity and identity. Fugard often stages characters struggling to survive in a world that seems bleak and meaningless. This leads critics to point out the influence on Fugard of Albert Camus's existentialism and the absurd in Samuel Beckett's work.[12] Fugard's characters also display strong emotions of "anger and

---

[9] Goetsch (1997) also sums up Fugard's concept of drama in relation to apartheid reality.

[10] Fugard is influenced by Ezra Pound's idea of image: "'An image is the presentation of a psychological and emotional complex in an instant of time.' To which he adds a remark about the 'sense of liberation, of freedom' that follows" (Fugard 1983: 77).

[11] Fugard has not written about South Africa's Indian population although he has occasionally mentioned his interaction with Indians in his *Notebooks* (cf. Fugard 1983: 68f.).

[12] This is repeatedly pointed out by critics. The works by Seidenspinner (1986), Vandenbroucke (1985), Walder (1984) and Wertheim (2000) are representative. See also Fugard's own reflection on these influences that continuously appear in his *Notebooks* and in interviews (for example, see Wertheim 2000: 21, fn. 9).

compassion" which express their opposition to the prevailing order (Walder 1984: 3). In addition, the strong sense of their reciprocal reliance emphasises the author's conviction that man is essentially a social being and needs the other to confirm his existence and identity. Fugard states that the "way into my life is through the 'other man'" (1983: 127) or, as the title quotation of this chapter reads, a "man's scenery is other men." Often the only thing his characters have left is each other. However, the dramatist also makes clear that even mutual support and recognition are hard to give and cannot be taken for granted. Walder concludes, "His plays make us aware not only of the South African dimension of man's inhumanity to man, but also of the secret pain we all inflict upon each other in the private recesses of our closest relationships" (1984: 2f.). However, Fugard is convinced that human beings can overcome their hellish existence through recognition of the other. In keeping with this liberal attitude,[13] he believes that the most important ingredient is awareness of the other's suffering, supplemented by responsibility, intimacy, compassion and love.[14] Given the reality of his society's inhumanity, it is not surprising that the author perceives himself to be, first and foremost, a "regional writer" who has only been able to write meaningfully about the "themes, textures, acts of celebration, of defiance and outrage that go with the South African experience" (1983: 8).

Fugard has created several plays in which he not only portrays the suffering of representatives from one of the many racial groups but also shows how apartheid affects interracial communication and interaction. He analyses the dynamics and possibilities of transgressive relationships to develop and strengthen identity in a society which has created only social roles that *per definitionem* promote alterity and forbid interracial contact. The characters' suffering becomes a sign, or even icon, for the pathological nature of apartheid society and its predefined social roles. As Albert Wertheim maintains with regard to Fugard's work,

> [...] the word "acting" has at once a theatrical and a political meaning. Theatre is a place to enact both realities and dreams, and it is thus a microcosm and a possible model for the world beyond the playhouse doors. If all the world's a stage, then the stage and the *acting* and *performance* it witnesses can also be played out in the world. (2000: 3)

---

13 Seidenspinner gives an account of Fugard's liberal attitude (cf. 1986: 98-108).

14 Cf. Fugard (1983: 127) and Goetsch (1997: 297f.). Fugard's liberal attitude has often been severely criticised by Marxists and militant blacks (cf. Kavanagh 1985).

This chapter focuses on three multi-racial 'protest plays' from the first half of Fugard's writing career. The so-called "Protest Theatre" voiced "disapproval or disagreement" with apartheid (Mda 1998: 257). Protest plays were mainly addressed to the oppressors with the aim of appealing to their conscience and thus did not go beyond criticising apartheid. Although these plays also presented to the oppressed solutions of how to survive under the apartheid regime, they never openly challenged or incited this part of the population to change their situation. Paul Goetsch's characterisation of Fugard's plays can be attributed to protest theatre in general:

> They are didactic but not propagandistic. Instead of issuing calls to action or impressing a clear political message on the audience, they challenge theater-goers to reflect upon their racial prejudices and political assumptions and to question their longing for easy solutions. (1996: 73)

In this sense protest theatre cannot be described as radical or militant.

The plays under review in this chapter all take place during the 1960s in the Port Elizabeth area and can be read as variations on the same theme. Fugard portrays coloured and white characters who suffer from apartheid's rigid definition of social roles and, consequently, the limited development of personal relationships and identity. In *The Blood Knot* (1961; revised version *Blood Knot*, 1985) Fugard examines the confrontation between two physically and mentally different individuals who are both affected by the hostility of racist society and are forced to recognise each other when they discover the meaning of their blood relationship. In *Statements after an Arrest under the Immorality Act* (1974) Fugard links the increasing human degradation in society to its legal context, which censors both platonic and physical interracial love as immoral and treats them as crimes. And in *A Lesson from Aloes* (1978) the playwright shows the negative effects of apartheid ideology on members of different racial groups who have all become socially and personally mutilated and suffer from an incapacity to interact.

2.2. In search of one's identity: *Blood Knot*

Some things are only skin deep, because I got it, here in my hands, I got beauty ... too ... haven't I?

Zach in *Blood Knot*[1]

An anonymous 1961 newspaper review claimed, "Theatre history was made in Johannesburg [...] when a White man and a Black man acted together publicly in the same play."[2] In the year of the new republic's independence and consequent entrenchment of Nationalist policies, Fugard staged *The Blood Knot* about two coloured brothers in which he himself took the part of Morris while his African actor-friend, Zakes Mokae, played the role of Zachariah. In this performance the difference between the Pieterson siblings is defined as racial in the most obvious way: Morrie is light-skinned while Zach is dark-skinned.[3] This visual difference is accompanied by differences in psychological, social and cultural terms.

Morrie is strict, controlled, rational, prudent, frugal, ascetic and devout – just as a pious Calvinist Afrikaner ought to be. He rejects all hedonistic elements in life and sets up plans for the future in his belief in delayed gratification. He possesses a modest degree of education (literacy and good manners) as well as a certain worldliness. He has seen other South African towns and cities apart from his home town, Port Elizabeth, where he lives in the poor coloured neighbourhood of Korsten with his brother. With the help of his most prized possessions, a Bible and an alarm-clock, he manages to impose order on their lives in the one-room shack.

Zach, by contrast, has never left the world of industrial Port Elizabeth. He is illiterate, spontaneous, sensual and he smells. He is not interested in religion or saving money for a future life, remembering instead his sex-, booze- and music-filled adventures with his jovial pal, Minnie, before Morrie's return to Korsten a year prior to the dramatic present. He works as some sort of park keeper or factory

---

[1] *Blood Knot*, 109. References to Fugard's revised version *Blood Knot* (1985) are marked *BK*. References to the original version *The Blood Knot* (1961) are flagged *TBK*.

[2] Anon. "Together on the Stage." Review from unknown South African newspaper. Found among the papers in the Fugard Manuscript Collection, Lilly Library, Indiana University, Bloomington, Indiana. See also Wertheim (2000: 18) for an imprint of this article.

[3] Morrie and Zach have the same mother. However, it is not clear as to whether they have the same father. The play itself gives no definitive clue to solve this puzzle. While Fugard thinks of them as biological brothers (cf. 1983: 10), Vandenbroucke (cf. 1985: 39) and Rutherford (cf. 1976: 268) take it for granted that they are only half-brothers. Most others critics comment on this topic but leave its outcome open.

watchman and earns the family's income – money which the house-tending Morrie saves for what he hopes will be their future: a two-man farm.

Although Morris is financially dependent on Zach, his verbal skills and articulateness secure him Zach's respect. Thus Morrie has control and the power to make decisions while Zach works hard and suffers to secure their survival. Martin Orkin suggests that the difference between the men can also be analysed according to their different attitudes towards their bodies:[4] Zach is sensual and manifests a natural attitude towards his body and his physical desires. By contrast, Morrie displays anxiety and guilt about human physicality and wishes to control and repress his bodily functions and urges.

Morrie's and Zach's characters represent stereotypical versions of the poor, white Afrikaner and the life-affirming black man. The brothers construct the role games they play around these social clichés and show how these can be used and altered effectively to exercise social and racial power. Stereotypes are revealed as ideological constructions (cf. Gilman 1985: 27f.).[5]

The fraternal hierarchical relationship of the light- and dark-skinned brothers, as Goetsch argues, mirrors the tensions and problems of racial co-existence in a South Africa where racist discourse is based on the construction of exclusive difference. However, the representation of the apartheid state and apartheid ideology in the brothers' differences is, at the same time, a distorted one (cf. 1997: 301). Looking through the racially tinted glasses of apartheid ideology, Morris and Zachariah are, first and foremost, both coloured, no matter how striking their differences in character and attitude may be. This is the lesson that the brothers learn in their isolated world of the Korsten shack. Their psychological and social differences are merely defined as illusory and invalid in the political, economic, social and racist world of South Africa. In the end the brothers are left with the option of incorporating these differences into their games and experimenting with them in theatrical fashion. It is in the course of these games and their role-playing that the men learn about the objective, given rules of social and public life. They are able to recognise their definitions of reality and dreams as subjective and impossible given

[4] See Orkin (1988; 1991: 81-107). His interpretation of *Blood Knot* focuses on the presentation of the body within the familial structure and the context of the state.

[5] See also Zijderveld (1987) for a definition of stereotypes and clichés as well as their function. Six (1987) describes the use of stereotypes in social psychology.

the world in which they live. They both reconcile themselves to their personal histories and identities through their various games and learn to live in the present.

2.2.1. Dreams

Both Morris and Zachariah are dreamers, but their dreams are of a strikingly different nature. While Zach relives his hedonistic past, Morrie dreams of a happy, alternative future on a two-man farm.[6] In Afrikaans writing the farm represents, as J.M. Coetzee explains, "the sacral place where the soul can expand in freedom" and the "little kingdom [where] a man can be his own master." He suggests that by extension the farm signifies the dream of the "'Free State' where the Afrikaners can take care of their own affairs in their own way" (1988: 175). The notion of the farm being far away from society in the beauty and safety of the land is important for Morrie. He shares his dream with Zach:

> [*Morris fetches an old map from the shelf over his bed.*]
>
> [. . .] A map . . . of Africa. [. . .] Look – there . . . and there . . . and down here . . . Do you see it? Blank. Large, blank spaces. Not a town, not a road, not even those thin little red lines. And, notice, they're green. That means grass. (*BK* 59)

Morrie's emphasis of the uninhabited area as a blank space is reminiscent of the narrator's description of the map of Africa in Joseph Conrad's *Heart of Darkness*.[7] Far from representing stereotypical colonial interests or a higher morality, however, Morrie's dream serves the same function as his failed dream of passing as white in that it represents his escape from an unaccommodating present.

In his previous attempt to 'try for white'[8] Morrie presented his camouflaged self to society. He has understood that no matter who he wishes to be, what counts is how society evaluates him. Erving Goffman calls this the virtual social identity attributed to a character, an effect which arises from normative expectations that are "righteously presented demands." He contrasts this with the actual social identity of

---

[6] Compare this difference to white Frieda and coloured Errol in *Statements after an Arrest under the Immorality Act*. In the discussion about how to spend the last 43 cents in his pocket Errol reveals his belief in instant gratification whereas Frieda is interested in saving for the future (cf. *SA* 87f.).

[7] "Now when I was a little chap I had a passion for maps. [...] At that time there were many blank spaces on the earth [...]. But there was one yet - the biggest, the most blank, so to speak - that I had a hankering after" (Conrad 1995: 21f.).

[8] South African English for 'pass for white.'

a person. A stigma then arises if a discrepancy between these two types of identities becomes noticeable. It is a discrepancy between stereotype and actual attribute (1963: 2; cf. 2-4). Had his 'colouredness' been discovered, Morrie would have suffered not only from legal prosecution but also from severe social stigmatisation.

Having realised how hostile society is towards passing, Morrie now desires to leave behind society and its categorisations as well as the space and time that society controls. He sees himself as a victim of society - as a man who is neither really white nor coloured and as an insecure, identity-less creature who believes that he can find peace of mind only in the asociality of a monastic and self-sustaining farm.

Morrie's dream of escape to the farm is threatened by Zach's desire to live, to experience himself as made of flesh and blood. His desire for women and sex not only characterises him as an individual and a social being but also shows that his longings are essentially human, realistic and possible to realise. No matter how asocial Morrie is or believes he can be, he cannot win an idealistic game against Zach, who behaves as a truly social being in a social reality. In addition, Zach's dream is in accordance with apartheid reality. Implied in his descriptions of his good times with his friend Minnie is the given that the men stay in their coloured areas and meet with coloured women. For Zach racial and social barriers are not an issue.

By contrast, Morrie's dream transgresses the social and racial barriers of a country whose rules are defined by apartheid. He does not realise, or for that matter want to realise, that whites are farm owners, whereas coloureds and blacks are usually never more than farm labourers.[9] The widening gap between Morrie's personally desirable but socially not permissible development is a direct result of apartheid law. However, apart from the fact that it is theoretically impossible to realise the dream socially, it is also a practical impossibility as it requires much suffering and denial in the process of attaining the goal. It is as if the dream itself were anchored in a large, blank space that cannot properly be accessed or inscribed. This can also be seen as a metaphor for Morrie's true coloured identity - in contrast to whites, who appropriate land and colour-in the large blank spaces on maps in their colonialist endeavours to demonstrate possession.[10]

---

[9] This theme also appears in *Sizwe Bansi is Dead* (1972) in the story of Jacob and is still topical in Fugard's post-apartheid plays *Valley Song* (1996) and *Sorrows and Rejoicings* (2001).

[10] Ampie Coetzee traces the Dutch settlers' "saga of land ownership" from Jan van Riebeeck in the mid-seventeenth century onwards and shows that a whole discourse on land and ownership

This juxtaposition of the brothers' dreams portrays Morrie as a masochist, ready to endure extreme personal and physical hardships for his dream. It is through Zach's reactions and his proximity to real life that the audience identify the illusory quality of Morrie's dream. As Russell Vandenbroucke points out, Morrie has merely exchanged the illusion of trying for white with the dream of the farm, failing to realise that he continues to remain mired in illusion (cf. 1985: 38). This dream is based on a subjective definition of the situation which does not correspond to objective circumstances. Society's refusal to tolerate the realisation of such dreams - both that of the farm and of passing to achieve racial integration - reveals its repressive character. Hans-Peter Dreitzel asserts that this repression results from the lack of open discussion about the relative legitimacy of social needs. The larger the discrepancy between the possible and the actual satisfaction of desires and needs, the stronger this repressive character becomes. However, this discrepancy correlates antithetically to the degree of self-determination of an enlightened people ("Selbstbestimmung der Gesellschaft" 1980[3]: 170; cf. 165-73). Although there is little evidence in the play for Morrie's passing, his anecdotes suggest that he has been able to pass successfully in white society at least for some time. Thus he knows what possibilities theoretically exist. It is from this knowledge and the resulting illusions about his position in society - the return of the repressed, so to speak - that he suffers.

2.2.2. Language games

Morris secures Zachariah's respect through his verbal skills. In a way he is a poet who always has the right word or the right quotation at hand. Wertheim calls Morrie an "artist, a Prospero, a playwright who seeks to control story and narrative" (2000: 22). This talent has a positive effect on Zach: he seems to be able to orient himself through Morrie's quotations and citations and appreciates the way in which words name things, feelings and concepts.[11] Even though Zach is aware of the fact that words can signify abstract concepts, these only carry meaning for him if they

---

developed: "Land is ownership, and in colonial times land was allocated according to the laws of the colonists, and disregarding the customs of the original inhabitants. The law and its justification or ownership was synonymous with power" (1997: 106). On a literary level J.M. Coetzee presents the development of South African landscape writing in English (cf. 1988). See also the collection of essays edited by Darian-Smith, Gunner & Nuttall (1996).

[11] Vandenbroucke (cf. 1985: 42) and Walder (cf. 1984: 57) also comment on Morrie's linguistic talent and its effects on Zach.

refer to a specific situation. His limited sense of abstraction is also revealed in the way in which he remembers these words. Nonetheless, he undergoes a learning process which equals a process of empowerment:

> ZACHARIAH: *Ja*. They call a man a boy. You got a word for that, Morrie?
>
> MORRIS. Long or short?
>
> ZACHARIAH. Squashed, like it didn't fit the mouth. [...]
>
> MORRIS. Prejudice.
>
> ZACHARIAH. Pre-ja-dis.
>
> MORRIS. Injustice!
>
> ZACHARIAH. That's all out of shape as well.
>
> MORRIS. Inhumanity!
>
> ZACHARIAH. No, that's when he [his boss] makes me stand at the gate. [...] He said, 'Go to the gate or go to hell ... Boy!' [...] Prejudice and inhumanity in one sentence!
>
> (*BK* 74f.)

It is obvious that Zach remembers words phonetically – not surprising given the fact that he is illiterate - and attributes each word to a specific context or occurrence. Derek Cohen suggests that these words render his life intelligible and provide "comforting formulas and reasons which in his ignorance he can only dimly feel" (1977: 78). In contrast to this, I argue that Zach becomes acutely aware of his oppressed state during these word games because he realises that many different words correctly describe his condition. Although all of these terms have slightly different meanings, they refer to the various forms of oppression to which Zach is subjected. Whether having to stand at the gate (which makes his feet ache) or being addressed by the anonymous term 'boy,'[12] he comprehends that each of these methods, from covert to overt, is degrading. However, the accumulation of insults and injustices allows the power of the whites over him to become even greater and more threatening. At the end of this conversation his awareness of his own situation has been raised, and he more clearly understands that he is being discriminated against on the economic, social, racial and psychological level. He now knows that society prescribes him a role and also defines this role without his being able to influence the definition. What apartheid society promotes as

---

[12] The term 'boy' derives from apartheid rhetoric and is used by racist whites to refer to black adults, whose maturity and manhood is denied with this name.

'objective reality' does not correspond to Zach's subjective judgement of the situation.

However, Morrie's abstract concepts and dreams cannot prevent Zach from living his life in the concrete here-and-now. Morrie soon feels threatened by Zach's persistent longing for Minnie and their 'good-old-times' with women and is forced to act. As he cannot exorcise Zach's concrete desires with the help of words, he must take other steps to avoid losing control over his brother's life. He persuades Zach to engage in correspondence with a female pen-pal. In this way Morrie steers his sibling's very real desires for women, which threaten his dream of the farm, to a more abstract and less dangerous level. Because Zach is illiterate, Morrie will also have to act as scribe and teacher and can thus control the letters' style and content. Zach is seduced at least temporarily because he can project his sexual desires onto his pen-pal Ethel. At the same time Morrie is satisfied that he has provided a theoretical and abstract outlet for Zach's physical desires without Zach fully seeing through the scheme.

Morrie thus asserts his superiority over Zach and uses his linguistic knowledge and education not only to teach Zach new things but also to raise his level of sophistication. Morrie can control his brother's relationship by introducing him to the kind of respectful behaviour prescribed by the epistolary code of conduct (cf. Wertheim 2000: 23f.). He uses these rules to censor 'Zach's' letters to Ethel, especially to curb all sexual remarks and allusions, thus depriving Zach of voice and agency.[13]

Morrie refers to a dominant yet invisible "they" (*BK* 69) as the rule makers. This is George Herbert Mead's "generalized other"; it is the unseen collective voice of authority, in this case white authority, which sets the rules for acceptable social behaviour of which acceptable epistolary behaviour is a function. The guards in Fugard, Kani and Ntshona's play *The Island* are an analogous manifestation of order imposed by the white generalised other (see Chapter 3). Morrie believes (or at least tries to delude Zach into believing) that polite behaviour and the rules of proper conduct are guarded and guaranteed by a higher abstract, possibly even religious, authority. He presents himself to Zach as being fully indoctrinated into the system of proper conduct, blindly following the prescribed conventions. Initially this may be an easy solution to keep Zach's mind off sex, but what Morrie

[13] King comments on the nature of voice bound by convention (cf. 1993: 41).

does not seem to realise is that he is censoring Zach with the help of a method that apartheid uses to control the lives of the various racial groups. While Morrie correctly perceives the apartheid system to be confining and inhuman, Zach has the same attitude towards the epistolary formalities. He believes that these rules control and deny his natural human instinct and the right to live according to his modest desires. As these systems operate on very different levels and scales, they are only partially comparable. Notwithstanding, both systems exercise psychological pressure that leads to self-censorship and to a limited existence of self.

2.2.3. Passing

Passing is a social strategy through which the performers attempt to disguise their stigma by employing techniques of information control in order to integrate into social groups they otherwise could not enter. Passing occurs in societies that are conceived around optical dichotomies (cf. Goffman 1963: 73-104). In the South African context skin colour becomes the distinguishing factor. As Amy Robinson maintains, the pass requires that the terms of the system be intact, for it is "precisely the presence of rigid and artificial institutional binaries that not only produces the pass but also solicits the social practice of passing" (1994: 735).

In the course of *Blood Knot* we learn that Morris has tried to pass for white in the past.[14] Apparently favoured by his mother and by his light skin colour, he has abandoned his dark-skinned brother because of the racial stigma that Zach carries. The archetypal Cain and Abel story about fratricide is now charged with fraternal and racial denial (cf. Wertheim 2000: 22). Morrie has never been able to shake off his guilt at having betrayed his brother and his blood and thus returned to the Korsten shack to do penance and ask for forgiveness. However, we come to realise that Zach does not really know why Morrie left him in the first place, what he did in his absence and why he decided to come back. In a probably unintentional yet brilliant pun Morrie tells Zach that he happened to be "passing this way" (*BK* 66). This illustrates the instability of his identity. He drops little hints throughout the play - often unobserved by Zach - that he encountered insurmountable psychological barriers when trying for white, and it had been these barriers that led

[14] Kruger traces the tradition of dramatic works about passing in the late 1950s and early 1960s that thematise the taboo subject of miscegenation. Besides *The Blood Knot* (1961) she mentions Lewis Soden's *Kimberley Train* (1958), Basil Warner's *Try for White* (1959) and Bartho Smit's Afrikaans play *Die Verminktes* (cf. 1999: 104).

to his failure to integrate into white society. In a similar fashion it becomes clear that he also feels displaced in the coloured environment: "No one recognized me after all those years. I could see they weren't sure, and wanting to say 'sir' when I asked them the way" (*BK* 67). It seems as if he had not yet, at the time of his return to Zach, found his racial identity. In this state of limbo his "passing this way" can be meant not only geographically but also racially and suggests that he was not able to do more than 'play' his colouredness, not having really internalised it.

This racial insecurity shows itself when Morrie tries on Zach's suit while his brother is sleeping (end of Scene One). It is more a performance of racial rather than fraternal 'drag' in the sense that Morrie does not just want to know what it feels like to be Zach but rather what it would feel like to be dark-skinned Zach: "You get right inside a man when you can wrap up in the smell of him. It prepared me for your flesh, Zach. Because, you see, your flesh has an effect on me. [...] I saw you after all those years . . . and it hurt, man" (*BK* 67). This is more than play-acting on stage, than donning a costume to slip into another role while maintaining one's own identity outside the role. This is an act of "transvestism" (Wertheim 2000: 23), not merely cross-dressing; it is an attempt to understand fully and to merge both psychologically and emotionally with Zach's identity instead of just playing the role of Zach in a detached way. It also allows Morrie to see himself with "new objectivity" (*ibid.*). Orkin asserts that it is Morrie's attempt to understand his brother's body in a way that racist apartheid discourse has prohibited him: not as an impure body but as the body of his blood brother (cf. 1991: 104). That is why this experience is so emotional for Morrie. He feels shame for Zach because he is so obviously coloured, but he also feels ashamed of himself for having betrayed his brother and his own identity by passing. Furthermore, Morrie's appearance in drag is itself visually interesting. Zach's suit is several sizes too large for Morrie and thus presents the audience with a grotesque image of a man who is literally and figuratively lost inside his own skin as well as inside his brother's coloured skin.

This act of transvestism shows Morrie who he *is* according to the racially-based apartheid laws. He is coloured, no matter how literally and figuratively ill-fitting this categorisation is. Yet he also realises that his attempt to try for white has shown him who he *is not* in terms of both social and personal identity and what restrictions this places on his life:

> I touched something else once, with my life and these hands . . . just touched it and felt warmth and softness and wanted it like I've never wanted anything in my whole life. Ask me why I didn't take it when I touched it. That's the question. (*BK* 73)

Morrie is most likely talking in concrete terms about his desire for a white woman but also in abstract terms about the desire to be white. He repeatedly alludes to two reasons why he eventually gave up passing, both of which are implied in the quotation above. First of all, although Morrie has been trying for white successfully for many years and might have been able to continue this game for much longer, his conscience finally catches up with him and makes him repent his fraternal treason. Secondly, he knows that he is transgressing 'objective' apartheid reality, namely official state-enforced laws, with his desire. These laws openly keep the blacks in their place and at a distance from white society by exercising prohibitions on mobility, labour and sex. Morrie has understood that these racist regulations protect the agency of whites while keeping the hands of the blacks tied and thus forcing them into the prescribed role of subaltern passivity. He sums up this attitude correctly in asserting that they "don't like these games with their whiteness" (*BK* 92) because these games place the whites into a passive object position (they are being duped), which is normally reserved for all the other racial groups. What blacks desire and how they would like to define reality is simply not relevant in a racist society. Morrie explains to Zach that the apartheid system not only judges blacks according to their deeds but more so that it is their "dreams that they drag off to judgement" (*BK* 92). With this statement Morrie teaches Zach about the contradictions of white fear of racial impurity through sexual contact, a fear which leads whites to openly mark racial difference on individual bodies.[15] This image of constant surveillance shows that Morrie has accepted the notion of the state as an omniscient observer that will inevitably discover the brothers' secret desires.

The theme of self-censorship is also addressed in Fugard's first apprenticeship play, *No-Good Friday* (1958), in which Willie, an educated black man, comes to accept the barriers imposed on him by a society that is built around skin colour:

> I used to lay awake and think. I'd say to myself, 'You're black.' But hell it was so dark I couldn't see my own hand. I couldn't see my blackness, and I'd get to thinking that maybe the colour wasn't so important after all . . . and because I'd think that, I could dream a little. But there was always the next morning with its light and the truth. (43)

---

[15] See Kruger (1999: 104) and Orkin (1988: 27f.) on this aspect.

Both Willie and Morrie have discovered the dangerous and illusory quality of racially transgressive dreams.

In *Blood Knot* the correspondence with Ethel gives Zach an opportunity to dream of passing, at least on paper. The men can deduce from her photograph that she is unmistakably white. Furthermore, the fact that she responds to his letter also shows that she never believes him to be anything other than white. Zach's interest in this epistolary relationship is fully re-established because he sees it as his chance to play at trying for white and to clearly flout South Africa's Immorality Act, which prohibits interracial sex and marriage. Zach refuses his brother's wish to burn the letter and avoid getting caught in an illegal game of racial transgression. He prefers the risk and thrill that accompany the forbidden. This changed situation clearly gives him new powers of articulation and confidence. Persuading Morrie to act as scribe, Zach dictates his response to Ethel with enthusiasm and authority over his brother, respecting what he learnt from him in order not to break any formal epistolary rules. However, Morrie eventually makes Zach understand and accept the fact that his black skin will always keep him in his place, no matter how deceptive his linguistic skills may be. Morrie forces Zach to exorcise his desire for white Ethel by acknowledging and accepting the limits imposed by his skin colour or what Fanon calls the "racial epidermal schema" (1967: 112): "Ethel is so ... so ... snow white [... and] I am too ... truly ... too black. [...] She's too white to want me anyway. [...] The whole, rotten stinking lot is all because I'm black!" (*BK* 94). Race thus again proves to be a marker of both social and personal identity. Zach, however, is not one to deplore his racial stigma for long: "Black days, black ways, black things. They're me. I'm happy. Ha Ha Ha! Can you hear my black happiness? [...] after a whole life I only seen myself properly tonight. You helped me. I'm grateful" (*BK* 94f.). He can quickly embrace his own identity and accept his life as it is.[16]

Once Zach has understood that his desires for Ethel are completely incompatible with all social norms, he then tempts Morrie into meeting as a passer with the young woman, who has vaguely announced her impending visit. Orkin emphasises the element of sexual potency and achievement inherent in the games of passing scripted directly around Ethel's presence (cf. 1991: 97). Or according to Goffman,

---

[16] Lewis Nkosi criticises Zach's easy acceptance of his place as well as the fact that this play, in his opinion, does not question whiteness as a standard (cf. 1983: 144f.). Mshengu (Robert McLaren Kavanagh) elaborates on Nkosi's criticism of Fugard and evaluates Fugard's theatrical activity from the perspective of race, class and culture (1982: 172-78).

"to be 'with' someone is to arrive at a social occasion in his company," meaning that the social identity of the partner can be used by the passer to define her or his own identity (cf. 1963: 47). Zach paints the scene of courting Ethel in such a clumsy and unrefined way that Morrie interferes and takes control over the make-believe scene, thereby getting drawn into this imaginative transvestism through the use of clothing and etiquette. Zach takes advantage of this dream-state to talk his brother into buying a new suit with the 'farm money' in order to meet Ethel as a 'white' man. This scheme gives Zach a lot of power. As Amy Robinson demonstrates, in triangular games of passing the greatest power is accorded to neither the passer (Morrie) nor the dupe (Ethel) but to the third character (Zach), who knows the true identity of the passer. Zach thus has the power not only to reveal this identity but also to secure it by forcing Morrie to keep up his façade (cf. 1994: 724; Wertheim 2000: 26).

Empowered by the illusion this game supplies, Zach buys a new suit for Morrie. He asks for "the outfit of a gentleman" (*BK* 102) and is abused by the shop-owner for aspiring to white standards. However, Zach is able – literally and figuratively – to save his skin in the second clothing store. Asked if he is the gentleman in question, he replies: "Do I look like a gentleman, Mr. Moses?" (*BK* 102). Hence he proves that he has no intention of challenging or transgressing apartheid's social categories. It is only when he shows the salesman his money that he is served. With this suit it is Morrie who can make a political statement. Joanne Tompkins looks into the significance of racial cross-dressing:

> In terms of the sartorial it is a small step to wear clothes associated with 'white' groups in order to 'pass' as white, but it is a significant political act to 'pass' and thereby breach social and political boundaries that are integral to the maintenance of the colonizer-colonized dichotomy. Here, the wearing of costume becomes a means of disputing the assumption that racial difference and the race-based hierarchies of apartheid are immutable. (1998: 190)

It is interesting to note that the salesman's fear of Zach requesting a suit for himself seems unfounded because, even if Zach wore the fancy clothing himself, his dark skin colour would still give him away. However, Helen Gilbert and Joanne Tompkins emphasise that "[...] the body is open to multifarious inscriptions which produce it as a dialogic, ambivalent, and unstable signifier rather than a single, independent, and discrete entity [...]" (1996: 205). It can be argued that by openly displaying a white social identity, a black person threatens the clear-cut categorisations in apartheid society and creates a Bhabhaesque hybrid which undermines the white-black dichotomy (cf. 1994).

Morrie continues to fight Zach's plan for him to meet Ethel because he knows that successful passing not only relies on the proper clothing and etiquette. It also requires a certain attitude and confidence that whites exhibit yet that he self-consciously admits to lacking: "The clothes will help, but only help. They don't maketh the white man. It's that white something inside you, that special meaning and manner of whiteness. [...] They look at things differently. [...] It's even in their way of walking" (*BK* 103f.). Morrie's point becomes clearer in the original version of *The Blood Knot* where he makes more elaborate comments.[17] He asks Zach: "Haven't you seen their eyes when *they look at you*?" (*TBK* 100; emphasis added). The power relationship between whites and blacks is present on an abstract level that is hard to grasp with words. Nonetheless, Zach knows that all racial relationships in South Africa are based on a hierarchy of power. Being white or black in a racially-loaded environment is never just *being* in the sense of existing *per se* but always *being* determined by the context of the racial other. Thus Zach also realises that skin colour carries social meaning.

Then Morrie shares another anecdote: he tells Zach an allegorical tale of following a man walking ahead of him on a deserted road in the *veld*:[18] "When I was even nearer he saw me coming and stood up, but when he saw me clearer he picked up a stick and held it like a hitting stick, stepping back for safety and a good aim ... so what could I do but pass peacefully" (*TBK* 103). This leads him to discover what Wertheim describes as an "epiphanous racial truth" (2000: 27)[19]: "It's in the way they walk as well" (*TBK* 103). The visible gives way to epistemological guarantee.[20] Again, the term 'pass' acquires a multi-layered meaning. Morrie painfully realises that he can never integrate into white society. He is convinced that 'whiteness' is a social quality that cannot be fully appropriated by a person

---

[17] Kim McKay (1987) offers a comparison of the 1961 version of *The Blood Knot* and the new 1985 version *Blood Knot.*

[18] '*Veld'* is Afrikaans for 'field' and signifies the vastness of the land on which Afrikaners traditionally built their farms.

[19] Wertheim also understands the tale to be allegorical (cf. 2000: 27f.).

[20] Robinson (1994) offers a new concept of discovering the passer that does not rely on the visibility of her or his stigma. Analysing how a member of the same original social group as the passer can identify the transgression, she emphasises the qualities of identity politics as a skill of reading behaviour that acknowledges multiple codes of intelligibility without necessitating ontological knowledge of the identity of the performer.

who did not grow up as a white member of society. So instead of passing *as* white, he is passing *by* whites and their society. In the end this rapprochement actually sends him back to where he belongs in the eyes of racist whites.

What becomes clear in Morrie's anecdote is that the body is racialised in the South African context. Orkin maintains that no matter how the brothers define their bodies within their private family structure, the state asserts its own authority over the identity of the human body and places all bodies in relations of domination and subordination (cf. 1988: 23).[21]

2.2.4. Social play

Morris and Zachariah engage in several role games in which they enact typical white and black social roles in daily life under apartheid. Robert King maintains that by engaging in this sort of activity, they are directing the spectators' attention to "acting as a technique for social control" (1993: 40).[22] These social performances are preceded by the re-enactment of a childhood game, the car ride, which shows them self-consciously playing themselves as children. Vandenbroucke argues that this scene is important because it allows the brothers to discover an objectivity towards themselves as well as the ability to be self-critical. In contrast to the self-deceptive quality of Morrie's dream of the farm, this self-deception now yields reflection and insight, allowing the men to begin excavating the truth about their identities (cf. 1985: 39).

Zach is able to teach Morrie how to act white and acquire the 'something special' that whites have because as a dark-skinned man he is a victim of white behaviour in daily life. He knows very well how he feels when racist whites treat him condescendingly and can thus coach Morrie to evoke these feelings. For his part, Morrie has already gathered plenty of experience in the technicalities of passing. By blurring illusion and reality and manifesting what King calls the "inseparability of drama and reality" (1993: 42), Zach and Morrie rehearse the following scene in which they enact the roles they have learnt in the outside world (cf. Vandenbroucke

---

[21] Orkin also points out how Afrikaner discourse made use of the purity/impurity distinction as a means of racial separation and discrimination: "The human subject is encouraged to believe fervently that impurity is more importantly to be located in the bodies around him/her rather than within his/her own body. Or if a member of the subordinate classes, the subject is defined by prevailing discourse, held in position, as impure" (25).

[22] King reflects on the self-consciously dramatic quality of *Blood Knot*.

1985: 40): Zach plays a cheeky peanut vendor from whom Morrie wants to buy some nuts. Zach deliberately ignores Morrie and his attempts at communication, thereby insulting his 'white' manhood. Tempted by Zach's insolence, Morrie finally succeeds in appropriating the white role when he brutally calls his brother "*swartgat*" (*BK* 106) or 'black arse.' Their game has turned into a racial confrontation that alienates the two brothers from each other. It also represents a primal confrontation of self and other. Light-skinned Morrie has shown that he is able to adopt white behaviour, attitude and language and transgress apartheid's racial barriers. In his exclamation he projects the hate he feels for himself onto Zach. His act as a white man is so convincing that Zach sees him with new eyes: "I thought I was looking at a different sort of man" (*BK* 106). It is the fear in the dark-skinned man's eyes, what Loren Kruger calls "the fearful gaze of his black (br)other," that triggers Morrie's white act and eventually causes Zach to erupt in violence (1999: 109).

Chris Wortham points to the brutal fact that scenes like this emphasise that coloureds, in a white-dominated land with an ideology based on racial hierarchy, cannot avoid accepting the "spurious symbolic associations" diffused by their oppressors. This leads to a "characteristic behaviour pattern among the coloured people of the Eastern Cape: they have a tradition of elaborate self-parody, at once mocking the whites by affecting exaggerated servility and mocking themselves in their degradation" (1983: 168f.).

This scene has a disturbing effect on Zach. Not only does it remind him of his social identity in apartheid society, but it makes him feel insecure about his personal identity as well. Orkin asserts that "prevailing discourse about the human body work[s] in ways that divide[s the brothers], lead[s] them to hostility and to fracture" (1988: 29). In a night-time dream-like scene Zach puts on Morrie's new suit and confronts their deceased mother in an imaginary dialogue. His ludicrous appearance offers a grotesque sight: no matter how much he tugs at the ill-fitting, much-too-small suit and pulls the hat to hide his face, he cannot cover up his dark skin. He proves what Morrie has already pointed out: clothes do not establish identity. Unlike Morrie, who has the right skin colour and is able to learn to play white, dark-skinned Zach is deprived of this chance. He reveals his need to hear from his mother that she loved him, too, although it seems she always preferred Morrie because of his light skin and the possibilities that this implied. Nonetheless, Zach's self-esteem depends largely on his sense of his own beauty and his conviction that beauty is more than superficial (cf. *BK* 108f.). However, because he can only confront his mother in racial and fraternal disguise, he thus acknowledges the power of white propaganda which praises whiteness and condemns blackness. Similarly, Morrie also feels insecure about his personal identity after his racist exclamation. Aware of the two social identities open to him in a society that is based on convincing play-acting, he nonetheless believes he has betrayed his brother and thus also himself.

When Ethel ends the pen-pal relationship with the news of her engagement, Morrie feels that a burden, which had almost made him flee from Zach once again, has been lifted from his shoulders. He is now freed from having to meet her as a white man who betrays his own brother and his blood and avoids the risk of being caught violating apartheid laws. Despite Morrie's hesitation, Zach now talks his brother into wearing the new suit, in which he looks just like a white man. As the stage directions indicate, Zach voices his request "*slyly*" (*BK* 113) as if he were plotting a new scheme. While secretly taking advantage of Morrie's desires and his vanity, Zach stresses that Morrie's dressing-up is merely a game luring the light-skinned man into his white role: "No harm done. We're only playing" (*BK* 113). Zach's evaluation of their activity shows that he has understood that taking on roles in apartheid society is never more than a form of play-acting. He then uses his raised awareness to teach Morrie what it is like to live in a coloured skin and be mistreated by whites with their stereotypical image of blacks. He does this by slipping into his own daily role. As keeper guarding the gates of a whites-only park Zach is required to chase the black children away. Because he is the director of this script, Zach teaches Morrie how to play a hard-line white whose behaviour emphasises Zach's invisibility vis-à-vis whites despite his servility ("That sort doesn't even see me" [*BK* 116]). With increasing aggression Zach and Morrie enact their respective racially-defined roles, summed up as "*Baas* Morrie and his boy, Zach" (*BK* 114). However, for them to be able to discover their true identities as blood-brothers, they must also brutally exorcise the memory of their mother[23] as a woman who raised her sons according to different racial ideals.

In his description of his stroll around the park Morrie displays a strong feeling of hatred for the park keeper and becomes aggressive. His peace of mind is disturbed by Zach's presence as a garbage collector in the park; it is as if his entry into the white man's sight threatens the latter's conscience. This scene represents one of the

[23] From a feminist perspective Kruger sees this exorcism as a sign for the non-agency and exclusion of black women from society (cf. 1999: 109f.).

inconsistencies in apartheid thinking: although blacks are needed as minimum wage employees, whites nonetheless wish them to be invisible so as not to remind them of their own immoral behaviour and guilt. Morrie cries: "What did you mean crawling around like that? Spoiling the view, spoiling my chances! [...] I hate you, do you hear? Hate!" (*BK* 120). This outcry not only comes from the white man who fears the black man but from a self-loathing Morrie who can escape neither Zach nor his own true identity. What makes their game so emotional is that the brothers both translate the hatred they feel for themselves into hatred for the other.[24] Zach also shows that he will not endure this maltreatment without taking revenge: he mimes locking Morrie into the park to torture him psychologically for his sins:[25]

> MORRIS: But it's getting dark. [...] And cold ... and I never did like shadows ... [*Pause.*] Where are you?
>
> ZACHARIAH: Behind a tree.
>
> MORRIS: But ... but I thought you were the good sort of boy?
>
> ZACHARIAH: Me?
>
> MORRIS: Weren't you that? The simple trustworthy type of John-boy. Weren't you that?
>
> ZACHARIAH: I've changed.
>
> MORRIS: Who gave you the right?
>
> ZACHARIAH: I took it!
>
> MORRIS: That's illegal. They weren't yours. That's theft. (*BK* 121)

This conversation is revealing in two respects. Firstly, it shows Morrie's inability to keep up the stereotypical role of the brutal white man, an important insight for him on his way to embracing his own coloured identity. His façade starts to crack when he realises that Zach is no longer playing the docile black but has taken on the other stereotypical black role, that of the disobedient, dangerous and rebelling native. Coplan sees Zach as bringing "the weight of black experience and desire for self-determination to bear on the absurd fantasy and genocidal reality of apartheid" (1987: 117). Secondly, the brothers' conversation shows that empowerment is

---

[24] Similar observations are also made by Coplan (cf. 1987: 116), Goetsch (cf. 1997: 302), Vandenbroucke (cf. 1985: 40) and Wertheim (cf. 2000: 32).

[25] Wertheim describes this scene in more vivid terms: "[...] it is a vision of angry black wish fulfilment, of locking whites up in their own area and attacking them for their sins" (cf. 2000: 32).

possible for blacks but that it requires a consciousness-raising on their part. Once this state of awareness is achieved, the whites will be in real danger. It seems that only violence can reduce this tension. In fact, Zach's physical attack on Morrie is only prevented by the ringing of the alarm clock which brings both men back to the reality of the Korsten shack. At least for now Zach is only "firing blank cartridges" (Green 1970: 343).

Through their deconstruction of racial roles, the two men force each other to see themselves with the eyes of white and black society. The brothers show to themselves, each other and the audience that apartheid is a form of theatre and theatrical performance. Morrie sums up the situation for Zach: "We were carried away, as they would say, by the game. [...] Mustn't get worried though ... it was only a game." (*BK* 122). This statement confirms that for the first time Morrie is able to see himself clearly and view their situation objectively. He shows that he has now come to understand and accept his real identity as a coloured as well as the blood knot that ties him to Zach as his brother. Zach meanwhile has succeeded in finding beauty in his own identity. Their denial of self has been exorcised in this nightmarish scenario, or as Rutherford suggests, their neuroses have been exposed and cured through Freudian analysis (cf. 1976: 281). Cross-dressing evolves into a Beckettian pastime that makes Morrie and Zach seem like the successors of Hamm and Clov or Vladimir and Estragon:[26] "I'm sure it's a good thing we got the game. Because we got a lot of time left, you know!" (*BK* 122). In the end Morris and Zachariah find themselves in an objective no-win situation. Left without dreams of a happy future and without a meaning in their life, they must continue hopelessly like so many blacks at the time. At least they now know who they are. As their identities are objectively defined by apartheid discourse, they can only assume subjective identities in their own theatrical performances. They will no longer delude themselves with dreams of escape but will pursue the game as an end in itself.

Morris and Zachariah, who live in a situation controlled by relations of domination and subordination, have understood that their social identity is defined and fixed by apartheid discourse. They are acutely aware of the fact that they cannot change reality and that in the eyes of the political regime they exist only as racialised bodies. Despite the fact that Morrie and Zach can experiment with multiple

[26] Many critics suggest this parallel (cf. Goetsch 1997: 302; Hodgson 1992: 210; Walder 1984: 55; Wertheim 2000: 32).

inscriptions of their bodies, they have realised they can only do so in private (cf. Biodun 1985: 103f.). It is through their theatrical games that the brothers comment on what Richard Schechner and Victor Turner would call the "major social drama" of apartheid (Turner 1990: 16). Because they are forced to perform in private, they lack a public audience which they could influence with their playful interpretation of role behaviour. It is only on the meta-level that the drama group performing *Blood Knot* can enlighten its audience about the oppressive nature of apartheid rule.

In the end it is the on-stage presentation of acting, the display of theatre-in-the-theatre that creates political awareness in the play's characters and the audience. In addition, taking a look at the performance history of this play, Fugard's appearance as Morrie in the original production beside his black actor-friend, Zakes Mokae, as Zach brings out the true hybridity of racial identities. The fact that Fugard, a white man, is playing a coloured character who is trying for white emphasises the theatrical quality of both the theatre and apartheid. As Wertheim concludes, "Fugard allows us to realize how theatre craft, dramaturgy, can be and is employed to create the theatre of apartheid; but he demonstrates as well how that same dramaturgy, in his hands, can also be employed as a forceful weapon directed against apartheid" (2000: 29).

2.3. The disintegration of public and private self

But they won't give me a chance to live.

Steve in *A Lesson from Aloes*[27]

Two plays in which Fugard examines the effect of apartheid on intimate relationships are *Statements after an Arrest under the Immorality Act* and *A Lesson from Aloes.* Both plays will be analysed under the same rubric – the disintegration of public and private self.

In *Statements after an Arrest under the Immorality Act* (1972/1974),[28] as in *Blood Knot*, Fugard explores the effect that the separation of the races and the clear-cut

[27] LA 77. References to *A Lesson from Aloes* are flagged *LA*.

[28] *Statements* premiered at The Space in Cape Town in 1972. A reworked version with the same name was first performed at the Royal Court Theatre in London in 1974. Although Fugard claims sole authorship, the versions evolved out of rehearsals with his actors. He emphasises Yvonne Bryceland's contribution to the rewriting of the script, the actress who played most of Fugard's leading female roles. This is documented by Vandenbroucke, who also gives an account of the genesis of *Statements* (cf. 1985: 132-34).

prescription of roles based on race have on individuals in South Africa. He does so by portraying the clandestine relationship between the white library owner, Frieda Joubert, and the coloured school principal, Errol Philander. Given the racial divisions, friendly contact between intellectually like-minded but racially different people are illegal. So are sexual relations between cross-racial lovers. Fugard complicates this situation by creating a 42-year-old spinster and a 36-year-old husband and father. This affair led reviewers to criticise the immoral quality of the relationship rather than the nature of the Immorality Act (cf. Cushman 1982 [1974]: 88; Joubert 1982 [1972]: 86). Wertheim argues that what is "perhaps not made clear enough or stated forcefully enough in the play is that both the Immorality and the Group Areas Acts, which haunt *Statements*, must bear the blame not merely for the racial transgressive sex but for the adultery as well" (2000: 70).[29] This evaluation foregrounds the fact that the highly restrictive nature of apartheid laws affects people in their personal development and deprives them of an identity-stabilising sense of self.

In a society which bases its politics on racial difference, interracial relationships can easily acquire political significance, even if the relationship takes place exclusively in the private sphere and the people involved have no intention of making their affair into an overt public or political statement. *Statements* explores how the public definitions of the various groups define individuals in racial and social terms. Frieda Joubert and Errol Philander desperately try to negotiate and alter these fixed definitions in the intimacy of their relationship. They attempt to create a private space of love, trust and self-realisation (*Selbstverwirklichung*), untouched by the oppressive public world. Ultimately, this turns out to be impossible and, after both characters are arrested, leads to their disintegration into insanity and self-annihilation.

In *Statements* whites and coloureds alike becomes victims. Thus Fugard challenges Morrie's claim to Zach in *Blood Knot* that the South African police are only on the side of the white members of society. As Robert Post asserts, Frieda's fate proves

[29] Wertheim quotes Fugard's comment on his own sense of self as an adulterer in the South African theatre scene as he works with both black and white actors (cf. 2000: 243f., fn. 6). It is interesting to note Fugard's own evaluation of his cross-racial collaborations in the theatre as adulterous instead of illegal. This could be meant to emphasise the fact that his choices are influenced by personal decisions and not by overt state criticism, just as Frieda and Errol's relationship is based on the restrictions that apartheid places on the individuality of the characters and how this effects their personal development.

that Morrie should have more accurately said that the police are on the side of those who obey the laws of apartheid (cf. 1985: 4).

A Lesson from Aloes (1978) analyses the dynamics of distrust and hostility and how this affects both character interaction and self-definition. Fugard creates the plot around the liberation struggle in the 1960s in South Africa and its suppression by the regime.[30] He shows apartheid's impact on human relationships. Again, the victims of apartheid suffer psychologically more than physically. Like Frieda and Errol, *Aloes*'s victims are representatives of different racial and cultural groups: the white Afrikaner, Piet Bezuidenhout, his wife of English descent, Gladys, and their coloured friend, Steve Daniels.[31] And again this play shows how the pressure of apartheid prevents the characters from maintaining healthy identities and from leading happy relationships that incorporate and support these identities and offer psychological strength. Despite the concrete political background, the play focuses primarily on the "interpersonal psychodynamics" and "psychological tensions" (Wertheim 2000: 117) that lead to mental breakdown, isolation and exile.[32]

2.3.1. *Statements after an Arrest under the Immorality Act*

The first half of *Statements* shows Frieda Joubert and Errol Philander in the affectionate post-coital moments they share in the darkness of the library office where they clandestinely carry on their affair. The dialogue centres on their relationship and how they perceive themselves and each other. Errol strikes a match:

> [*A match flares in the darkness. She scrambles away.*]
>
> WOMAN. No! [. . .]
>
> [*The match dies. Darkness.*]
>
> MAN. Is it me or you?
>
> WOMAN. You don't understand.

---

[30] Errol Durbach describes the political background into which the three characters are placed (cf. 1989).

[31] Biodun asserts that all of Fugard's characters are presented in a state of "*confined* victimhood, the whites being no less victims of their rigid, cast-iron restrictions then the other races and communities" (1985: 101).

[32] See also Wertheim (1988).

> MAN. Understand what? There is seeing, and being seen. Which one are you frightened of? Me or you? [...] What about me? I want to be seen. I want you to see me.[33]

Errol's sense of self and his own value as a human being depend on Frieda's visual recognition, not just her tactile and verbal communication in the dark. It is only when he moves towards the moonlight that he shares a personal experience with her. 'Seeing' and 'light' become metaphoric; they stand not just for the human sense of sight but for the total understanding of an individual in their personal identity. When he asks her: "Do you think I just want to *see* you? Do you think I just want to look? [*Pause.*] I do" (*SA* 84), he shows that he wants Frieda to acknowledge his existence as an individual by looking at him. 'Seeing' takes on a political dimension (cf. Crow 1992: 159). At the same time he also confirms both his own self as well as hers by looking at her. In his eyes seeing and being seen should be reciprocal. Yet this is exactly what he believes is missing in the relationship.

Frieda's retreat from the light of the match and the moonlight shows her insecurity. She is embarrassed by her naked body which points to the fact that she has not yet developed a stable sense of self. Consequently, as she lacks personal stability, she cannot truly connect with Errol. In the indeterminacy of darkness she defines herself not in visual but in spatial and relational terms. She self-consciously confirms her own existence and her special place in his life when she rebukes him for waiting a year to relate a decisive experience he has shared with no one: "I'm not no one. I'm also me. I'm the other person on the floor. With you" (*SA* 85). Her words confirm their relationship, but her different definition of it clearly shows that her approach to constructing identity is not based on sight.

As Lothar Krappmann asserts in his sociological theory of identity, every interaction consists of the two-step process of getting to know the partner in the interaction and recognising the expectations that society assigns to the situation. He maintains that an individual's identity relies on their possibility of negotiating proposed definitions of identity and that the subjective interpretation of identity is a requirement for successful social interaction. An individual cannot interact successfully with others by merely adopting society's expectations and interpretations because in the long run they do not express all aspects of the individual's behaviour or social biography (cf. 1982^6: 34-42). Errol and Frieda's

---

[33] *SA* 82. References to *Statements after an Arrest under the Immorality Act* are flagged *SA*.

discussion on 'seeing' and 'light' shows that each character has differing expectations. These result from their different strategies of defining self and other as well as from their failure fully to understand each other. Their interaction fails to evolve as a process of reciprocal negotiation leading to an agreement either about the identity of the partners or about their definition of the situation. Errol's unclear sense of identity is a result of Frieda's inability to understand the importance he attributes to the sense of sight for constructing his private self in their relationship.

Errol's unstable sense of self also results from the nature of apartheid's oppressive social norms and roles that undermine his ability to develop a balanced and healthy public identity. According to Hans-Peter Dreitzel, human behaviour follows certain aims and rules imposed by society which are institutionalised in social roles. When these rules cannot be followed, disruptions of behaviour become unavoidable. These problems result from inadequate social norms and point to the socio-pathological phenomena of social roles (cf. Dreitzel 1980³: 32f.). Errol suffers from the fact that apartheid's regulations assign him social roles based on race and thus also fix his social position. These roles do not allow him to develop personally and socially according to his talents and aspirations. For example, it is illegal for him to visit the whites-only library to study for his correspondence course although he needs the books that he can only access there. Furthermore, Errol and Frieda share similar interests while Errol and his wife do not seem to fit well together intellectually. Yet he belongs to his family in racial terms according to apartheid ideology. Personally he feels a moral obligation to secure his family's economic survival. It is this motive, not political reasons, that would lead him to reject a future life with Frieda even if society was based on racial equality. The couple perceive their relationship as adulterous while state law publicly defines their illicit relationship as miscegenation. Fugard writes in his journal: "Errol. If they catch you, you will feel shame. Yes you will. This country has made [...] us marry our skin colours. Our real crime is adultery."[34] The restrictive nature of roles under apartheid is responsible for these incongruities and the fragmented identities that develop under such circumstances. Similarly, Errol and Frieda's inability to agree on terms for accepting each other is also a result and a further indication of the socio-pathological quality of existing roles and norms.

[34] Unpublished notebook entry, 17 November 1971. Fugard manuscript collection, Lilly Library, Bloomington, Indiana, Journal 10.

Errol's relationship to Frieda is based on the interplay of revelation and concealment.[35] Adultery and miscegenation force him to be prudent when walking to the library. To avoid suspicion in the community, he often hides in the mud[36] under the bridge when cars pass, a symbol for his own sense of immorality as well as his ideologically prescribed place under apartheid. Errol's dilemma is doubled: he is known by the coloured people in his social roles as school principal, husband and father; he is also racially identifiable by the white population of the town as an intruder into white space when he approaches the library. This means that on his way to Frieda he is not able to slip into another role to hide parts of his identity by means of passing, role-play or disguise. Instead, he must consciously become invisible and momentarily erase his existence and identity. It is therefore all the more plausible that he tries to base his private identity on the sense of sight.

Despite the obvious intimacy and like-mindedness of the couple, an unbridgeable distance between the characters highlights the collision of two incompatible worlds. Whenever Errol returns to his home in the location, the difference between their worlds becomes painfully clear to him. With Frieda he experiences a life and dreams that are not open to coloureds in South Africa. By contrast, his own world consists of *braks*[37] and dispossessed people whose poverty has figuratively reduced them to rags: "I don't mean their clothes. The people inside look like rags" (*SA* 91). This anticipates his own loss of identity after the arrest.

Frieda reveals her distance from Errol's world in her use of exclusionary possessive pronouns. She offers him *her* water[38] and she does not know that he doesn't drink milk to still his thirst, but, as he tells her, "When *we*'re thirsty, *we* drink cooldrink" (*SA* 87, emphasis added). She has to make sure he enters *her* library secretly. In

---

[35] Robert Baker-White comments on this dyad in his analysis of authority and *jouissance* in *Statements* (cf. 1992: 234f.). The trope of the 'seen' and the 'unseen' is also prominent in Frieda's descriptions of the library's neighbour, Mrs. Buys, who sneaks around her quince trees and visits the library alarmingly often. Mrs. Buys's statement to the police that leads to the lovers' arrest adds emphasis to the fact that visible concealment of an action can actually render the ongoing event more visible: after "forty-five minutes of darkness [... the library's] back door opened and Philander came out" (*SA* 95).

[36] Margarete Seidenspinner explores Fugard's use of the wasteland metaphor in his plays (cf. 1986: 238).

[37] 'mongrel dogs'

[38] MAN. [...] The reason I don't want your water is just because Bontrug [the location] is thirsty.

WOMAN. And that is not pride.

MAN. No. Exactly the opposite. Shame. (*SA* 91)

fact, she even had to initiate their sexual union, both of them knowing that his advances towards her could easily be classified as a serious crime: the rape of a white woman. Errol refuses Frieda's offer of water "because it is a gift bearing the distinct odor of white patriarchy and charity towards inferiors" (Wertheim 2000: 76).[39]

For Errol the epiphanous "comprehension [...] of life" (*SA* 84) and eternity he acquires through his studies is inapplicable to life in the location of Bontrug. He has learnt that the world of science is nothing more than a dream, as is his relationship with Frieda. He feels lost, suffers from the desolation and lack of personal and social development characteristic of coloureds and despises Frieda's world for emphasising this material and intellectual poverty. He feels ashamed of his colour, his background and the limited possibilities that his life has to offer. However, he also feels shame and guilt for slipping into a better world with Frieda, a world that allows him, at least temporarily, to deny his publicly defined social identity: "That's how I walk now between Bontrug and the town ... one way guilty, back with [shame]" (*SA* 91). The interplay of pride, guilt and shame represent the irremediable fault in their relationship. It is as if Errol's wish to fill the room with light is his attempt to give birth to a better reality.

The privacy of the relationship presented in the first half of the play is suddenly interrupted by the appearance of Sergeant du Preez reading to the audience his statement on the apprehension of Frieda and Errol.[40] As Robert Baker-White argues, the sergeant's heavy and authoritarian discourse, by virtue of its being "*dictated to the audience*" (*SA* 94), implicates both the "audience in the power structure against which the lovers struggle" as well as the "very theatrical action of the play in the process of arresting the two" (1992: 238f.). The man and the woman are turned into lifeless data, consisting of their addresses, racial classification, marital status and police record. The statement ends with a sequence of six camera

---

39 Wertheim classifies the nature of their relationship as "inflected with archetypes of patriarchy." He goes on to assert that the Immorality Act not only undermines sexual mutuality but even manipulates their intimate relationship by "tainting it with a grotesque replication of apartheid's textures of power and the archetypes of racism." Frieda acquires the white, active, masculine, dominant role while Errol is forced into the position of the subaltern, passive, feminine (cf. 2000: 75).

40 The public voice, represented by this policeman, completely alters the tone, style and structure of the play and moves it away from realism. Vandenbroucke vaguely describes the second half as "something quite different," emphasising the lyrical and abstract elements (1985: 137). Baker-White classifies it as a "fractured and repetitive" or "dystopian, agonized montage" (1992: 229).

flashes that capture the naked couple in grotesque, animal-like behaviour. The stage directions describe "*the man and the woman tearing apart from their embrace; the man then scrambling for his trousers, finding them, and trying to put them on: the woman, naked, crawling around the floor, looking for the man*" (*SA* 96). These six flashes, which are followed by a bright light shining on the couple, destroy everything they have intimately created. The police hide behind these lights and thus become, in the words of Vandenbroucke, a "disembodied presence, an unseen nemesis" (1985: 139).

This effect is similar to the threatening presence of the unseen prison guard Hodoshe in Fugard, Kani and Ntshona's play *The Island* (see Chapter 3). As the source of these lights seems to be located in the audience space, the direct implication of the spectators in this scene becomes obvious (cf. Baker-White 1992: 238). The spectators' attempt to make sense of the lovers' fractured, poetic and self-revelatory words in the presence of the police foregrounds the need to add stability to the couple's speeches. Yet such an approach will lead to a sense of closure which ultimately reinforces the spectators' power over the victims. It also shows how the lovers become outcasts in the eyes of society and, in contrast to the characters of *Sizwe Bansi is Dead* and *The Island*, lose all power of resistance to officialdom. Thc bright light that shines mercilessly on the couple, pinning them to the wall, contrasts strongly with Errol's wish to be able to see Frieda and be seen by her in the intimacy of the library. It is as if the light now blinds the characters and deprives them of the ability to see clearly - a symbol of their continuous disintegration.

The destruction of the lovers' relationship is represented by the fracture in their language and stories, and in the fragmentary and montage-like quality of their action after the arrest. Their language now reveals more about their inner selves, their secret desires and their personal insecurities than during their private dialogue. The humiliation and degradation of their exposure raises their self-awareness even more. At the same time it annihilates the two as lovers and as human beings. They are deprived of their individuality and private selves while being reduced to their public definition as bodies in a society based on race classification.

The police make it clear to Frieda that apartheid discourse defines Errol's interest in her as based exclusively on her skin colour. She is unable to cope with this exposure and confesses to their relationship. Her language evolves from an animal-like "*almost incoherent babble*" (*SA* 96) to a hysterical revelation and self-justification of the intimacy of their affair in the attempt to save her private sense of self.

Errol, by contrast, intervenes and, as the stage directions reveal, starts behaving like the stereotypical coloured. In this way he conforms to his public identity: "*The man's 'performance' has now degenerated into a grotesque parody of the servile, cringing 'Coloured'* (*SA* 99). He denies their intimacy, addressing her as "Miss Frieda Joubert," next as "Miss Frieda," and then in a detached manner as "lady" and "Miesies" (*SA* 98f.) until she turns mad in her inability to cope with his denial of her as his lover. This behaviour can be seen as Errol's attempt to save his own skin in front of the police. The theatricality of the roles defined by apartheid is once again emphasised.

Dreitzel claims that people individually adapt their behaviour to certain roles and situations. This allows them to develop a defence mechanism against the social roles' frustrating expectations. Every role puts pressure upon the individual by dictating norms of behaviour. Consequently, any personal contribution to role behaviour is limited because the domains of action in which it is exercised are structured according to power relations and status hierarchies (cf. Dreitzel 1980[3]: 225f.). In his performance Errol erases his identity in his relationship with Frieda, possibly in an attempt to protect it by closing it off to outer interpretation and manipulation. However, in the end he is not able to keep up the role of a subaltern coloured who merely has an economic relationship to Frieda, but he rises to acknowledge the personal disintegration of his private sense of self that the dominance of external power provokes.

The arrest physically and psychologically strips Frieda of Errol. She knows that she is no longer allowed to define herself through him but that she must succumb to the public definition of her identity: "In every corner of being myself there is a little of you left and now I must start to lose it. I must be very still, because if I do anything, except think nothing, it will all start to happen" (*SA* 105). Her words describe the conflict between her wish to freeze the passing of time and the disintegration of their relationship and lives. As in the darkness of the library she tries to define herself in relational terms through his presence. However, when this is no longer possible and Errol is thus unable to define himself through her recognition of him, both of their psyches disintegrate.

In the process of the arrest and interrogation Errol is punished with emasculation; he is deprived of his manhood, his virility and his sense of self. Fugard reflects on this in his journals: "Every arrest under the Immorality Act a vestigial re-enactment of the castration ritual."[41] In Errol's final speech he realises that he has lost his ability to love and now defines his life as worthless, a shell around emptiness. He relives his conflict of standing between his family and Frieda and hearing Frieda tell him that their relationship is useless and that they will be caught. This echoes Frieda's acceptance that she cannot hold on to him and that by denying him, she effaces his existence : "I am here. You are not here. I know that without trying to find you, [...] because nothing can be here except me" (*SA* 105). He describes the process of being discovered by the police, emphasising the inhumanity and life-annihilation that he experiences in the process. The irony of this situation is that in the eyes of apartheid Errol is nothing, but he is arrested nonetheless. Post concludes, "As long as he does not break the law, the government treats him as nothing, but when he does break the law, he suddenly becomes some*thing* (not necessarily some*body*)" (1985: 5). Errol knows that all that is left of him in the end is emptiness: "They arrest it all the same. Now I'm here. There is nothing here" (*SA* 108). Fugard sums up Errol's dilemma: "The man's predicament then not just the personal torment and guilt of the adulterer – the ultimate question is again articulated. What am I? It is not his heart and undivided love that create his dilemma - but a system, a society" (1983: 194). In a similar vein Derek Cohen evaluates *Statements* as "a total image of the flinty cruelty of South Africa's institutionalized racialism" (1980: 160).

The interrogation scene shows that the lovers' flawed identities and sense of self, which finally prevent them from achieving complete mutual recognition, result from the fact that the roles available in the apartheid state are all pathological. It is not possible to create healthy, self-defined roles and successfully live them because public racial and social pressure is too great. The characters' self-immersion and personal isolation highlight the power of the inhuman and destructive nature of apartheid ideology over the mind.

2.3.2. *A Lesson from Aloes*

In *A Lesson from Aloes* Fugard presents the strategies employed by three characters in an attempt to survive after being 'burned and scarred' by life under apartheid. As

[41] Unpublished notebook entry from 1972 (no exact date). Fugard manuscript collection, Lilly Library, Bloomington, Indiana, Journal 11.

he puts it, the play "examine[s] and question[s] the possibility and nature of survival in a country for which 'drought', with its harsh and relentless resonances, is a very apt metaphor" (1982 [1980]: 67). Piet and Gladys have invited Steve and his family, who are leaving the country on an exit permit, for a farewell dinner. Steve has been involved in anti-apartheid activities and had been under house arrest because an anonymous informer had reported to the police that he had violated his banning order. He arrives at the Bezuidenhout house alone, and the confrontation of the three characters with each other and their past leads to a destabilisation of both the marital relationship and the male friendship. As the characters are to varying degrees all left with incomplete and insecure identities, they are unable to engage in relationships from which they can draw strength. This leads to the disintegration of their sense of self and their relationship with society. At the end of the play they have all retreated into different forms of isolation and have become indifferent and apathetic to the plight of others: "Scarred by apartheid, each inhabits a small corner of hell and imagines it to be an exclusive and personal domain" (Durbach 1989: 8).

Piet Bezuidenhout, the liberal grass-roots Afrikaner, relates how drought forced him off his land when he was a young man. His last memory was that of the funeral for the baby of one of his African workers. The infant's death moved him deeply and revealed his personal sense of shame and failure (cf. *LA* 54). While participating in the coloureds' bus boycott where he met Steve, he witnessed their defiant display of dignity which revived him, introduced him to the world of political action and raised his consciousness: "My first lesson from Steve [...]. There's nothing you can do to stop a drought, but bad laws and social injustice are man-made and can be unmade by men" (*LA* 35). However, the betrayal of the men's commitment to the "cause" led to Steve's ban and house-arrest. It becomes clear during the course of the play that the comrades believed and still believe Piet to be the informer. Once again, as is the case for the characters in *Statements*, the public definition of a character's identity is too strong to be negotiated, even among groups who oppose the reigning ideology: Piet is a white Afrikaner and thus linked to the group responsible for the implementation, execution and preservation of apartheid. He has been excluded and shunned by his fellow fighters on the basis of prejudice and stereotype. It can be assumed that he is one of a few whites in the resistance movement and thus easily rendered the scapegoat, despite his liberalism. Ultimately, his personal evolution from the white *Baas* on his farm to a fighter for the 'cause' apparently does not convince the comrades. Their behaviour shows that they have internalised apartheid's rigid definitions of identity. Piet cannot develop personally in opposition to the given definitions of identity. In this situation the price Piet has to pay to live in his own country becomes very high. Hardened and alienated from his friends, he is left in isolation and retreats from society to survive amidst his drought-resisting aloes.

Piet, the hobby-botanist, who zealously classifies his aloes in an attempt to bring order and control into his world, draws strength from the plants' hardiness in a stoical determination to endure. At the same time he avoids naming and categorising the reasons for his exclusion from society: suspicion and distrust. During Steve's visit Piet orders his friend to stop putting words in his mouth and tells Gladys to let him speak for himself (cf. *LA* 66f.), yet he refuses to talk about the rumour of his being the informer. When his wife suggests - and Steve readily believes - Piet's guilt, he acknowledges that there "wasn't anything left to say" (*LA* 77). He alludes to the impossibility of reconciliation after his friend has doubted his innocence: "If you could have believed it, there was no point denying it" (*LA* 77). For him personal trust is the basis of all interaction and represents the only possible strategy to unite groups that the state's ideology strives to keep apart.

Disillusioned, Piet has repudiated his previously-held belief in the possibility of changing mankind in order to fight social injustice. He now holds human nature responsible for creating the chasm between the once-allied groups engaged in the struggle: "I don't accept it easily, but there is nothing else to do. I can't change human nature" (*LA* 21). Nonetheless, according to Durbach, Piet knows that only a change in human nature that has been grounded in the "psychopathology of apartheid to deny love and trust and faith as the only strategies for resistance" can make effective action possible. "And," as this critic concludes, "what possible action can be taken when the greatest contest of the country is the havoc wreaked on human nature by the operation of the Nationalist Party regime on human connections?" (1989: 18). Seen in this light, Piet's isolation results from his inability to clearly fit into the political groups in his country and appropriate apartheid society's pre-defined roles: he is rejected by the Afrikaners as a "kaffirboetie" or 'nigger-lover,' suspected of treason by the coloured liberals and dismissed by the left wing because of his inaction (cf. Durbach 1989: 19). Thus Piet is associated with the unidentifiable and unclassifiable Aloe Anonymous that he holds in his hands at the beginning and end of the play. Like the aloe he does not conform to an existing scheme - fixed categories that result from stereotype, cliché and prejudice and that irrevocably define people break down. This emphasises "the necessary persistence of variation in man and plants, even under *apartheid*" (Munro

1981: 476). The Aloe Anonymous can also be read as "an existential statement of the uniqueness of individual human response to adversity" (Wortham 1983: 180). The image of the unclassifiable aloe then suggests that new and flexible forms of character and opinion are natural and could lead to an open-minded society. However, Piet confines his aloes in jam tins just as he is resolved to go through life in his own asocial tin of isolation (cf. Roberts 1982: 29), not yet understanding the freedom that the new aloe symbolically offers him. As Piet's naming of his aloes resembles apartheid's oppressive strategy of racial categorisation, the lone aloe's resistance to final identification points to a need for tolerance, free development and variety. While he emphasises his need to name his aloes in order to "feel a little bit more at home" (*LA* 4) in his world, the lesson from the single anonymous aloe could be that he should rethink his own position. His desire to order and fix his world may not be the best way to create a sense of belonging, especially since his horticultural hobby has only strengthened his increasing retreat from society.

The Aloe Anonymous has also been interpreted as a symbol for Piet as the saviour. Durbach goes so far as to suggest that Piet is the "unnamable first specimens [*sic*] in an evolutionary, grass-roots change that begins with one ordinary and unremarkable individual finding his 'home' in a world not programmed for his survival" (1989: 19). Similarly, Coleen Angove suggests that "Piet represents the Afrikaner's movement into a new awareness of his roots in African soil, but with consideration for those with whom he co-exists" while combining preservation and change. This critic does not read Piet as embodying the Afrikaner stereotype but calls him a maverick who "rebels against stifling conformity within his cultural group in a quest for meaningful change" (1989: 56, 63). Contrary to this view, other critics have emphasised Piet's Afrikaner qualities such as his hardiness and his will to survive droughts like the aloe. They suggest that "these traits, which helped build and maintain apartheid, may, in the hands of people like Piet, also become that system's undoing" (Wertheim 2000: 134; cf. Oberle 1996: 216). All of these interpretations are very optimistic but do not appear to take into account his loss of social roles (friend, comrade and husband) during the dinner party. Although Piet's identity seems stable compared to that of the other characters (cf. Roberts 1982: 29), his stereotypical Afrikaner stubbornness and unassailable faith in himself point to the probability that his sense of self might not be more than a form of self-protecting denial of reality.

Alternatively, it is also possible to evaluate Piet as a victim of society who is both "personally and politically isolated" and stands little chance of ameliorating his situation (Wertheim 2000: 134; cf. Seidenspinner 1986: 339; Weales 1993: 506).[42] It must be taken into account that the comrades' distrust leads to Piet's stigmatisation and public denial of what Goffman calls his "actual social reality," confining him to a "virtual social reality" (1963: 2, original emphasis changed) and consequently rendering him increasingly isolated. According to Dreitzel, it is possible to see Piet's isolation not as one of his own choices but as a result of disrupted role behaviour as it arises in situations of stigmatisation. An outside group, in this case Steve as the representative of the comrades, appropriates the power to interpret Piet's character and refuses to recognise his full value as a role player by discrediting his social attributes. Piet is thus deprived of his position and public roles in society and in his social group, which leads to his increasing isolation from public life and forces him to retreat into privacy. The fact that he suffers from the exclusion from social behaviour then accounts for his isolation (cf. 1980[3]: 233-35).

Steve Daniels, Piet's former comrade and friend, represents the politically conscious and active coloured liberal who asserts his belief in human equality through his fight for the rights of his people. His support of the 'cause' resulted from his family's suffering under apartheid legislation, specifically the Group Areas Act. Steve witnessed his father's unsuccessful legal fight against the order to leave his home after the area had been declared white, an unfair struggle in which the old man lost both his fortune and his soul. This incident raised Steve's political consciousness and led him to join an anti-apartheid group. Whereas the old man was indoctrinated by apartheid's views and accepted his public definition and identity ("Ons geslag is verkeerd"/"our race is a mistake"), Steve affirmed his own sense of self: "[...] we have only ourselves to blame if we let them walk over us" (*LA* 64). However, broken under torture by the police several years later, he, too, ends up feeling deprived of his own identity. Instead of portraying himself as a political victim, he now focuses on the personal effect that the torture had on his psyche: "They had laughed at my manhood and every reason I had for diving out of that window" (*LA* 72). He has lost the ability to work and thus provide for his family because his hands - the tools of the bricklayer and mason - have become soft and "might as well fall off for all they mean in my life now" (*LA* 67). Just as Errol

---

42 Durbach reflects on the notion of Piet as victim: "It is a curious 'victim,' however, who refuses to compromise his humanity, who chooses his mode of survival – neither compelled by the State into exile, nor driven ineluctably into insanity – and whose pessimism is held in a delicate balance with an absurd form of hope" (1989: 19).

Philander is broken under psychological torture and emasculated in *Statements*, Steve is left symbolically castrated and deprived of his sense of self and his sense of purpose in life (cf. Vandenbroucke 1985: 171). His re-evaluation of the comrades' struggle reveals that his opinions and views have been redefined according to the reigning ideology. This is shown in his distinction between boy scouts, rough boys and men: "We were like a bunch of boy scouts playing at politics. Those boer-boys play the game rough. It's going to need men who don't care about the rules to sort them out" (*LA* 68). Steve sees himself as an amateur scout, failing to adopt the force and ruthlessness of rough "boer-boys" or real "men" who could effect change. Despite his love for his country, he feels that exile in England is the only solution to secure his family's safety and continuation. He thinks it more important to offer his children a better future and risk his own complete alienation in a strange place than to hold on to what he perceives as an impossible dream.

Steve attaches many hopes and fears to his reunion with Piet. He wants to test the quality of their friendship and brotherhood as well as the viability of the liberal dream that Piet still adheres to. Yet Steve is also reluctant to visit the Bezuidenhout home because he is not sure of Piet's innocence. Half-fearing that the invitation represents a trap and relying on liquor for courage, Steve is ready to believe the worst of his once-close friend. In the course of the evening Steve's despair and fear of involuntary exile transform into an extreme bitterness that robs the former comrades of any common denominator. "If I had a white skin, I'd also find lots of reasons for not leaving this country" (*LA* 67). In this exclamation he defines their lives exclusively through race and appropriates apartheid discourse in his open challenge of the collaboration of black and white liberals in South Africa. He also self-righteously implies that his plight is exclusive, denying even the possibility of Piet's victimisation under apartheid. Durbach asserts that the meeting of Piet and Steve merely highlights the interlocking tragedies of cunningly programmed alienation and disillusionment in a country where *not* to be imprisoned is as heinous a penalty as banishment. One exile leaves his "home," shamed by his betrayal of fellowship and trust. The other remains "at home, exiled forever in his [...] cave of suspicion and fear" (1989: 12f.).

This critic concludes that the insidious engendering of doubt and suspicion does a much more effective job than Acts of Parliament in destroying relationships. By characterising the men's camaraderie as a "charade of friendship," he emphasises the theatrical quality of their behaviour (Durbach 1989: 12). Again, the oppressive nature of regime ideology reduces human interaction to an enactment of stereotypical roles and thus foregrounds the artificiality promoted by apartheid.

Gladys Bezuidenhout's fate is to some extent more personal than that of either Piet or Steve, whose bodies have become politicised and racialised in the struggle as the liberal-white/pseudo-informer and the coloured victim of apartheid:[43] "I've got my own story. [...] I've discovered hell for myself" (*LA* 74). Gladys is a shy and insecure woman of English descent who suffers from the harsh South African climate and landscape. It is only when she meets Piet that she learns to survive by developing confidence and trust in herself and others as well as believing in the purpose of life. Keeping a diary has become her way of learning to establish her own identity, of developing and exploring thoughts and secrets. Nonetheless, her allegiance to England, which she has never visited, and the implied rejection of South Africa is visible in her attempt to Anglicise the world. She calls her husband Peter and prefers roses to aloes.

When the Security Branch searches the Bezuidenhout house because of Piet's involvement in the 'cause,' the men read her diaries. Similar to *Statement*'s Frieda Joubert, who is psychologically 'raped' by the police, Gladys experiences this violation of her privacy as 'rape' by the Special Branch and as betrayal by Piet who fails to interfere.[44] This event causes her to lose all trust in other human beings. Her social position as wife of a political activist automatically victimises her. For her the private becomes political and shows how apartheid permeates even the lives of characters living on its fringe. Fugard surmises from his own experience of a house search by the police "'that the system here in this country, this society, involves the rape of an individual and his privacy'" (qtd. in Seidenspinner 1986: 148).

Displaced and alienated from her environment, Gladys withdraws into herself and is treated with shock therapy in a mental institution. She is not able to recover from the psychological scars inflicted upon her by the police, the hospital and her husband. It is as if her life has been reduced to the receipt which Piet obtained when the police confiscated her journals. Consequently, her sense of self is weak and fragile. She attempts to erase the past by ordering Piet to tear up the receipt but is

---

43 Fugard compares the three characters: "Piet and Steve are victims of a system they have tried to resist, something man-made, whereas Gladys is God's victim" (Benson 1997: 115).

44 Munro suggests the betrayal of Gladys as a double rape: the loss of her diaries and Piet's inability to protect her. "It is not too much to see the aloes as grotesque thorny phallic symbol opposed to female secretiveness in this context" (1981: 476).

unable to forget what has happened. Paranoid, she not only fears the return of the police but also retreats from personal contact with her husband. The revelation of her inability to keep a diary and her frantic attempt to hide the blank notebook represent her loss of trust in her environment and her incomplete sense of self. The dark sunglasses she wears and her frequent retreats to her bedroom also symbolise her wish to conceal her inner self and avoid any kind of exposure to the outside world which she perceives as "turgid with violence" (*LA* 17).[45] Her life is as void of meaning as the empty white pages that she constantly repositions. They become a metaphor for her identity.

Unable to annihilate the past by tearing up her diary receipt, she finally deals with the past events and their consequences by openly confronting both men at the farewell dinner. She forces Steve to deal with his own suspicion about her husband and challenges the guest with the image of Piet as a stereotypical Nationalist Afrikaner. She almost succeeds in making Steve believe that Piet is the informer: "Careful, Steven! He looks like one of them, doesn't he? The same gross certainty of himself! He certainly sounds like them. He speaks English with a dreadful accent. What else, Steven? He's poor enough to do it for money" (*LA* 73). The fact that she foregrounds the act of enumerating stereotypical characteristics and even invites Steve to join in emphasises the constructed character of her accusation. Yet her attempt to make him aware of the danger of believing in stereotypes and how easily they create scapegoats and destroy friendships bitterly fails. Shocked and hurt that he takes her comments about Piet at face value, she confronts the dinner guest:

> My reason for telling you an ugly lie, which you were ready to believe! ... [*sic*] is *my* business. I accept, Steven, that I am just a white face on the outskirts of your terrible life, but I'm in the middle of mine and yours is just a brown face on the outskirts of that. Do you understand what I'm saying? I've got my own story. I don't need yours. I've discovered hell for myself. It might be hard for you to accept, Steven, but you are not the only one who has been hurt. Politics and black skin don't make the only victims in this country. (*LA* 74)

Despite the given that she is, of course, a victim of apartheid and politics, her last remark focuses on the personal nature of her experience. It alludes to the fact that she holds Piet responsible for her plight because of his failure to protect her diaries

[45] Erik Erikson argues that the inner space corresponds to womanhood as outer space corresponds to manhood, both biologically and consequently also socially (cf. 1974: 261-94). Munro also comments on this aspect (cf. 1981: 476).

and support her during her shock therapy. Revealing her paranoia and resulting inability to acknowledge his care, she now implies that he has not fulfilled his duty as her husband. She turns on him with vehemence: “I don’t need you to protect me anymore! You never did, anyway” (*LA* 75). She suffers from the fact that he does not revenge himself on those who betrayed him, neither to rehabilitate himself nor to defend and rehabilitate her. His tragic acceptance of his fate provokes her to violate him and take revenge by suggesting that she, too, believes him guilty. Unable to cope with her life and recognising her growing displacement in a country she fears and hates, she voluntarily prepares to return to the protection of her ‘English’ place of exile - Grahamstown’s Fort England Clinic - in her attempt to flee from a country she has never called her home.

Robert Greig maintains that Fugard’s plays are generally “concerned with people who are managing to live, with the validity of the choices they make, with showing how those choices may seem to be laid down by apartheid.” This evaluation leads him to observe that *Aloes* particularly “examines the quality of life for those who are struggling towards the possibility of choices” (1982 [1978]: 101). Although all three characters in *A Lesson from Aloes* oppose apartheid and wish to flee from it, they must recognise that their different lifestyles and attitudes are all strongly controlled and shaped by apartheid ideology.

Piet, Steve and Gladys are recognisable types. They embody stereotypical character traits of different groups in South Africa. The play shows that the characters are unable to develop a healthy personality free from stereotypical behaviour. Yet, what is more, they assign each other the roles apartheid creates through racial stereotyping and thus help to promote the state’s aim of separating and engendering hostility among the different groups. Munro believes that the play shows “how thoroughly *apartheid* and the looser social attitudes on which it is premised permeate every aspect of South African life” (1981: 477).

Michael Collins evaluates *Aloes* positively as a play in whose world of cruelty and suffering “Small things, ordinary things, affirm the dignity, the beauty, the decency of human life” (1983: 370). Despite the characters’ essential goodness, it must not be overlooked that their attempts to bond and help each other are doomed to fail because society is so effective in controlling and confining individual development. The characters experience alienation from one another, and this is revealed as their inability to engage in healthy role behaviour and relationships. Instead of profiting from the reciprocal nature of relationships and the possibility of negotiating their own and the other's self-definition in their interaction, the characters focus on their differences. In the end society forces them to take care of themselves and leave each other to their own devices. Their retreat into isolation, exile and insanity marks the only way to openly reject apartheid ideology. However, this form of resistance is ineffective and proves the system's success in removing oppositional spirits from public life and destroying their sense of self. *Aloes* foregrounds how strong the grip of apartheid is on its subjects who not only betray each other but also themselves.

2.4. Conclusion

(The) Blood Knot, *Statements after an Arrest under the Immorality Act* and *A Lesson from Aloes* are quite different plays that all explore the same questions: How can people live in a society in which identity and role behaviour are pre-defined and fixed, and still develop a positive definition of self? Or, can identity construction be possible in a multi-racial, multi-cultural country, whose regime openly promotes racial cleavage and oppression?

Athol Fugard offers three different answers in the works presented here. All his characters seek friendship, love and trust in interracial relationships. Written in 1961, *The Blood Knot* ends with the contrast between the coloured brothers' outward acceptance of their racial and social definition and their place in society as well as their private, racially transgressive role-play. The play explores the non-reconcilable definitions of identity that exist in apartheid reality and are possible in the world of make-believe. On the performance level Fugard and Zakes Mokae as actors were revolutionary as they challenged apartheid's practice of racial separation by stepping over racial boundaries. A white and a black actor played two coloured brothers who play white and black roles and simultaneously embrace their coloured identities. Thus on various levels (*The*) *Blood Knot* emphasises the artificiality and theatricality of roles based on race as well as the individual's need for the freedom to negotiate and play with the given definitions of roles and identity. By the seventies Fugard was exploring how apartheid had succeeded in preventing members of different groups in society from trusting and relying on each other without any twinges of fear, doubt or suspicion. *Statements* and *Aloes* suggest that social pressure eventually hinders the development and duration of healthy interracial relationships and that subsequent state intervention leads to the disintegration of identity.

All three works clearly show that the roles available in apartheid South Africa are pathological and thus point to the illness of society itself. Because the action of each play takes place during the 1950s and 1960s, although the plays were written over a time span of two decades, it could be claimed that this period marks the final consolidation of this pathological society. The answer to the question of whether healthy and strong identity construction is possible in apartheid South Africa must be 'no.' Yet Fugard has become more optimistic in his later plays such as '*Master Harold' ... and the boys* (1982), *My Children! My Africa!* (1989) and *Playland* (1992).[46] He offers small scenes that point at least to the possibility for change in society. Throughout the final decade of apartheid, up to the election of Nelson Mandela as President in 1994, Fugard continued to define love, education and sane role behaviour as the keys to the difficult and slow dismantling of racial barriers.

---

[46] See Collins (1983) and Goetsch (1997).

3. "Acting and role-playing as a means for survival"[1] in *Sizwe Bansi is Dead* and *The Island*

> [...] in much of Fugard's drama, the focus is on the theatricality of *apartheid*, and the effect in this case is not only to reveal its injustices and inhumanity but to promote the statement that 'acting' [...] is a necessary weapon of black struggle [...].
>
> Brian Crow[2]

3.1. The collaboration of Athol Fugard, John Kani and Winston Ntshona

In the early 1970s Athol Fugard and his African actor-collaborators John Kani and Winston Ntshona created two plays in workshop, *Sizwe Bansi is Dead* (1972) and *The Island* (1973), in which they addressed the same topic: the (non-)status of blacks in contemporary South African society. Their common effort, as Martin Orkin emphasises, provided "a new impetus to South African theatre" by showing how group improvisation and workshop brought together theatre practitioners and crossed the social and racial boundaries aimed at isolating them (1991: 159).

Sizwe Bansi is Dead and *The Island* belong to the group of 'protest plays' that openly condemned apartheid. However, as these plays both use techniques of agitprop theatre to raise the consciousness of their white or black audiences (cf. Wertheim 1988: 211f.),[3] they anticipate the style of the more radical 'resistance theatre' created in the light of the Black Consciousness Movement in the 1970s and early 1980s (cf. Chapter 4).

Sizwe Bansi is Dead and *The Island* introduce characters who master oppressive reality and resist and subvert apartheid's ideological practices. In contrast to the social invisibility of blacks, African actors who appear on the theatre stage force their (white and non-white) audiences to look at them and acknowledge their existence. The spectators of anti-apartheid theatre are confronted simultaneously

---

[1] Wertheim 2000: 81, capitalisation changed. Walder has used a similar phrase: "Acting as a means of survival" (1993: 421).

[2] Crow 1992: 157.

[3] Walder argued in 1993 that the plays' "lasting popularity as well as their influence – most drama from South Africa today bears their mark – demonstrates how they also transcend the limitations of immediacy, or agitprop" (1993b: xxx).

with the characters' vitality as human beings and the actors' histrionic creativity as they perform a variety of roles. The theatre becomes the domain where the black South African is able to escape their apartheid-imposed definition of identity in terms of mere functionality. Instead, they exist not only *through* the gaze of others but also *in* the gaze of others. This duality is implied in George Herbert Mead's assertion that identity is formed by the ability to see oneself with the eyes of the generalised other (cf. 1957[15]: 156). The fact that black people are only recognised in their individuality in the theatre is ironic because on stage they are not themselves but play other roles. The closest the actors can then get to presenting their own self is by playing themselves. However, this still implies a mediated presentation of self.

Brian Crow argues that Fugard's belief in the precedence of the actor over both audience and text allows the actors to present a truth that is "more than an accomplished mimicry of emotion or the assured interpretation of a role; it is nothing less than the actor's attempt to communicate what cannot normally be expressed, a confrontation with self." Crow implies that a convincing theatrical act can only grow out of social experience and that the actor must genuinely be creative, not simply mimicking their own experience, but transcending it, to explore the depths of human existence (1992: 151, cf. 157). In his introduction to the 'Statement plays' Fugard emphasises that "[...] in the absence of words on paper [...] personal truth has been our only capital" (1986: n.p.).[4]

This approach to theatre and acting can be seen in Fugard's reflections on an acting exercise with Kani and Ntshona in September of 1972 when the trio was rehearsing *Sizwe Bansi is Dead.* Fugard asked his two actors to respond to a scene in the lounge of a local hotel: "[...] our basic challenge [...] consisted of one table, one chair and their relationship to it as 'the servant'. Obviously the table and chair (empty) is a symbol of whiteness; they are black" (1983: 202). This exercise, rooted in segregated apartheid reality, shows to what extent both people and objects carry political and racial meaning in the South African context. Fugard describes the men's relationship to the table and chair as "subordinate, resentful, dependent" (1983: 202).

---

4 The so-called 'Statement plays' include, besides *Sizwe Bansi is Dead* and *The Island*, *Statements after an Arrest under the Immorality Act* (1974), which was written in conventional fashion but rehearsed with workshop techniques (cf. Chapter 2.3).

The valuable questions that this acting exercise provoked are contained in Fugard's summary of Kani's experience: "[...] who am I? Where am I? Who is where? The mask and the face behind the mask. The ontological dilemma arising out of 'role' playing" (1983: 202). Black life is characterised as a dialogic existence in histrionic terms. Blacks are forced to take on masks in the presence of whites because the prescribed roles and forms of behaviour in South African society correspond to neither natural nor dignified existence. They are forced to transform into actors by the very inhuman definition of identity offered to their public self under apartheid. However, Kani's evaluation also makes clear that the private self of Africans differs from their public definition: there is a face behind the mask which is looking for an identity independent of external white prescription. It is on the stage that this conflict can be enacted. By slipping into different roles and moving away from techniques of realism and naturalism, the actor is able to try on various identities: "The self as the play of masks; society as a 'theatre' in which 'actors' perform their 'roles'; being as the dialectic of self and other" (Crow with Banfield 1996: 102).

In accordance with Camus' definition of the actor as someone who transcends the boundaries of a theatrical functionary, Crow suggests that sincere and effective play-acting, as created by Fugard, is about becoming a "modern hero, free to explore and affirm his own being and to make and remake himself in his own desired image" (1992: 151). From this point of view play-acting in the South African context is as such not only about presenting other characters and their life stories on stage but also about using this opportunity to experiment with different identities. Thus acting is seen essentially as a means for evading prescriptive concepts of self in favour of self-exploration and self-definition. These ideas explain why, for example, it is important for John in *The Island* to bring Winston to a full understanding of Antigone's plight and to recognise the parallels between her story and their own fate. When at the end Winston takes off his wig and speaks both as Antigone and himself, he has transcended the state-defined boundaries in favour of an existentialist affirmation of his identity.

In *Sizwe Bansi is Dead* and *The Island* acting is a central metaphor. Commenting on the famous improvisational monologue of *Sizwe Bansi*'s protagonist Styles, Albert Wertheim concludes that with "its theatrical image, it becomes clear that the scene is most importantly about acting and role-playing as a means for survival"

(2000: 81).[5] Styles takes on various roles in South Africa's racial hierarchy, a strategy which allows him not only to analyse and understand the functioning of apartheid society but finally to resist and subvert it. Styles's anecdotes prepare the scene for Sizwe and Buntu's "extreme and horrifying social theatricality", the exchanging of Sizwe's identity with that of a dead man in the name of mere survival (Crow 1992: 156).

Wertheim also suggests that in *The Island* acting is conceived of as a means of acting out one's life, as a manifestation of survival and as a basis for political action (cf. 2000: 88). The most obvious form of acting in *The Island* is the prisoners' improvisational performance of Sophocles' *Antigone.* John and Winston present the confrontation between Antigone and King Creon, which is staged as a play-within-the-play.[6] The significance of the *Antigone* performance lies as much in its preparation as in its interpretation by the actors. In addition, the two men improve their meagre existence in inhuman circumstances with games that involve the enactment of their own social roles. In order for the nature of their lives to be conveyed appropriately to the members of the theatre audience, the spectators of both plays are drawn into the reality of the on-stage performance.

This chapter proposes an interpretation of the two plays created in workshop by Fugard, Kani and Ntshona as a set of instructions for survival through playacting. Theatre is seen as the manifestation of the social theatricality of being. The context is the grim reality of life in apartheid South Africa during the early 1970s.

3.2. Seeing through the status-quo: Black life under apartheid rule

The performance of *Sizwe Bansi is Dead* displays the multiplicity and ambivalence inherent in the reigning power structures in apartheid South Africa. By taking on different roles, especially roles of representatives of the white ruling class, the protagonist Styles is able to show how one can undermine white authority and free oneself from oppression. In a similar fashion *The Island*'s characters, the prisoners

[5] Biodun describes Fugard's dramaturgic device as "*role-deconstruction* and *role-construction.*" This device leads to a "thoroughgoing *de-totalisation* of the inhuman claustrophobic space initially encountered on the surface level of Fugard's plays" because the "artificial, fragmented totalisations of experience" created by apartheid are "negated" (1985: 102f.).

[6] Durbach (1993), Foster (1977) and Mackay (1989) offer a comparison of Sophocles' *Antigone* and its performance in *The Island.*

John and Winston, refuse to let the system subject them to its total control.[7] The men manifest a strong urge to live and maintain their existence as human beings in a social web in spite of, or due to, their isolation from society.

3.2.1. Resistance and subversion through role-play in *Sizwe Bansi is Dead*

Styles first appears on stage reading a newspaper. After some remarks on articles in the daily paper he performs a series of sketches in which he re-enacts past experiences decisive for his personal development. These implicitly characterise him as a bright, versatile, cunning man.

An article about a car plant expansion prompts Styles to tell the audience about his time as a worker at the Ford motor plant in Port Elizabeth. He narrates and partially re-enacts what happened on the day an American Ford heir[8] came to visit the factory. Styles plays several roles - himself, the General Foreman Baas Bradley, the 'big baas' and Mr. Ford - and defines the audience as his African co-workers. André Brink believes that this method is effective in enlarging the "scope of the character's involvement in the narrative" (1993: 443). Role-play thus realises the plurality already suggested in Styles's very name (cf. 1993: 443).

As the stage directions indicate, Styles not only mimics Bradley's language ("*heavy Afrikaans accent*")[9] but also re-enacts his baas's gestures, movements and actions. Styles describes his boss as a gullible, easily-duped, harmless man. He suggests that he has deciphered Bradley's character and can use it to his own advantage: "Good man that one, if you knew how to handle him" (*SB* 4). He then switches from telling to showing in order to display Bradley's nature more effectively. For example, he captures his boss's treatment of the workers in preparation for Mr. Ford's visit during General Cleaning, "[s]*lapping his hands together as he urges on*

---

[7] *The Island* was originally called *Die Hodoshe Span* ('The Hodoshe work-team') after a warder on Robben Island nicknamed Hodoshe (Xhosa for 'carrion fly'). The title of the then still unscripted play was "usefully obscure" because it was illegal to talk about prison conditions in public (Walder 1993b: xxix). *Die Hodoshe Span* consisted of two characters, Bonisile and Zola, who spoke Afrikaans and Xhosa. It played to small audiences during its short private run in South Africa before it premiered as *The Island* in Britain. There John Kani and Winston Ntshona decided to use their own names in the play and switched to a predominantly English dialogue (cf. 1993b: xxix).

[8] For a reading of this scene as a comment on multinational business interest see Seymour (1980: 279).

[9] *SB* 4. References to *Sizwe Bansi is Dead* are flagged *SB*.

the 'boys.'" Styles as Bradley directly addresses the audience as the "boys": "'Come on, boys! It's got to be spotless! Big day for the plant!'" (*SB* 4). This behaviour makes clear that although Bradley adopts apartheid discourse, he does not treat the workers in a specifically condescending manner. Instead, he appears excited and completely focused on the reception of the important visitor. The big boss seems to use the discriminatory terms of apartheid rhetoric in a nicer way. He turns the degrading "boys" and "John,"[10] terms which deny the workers' individuality, into a more affectionate and conspiratorial "my boys" (*SB* 4). This behaviour reflects the double dependence of the supervisors on the workers. Firstly, the African men must work hard and quickly to clean the plant and make it presentable. Secondly, the supervisors must ensure that the workers do not voice any discontent about the poor working conditions in the presence of the American visitor. They all know that ultimately Mr. Ford would find the white men responsible for failing to keep the Africans in their place and thus negligent in ensuring the proper functioning of the plant. This is why Bradley demands of Styles that the workers "must try to impress Mr Henry Ford that they are better than those monkeys in his own country, those niggers in Harlem who know nothing but strike, strike" (*SB* 7). The black men, who are usually placed at the bottom of the human and social hierarchy, move up one position: they are at least "better" that the American "monkeys." This also implies, however, that the African men are usually considered no more than circus animals which can be trained, an observation that Styles also makes.

The irony of the monkey image is that Henry Louis Gates Jr. sees the African-American figure of the Signifying Monkey as a cunning trickster figure who is able to outwit his opponents with creative language usage. The Signifying Monkey is not only a character in a narrative but more importantly stands for a rhetorical strategy. It is a master-trope that comprises other black tropes or creative uses of language (the vernacular), such as the obscuring or displacement of meaning or free language play. It represents the "principle of self-consciousness in the black vernacular." In relation to white or 'standard' language usage, this rhetorical strategy is subversive, even mocking (Gates 1988: 53; cf. 44-88). In a similar fashion Styles makes use of the instability of meaning and the creativity of language to poke fun at and look down on the white men, especially when he acts as translator between them and the African workers (see below).

[10] 'John' is a generic name used by whites to address Africans.

The supervisors, knowing that they themselves have wilfully neglected their obligations to provide basic human working conditions and the necessary safety measures, now scurry to do so. They kneel on the floor to paint lines for safety precautions, thereby exposing themselves to the view of Styles and his colleagues. As they do not speak Xhosa, the native language of their workers, they depend on the linguistically versatile Styles for translation. Bradley asks him:

> 'What do you say in your language for this? Eye Protection Area.'
>
> It was easy, man!
>
> *'Gqokra Izi Khuselo Zamehlo Kule Ndawo.'*
>
> Nobody wrote it!
>
> 'Don't bloody fool me, Styles!'
>
> 'No, sir!'
>
> 'Then spell it ... slowly.' (*SB* 5)

In this situation Bradley recognises Styles's power over him: he has no way of checking if Styles is giving him the right answer or if he is mocking him. The baas's cursing and threatening only highlights his dependency. That he must ask Styles to spell the words slowly is a further act of accepting Styles's temporary superiority. In this moment of role reversal the intellectually higher position of the African man is mirrored in the spatial arrangement of the characters: "That was my moment, man. Kneeling there on the floor ... foreman, general foreman, plant supervisor, plant manager ... and Styles? Standing!" (*SB* 5f.). In this encounter the authority of the management is, in Homi Bhabha's terms, threatened in that its look of surveillance is returned as the "displacing gaze of the disciplined" (1994: 89; cf. Chapter 3.4.2).

This scene clearly has a comic and satiric quality. The exposure of white characters played by black actors is a typical element in anti-apartheid drama to criticise the dominant order.[11] Despite the comic tone of this scene, it is to be taken seriously. It reflects the actual working conditions in the motor plant: poor social conditions, machines which are dangerous to handle and a lack of basic safety precautions.

---

[11] Ron Jenkins points out, "In the twentieth century the Union of South Africa offers no single clown figure as representative of the black and colored peoples' battle against apartheid. Yet a powerful presence in this struggle is the variety of clown figures mocking the absurdity of the dominant white order" (1998: 419). Percy Mtwa also uses this strategy in *Bohpa!* (see Chapter 4.3).

Furthermore, the inability of the employers and employees to engage in even basic communication is pointed out. The whites are implicitly criticised for deeming it below their dignity to learn any words in an indigenous language although it would promote the smooth functioning of the factory if they mastered at least the work-related vocabulary in Xhosa. The fact that the workers don't speak English is a result of separate development and Bantu Education. By denying Africans the possibility of learning English, the state prevents them from gaining access to upward mobility, from moving from shop-floor labourer into management. Fanon asserts, "A man who has a language consequently possesses the world expressed and implied by that language. [...] Mastery of language affords remarkable power" (1967: 18). Language competence and knowledge of the culture in which this language is spoken go hand in hand.[12] Hence Styles's fluency in English also implies that he knows and understands the English (read: white) way of thinking in apartheid South Africa. And, as H. Douglas Brown suggests, second language learning can often be equated with second culture learning.[13] Myles Holloway's evaluation of the workshop plays by Fugard, Kani and Ntshona as "a fusion of cultural and social knowledge" also shows that language, culture, and society are interwoven fields (1993a: 18).

During Mr. Ford's visit Styles observes the managers' servile eagerness to please. The white men are so engrossed by the visitor's presence that they neglect their surveillance of the African workers. Styles seizes this opportunity to reverse the usual order of perception: "We were watching them. Nobody was watching us" (*SB* 8). Freed from the oppressing gaze, he is able to recognise his supervisors' dependence on the American boss's satisfaction:

> [...] the bloody lot [supervisors] were there ... like a pack of puppies!
>
> [*Mimics a lot of fawning men retreating before an important person.*]
>
> I looked and laughed! 'Yessus, Styles, they're all playing your part today!' (*SB* 8)

---

[12] Scholars interested in second language teaching and acquisition have widely commented on the interdependence of language and culture. See for instance Swiderski (1993) or the collection of essays in Valdes, ed. (1986).

Edward Sapir pointed to the quality of language as a guide to social reality in the first half of the twentieth century. Harry Hoijer quotes from Sapir's work: "The worlds in which different societies live are distinct worlds, not merely the same world with different labels attached." (1964: 142). Original source: Edward Sapir. 1929. "The Status of Linguistics as a Science." *Lg.* 5: 207-214, here 209.

[13] Brown (1986: 33). In addition, the language learner is seen and must be made aware of themself as, first and foremost, a cultural being (cf. Valdes 1986: vii).

With this last remark Styles makes clear that he is only pretending to respect his bosses' superiority with his behaviour. He is clearly playing a role.

Styles takes revenge on Bradley by secretly mocking him in the presence of the other employees. Yet Styles is conscious of the fact that he must play along according to the prescribed rules in order to occupy his more privileged position of translator, just as his supervisors make gestures of subservience to their own boss. Styles's pantomime makes clear, as he gleefully remembers the scene, that Mr. Ford's visit consists of three enormous strides in, a courtesy look around and three enormous strides out without talking to anyone or really looking at the plant (cf. *SB* 8f.). Their invisibility in the eyes of Mr. Ford engenders in the white men a feeling of degradation – they are, in fact, being treated exactly the way they treat their black workers - which they overcome by re-asserting their position of authority and power over the Africans. They double up the speed of the assembly line to make up for lost production during General Cleaning.

The image in Styles's last comment ("they're all playing your part today") can be connected to the theatrical quality of the scene as a whole (cf. Wertheim 2000: 81). The theatre stage represents the plant which itself is turned into a stage for the arrival of Mr. Ford. In the phase of setting up the stage the supervisors themselves take on the roles of the technicians and stage manager. They are responsible for turning the dirty and unsafe plant into a clean, safe and well-structured 'plant stage.' Baas Bradley as director issues the workers their costumes, i.e. new working uniforms, before the white men prepare for the show: "I could see them – Mr 'Baas' Bradley, the line supervisor [...] brushing their hair, straightening the tie. There was some General Cleaning going on there too" (*SB* 8). The bosses commit a major 'error' in allowing the African men to see them here in positions of subservience to Mr. Ford. Styles realises at once that he is witnessing backstage behaviour. Goffman would say that the white men's "front" breaks down. Instead, they give access to their "back region." The supervisors usually display a commanding presence when in the workers' field of sight. However, their strategy breaks down in preparation for the visit. By appearing subservient and overtly anxious to make a good impression, they become vulnerable and lose some of their authority over the Africans. Control of the back region, while keeping up a certain impression with the audience of the front region, is an important strategy for achieving dramaturgical success and maintaining information control. Goffman emphasises that "[...] the audience must not acquire destructive information about the situation that is being defined for them. In other words, a team must be able to keep its secrets and have its secrets kept" (1959: 141).

Later in the same scene Bradley asks Styles to translate while he goes over the 'script' with his workers. He thus plays the role of the director who makes sure that everybody has memorised their lines. At the same time he also takes on his 'real' role as their boss, treating them in a condescending manner as if they, like the machines, needed proper tuning:

> 'Styles, tell the boys that when Mr Henry Ford comes into the plant I want them all to look happy. We will slow down the speed of the line so that they can sing and smile while they are working.'
>
> 'Gentleman, he says that when the door opens and his grandmother walks in you must see to it that you are wearing a mask of smiles. Hide your true feelings, brothers. You must sing. The joyous songs of the days of old before we had fools like this one next to me to worry about.' (*SB* 7)

Styles uses this opportunity to educate his fellow-workers (and by extension the audience), enlightening them about the reality of their oppression. Hilary Seymour argues that he strategically exposes Bradley to ridicule. By making the official mythology look absurd and grotesque, he destabilises the binary opposition of white superiority versus black inferiority. Furthermore, he sharpens the self-awareness of his colleagues, thereby drawing their attention to socio-economic realities (cf. 1980: 282). Styles's remarks make clear that he identifies the behaviour that is required of the Africans as humiliating and thus re-defines it, turning it into mere play-acting. The conversion from "smile" to "mask of smiles" signals a difference between appearance and reality and emphasises that the workers are to suppress their true feelings and perform in false consciousness.[14] In fact, Styles's 'interpretation' of Bradley's words is very effective. His fellow-workers are so quick to learn that Styles himself runs into danger:

> 'Say to them, Styles, that they must try to impress Mr Henry Ford that they are better than those monkeys in his own country, those niggers in Harlem who know nothing but strike, strike.'
>
> *Yo!* I liked that one too.
>
> 'Gentlemen, he says we must remember, when Mr Ford walks in, that we are South African monkeys, not American monkeys. South African monkeys are much better trained....'

[14] Seymour offers a similar reading of this scene (cf. 1980: 282f.).

> Before I could even finish, a voice was shouting out of the crowd:
>
> 'He's talking shit!' I had to be careful!
>
> [*Servile and full of smiles as he turns back to Bradley.*]
>
> 'No, sir! The men are much too happy to behave like those American monkeys.' (*SB* 7f.)

Here Styles slips into the role of the teacher and leader of his fellow Africans but fails (or refuses) to seize this moment of heightened consciousness to initiate a strike or revolt in the factory. Seymour suggests that the games he plays at the expense of Bradley "have more entertainment than politicising value" and serve a cathartic function, "allowing frustrated workers to let off steam, to release tensions partially and temporarily" (1980: 283).

Brink offers a different reading of Styles's role-playing and attributes special importance to his impersonation of Baas Bradley. He argues that it allows Styles to present the "all-encompassing yet invisible System" (1993: 443) on stage, a strategy which makes it easier to communicate to the audience the full effect of the people's suffering and their possibilities of subversion and resistance. On the one hand, it demonstrates the possibility of subverting the system's representative by appropriating him in a "totemizing function" (Brink 1993: 444) and thus shows that the Baas, too, can be dominated and manipulated. Seen in this light, the ability to stage and play the system's representatives gives relative power. On the other hand, Styles's representation of Bradley also signifies the latter's omnipresence. In other words, his physical presence is not necessary for his image to occupy the minds of his workers; they have internalised Bradley's gaze. This confirms Foucault's claims (following Bentham's concept of the panopticon) that a gapless system of surveillance must suggest to its subjects that they can be observed at all times (cf. 1981b).[15] Brink also stresses that Styles's role-play functions as a "startingly effective demonstration of Derridean presence of absence and absence of presence" (1993: 443). He goes on to assert that Styles can only temporarily transcend the psychological omnipresence of the system's representatives: "Through play-acting, and only through play-acting, can the actor, in the primary sense of 'actant,' enter into a full understanding of the System, which helps to subvert it from the inside – even as it confirms it" (1993: 444). However, despite all controversy surely inherent in *Sizwe Bansi,* the more important point that Styles's play-acting makes is

[15] Bender calls this concept "isolation under inspection" (1987: 225).

that "[...] if blacks can play white roles convincingly on stage, they understand those roles and could easily, were the society a just one, take on those roles off stage, in real life" (Wertheim 2000: 80). Here lies the effectiveness and real threat that *Sizwe Bansi* extends to white minority rule.

In the performance enacted for Mr. Ford's benefit he does not see the factory in its natural state but in a stylised version, filled with otherwise missing props and disguised characters putting on an act. The usual work routine is rewritten and turned into a musical about the happy docile African. The speed of the assembly line is slowed down so that the labourers can sing and smile while working at a humane pace with their new tools. It is of course ironic that the songs being sung stem from the resistance movement.[16]

By adding music and song, this scene can be read as an implicit criticism of the black South African musical which is primarily designed for white audiences. Andrew Horn refers to this form as "Theatre of Exploitation" (1986: 213). Anthony Akerman comments on the nature of the black musical: "Song and dance, traditional forms of cultural expression in Africa, were viewed through racist eyes as 'inherent characteristics'. This theory is still subscribed to, and 'innate rhythm' presents itself as raw material from which profit can be made" (1977/78: 67). This process would also correctly describe the essentialist image of blacks that the managers want to convey to Mr. Ford: happy natives, whose singing is natural and whose rhythmic work on the conveyor belt represents their dancing motions. Russell Vandenbroucke's review of *Ipi-Tombi*,[17] a 1974 black musical designed for white audiences, points out that it is based on "white attitudes and prejudices" and "sugarcoats the bitter realities of contemporary South Africa" (1976: 68; cf. 1977/78: 50; Mda 1996: 196f.).[18] In a nutshell this is the strategy of the white managers facing the American visitor.

Throughout the whole improvisational passage Styles repeatedly alludes to capitalism's exploitation of subalterns and realises that this is a worldwide truth. Instead of presenting the apartheid system in terms of racial oppression, his

---

[16] The song translates as "There are the black men, Vorster. Be careful, there are the black men, Vorster" (Pieterse 1982 [1976]: 200). Fugard also gives a literal translation in the glossary: "work steady, the train is coming" (1986: 109).

[17] The title *Ipi-Tombi* is Zulu and translates roughly as 'Girls! Where!' (cf. Kruger 1999: 137).

[18] Intriguingly, several of Vandenbroucke's paragraphs reappear in the exact same wording in Akerman's article, without being marked as a quotation.

comments clearly identify economic exploitation as the source of dehumanisation and oppression and thus create, as Brink asserts, a "more problematic ideological subtext" (1993: 441).[19]

Wertheim attributes Styles's recognition to his observation of the performance for Mr. Ford (see quotation below). Styles analyses the role played by the white South African managers, the African workers and, last but not least, by the American capitalist himself. By enacting and narrating these disparate roles, he brings himself to see his own situation "clearly and with perspective" (2000: 81). He concludes:

> I said to myself:
>
> 'Styles, you're a bloody monkey, boy!'
>
> 'What do you mean?'
>
> 'You're a monkey, man.'
>
> 'Go to hell!'
>
> 'Come on, Styles, you're a monkey, man, and you know it. [...]'
>
> I was right. I took a good look at my life. What did I see? A bloody circus monkey! Selling most of his time on this earth to another man. (*SB* 9)

Here Styles decides to resign from the Ford plant after playing yet another role game. In a dialogue of split consciousness his enlightened self fights off all attempts by his less courageous and less independent side to ignore his obvious condition. However, the former succeeds in convincing the latter that only drastic measures can free him from his position of servitude. He comes to understand that he does not exist as a 'real' person in the eyes of whites. Yet the life-affirming and regime-critical theatrical experience that Styles presents to the audience draws attention to the contradictions and inhumanity of white ideology. Realising that his

---

[19] This perspective on reality allows Styles to overcome his oppressed state by resorting to private enterprise – a photographic studio. Seymour criticises Styles for the "fundamental passivity and pragmatism" (1980: 277) of his individual response. She reproaches him for not developing his talent as spokesman for his African co-workers, choosing instead to retreat from public commitment to favour his personal assertion. In fact, several critics approaching from a Marxist point of view point out that Styles depends on his appropriation of and capitalisation on the practices of apartheid for his rise to the black petty bourgeoisie, for example, by taking reference book photographs. "Instead of highlighting the contradictions and absurdities of industrial apartheid, he becomes a skilful manipulator of individual sensibilities, a public relations officer retailing acceptance of the status quo" (Seymour 1980: 280). For such a reading of *Sizwe Bansi* refer to R.K. (1973: 125), Seymour (1980: 277-86) and Piniel Viriri Shava (1989: 135). Seymour's main criticism is that "statements on racism which ignore its class basis are not in essence radical" (1980: 275).

games of resistance have raised the consciousness of his co-workers, he has fulfilled one of his tasks. However, these games have remained mere games without having any effect on his own material and psychological situation. Consequently, he did not and cannot reach his other goal, the improvement of his own fate, by staying in the Ford plant. Having come to this conclusion through his role-play and social theatricality on the job (after all, what better way is there to see one's own situation clearly than by playing it out oneself), he resigns his position and opens up a photographic studio.

3.2.2. Rehearsing social roles: Keeping up with 'real' life on the Island

Turning from the factory in *Sizwe Bansi* to the prison in *The Island*, it can be said that one aim of apartheid's prison system seems to be to deprive prisoners of their humanity. Methodologically this implies stripping the men of the opportunity to function as they did in society. By refusing to let them enact and live their social roles, an attempt is made to deny their personal identity and eventually annihilate their sense of self.

Similar to the depiction of oppression in literature about totalitarian regimes, for example in George Orwell's dystopia *Nineteen Eighty-Four*, the men are stripped of their manhood and are either reduced to weeping, vulnerable babies or to animals. While being transported from Port Elizabeth to Cape Town by police van, the convicts are crammed together and tied to one another. They therefore cannot prevent themselves from urinating on each other. The stage directions of Fugard's unpublished draft version of *The Island* describe the two men as being "ground into animal-like submission by their labour [...] Their movements are almost those of unfeeling robots." Back in the prison Winston "crawls around the cell like a wild animal as his rage and anger mount."[20] After their three-legged run and the beatings by their guard Hodoshe John attempts to clean Winston's wounds with his urine. According to Wertheim, John's gesture symbolises "the transilience of inhumanity and animal function into human caring." He goes on to analyse the chiasmic nature of this theme: "Hodoshe exemplifies the prison guards whose humanity devolves into animal behavior, whereas the prisoners, Winston and John, create their humanity out of the very bestiality that has been forced on them" (2000: 92). It is

---

[20] Both quotations are from Fugard, Unpublished draft version of *The Island.* Fugard manuscript collection, Lilly Library, Bloomington, Indiana. Act II, pp. 1f. The references to their animal-like behaviour have been omitted in the published version.

significant that the gaoler's nickname, Hodoshe, means 'green carrion fly.' This refers to an insect that makes irritating noises and stings living beings just as the guard maltreats the prisoners every day and makes sure that they feel they are at his mercy.[21]

John and Winston are well aware that they are meant to resemble children in their prison clothes which consist of khaki shirts and short trousers. They attempt to downplay the degradation they experience during the sand shipping torture. Hodoshe forces both prisoners to fill wheelbarrows with sand and empty them where the other man is digging so that both piles of sand never dwindle. John and Winston relate this to their own children's enthusiasm for playing on the beach. However, they come to realise that their comparison is inappropriate. In the context of Robben Island sand shipping cannot convincingly be redefined as a child's game of building sandcastles and playing on the dunes. The two men are not able to align their situation with the carefree and happy existence of children. Instead, they risk being reduced to babies not yet able to think and act on their own. John exclaims, "I'm a man, brother. A man! But if Hodoshe had kept us at those wheelbarrows five minutes longer...! There would have been a baby on the Island tonight. I nearly cried."[22] Furthermore, the guard almost succeeds in driving the friends apart and turning their bond of solidarity and reciprocal recognition into a relationship of hate and competition.

John and Winston pass the time by taking each other to the bioscope[23] in the evening. In turn they recreate the movies they have seen through words and gestures. Thus they not only entertain one another but also keep alive their memories of life outside the prison walls and reaffirm their human spirit. Theatricality takes on an affirmative value (cf. Biodun 1985: 102f.). They also establish imaginary contact with their friends and families on the mainland using a tin cup as a telephone receiver to enact a conversation with them. John, who initiates this game, is so convincing in his words and gestures that he draws Winston into his make-believe, hereby giving proof of his great acting talent and subjecting his friend to the (deceptive) power of the imagination. Their one-sided

---

[21] Harlow discusses the significance attributed to the nicknaming of the guards by prisoners (cf. 1987: 128).

[22] *IL* 49. References to *The Island* are flagged *IL*.

[23] South African English for 'cinema.'

conversation reveals a strong emotional bond with their community.[24] Once Winston returns to the reality of their situation, his misery is foregrounded in the juxtaposition of their prison life with their home life. Although both men suffer emotionally from their memories, it is important that they remind themselves of their family ties and personal connections outside their cell walls.

By acting out a conception of identity, the men perform a memory which ceases to belong to the past and becomes an ongoing present. "Performance always unfixes," as Lesley Wade Soule asserts (1998: 42). This scene shows that memories can live on only if actively shared and not kept locked up passively in the mind. Furthermore, by enacting the roles of friends, husbands and fathers that they would normally be playing outside the prison walls, they show that they could easily re-adopt them if set free. This emphasises the fact that roles are acquired through socialisation and can only be exercised in the context of their respective social groups. Hans-Peter Dreitzel shows how an individual's loss of contact with other people in a specific milieu leads to their relative deprivation, disruptions of role behaviour and exclusion from their group (1982[6]: 231-34). By practising the roles they would normally occupy in life outside of the prison walls, John and Winston avoid running the risk of becoming alienated from their group's norms. If and when they are set free, they could then re-integrate into their group.

In their personal interaction in the cell the two men behave in a human way and take on roles appropriate to the situation and context. After being beaten by Hodoshe on the beach, the prisoners return to their cubicle and examine their wounds. The blood on John's ear alarms Winston. The stage directions indicate their care for one another in the language of acting and role-playing. "*In a reversal of earlier roles Winston now gets John down on the floor so as to examine the injured ear*" (*IL* 48). They tend to each other's injuries just as parents would look after their children or partners would care for their mutual well-being.

It becomes clear in the course of the play that John and Winston draw strength from their solidarity as well as from their shared memories of their community. Vandenbroucke insists that "[...] John and Winston are literally manacled hand and foot. However, their spirits are free to return to shore and unite with their people"

---

[24] Vandenbroucke's interpretation of *The Island* attributes great significance to this communal bond: "It is this solidarity (rather than the dramatization of prison's horrors) that makes *The Island* more political than any other Fugard play" (1985: 131). The term "Fugard play" is, of course, ill-used as Fugard does not claim sole authorship.

(1985: 131; 1992: 310). John confirms, "People must remember their responsibilities to others" (*IL* 56). This personal bond between the two men can be seen as a microcosm of the play's larger racial bond. This is also alluded to in *Sizwe Bansi is Dead* when Buntu tells Sizwe that Robert, their "brother" (*SB* 43), is wishing him luck (cf. Vandenbroucke 1985: 130; 1992: 309; Orkin 1991: 160).

The aim of the prison system is to disrupt the men's human, rational and caring behaviour as well as their solidarity. Winston and John continually call each other "*broer*," a socially coded expression of comradeship (cf. *IL* 49, 52, 63). But the bond of brotherhood between John and Winston is put to the test in the 'sand shipping' scene. After a long day of hard work John has difficulty in calming Winston and distracting him from his feelings of rage and pain, which wake in him the urge to complain to Hodoshe. They admit that they developed feelings of hatred for one another during this futile labour of shipping sand on the beach. To them the incessant hum of the carrion fly and the invisible 'presence' of Hodoshe signify death. E. Anne Mackay argues that this image of death is also present in their never-ending sand shipping. The prisoners are, if not burying themselves, at least interring each other's endeavours under the loads of sand (cf. 1989: 153). However, John and Winston are emotionally strong enough to overcome these destructive feelings by analysing the situation rationally. They finally realise that the purpose of this torture is to break their emotional and physical stability. Winston admits, "If he were God, he would have done it. [...] Broken us." However, he reasserts his own strength by placing himself above their tormentor: "Men get tired. Hey! There's a thought. We're still alive because Hodoshe got tired." The memory of Hodoshe's torture no longer seems to affect Winston. He is able to face John "*with calm resignation*" (all *IL* 49) and accept his reaffirmation of their brotherhood.

John and Winston's brotherhood is put to an even greater test when John learns from the wardens that he is to be released in three months' time.[25] According to the stage directions, "*Winston explodes with joy*" at first (*IL* 64). However, once he realises the consequences that their separation will have, he develops feelings of envy and anger. Using his story-telling and play-writing abilities, he 'rewrites' the sketch of the phone call to their friends and family. He torments John with a tantalising narration about his first evening back home in New Brighton with their

[25] We do not learn why John's sentence has been reduced whereas Winston's has not. Mackay suggests that this is Fugard's mirroring of the fate of Antigone's brothers. One is given a state burial, the other is denied this ceremony. She believes that it is the sense of "fundamental *wrongness*" about the difference that is important (1989: 153).

mates in the local pub. He concludes, "You stink, John. You stink of beer, of company, of *poes,*[26] of freedom ... Your freedom stinks, John, and it's driving me mad. [...] You will laugh, you will drink, you will fuck and forget" (*IL* 71).

After giving vent to his jealousy, Winston is able to overcome these feelings and accept his fate of interminable imprisonment on Robben Island. Fugard reflects in his *Notebooks*, "The fusing of Hopelessness (metaphysical predicament) and Hope (Historical predicament) ... the reality, the Truth that is both, even as a coin is both heads and tails" (1983: 206). John's upcoming release underscores the pointlessness of Winston's existence without his friend. Fugard's notes in the draft version of *The Island* also highlight this aspect: "For the men sentenced to 'Life' that weekend is the moment when Sisyphus first realises what the Gods have done to him ... that he will in fact never succeed. Pessimism and courage experience their first moment of consciousness."[27]

Winston projects himself into the future and imagines that he will resemble the broken spirit, Harry, one of their co-prisoners:

> WINSTON. [...] Look into his eyes, John. Look at his hands. They've changed him. They've turned him into stone. Watch him work with that chisel and hammer. Twenty perfect blocks of stone every day. Nobody else can do it like him. He loves stone. That's why they're nice to him. He's forgotten himself. He's forgotten everything ... why he's here, where he comes from.
>
> That's happening to me John. I've forgotten why I'm here.
>
> [...] what do I count? My life? How do I count it, John? One ... one .... another day comes ... one ... Help me, John! (*IL* 71f.)

In this short speech Winston touches on several strategies that the system employs to break its subjects' will and individuality. He fears that he will lose his ability to think rationally and keep track of time or suffer from loss of memory and self-recognition. If so, his life would no longer develop with a sense of direction but continue meaninglessly into Sisyphean infinity, a "living death" (*IL* 77).[28] Forgetting means no longer reflecting on the past or being able to use it in the present. To some extent this will happen to Winston once he is deprived of John's

---

[26] Afrikaans for 'cunt.'

[27] Fugard, Unpublished draft version of *The Island.* Fugard manuscript collection, Lilly Library, Bloomington, Indiana. Act I, n.p.

[28] Mackay offers an analysis of the fluctuating reversal of the concepts of life and death (cf. 1989: 153f.). Wertheim explores the influence of Camus' myth of Sisyphus on *The Island* (2000: 94f.).

company. Their common background has helped both men to stay conscious of their development and fate. It seems to Winston, however, the he will endure his existence more easily if freed from the taunting memories of the happier times with his friend, John. He therefore actually hopes that amnesia will heal his wounds. However, he has not yet reached this state of mind and (as the stage directions emphasise), compared to old Harry, he is aware of his fate and consciously accepts it:

> [*John has sunk to the floor, helpless in the face of the other man's torment and pain. Winston almost seems to bend under the weight of the life stretching ahead of him on the Island. For a few seconds he lives in silence with his reality, then slowly straightens up. He turns and looks at John. When he speaks again, it is the* voice of a man who has come to terms with his fate, *massively compassionate.*]
>
> [...]
>
> *Nyana we sizwe*[29] ... it's all over now. [...] Forget me ... because I'm going to forget you. (*IL* 72)

According to Jack Goody and Ian Watt, all elements that have lost their significance in the present are eventually forgotten and completely removed from memory, a process they call 'homeostasis' or 'structural amnesia.' Furthermore, in an essentially oral culture the individual views the past through the eyes of the present because no written collections or chronological statements about the past exist (1986: 72f.). Homeostasis is the fate that most likely awaits Winston once his contact to John is broken. As Winston has no way of recording the years spent with John other than through memory, once the process of forgetting has set in, he will have no objective written proof of their time together. By forgetting their games and thus ceasing to imagine life outside of prison bars, Winston runs the risk of physical death or total social exclusion and consequently social death.

3.3. Preparing for future survival

Sizwe Bansi is Dead's protagonist, Styles, and *The Island*'s prisoners, John and Winston, experience different forms of life under apartheid, all inhuman in their own way. Yet all three characters manage to affirm their humanity and vitality and their solidarity with their families and/or broader communities. It is their will to

---

[29] Xhosa for "brother of the land"; Winston and John use this slogan throughout the play to affirm their brotherhood.

live and their affirmation of a commitment to the struggle that allows them to face all odds.

3.3.1. Playing (for) life in *Sizwe Bansi is Dead*

3.3.1.1. Alternative historiography

Styles's New Brighton photographic studio is his "strong room of dreams" (*SB* 12). It is here that Styles defines himself as a historiographer, capturing the size, variety and individuality of the township population in black and white: "My people [...] who would be forgotten, and their dreams with them, if it wasn't for Styles. [...] Walk into the houses of New Brighton and on the walls you'll find hanging the story of the people the writers of the big books forget about" (*SB* 12f.). It is significant that he directly addresses his audience: "That's what I do friends" (*SB* 13). Having lost their role as the fellow-workers in the Ford motor plant, the audience now acquire a new role in the play - that of bearing witness. Styles presents several pictures to his spectators and explains the story behind each photograph. Again, he slips into diverse roles and brings the inhabitants of the township to life. Ntshona expands on Styles by explaining:

> Whenever one is involved in all he is doing, he is selecting from life, from his immediate surroundings, the themes that affect his life, because in the overall end of it all, what you're going to see on stage is never no ghosts, no apparitions; those are human beings talking about their lives, their immediate surroundings. (Kani & Ntshona 1976: 8)

With this method Styles is able to people the "bare stage with what seems like the entire New Brighton community [...] in a *tour de force* of mime, improvised dialogue and remembered gesture" (Walder 1984: 84). It must not be forgotten that because of the Group Areas Act, few white audience members would have been fully aware of the reality of black life. As Fugard himself emphasised, "I've not been allowed inside a black township for many years, so I am very dependent on the two actors for a basic image, a vitality, an assertion of life" (1973a: 35). And assertions of life is what Styles offers: the broad smile of a 48-year-old African, who passed his Standard Six Certificate through correspondence courses, and the voices of a large family shouting "cheese" into the camera: "[...] there it was – New Brighton's smile, twenty-seven variations" (*SB* 15).[30]

Two different concepts of historiography underlie this scene. On the one hand, Styles merely documents the New Brighton community in his photos. On the other, he deconstructs, in Derrida's sense of the term, traditional historiography to the extent that he rehabilitates what white South African historical tradition has repressed and thus offers a new interpretation of history.[31] His photographs become the record of the poor and illiterate non-whites and form a visual chronicle of life in South Africa under the laws of apartheid. These pictures of the dispossessed create a dialogue with the spectators and make them aware of the reality of society in an attempt to undermine the dichotomy of visible whites versus invisible non-whites (cf. Wertheim 2000: 82).

Fugard uses the idea of photography in all three plays discussed in Chapter 2. In *Statements after an Arrest under the Immorality Act* he explores how a police photographer invades personal privacy and paralyses the dynamics of a multi-racial relationship by degrading it to black-and-white still photographs. In *Blood Knot* the coloured brothers, Morrie and Zach, realise that they have been corresponding with a white girl when they receive a snapshot from their pen-friend. This photo represents reality. It makes Morrie aware of their behaviour as a transgression of apartheid's code of conduct while Zach wonders how his light-skinned brother can evade the truth by passing, i.e. using the power of the deceptive appearance. In *A Lesson from Aloes* the coloured character, Steve, shows his white friends a picture of his father and himself. While the photograph itself brings back joyful memories of his father, Steve knows that the snap only captures a certain moment in life and does not mean eternal happiness. He recalls his father's tragic downfall from a proud to a broken man as a result of apartheid's racist laws, reminiscent of the fate of Styles's father (see below).

In the scene from *Sizwe Bansi* the audience recognise the life-affirming smile of the twenty-seven family members and thus the power of life. The spectators, however,

---

[30] Walder explains that the actors Kani and Ntshona, who both grew up in New Brighton township, were able to achieve "immediate local recognition" for *Sizwe Bansi* and "comment on personal history and current issues" with the help of improvisational techniques and the play's story-telling structure (1993a: 421).

[31] These two concepts of historiography can be compared to those proposed by Dominick LaCapra. He differentiates between documentary reconstruction of the past and dialogue with the past (cf. 1983: 27).

are not allowed to enjoy this impression of happiness. When the eldest son comes to collect the photographs, he laments his father's death. Styles is forced to play a further role, that of the friend offering consolation. When he repeats his words of condolence to the man, he turns to the play's viewers and includes them in the group of mourners. This allows Styles to slip into the role of a leader of the people who preaches about the meaning of life and death: "You must understand one thing. We own nothing except ourselves. This world and its laws, allows us nothing, except ourselves. There is nothing we can leave behind when we die, except the memory of ourselves" (*SB* 16). This speech can be read as a harsh condemnation of apartheid and the meagre life it forces its non-white subjects to endure. However, it can also be seen as an explanation of the importance that family ties and friendships carry. Life for the deprived is characterised as the basic struggle for existence in a world that "allows us nothing, except ourselves." The preservation of their memory is thus of great value because it reinforces their humanness and their sense of dignity. This positive image is contrasted with the regime's treatment of Styles's father. After fighting in World War II,

> they stripped him at the docks – his gun, his uniform, the dignity they'd allowed him to have for a few mad years because the world needed men to fight and sacrifice themselves for something called Freedom. In return, they let him keep his scoff-tin and gave him a bicycle. Size twenty-eight. I remember, because it was too big for me. When he died, in a rotten old suitcase amongst some of his old rags, I found that photograph. That's all. That's all I have from him. (*SB* 17)

This anecdote serves several functions. The identification of discrimination and segregation with black poverty and death even before the rise to power of the National Party in 1948 and the official implementation of apartheid is contrasted with the necessity for political consciousness and empowerment based on memory.[32] Styles has seen through the state's strategy of merely using its population for its own (i.e. white) self-defence. The memory of his father keeps alive in him the awareness of his own oppression as well as the will to actively fight for his survival. The photograph presents Styles with a fixed image of his father and serves as constant reminder of the reality of life in South Africa. This explains the importance Styles attributes to his pictures and the memories they convey. This is why he tries to teach his customers that they must cherish their

[32] 'Memory' is used in in Assman & Assman's sense of communicative and cultural memory (cf. 1988: 29).

snapshots as affirmations of life and defy the state's treatment of them as ghosts, as Buntu also explains later to Sizwe (see Chapter 3.3.1.2).

The first half of the play, Styles's improvisation, has an important structural function in *Sizwe Bansi is Dead.* It does not merely precede the second part, which lends the play its name, but "surrounds it and contextualises it" (Brink 1993: 445). In this second part the spectators, Styles's co-conspirators and friends, witness the story of Sizwe Bansi who saves his own life with the help of a dead man's passbook. Sizwe replaces the picture of the deceased Robert Zwelinzima with a photograph of himself. It is against the knowledge acquired in the first part that the audience are asked to judge the second part. According to Brink, "Styles does not merely establish a prologue to the play, but rehearses the conditions for its interaction with the audience" (*ibid.*).

Thus far all the characters that have populated the stage have been brought to life through Styles's role-play. In the second part of the play another character comes on stage. Styles announces the appearance of Sizwe Bansi, who is anonymously called "Man" in the script. His Xhosa name translates as "large nation" (Vandenbroucke 1985: 119) or "the people are strong" (cf. Orkin 1991: 162). Styles does not announce a human being but a "Dream" (*SB* 17). In other words the photographer does not interact in a neutral manner with a man who has come to have his picture taken but actively stages him. To this extent it becomes apparent that Styles's studio is a "strongroom of dreams" because he not only defines his customers as dreams but, more significantly, induces in them the feeling that they can be what they want to be. Thus he is actually imagining and reshaping their lives. Vandenbroucke stresses the manipulatory aspect of this process as well as the fact that Styles is creating his own subjective picture (cf. 1985: 121). Seen in this light, the content and form of the story that Robert/Sizwe relates (see below) are certainly also influenced by Styles's view of the world and his treatment of his client. The photographer transforms a hesitant and identityless Robert/Sizwe from a static image, a "snap" or "card," into a dynamic "movie" (*SB* 18, 20).[33] Moreover, Styles manages to imbue his client with life by pulling him out of his anonymity and placing him in his context. By asking about his family and his job at the company Feltex, Styles gives Robert/Sizwe a context. For Styles this task is clearly great fun. The stage directions indicate that he is "*now really warming to the*

[33] Styles creates an impression of movement/action by having his client walk towards him as he takes the picture, hence "movie."

assignment" (*SB* 19), physically and psychologically dressing up Robert/Sizwe for the shot. The photographer urges his client to make use of his "props," namely his hat, pipe and cigarette, and encourages him to smile for the sake of his wife back in the homeland so that she will feel reassured about her husbands' success in the city and his ability to provide for the family. Styles makes Robert/Sizwe understand that he must seize this opportunity to present the most positive self-image possible. Pierre Bourdieu has pointed out this characteristic of portrait photography:

> Looking at the person who is looking (or who is taking the photograph), correcting one's posture, one presents oneself to be looked at as one seeks to be looked at; one presents one's own image. In short, faced with a look which captures and immobilizes appearances, adopting the most ceremonial bearing means reducing the risk of clumsiness and gaucherie and giving others an image of oneself that is affected and pre-defined. Like respect for etiquette, frontality is a means of effecting one's own objectification: offering a regulated image of oneself is a way of imposing the rules of one's own perception. (1990 [1965]: 83)

Styles assures Robert/Sizwe that it is perfectly acceptable to carry a newspaper in the photograph despite his illiteracy: "That is not important. You think all those monkeys carrying newspapers can read? They look at the pictures" [*SB* 21]). Important for the picture is only the impression conveyed. He thus implies that the photographic representation of society is always "the representation of a *represented* society" (Bourdieu 1990 [1965]: 84).

Styles conjures up for Robert/Sizwe the image of the successful future Chief Messenger at Feltex. To do this, he uses the photograph of a map of the world and the poster of a futuristic city as backgrounds for the "card" and "movie." Styles is "*carried away still further by his excitement*" (*SB* 20), transforming his commission to take a simple picture of his client into the self-imposed assignment to create a hero: an image of self which Robert/Sizwe can look up to and from which he can draw strength. Although Robert/Sizwe is the centre of Styles's attention, the latter occupies the dominant position. Here again the photographer can be seen playing a role. As stage manager and director he is responsible for conveying the atmosphere of the scene to an inexperienced actor who has difficulties slipping into his role.[34] By staging Robert/Sizwe according to his own image, Styles succeeds in

[34] Wertheim also points out that "[...] in his role as photographer/historiographer, Styles arranges and directs those who have come for a sitting much as the playwright and director stage-manage their actors" (2000: 82).

transforming him into his dream and teaches him to smile at his own potential and the future that now becomes possible.

It is legitimate to ask whether Styles is actually doing more harm than good by planting ideas in Robert/Sizwe's head. On the one hand, he could be seen as a devil tempting his victim with possibilities that might never come true. On the other hand, Styles seems to be suggesting that dreams and hopes are necessary for survival in a society that openly reduces the essence of black human life to a number in a passbook. Styles shows that he is aware of this situation and thus acts as a model for those people who recognise this reality and are able, in their enlightened state, to help their fellow countrymen and -women.

3.3.1.2. Of dreams of life and ghostlike deaths

As the stage directions indicate, Styles's photo of Robert/Sizwe is not an ordinary one as it embodies the life story of the client: *The camera flash goes off; simultaneously a blackout except for one light on Robert, frozen in the pose that will appear on the picture. We are in fact looking at the photograph. It 'comes to life' and dictates the letter* [...] (*SB* 22). In fact, Robert, who now goes back to calling himself Sizwe, starts his letter to his wife by proclaiming that "Sizwe Bansi, in a manner of speaking, is dead!" (*SB* 22). This apparent contradiction – a photo coming to life and announcing its own death – sets the tone for the encounter between Sizwe and his friend Buntu, a wise and experienced man who reminds the audience of Styles (and not only because the two roles are played by the same actor). Buntu means "humaneness" or "humankind" and functions as a telling name (cf. Vandenbroucke 1985: 119; Wertheim 2000: 86). As his work permit has been revoked, Sizwe seeks Buntu's help. Illiterate and completely unaware of the political and existential meaning of the passbook, Sizwe is dependent on other people's analysis of and reaction to the situation as a way of understanding his condition. The police arrested him in a raid and took him to the Labour Bureau: "I was made to stand in the passage there, with everybody looking at me and shaking their heads like they knew I was in trouble" (*SB* 24). By making the gestures of stamping the passbook and recording information, Buntu vividly explains to Sizwe the implications of the stamps in his pass. He has been endorsed to his home town, King William's Town, as a result of Influx Control which means that he loses the right to look for work in Port Elizabeth. The two men comment on the hardships of black life in South Africa in a few anecdotes that are at once comic in their narration but also extremely disillusioning in their meaning. The pointless bureaucratic journeys to find a job and housing in the city reiterate Styles's difficulties in getting administrative permission to open his photographic studio. Answering Sizwe's question about why there is so much trouble, Buntu responds by telling the story of the life and death of the migrant farmer, Outa Jacob: "That's it, brother. The only time we'll find peace is when they dig a hole for us and press our face into the earth" (*SB* 28). This comment alludes to Robert Zwelinzima's death. He has found peace in death, and thus if Sizwe uses this man's passbook and identity to survive, it does not affect the deceased's peace but offers another man a chance to continue living. Life and death are two sides of the same coin.

Although Buntu understands that altering the dead man's passbook is Sizwe's only hope, Sizwe himself fears that this will mean the loss of his own identity. "To give up his name is the only thing truly Bansi's own," Vandenbroucke argues. "He perceives the choice between his card and identity and those of the dead man as one between personal dignity and survival itself" (1985: 121). And at first Sizwe chooses dignity. Yet personal dignity is a concept which he had learnt only that same evening. Leaving Sky's bar[35] completely drunk, Sizwe's comments to the audience reveal that the people he encountered with Buntu succeeded in building up his own self-image - although one may assume that in his state of drunkenness he was actually more the butt of their jokes. Be that as it may, he writes in his letter to his wife and then asks the audience:

> And it wasn't just your husband Sizwe sitting there with all the most important people of New Brighton, but *Mister* Bansi.
>
> [*He starts to laugh.*]
>
> [...]
>
> Do you know who I am, friend? Take my hand, friend. Take my hand. I am Mister Bansi, friend. Do you know where I come from? I come from Sky's place, friend. A most wonderful place. I met everybody there, good people. [...]
>
> I'm not just Sizwe no more. He might have walked in, but Mr Bansi walked out! (*SB* 29f.)

This shows that his perception of self depends on the identity that the others give him. The social status he occupies is also defined by the social group with which he comes into contact. Sizwe begins to see himself with the eyes of his environment

---

[35] The name 'Sky's' is another reference to the domain of dreams.

(Mead). In his drunken state he talks to himself and perceives himself as a 'doubled' being, the worthy Mr Bansi and the clumsy "fool Sizwe" (*SB* 32). However, this self-assertion is only temporary. Reflecting on the circumscribing nature of the passbook, he loses his sense of direction (*Sizwe is lost. He wanders around, uncertain of the direction to take* [*SB* 31]), a fact which mirrors the inner loss of his sense of self. Again, Sizwe reduces his identity to the name in his passbook. When he and Buntu first stumble upon Robert's corpse, he observes:

> That passbook of his will talk. It talks, friend, like mine. His passbook will tell you. [...] My passbook talks good English too ... big words that Sizwe can't read and doesn't understand. Sizwe wants to stay here in New Brighton and find a job; passbook says, 'No! Report back.' [...] They said: Book of Life! [...] They told us lies. [...]
>
> Wherever you go ... it's that bloody book. [...] Go to hospital to die, it lies there too! (*SB* 33, 35)

What Buntu wishes to teach Sizwe is to give up the equation 'name equals body equals self': "What's wrong with me? [*Starts to tear off his clothes.*] Look at me! I'm a man. I've got legs. I can run with a wheelbarrow full of cement! [...] I've got a wife. I've got four children" (*SB* 35). In his naked state Sizwe addresses the audience with essentialist questions about human existence in liberal terms: "What's happening in this world, good people? Who cares for who in this world?" (*SB* 35). The key to survival turns out to be adopting Robert's identity, his name and his passbook, which contains a valid work seeker's permit. However, things are not as easy as they may seem, for Sizwe's adherence to his own name leads to a reductive and inflexible definition of identity. "How do I get used to Robert? How do I live as another man's ghost?" (*SB* 38). It is Buntu's words that make Sizwe really understand for the first time that the apartheid system does not perceive him as a man but only as a number:

> When the white man looked at you at the Labour Bureau what did he see? A man with dignity or a bloody passbook with an N.I. number? Isn't that a ghost? When the white man sees you walk down the street and calls out, 'Hey, John! Come here' ... to you, *Sizwe Bansi* ... isn't that a ghost? Or when his little child calls you 'Boy' ... you a man, circumcised with a wife and four children ... isn't that a ghost? Stop fooling yourself. All I'm saying is be a real ghost, if that is what they want, what they've turned us into. Spook them into hell, man! (*SB* 38)

Buntu points out that if blacks are just faceless de-individualised beings, their names mean nothing to the state. These are the terms in which people may address each other in apartheid society – the fundamental condition of social theatricality (cf. Crow 1996: 106). Thus Buntu appeals to Sizwe's common sense to perceive that he is in a crucial life-and-death situation and that bodily survival is more urgent than nurturing his soul:

> Shit on names, man! To hell with them if in exchange you can get a piece of bread for your stomach and a blanket in winter. Understand me, brother, I'm not saying that pride isn't a way for us. What I'm saying is shit on our pride if we only bluff ourselves that we are men.[...] Take mine and give me food for my children. (*SB* 43)

Buntu finally convinces Sizwe to take on Robert's passbook identity and thus defy the Pass Laws. Sizwe learns that his current definition of self is superficial and comes to understand that human identity transcends a mere name, number or passbook identity. By playing with the rules laid down by apartheid, he hopes to beat the regime with its own weapons. Consequently, his life now depends on convincing play-acting. Taking on another man's identity is the ultimate act of versatility required of the protean, social actor. In accordance with apartheid's definition of non-white identity Sizwe is now reduced to Robert's Native Identification number, which he must be able to recite like a robot to avoid suspicion. Buntu preaches, "Burn that [number] into your head, friend. You hear me? It's more important than your name" (*SB* 39). He teaches Sizwe his new number and simulates little encounters with official representatives of the state and society. Similar to Styles's quick change of roles in the first part of the play Buntu's comic versatility permits him to slip from being a policeman to a salesman to an employer etc. He helps Sizwe respond to his new public identity as Robert by making him recite the new number on several occasions.

With this rehearsal of Sizwe's future role the theatrical quality of *Sizwe Bansi is Dead* is reinforced once more. However, at this point the performance has lost the original light-heartedness of the first scenes. It seems as if all the early playfulness merely went on to set the tone for Sizwe's story and prepare the audience for harsh reality. Styles's role-playing raises his self-consciousness and then allows him to heighten the consciousness of his fellow-workers and the spectators. As Sizwe's teacher Buntu helps imbue Sizwe's role as Robert with existentialist significance. Although Sizwe knows that he has discovered a mechanism for survival, he nonetheless perceives his change of identity as nothing more than a game of charades. To put it in Goffman's terms, the success of a performance relies on the witnesses' conviction that the performers are sincere. What is important is who one appears to be, not who one really is (cf. 1959: 71). However, Buntu and Sizwe are aware that it is only a matter of time before the new Robert's true identity is discovered. The real Sizwe Bansi can be resurrected if there is a fingerprint check. And as Sizwe foresees, "A black man stay out of trouble? Impossible, Buntu. Our skin is trouble." (*SB* 43). Thus the final image of the play, that of a smiling Robert/Sizwe being photographed by Styles, is deeply ironic: we know what this smile disguises and that it is mere play-acting.

3.3.2. Life and death: Simulation and reality in 'The Island Theatre'

Throughout *The Island* John and Winston frequently talk about their upcoming production of *Antigone* at the prison concert. John, who proposes this scheme, finds it difficult to help Winston to understand the plot and make him agree to participate in the performance. Their conversation reveals the two men's divergent interpretations of *Antigone*:

> JOHN. [...] Antigone buried Polynices. The traitor! The one who I said was on *our* side. Right? [...] Stage two is Pleading. What does Antigone plead? Guilty or Not Guilty?
>
> WINSTON. Not Guilty.
>
> JOHN. [*trying to be tactful*]. Now look, Winston, we're not going to argue. Between me and you, in this cell, we know she's Not Guilty. But in the play she pleads Guilty.
>
> WINSTON. No, man, John! Antigone is Not Guilty...
>
> JOHN. In the play...
>
> WINSTON. [*losing his temp*er]. To hell with the play! Antigone had every right to bury her brother.
>
> JOHN. Don't say 'To hell with the play'. We've got to do the bloody thing. And in the play she pleads Guilty. Get that straight. Antigone pleads...
>
> WINSTON. [*giving up in disgust*]. Okay, do it your way.
>
> JOHN. It's not my way! In the play...
>
> WINSTON. Guilty!
>
> JOHN. Yes, Guilty! (*IL* 53)

John reads Sophocles' plot as a performance of resistance to the state similar to Jean Anouilh's version of *Antigone* as resistance to Nazi-occupied France. He identifies with Polynices, whom he understands as a "traitor" in the eyes of the state. John believes that Polynices is in a position comparable to (black) South African dissidents who oppose the regime by burning their passes (the one on "our side"). By burying the traitor and thus defying the state, Antigone aligns herself not only with her brother but with all people who suffer from unjust laws. Winston, by contrast, reads the text in a literal, semantic sense. He recognises that ethical justice does not take place in the plot, and he is unable to cope with the apparent arbitrariness of the portrayed legal system. For him their investment in the performance of *Antigone* equals the tasks imposed on them by their unseen guard: "Learn to dig for Hodoshe, learn to run for Hodoshe, and what happens when I get back to the cell? Learn to read *Antigone*!" (*IL* 52). He refuses to accept John's summary and interpretation of the plot and suspects his friend of falsification ("do it your way"). However, as Robert Green points out, South African society is one which "defiles semantics, which rewrites, for instance, the rich associative power of the word 'homeland' [used in *Sizwe Bansi*]" and thus abuses "historical and verbal confidence" (1976: 171). Seen in this light, John is fighting the system with its own weapons.

It has become clear that Winston's failure to understand the meaning of the *Antigone* plot threatens to destroy the performance, for how can an actor who does not identify with his role act convincingly? That is why John must lead Winston to a true understanding of the implicit subversiveness of the play and the fact that Antigone's fate can be read as a metaphor for their own plight. John seems to be aware that as an actor his success and credibility depend on how closely he identifies with the role he is playing. Reminiscing about a performance of *Antigone* that he had seen (or even participated in himself), he explains to Winston how the actor playing Creon had convincingly slipped into his role: "Should have seen him, Winston. Short and fat, with big eyes, but by the time the play was finished he was as tall as the roof" (*IL* 54).[36]

However, John commits a major error in his treatment of Winston which almost jeopardises their performance. When Winston, dressed as Antigone, appears wearing a wig, necklace and false breasts, fabricated from bits and pieces that the two men have been able to collect and stash away despite constant surveillance, John bursts out laughing. As Fugard's draft version of this scene reads, Winston already feels awkward before his friend sees him: he is "standing solemnly and self-consciously against a wall." This element of travesty (cf. Brunkhorst 1998:

[36] This is in fact autobiographical. Kani and Ntshona were members of the drama group Serpent Players, who performed *Antigone* in New Brighton, a township outside Port Elizabeth, in 1965. Kani played the role of Haemon, Creon's son (cf. Solberg 1999: 224).

135) with Winston in drag is undoubtedly a hilarious sight. Again, it says in the early draft, "It is impossible not to [laugh],"[37] justifying (or excusing) John's reaction. Notwithstanding, John clearly goes overboard when he treats the vulnerable Winston-as-Antigone as a sex object. Winston, who does not yet identify with his role as Antigone in this scene, takes the assault personally. We already know from an early incident in the play that Winston refuses to fulfil what he considers to be the role of a woman, exclaiming to John: "You got no wife here. Look for the rag yourself" (*IL* 50). Despite all attempts on the part of John to placate Winston, the latter feels deprived of his masculinity through which he defines himself: "Here's Antigone ... take these titties and hair and play Antigone. [...] I'll have my balls and play Creon" (*IL* 61). As his sexist terminology reveals, for him Antigone is characterised by her anatomy and appearance, not by the character traits revealed in her words. He only sees her as a woman in a strongly patriarchal society and completely overlooks her universality and the a-historicity of her story of defiance against the state. Winston exclaims, "I didn't walk with those men and burn my bloody passbook in front of that police station, and have a magistrate send me here for life so that he [John] can dress me up like a woman and make a bloody fool of me" (*IL* 63).[38] Winston clearly rejects the opportunity of role-play in a theatrical context. In fact, he does not distinguish between himself as actor and himself as character, and perceives role-play as a threat to his masculine identity. What is more, John fails to make him understand that Antigone's defiance of the state is clearly parallel to their own conscious passbook burning and, furthermore, that oppression and its resistance transcend all sexist, gender, racial, ethnic and cultural barriers.[39]

Winston's second important argument for refusing to slip into the reality of the play and take on Antigone's role is that the "Bloody thing never even happened. [...] Fuck legends. Me? ... I live my life here! I know why I'm here, and it's history, not legends. I had my chat with a magistrate in Cradock and now I'm here. Your Antigone is child's play, man" (*IL* 62). In the draft version of this play Winston

---

[37] Fugard, Unpublished draft version of *The Island*. Fugard manuscript collection, Lilly Library, Bloomington, Indiana. Act II, p. 1.

[38] It is interesting that in the draft version Fugard has Winston exclaim: "[...] dressed up like a bloody circus monkey." (Unpublished draft version of *The Island*. Fugard manuscript collection, Lilly Library, Bloomington, Indiana. Act II, p. 2). Note the intertextuality between this version of *The Island* and *Sizwe Bansi* (9) where Styles refers to himself with the same animal metaphor to signify his relationship to his boss at the Ford motor plant.

[39] Mackay (1989) offers a detailed comparison of the prisoners and Antigone.

juxtaposes 'make-believe' legends and 'real' history and refers to Antigone as "the lady who never was. She's got nothing to do with us."[40] It appears that Winston only believes in the power of history and facts while rejecting legends as irrelevant and impotent make-believe. In his state of rage he blindly relies on and accepts the power of the written legal word in South Africa and denies that any forms of tradition deriving from an oral source (such as myths, legends, folk tales) can convey truths and insights about the human condition. Dismissing legends as "child's play," he falls into the apartheid system's trap by failing to recognise the topicality of the *Antigone* legend - which must figuratively be seen as oral - and its similarity to the fate of his black people. This leads him to deny his own oral history and culture in favour of legal Western written culture. Walter Ong claims, "A present-day literate usually assumes that written records have more force than spoken words as evidence of a long-past state of affairs, especially in court" (1982: 96). John immediately sees the danger in Winston's ideologically tainted outburst and reproaches him for letting himself be drawn into bowing down to the system: "Hodoshe's talk, Winston! That's what he says all the time. What he wants us to say all our lives. Our convictions, our ideals ... that's what he calls them ... child's play" (*IL* 62). Here John is able to link the discussion about *Antigone* to their own plight.

The only way John can entice Winston into playing the role of Antigone is by explaining the nature and functioning of theatre. In his attempt to create peace with his friend he states, "I wasn't laughing at you" (*IL* 60), thereby implying that he can differentiate between actor and character. John fears that like Winston the co-prisoners watching the performance at the concert may also fail to make this distinction, seeing in Winston not Antigone but a man making a fool of himself as a cross-dresser. Notwithstanding, he is sure that if appearances do not convey the message, Antigone's words will make an impact on the prison audience:

> JOHN. [...] When you get in front of them, sure they'll laugh... Nyah, Nyah! ... they'll laugh. But just remember this brother, nobody laughs forever! There'll come a time when they'll stop laughing, and that will be the time when our Antigone hits them with her words. [...] You think those bastards out there won't know it's you? Yes, they'll laugh. But who cares about that as long as they laugh in the beginning and listen in the end. That's all we want them to do ... listen in the end. (*IL* 61f.)

---

[40] Fugard, Unpublished draft version of *The Island*. Fugard manuscript collection, Lilly Library, Bloomington, Indiana. Act II, p. 10.

With these words John makes it clear that from the point of view of the play's production the content of Antigone's speech is a more important element of their play than Winston's performance as an individual. Barbara Harlow states that the experience of detention, as described by political prisoners in their memoirs, is influenced by the ideal of collective resistance. Communication, she argues, plays an important role in creating and preserving solidarity among the detainees (cf. 1987: 119f.). This is the approach that John takes when he first decides to stage the Greek play. Antigone's speech is meant to remind the prison audience of their opposition to apartheid in the name of justice and humanity. John thus defines their struggle as one against a common enemy.

The scene presented above is also important with regard to the real theatre audience. Surely some spectators will not be able to prevent themselves from joining in John's laughter in the presence of Winston in his grotesque disguise. They are thus also responsible for 'hurting' his feelings and causing him to undergo a destabilisation of identity. However, in this regard the audience are permitted greater freedom in their reactions and the possibility of evolving and maturing. Initial spontaneous laughter will fuse into a conscious and mature understanding of the actual performance of *Antigone* and its recognition as a metaphor for the condition of the black South African. They will thus follow Winston's personal development and be prepared to identify with his fate in the end.

Despite John's attempts to explain the nature and the functioning of theatre as well as the similarity of Antigone's story with the black South African narrative of resistance, Winston only comes to terms with the legend when he relates his personal fate to that of the heroine. John's upcoming release makes him aware of the arbitrariness of freedom and the absurdity of his own life-long incarceration.[41] He is able to link this Beckettian absurdity to Antigone's fate, finally understanding why and accepting that she pleads guilty.[42] It is at this point that he is willing to play the female role in the prison concert. This process confirms Martin Esslin's observation that "Play is a simulation of reality. That, far from making play a frivolous pastime, in fact emphasises the immense importance of all play activity for the well-being and development of man" (1977: 19).

---

[41] See Wertheim's reading of *The Island* in terms of Camus' *The Myth of Sysiphus* (2000: 93-98).

[42] Durbach provides an analysis of the Beckettian elements in *The Island*, especially a comparison of John and Winston to *Waiting for Godot*'s Vladimir and Estragon (cf. 1993: 244-47).

Winston compares Antigone's defiance of the Greek state in the name of God's laws to their own opposition to the South African passbook system in the name of human and civil rights, thereby justifying their actions through analogy. Antigone does not question Creon's ruling, arguing instead for human and honourable action in a distinctly South African vocabulary which reinforces the immediacy of the topic:

> Your threat is nothing to me, Creon. But if I had let my mother's son, a Son of the Land, lie there as food for the carrion fly, Hodoshe, my soul would never have known peace. [...] I buried my brother. That is an honourable thing, Creon. All these people in your state would say so too, if fear of you and another law did not force them into silence. (*IL* 76)

Once Winston fully identifies with the female heroine, which means that he has understood and come to terms with his own destiny, he is no longer able to play the role. In contrast to Sizwe Bansi, who can at least temporarily survive in the role of Robert Zwelinzima, Winston cannot escape reality through role-play. Taking off his wig, a sign of his falling out of the role, he still speaks the heroine's words: "I go now to my living death, because I honoured those things to which honour belongs" (*IL* 77). However, these lines are exclaimed by Winston as himself and not Winston as Antigone. He reaffirms his commitment to struggle in the name of brotherhood, addressing his co-prisoners and audience members as "Brothers and Sisters of the Land" (*IL* 77). Crow evaluates Winston's transformation:

> [...] the performance [of *Antigone*] is also crucial, dramatically, in helping Winston transcend his despair [...]. The ability to 'act', to assume a new identity however temporarily, is here as in *Sizwe Bansi* a form of self-protection and a strategy for survival, allowing its exponent as well as its audience (the real one as well as the imagined prison audience) to achieve an understanding and a renewed commitment to struggle in spite of the horror of the situation. (1992: 157f.)

At first, by playing a role, Winston is able to regard his own situation from an external vantage point. He infuses a character with life and thus manifests his own vitality and flexibility. Similarly, his ability to take on other roles provides a perspective from which he can redefine his identity and accept his fate of "living death" (*IL* 77). Winston adopts the knowledge he acquired in his role as Antigone to his life in prison and in future will consciously 'perform' his life as a detainee. For him reality and stage reality have begun to influence each other (cf. Turner 1990: 16). He is no longer afraid that his own self will be extinguished by his continued incarceration and turned to stone like that of Harry. He accepts his imprisonment and all its consequences but for the moment can draw strength from the fact that the system's failure to break him amounts to his renewed contribution to the struggle against apartheid in the name of "our struggle [...] our slogans, our children's freedom" (*IL* 72). Winston succeeded in asserting the "indestructibility of the human spirit" (Fugard, Kani & Ntshona 2000: 32). And like Sizwe he has at least found temporary peace.

3.4. Seeing and being seen: The role of the audience

In both *Sizwe Bansi is Dead* and *The Island* the live theatre audience are accorded a role in the performance. The spectators are not allowed to settle back in their seats and enjoy the show from this removed vantage point. Rather, the actors on stage draw the audience into the performance in a way that makes clear that the spectators' involvement is necessary for the plays to be convincing and to fulfil their aim of bearing witness and criticising reality.[43]

3.4.1. Audience participation and identification

In *Sizwe Bansi is Dead* Styles entertains the audience with an improvised monologue in which he comments on articles in the daily newspaper. Upon entering the stage, he mentions Chinese interests in Africa and, as the stage directions indicate, "*Stops abruptly. Looks around as if someone might be eavesdropping on his intimacy with the audience*" (*SB* 3). He transforms the audience into an active witness of the potentially dangerous political remarks about communism that he might make. By highlighting the need for secrecy, he makes the spectators aware that he is fully conscious of what, in the eyes of the apartheid regime, would be deemed subversive. His behaviour suggests a certain routine. He is not only used to making such political comments but also seems to take for granted the presence of potential eavesdroppers waiting to report him if he transgresses the limits of discretion. Thus Styles invites the spectators to become either his co-conspirators or spies. He thereby attributes to each person either the role of friend or foe, placing the two resulting groups in binary opposition.

---

[43] Orkin also points out the plays' emphasis on direct communication (cf. 1991: 159). He quotes Fugard's *Notebooks*: "Addressing the audience [...] how, sincerely, do we want to 'talk' to them" (1983: 186). The actor-spectator-relationship must be reciprocal and equal to ensure success.

This gesture is significant both on the levels of real life and drama-internal reality. In regard to real life the actor in the role of Styles is speaking in the name of the drama group when he acknowledges the presence of members of the security police among the audience. They are defined as spies, threatening the success of the apartheid-critical performance in effort to quell dissidence and guarantee state security. In an interview in 1973 Fugard talks about the acting group's encounters with the police:

> We've been hauled off the stage a number of times. [...] we continually ran into trouble in our attempts to play *Sizwe Bansi* to white audiences in South Africa. We were stopped every time. [...] We had long since learned to cope with not playing publicly to white, but we had *never* run into trouble with playing to coloured: but, on this occasion, with two *black* actors playing to a *coloured* audience, the police came in about five hours before the first performance to say that if we were to proceed, we would be prosecuted. (1973a: 34)

However, this did not stop Fugard, Kani and Ntshona from putting on the show. Seen in this light, the gesture of secrecy is actually a sign of defiance and battle. If the actors are hindered from speaking out loud, they will find other means of reaching their intended audience and getting their message across. Kani emphasises, "The link between audience and actor is, in my opinion, a continuation of the link between the artist and his community" (1988: 56). By having to resort to secrecy and whispering, they are actually reinforcing the bond between actor and audience and thus safeguarding the subversive nature of their performance.

Fugard also states that the "experience belongs to the audience" and, echoing Grotowski's concept of 'poor theatre,'[44] that "the full and unique possibility of this

---

[44] Grotowski places the actor, the "*spiritual and scenic technique of the actor*" (1967: 60), at the centre of theatre art. An actor performs a "*spiritual process*" in which he or she gives him- or herself using a technique of trance, "an integration of spiritual, psychic, and physical faculties climaxing in a 'penetration' from and by the actor's intimate instinctive psyche." This means that the actor's body as such disappears; what the spectators see is only the "visible reflection of spiritual impulses" (1967: 61).

Grotowski's theory of theatre is based on two concepts, 'poor theatre' and 'performance as an act of transgression.' 'Poor theatre' signifies a theatre that focuses on the "actor-spectator relationship of perceptual, direct, 'live' communion" (1967: 62). It renounces make-up, autonomic costume and scenography, a separate stage, lighting and sound effects. The aim of poor theatre is to not create theatre as a synthesis of diverse artistic disciplines but to strip theatre of everything that is not essential to it. This means that the focus lies on the actor who is able to bring the text to life with her or his body (1967: 62f.). With the concept of 'performance as an act of trangression' Grotowski refers to his conviction that theatre is able to challenge itself and its audience by questioning stereotypes and thus transgressing social taboos. People attempt this because they strive to find their truths. Myths play an important role in this theory because

experience needs nothing more than the actor and the stage, the actor in space and silence" (1986: n.p.). Following Grotowski's ideas, Fugard is able to involve the creative abilities of his actors in the process of production and thus establish this desired "more immediate and direct relationship with the audience" (Fugard 1986: n.p.). The actors sacrifice themselves to the spectators in order to initiate in them a process of raised consciousness (cf. Walder 1984: 78).[45] This leads not only to the expression of a daily experience of suffering and protest by the subalterns in his plays but also to the continuity of that protest in the work of black theatre groups. Fugard stated in 1973:

> Four years ago I asked, in despair, who else, apart from Serpent Players,[46] will break the conspiracy of silence? Since then, this circuit has flourished; [...] These are people with the desperate need to triumph in the articulation of their grievances, the articulation of something that has been smothered, that the society has attempted to silence. (1973a: 35)

Not only did theatre groups and actors begin to express themselves and bear witness to their suffering, but the local audiences also had to learn to accept the plays' content. Fugard describes the response of a New Brighton audience to *Sizwe Bansi* as a "near-riot as people reacted 'with disbelief, panic and fear that these things were actually being talked about out loud and then there was joy, that this was a celebration of small things in their lives'" (Walder 1984: 87; cf. Fugard 1982).

When examining the interpretation of Styles's gesture to the audience from a play-internal perspective, this incident can be read as an attempt to pull the spectators out of their traditional position as mere observers and offer them roles in the performance. The protagonist prepares the members of the audience for the general atmosphere of the play and forces them to decide for themselves if they are comfortable with the themes that will be addressed. By opting to stay for the performance, the audience have agreed to Styles's terms of engagement. This means that they must again choose between identifying themselves as eavesdroppers or as Styles's co-conspirators, this time on the level of the play's

---

Grotowski believes that confrontation with myth and one's roots is possible in theatre whereas identification with them is not (1967: 64).

[45] O'Sheel (1978) traces Grotowski's influence on Fugard.

[46] The Serpent Players are a group of black amateur actors from New Brighton, who asked Fugard to help them start a drama group in 1963. Accounts of this are given in numerous texts. See for instance Fugard (1973a), Solberg (1999: 223f.) and Walder (1984: 79-83).

reality. Most likely they will identify with the latter role and thus become Styles's friends and confidants. It is on this process of identification that the interpretation of Styles's monologue presented above is based.

The dialogic quality of Styles's monologue is maintained throughout the improvisation by exclamatory words such as "hey," "man," "friend" (*SB* 4, 12), which serve to constantly remind the audience that he is addressing them directly as his co-conspirators. Consequently, Styles no longer needs to make his politically subversive comments. After his secretive gesture he does not take up his remarks about China but dismisses the topic: "No comment" (*SB* 3). Thus this subject is not important in terms of its content but more so in the function it serves. This interaction between character and audience also sets the tone of the play and emphasises the nature of the theatre as a *locus* of acting and role-playing.[47]

In *The Island* the theatre audience is also invited to take on a role in the performance. Besides watching both the play and the play-within-the-play as visitors in the theatre, they simultaneously also become the play-within-the-play's *direct* audience. The audience is prepared for this double role during the course of the play. Wertheim points out that John and Winston are asleep on their small cell floor as the audience members walk into the theatre to take their seats. In other words the play is already in action when the spectators arrive (cf. 2000: 89).[48] The reason for this type of beginning may be to reinforce the importance of the spectators in their role as witnesses. It seems as if the characters are on stage all the time and that they exist even when no viewers are present: only the arrival of the audience infuses them with life and allows them to tell their story. Thus the mime sequence which initiates the performance as such can begin. It is announced by a wailing siren. The mime lasts for approximately ten minutes,[49] an endless-seeming time span considering the action being presented. The two prisoners engage in "*back-breaking and grotesquely futile labour*" (*IL* 47), filling wheelbarrows with sand and respectively emptying them where the other man is digging so that both piles of sand never dwindle. The Sisyphean quality of this labour is alluded to in the stage directions which classify it as "*interminable*" (*IL* 47). It is important that

---

[47] Wertheim also comments on the function of Styles in drawing the audience into the play (cf. 2000: 80).

[48] The introductory stage directions state that "*the prisoners sleep on the floor*" (*IL* 47).

[49] As estimated by Wertheim (cf. 2000: 89). Foster describes this scene as five minutes long (cf. 1977: 10).

the audience grasp the futility of the work portrayed in this mime as well as understand that despite all the stagedness, this is a representation of the arbitrariness and dehumanisation of prison reality:

> The audience's restiveness and their failure to understand why actions are taking place or punishments inflicted make the theatre a microcosm of the prison world. "What am I doing here? What does all this mean?" runs through the minds of the spectators – and then they realize that these are the thoughts of the prisoners who must endure the monotony and pointlessness (not to mention the physical abuse) not for ten minutes but for years without end. (Wertheim 2000: 90)

Thus during the opening scene of *The Island* the audience transcend their role as passive viewers of a stage action that merely mirrors reality and step into the roles of participants. The initial pantomime denies the spectators the possibility of hiding behind the safety-net of a fixed and thus interchangeable, traditional audience-actor-relationship. In order to decipher the intention of this scene and really identify with the men's plight, the viewers must comprehend the senselessness of the action on stage. More importantly they must recognise the fact that the two prisoners are suffering not only from the physical exertion required to perform this task but more particularly from the mental pain that is inflicted upon them. If this identification takes place, then the members of the audience participate in the men's suffering and form a *communitas* (Turner) with the characters in their common disapproval of the apartheid state. However, should the spectators refuse to be drawn into the stage reality, then they would be "sadistically" observing the action from a vantage point similar to that of the unseen prison guard (Wertheim 2000: 90; cf. Crow 1996: 19). This self-distancing would then lead to a different understanding of the performance and most likely also result in a theatre experience reduced in its emotional intensity and identification process.[50]

The reason the spectators' decision to identify (or not) with the men is important for the interpretation of *The Island* as a whole becomes clear in the last scene in which John and Winston perform *Antigone* at the prison concert. Lesley Wade Soule's concept of identity creation in the theatre is useful for explaining the relationship between spectator and performer that is established during the performance of the play-within-the-play. She asserts that the "idea of identity as

---

[50] John Bender (1987) traces and compares the historical relationship between audience and fiction (literature) to prisons and citizens. See particularly his chapter on "The Aesthetic of Isolation as Social System."

interaction is inherent in the theatrical" and analyses how the process of mirroring[51] can create identity in the theatre.

Soule distinguishes between mediated one-way mirroring and reciprocal mirroring (1998: 43). Mediated one-way mirroring refers to the audience's understanding of the stage action as a mimetic mirror image of their own world. By identifying with the actors, the spectators also identify themselves. By contrast, direct, unmediated reciprocity between performer and spectator is intercepted by the theatrical foregrounding of fictional identities. This kind of mirroring happens, for instance, when the performers respond directly to the spectators' reactions to the action. In this process the spectators come to recognise their identity as collaborators in the theatrical transaction. By analogy, performers also create their identity through the audience's responses. Identity is understood as an external and objective individuality compared to the internal, subjective self (cf. 1998: 42f.).[52] Identity creation is dissociated from an interiority of feeling. Instead, as Robert Weimann maintains, identity is considered to reflect and even form the transaction as well as to be structured and evaluated through a negotiation with the audience (cf. 1981: 30; Soule 1998: 42). It is both the balanced relationship between spectators and performers and their joint engagement that makes the production of identity possible. Soule emphasises, "What is central to this view is the process of discovering and creating in the course of the performance progressively complex and processual interactive identities." This reciprocal and processual interaction compares with social interplay (1998: 45, cf. 43-45).

Taking Soule's terminology into account, how best to describe the interaction between actors and spectators in *The Island*? In the play's last scene John, not yet in his costume as Creon, addresses the audience with an introductory speech:

---

[51] Referring to the concept of mirroring as used in theories of child development, Soule points out two different patterns of behaviour: First, when children seemingly imitate the actions of adults and each other, they do not actually mirror it. Instead, in the enactment they assimilate it for their own purpose: the acting out of themselves. She concludes that this strengthens the feeling of self instead of leading to an awareness of personal identity. Second, children use other people as their mirror instead of copying their behaviour. They perform an action and then, deducing from the mirror's reaction to their behaviour, come to understand and interpret what they have done. This also leads to the formation of an idea of who they are. The partner of the interaction proceeds in similar fashion, perpetuating the interactive exchange and leading to a process of reciprocal mirroring (cf. 1998: 42).

[52] Differentiation between internal, subjective self and external, objective identity (or individuality) can be traced back to Elizabethan theatre. See for example Edward Burns' evaluation of Elizabethan theatre: individuality as outside and as external character versus interiority and inner self (1990: 139).

"Captain Prinsloo, Hodoshe, Warders, ... and Gentlemen!" (*IL* 73). His greeting as well as his body language (a step forward) are directed at the live theatre audience. Just as the audience are transformed into Styles's co-conspirators in *Sizwe Bansi*, the spectators are now invited to assume the roles of either the unseen co-prisoners *or* guards.[53] Most audience members will have already identified with the prisoners long before this final scene, and they are now rewarded for their loyalty and support as co-prisoners with the attribute "gentlemen," which clearly distances them from the official representatives of state oppression. The threatening presence of the guards is emphasised in their triple address ("Captain Prinsloo, Hodoshe, Warders").

By taking on this role of co-prisoners, the spectators as members of the play-within-the-play's audience empower Winston and John in their performance at the prison concert. Because of the knowledge the viewers have gained watching *The Island*, they expect that apartheid will also be condemned in the performance of *Antigone*. The spectators are made to feel that they are under constant scrutiny by prison officials, whose invisibility makes the situation all the more uncanny. The power of suggestion is most potent at this point in the performance. The audience may even begin to understand the feeling of the threat and arbitrariness of the power exercised over the prisoners. Thus the spectators' support of and alliance with John and Winston reinforces the characters-as-actors in their defiant action, contributing to the growth of their courage and self-confidence. It is this reciprocal relationship between the actors and their audience that helps Winston to accept his role as Antigone and finally identify with her plight. As John had prophesied, the audience may laugh at Winston's appearance at the beginning, but they will listen to him as Antigone in the end.

John and Winston do not read *Antigone* as a Hegelian synthesis of ethical forces in a tragic struggle in which Creon symbolises the Aristotelean tragic hero. Instead, they see it as the indictment of a political system that denies humanity and dignity to its subjects in the name of the law (cf. Durbach 1993: 242; Foster 1977: 15f.). In the role of the Greek ruler Creon John enlarges the scope of the prisoners' adversaries. He turns Creon into a symbol for the South African state that victimises Antigone in the name of apartheid: she is "arrested" and will be taken

[53] In contrast to Lauri Anderson, who posits that the audience are "simultaneously the incarcerators and the incarcerated" (1986: 5), I argue that this choice is one of exclusion. However, Anderson is thus able to claim that the role of the spectators as prisoner and guard highlights the dual nature of man – as victimiser and victim.

"straight to the Island [...] for life" (*IL* 73, 77). These words clearly refer to John and Winston's own fate and can thus be regarded as "reflexive and metatheatrical" (McNaughton 1994: 227).[54] As the play *seems* to reinforce state justice, Antigone's words and actions will keep the 'prison guards' in the play-within-the-play's audience from censoring and stopping the prisoners' performance. However, those spectators who have slipped into the role of co-prisoners see through the façade and recognise the polyphonic quality of the discourse.

This difference in perception can be explained in theoretical terms. Soule claims that there is a need to differentiate between identity and character.[55] Once identity is fixed as a fictional dramatic character, it loses its capacity as a changing social interaction. Characters are thus "significations of 'absent identities'" (1998: 44) and hinder the social creation of performance identities by audience and actors. Character permanence also makes reciprocal mirroring impossible and creates alienation between the spectator and performer. The 'guards' in the audience see Antigone as a character according to Soule's definition. In fact, this is also how Winston initially perceives Antigone when he refuses to play her role because he fails to recognise the power he can gain from her identity. However, as Soule argues, once freed from a concentration on character, performers are able to utilise their own subjectivity to create an interaction with the audience. A dramatic character is now recognised as a theatrical identity that enables identification and consequently also allows a reciprocal mirroring process to take place. The authority attributed to a character does not come from its fixity but from the performers and spectators who create a collaborative performance identity on the basis of a character (cf. 1998: 44-46).

Performance identity is the creation through play of a lifelike model of identity as cultural interaction. Parts of it will inevitably be taken as significations and meanings will be constructed around them. Like the textual character, however,

---

[54] In his introductory speech John also transforms Creon into a symbol for all compliant blacks when declaring, "Creon's crown is as simple, and I hope as clean, as the apron Nanny wears. And even as Nanny smiles and is your happy servant because she sees her charge .... your child! ... waxing fat in that little cradle, so too does Creon – your obedient servant! – stand here and smile" (*IL* 73). In this audience address John also condemns all supposedly liberal whites who believe that the smile of their servants is a sign of genuine happiness and thus exposes white hypocrisy.

[55] Drawing on pre-modern popular comedy practice as well as on modern reader response theory and deconstructionism, Soule supports the notion of taking direct interest not in a text itself but in what performers and spectators do with a text. She defines the text as a "site of collaboration" (1998: 45) whereas characters only acquire secondary importance (cf. 1998: 44f.).

these will be fragmented by-products, just one group of components in the overall identity process. Any initially fixed fictional identity ('character') is bound to be destabilised by the multiple interplay of performer and spectator (Soule 1998: 45).[56]

Winston-as-Antigone undergoes this process of the destabilisation of identity. All audience members who identify with the prisoners and are engaged in a process of reciprocal mirroring with them pull Winston out of his fixed fictional identity as mere character (the identity-less prisoner that the guards perceive him to be). He is brought to an understanding of Antigone's fate as a mirror of his own situation and comes to terms with this. Spectator-performer-interaction, operating on both the level of *The Island* as well as on the level of *Antigone*, can thus be considered a form of successful resistance to and defiance of apartheid.

Audience members who have identified with Winston and John from the beginning will imaginatively take on their role as co-prisoners and undoubtedly recognise and support the men's criticism of the apartheid state. Wertheim suggests that Fugard, Kani and Ntshona are able to enlarge the scope of their play by way of this process of identification. The 'Island' does not just designate Robben Island off the coast of Cape Town but – with all audience members as the characters' co-prisoners - signifies South Africa as a whole (cf. 2000: 98).[57]

In *Sizwe Bansi is Dead* and *The Island* the theatre audience are accorded a role in the performance through the words and gestures of the actors. In both performances the spectators are forced to choose between conspiracy with the characters in their defiance of the apartheid state or opposition to their apartheid-critical opinions and manoeuvres, thus aligning themselves with unseen pro-apartheid representatives. Fugard, Kani and Ntshona clearly define the audience as an essential element in their performances. The spectators are denied a passive and consumptive attitude towards the play. They are made to experience this kind of theatre as active and participatory witnesses in the South African context. The analysis above has shown that these plays are not only about documenting black life under apartheid, but more particularly they are about exerting effects on the audience and making them

[56] The deconstructionist element of Soule's approach is clearly recognisable in this quotation.

[57] Wertheim also argues that John and Winston's use of their own names in *The Island* shows that their performance has metaphoric value. As citizens of the apartheid state they are incarcerated as much as the characters of both the Ancient Greek and the South African plays. The absurdity of the laws and regulations condemned in both *Antigone* versions can be experienced in daily life (cf. 2000: 98).

aware of the "rigorous curtailment of the potential for social expressiveness between the races" (Crow with Banfield 1996: 103).

John Kani is convinced that "[...] theatre which separates itself from its audience and by implication, the community, is bound to wither and die" (1988: 56). It has become clear in the ideas presented above that this statement requires further precision. An audience also cannot separate itself from the actors and the performance. Actors and spectators engage in a reciprocal relationship that ensures the success of the performances.

3.4.2. Resistance and subversion through the fractured gaze: A post-colonial reading

By definition a theatre audience gazes at the action performed on stage. However, this gaze is never neutral and uninvolved but, as Helen Gilbert and Joanne Tompkins emphasise in their seminal study on post-colonial drama, "[...] implicated in that action of watching theatre is an authoritarian gaze of watching *over* other(s)" (1996: 248). *Sizwe Bansi is Dead* and *The Island* resist and subvert traditional definitions of the gaze in the theatre by destabilising the concept of surveillance.

The authoritarian gaze exercised in the defined and delimited location of the theatre strongly resembles the imperial gaze of the colonisers over the colonised. As Homi Bhabha asserts in his essay "The Other Question," colonial discourse's "predominant strategic function is the creation of a space for a 'subject peoples' through the production of knowledges in terms of which surveillance is exercised" (1994: 70). Thus the colonised are produced as "a social reality which is at once an 'other' and yet entirely knowable and visible" (1994: 70f.). Imperialism's strategy of surveillance and representation constructs the Other as an object of both knowledge and power. This appears to fix the colonised in a position of paralysis. Yet Gilbert and Tompkins repeatedly exemplify that post-colonial theatre has developed many ways of staging "empowering subjectivity" (1996: 248) and undermining the authority of the gaze.

In his reading of Michel Foucault's concepts of power and discourse Bhabha emphasises that *pouvoir* and *savoir* do not draw up symmetrical or dialectical relations of the self/other sort which are threatened by potential subversion or inversion. By contrast, as "[s]ubjects are always disproportionately placed in opposition or domination through the symbolic decentring of multiple power relations" (1994: 72), he argues that relations of power and knowledge must be recognised in their ambivalence.

As has been asserted above, Styles's initial gesture of intimacy classifies the audience as either his co-conspirators or potential eavesdroppers, even spies. The categorisation depends on the spectators' willingness to be drawn into the drama-internal reality and to accept Styles's regime-critical comments. It can be expected that the majority of the audience will accept the role of Styles's conspirators. In contrast to the spectators-as-characters, the (minority of the audience) members who do not enter into the play's reality are automatically classified as representatives of the apartheid state and are only able to witness the play indirectly. For them the performance is exclusively meta-theatrical and becomes a play-within-the-play. In their effort to identify and report any subversive elements they are forced to direct their attention not only to the action on stage but simultaneously also to the surrounding audience who are watching the play. Their visual focus is forced to take on two sites. Hence their traditional unilateral sightlines are disrupted, and their gaze is fractured. Echoing Bhabha's claim that the "ambivalence of civil authority circulates as a 'colonial' signifier that is *less than one and double*" (1994: 97), Gilbert and Tompkins highlight the fact that in this position the viewers are forced to double their gaze, neither of which is ever more than an incomplete version. Consequently, as two object *loci* are never identical, the words and actions on stage speak twice - both in an unmediated fashion and also mediated by the reactions of the audience (cf. 1996: 250).[58] Returning to Bhabha's assertion, this supports his rejection of a unitary dialectical self/other relation which can be inverted through subversion and reinforces his Foucauldian argumentation that a multiplicity of decentred and unstable power relations are at work.

In *The Island* meta-theatre acquires the function of a tool for survival and protest. By slipping into different identities, John and Winston's private 'cinema' allows them, after a day of hard labour and torture, to escape the prison reality and the threatening gaze of their unseen guard, Hodoshe. Instead of confronting their tormentors, as the other inmates do, with complaints about their inhuman living conditions and thus becoming the target of more torture, John decides to stage *Antigone* as their form of protest and regime criticism. Gilbert and Tompkins argue

[58] See Gilbert & Tompkins for an analysis of post-colonial drama's use of the fractured gaze (cf. 1996: 250-53).

that the private games evade the guard's gaze while the play actively subverts his gaze (cf. 1996: 251). Again, as in *Sizwe Bansi*, the representative of the system may be omni-present, but his gaze is ironically caught and fractured in a complex system of multiple gazes: Hodoshe must watch over John and Winston on the prison-stage and also over the prisoners (played by the audience) as spectators of *Antigone*. What is more, Hodoshe must screen the other unseen guards who are watching the prison concert while they keep their eyes on the other inmates. The live audience members who do not sympathise with John and Winston but identify with the guards are in a position comparable to that of the spectators who refuse to be defined as Styles's co-conspirators. It is their task to identify and punish any subversive behaviour. This means that besides observing the action on stage, they must simultaneously also watch the surrounding audience whose members themselves are watching the play-within-the-play. The sightlines of the spectator-guards are disrupted, and their gaze is fractured. To take this one step further, audience members who identify with Hodoshe - and thus follow him in supervising the other guards as well as the prisoners - quadruple the fractured state of their gaze. Through their own split and doubled gaze they watch others whose gaze is also split and doubled. This leads to a complete destabilisation and dislocation of the locus of power.

Bhabha also argues that relations of power and knowledge must be recognised in their ambivalence, a quality which then makes it possible to account for and explain the origin and nature of destabilising elements such as the stereotype (cf. 1994: 72). The stereotype is effective in defining the Other to the extent that it forces her or him to turn away from herself or himself in the recognition of difference and to identify instead with the unattainable ideal of the colonisers, an effect for which Frantz Fanon also gives numerous examples (cf. 1967). This behaviour is characterised by the fact that the colonised accept the imposed definition. The stereotype is thus clearly recognisable as a strategy of surveillance because surveillance relies on "'the *active consent* which is its real or mythical correlate [...] and establishes in the scopic drive [the pleasure in seeing] the illusion of the object relation'" (1994: 76).[59] However, Bhabha goes on to point out that stereotypes also stage a definition of the native which they disrupt (cf. 1994: 82). The colonisers' perception of the colonised turns out to be illusory and the resulting stereotype a

[59] Quoted from C. Metz. 1982. *Psychoanalysis and Cinema: The Imaginary Signifier*. London: Macmillan, p. 62f.

mere projection of the colonisers' desire and fantasy. To give an example, in *Sizwe Bansi is Dead* the white management presents the African workers as happy, docile, singing natives to Mr. Ford while the employees see through the scheme and actually only wear a "mask of smiles" (*SB* 7). The contradiction of white desire and reality results from a disavowal that denies the Other's difference while creating forms of "authority and multiple belief that alienate the assumptions of 'civil' discourse" (1994: 91). Hence the stereotype is a discursive element with which it is possible to disguise the violation of enlightened and rational ideas and formally normalise a discourse of splitting. This split is produced by mimicry's construction around the concept of ambivalence: "[...] colonial mimicry is the desire for a reformed recognizable Other, *as a subject of a difference that is almost the same, but not quite*" (1994: 86). While the Other is appropriated in a strategy of discipline, their difference simultaneously threatens the established disciplinary powers. The translation scene between Baas Bradley and Styles exemplifies this threat in a more obvious way. The cultural, racial and linguistic difference which causes the reversal of dependence menaces the narcissistic quality of the whites' power and thus illustrates Bhabha's assertion, "The ambivalence of colonial authority repeatedly turns from *mimicry* – a difference that is almost nothing but not quite – to *menace* – a difference that is almost total but not quite" (1994: 91).

Styles carries the function of the mimic man[60] in his role as interpreter. He is the management's ally in preparing the motor plant for Mr. Ford's visit and thus is turned into the recognisable Other. Yet he is kept in his place through a difference that is "almost the same but not quite." However, Styles recognises that the relative power accorded him in his position as translator can be used for subversive action. In the presence of his fellow-workers he highlights the African difference as "almost total but not quite." He refuses to let his men believe in and be fooled by the stereotyped image they must present to Mr. Ford, and he makes them aware of their own power.

It must not be forgotten that Styles is the only character on stage. This specific scene is turned into a narrated play-within-the-play, and the performance as such becomes multi-layered. It is highly probable that the audience will also take on the role of the African workers whilst remaining in their role as Styles's spectator-accomplices, watching him narrate or enact several other identities. This resembles the spectator-actor-conspiracy in *The Island* where the audience are likely to slip

[60] As defined by Bhabha in "Of Mimicry and Man."

into the role of co-prisoners during the prisoners' recital. At the same time they retain the role of audience members who generally oppose apartheid's practices and sympathise with the two suffering African men. In both *Sizwe Bansi* and *The Island* forms of meta-theatre create a location from which it is possible to evade the threatening gaze of apartheid's representatives (or that of those audience members who potentially identify with this role). Thus it is possible to escape the prison panopticon, be it the Ford motor plant or a real gaol, in two ways. Firstly, the actors succeed in freeing themselves from their oppressor's gaze by fracturing and doubling it and by drawing the members of the audience onto their side. The actors strengthen their own action of resistance and subversion by enlarging the group of people who oppose the system. Secondly, besides creating strength through numbers, they entangle the system's representatives in a spectral web of intersecting gazes, thus destabilising the latter group's *locus* of power.

Soule's concept of reciprocal performer-spectator-mirroring posits that any character, i.e. any initially fixed fictional identity, can be destabilised by the multiple interplay of actor and audience members (cf. 1998: 45). The interpretation of *Sizwe Bansi is Dead* and *The Island* that results from her theory ties in with this post-colonial reading in that both approaches highlight the power of subversion that can be attained by the collaboration between actor and spectator. Viewing the post-colonial interpretation through the eyes of Soule's theory, it becomes clear that the plays' protagonists succeed in manifesting an identity that opposes the (non-)identity given to them by the system. According to apartheid ideology, Africans are identity-less creatures outside of their prescribed roles as the dependants of whites. Whether labourers in the industrial sector or prisoners, they are denied both individuality and identity development by the system. Instead, Africans are considered to have a fixed character, in Soule's sense of character as an absent identity. However, in the two plays the protagonists are able to symbolically break free from these constraints and processually and interactively develop their identity. This demonstrates not only that humans are social beings in need of contact with other humans but also that all positive definitions of identity presuppose the negotiation (not forced, unilateral implementation) of roles in society - a conclusion which echoes both Mead's and Goffman's conceptions of identity.

3.5. Conclusion

By bringing various characters to life on stage with their role-play, John Kani and Winston Ntshona are able to portray the variety and vitality of black life and thus act as Fugard's bridge to township life. In addition, this role-based approach to theatre allows them to suggest that understanding whites through mimicry (and, consequently, looking through their façades) can be a successful strategy for survival in the prescribed social theatricality of apartheid reality. However, the heightened consciousness of the audience seems to rely strongly on being accorded a role in the performance and hence being drawn into the drama-internal reality of the play. As Grotowski says, theatre can live without make-up, costumes, a stage set, a separate stage, lighting and sound effects, but it cannot live without the actor-spectator relationship (cf. 1967: 62).

Barbara Harlow maintains that in "the prison memoirs of political detainees, the 'power of writing' is one which seeks to alter the relationships of power which are maintained by coercive, authoritarian systems of state control and domination" (1987: 133). The characters of *Sizwe Bansi is Dead* and *The Island* are all prisoners of South Africa's apartheid rules and regulations. Through acting and role-playing the characters express their condemnation of the status-quo and rebel against their current situation of complete powerlessness. In doing so, they manifest, with their social theatricality, the strength that can be won through resistance and prove that this strength brings about a shift in the power structure. Whether it is Styles's anecdotes about his time at the Ford motor plant, stories about his clients in the photographic studio, Sizwe and Buntu's swapping of Sizwe's identity with that of the dead man Robert, John and Winston's private cinema or their presentation of the dialogue between Antigone and Creon in Sophocles' *Antigone*, all these actions can be considered alternative forms of 'writing.' They challenge the system of domination and give proof of the characters' vitality and humanity as well as their will to live and be recognised as full and equal human beings. It is here that these plays, with their protean and versatile black characters, reject the ideological concept that blacks have no identity.

Compared to the plays by Fugard discussed in Chapter 2, the collaborative workshop plays *Sizwe Bansi is Dead* and *The Island* offer a far more optimistic ending, despite the fact that both Sizwe and Winston have no long-term solution to their problems. For instance, while Zachariah and Morris in *The Blood Knot* decide to move their racially transgressive role games from a public environment to the privacy of their township shack in order to avoid all open conflict with the state, Sizwe is prepared to adopt Robert Zwelinzima's identity in public so that he can survive under the repressive regime. And Winston, for his part, draws strength from his and John's defiant interpretation of *Antigone* and their presentation of this play at the prison concert. Although both Sizwe and Winston cannot change their situation in the long run, they at least stand up for themselves and temporarily attempt to outwit the regime with its own weapons. In this act they go one step further than Morrie and Zach.

Fugard, Kani and Ntshona's two plays were the first South African "plays of social comment" (Larlham 1985: 81) to be strongly critical of the restrictive political and social conditions that determined the existence of black South Africans under apartheid. That is why these protest plays functioned as a model and an incentive to many black playwrights. However, those playwrights and critics committed to the philosophy of Black Consciousness did not feel that the portrayal of the black man's burden, as accurately as Fugard and the actors may have presented it, was sufficient to stimulate the black audience into thinking positively about themselves. For instance, Robert Zwelinzima alias the 'new' Sizwe Bansi was seen as too "shuffling, unintelligent, and unconscious; not proud enough or admirable enough to represent black sufferings, values, and aspirations" (Coplan 1985: 215).

The increase of theatre productions by black practitioners after the tour of *Sizwe Bansi is Dead* and *The Island* led to the development of more aggressive plays in which the black characters were no longer prepared to live under apartheid. This theatre of resistance initiated by the Black Consciousness Movement went beyond this mere portrayal of black suffering. Instead, it propagated a strong and active challenge to the state. (cf. Brink 1997: 168; Larlham 1992: 46; cf. Mda 1998: 257, Steadman 1991: 84). This change in tone and content is explored in the following chapter.

4. Black (Consciousness) Theatre and the Fight for Liberation

> The Revolutionary Theatre should force change; it should be change.
>
> LeRoi Jones[1]

4.1. The Black Consciousness Movement and culture

The Black Consciousness Movement (BCM) came to prominence in South Africa in the 1970s. It is considered to be the first "black politico-cultural movement" to issue its "own guidelines in the name of South African blacks as to what blacks should approve and condemn, what they should support or resist." It developed in the "nationalist tradition of black political struggle in South Africa, gave decisive emphasis to racial/cultural factors and to the common interest of all blacks, i.e. black Africans, 'Coloureds' and 'Indians'" (Kavanagh 1985: 146, 145). The BCM is a direct reaction to the failure of white liberalism in South Africa in the 1960s and a rejection of white supremacy (cf. Gwala 1984: 40; Sole 1983: 38; Sono 1993: 2).

The ideas of Black Consciousness (BC) were derived from various intellectual, political and ideological developments in twentieth century America and Africa including writings by Aimé Césaire, Leopold Senghor, Frantz Fanon, Paolo Freire, W.E.B. Du Bois and Marcus Garvey. The Négritude school, the Africanist and Pan-Africanist movement[2] as well as the Marxist liberation movements in China, Guinea-Bissau, Mozambique and Angola contributed to the movement's "eclecticism" and contradictory assertions (Kavanagh 1985: 158; cf. Snail 1993: 95-128; Steadman 1985: 106).[3] According to Ian Steadman, the BCM adopted

---

[1] 1966: 210.

[2] "According to Biko [Steven Biko, the first leader of the BCM] and others it was the evolution of Africanist and Pan-Africanist ideology and its advocacy of withdrawal from association in the same organization with those who were not of the nationalist culture – in this case, black African – that opened the way to the reinstatement of the political context of African history, traditional culture and especially language, and to the conversion of the struggle from an élitist activity directed at securing a 'place' in white society for the few, into a mass activity directed at the complete take-over of the state and the restructuring of the society according to what was perceived to be the needs and culture of blacks" (Kavanagh 1985: 151).

[3] On the class aspects of the BCM see Kavanagh (1985) and all articles by Sole (for example, 1987a: 57-68).

principles for a "two-pronged struggle against apartheid." On the one hand, it appropriated Third World philosophies of a common diasporic struggle against colonialism and imperialism. On the other hand, it adopted an Afro-centric search for a black identity with Africa as its centre (1998: 60f.).

Themba Sono identifies as the BCM's major external and immediate influence the American Black Power Movement of the 1960s and points to the "philosophical, ideological and historical linkages" between the doctrines of the two movements (1993: 33, cf. 2; 34). The American Black Power Movement has been described as "the collective thrust of these [African-American] activists toward racial pride, strength and self-definition" (Van Deburg 1992: 2). The Black Power or Black Liberation Movement followed Malcolm X's call for "Self-Determination, Self-Respect, and Self-Defense" and grew out of the Civil Rights Movement, the non-violent struggle for democracy led by Martin Luther King (Baraka 1989: ix). The programme of BC echoes these radical African-American ideas, especially the notion of the importance of a militant cultural struggle in the programme of political consciousness-raising in order to reach political and psychological liberation (cf. Steadman 1998: 60). The ideas of Black Theology – the need of the black population to draw strength from their rediscovery of God and their celebration of Christ's identification with the oppressed - also fell on fertile ground in South Africa (Fatton 1986: 107-19; Hayes 1996). Writings by James Baldwin, Eldridge Cleaver, Malcolm X and Eliijah Muhammad shaped the BCM ideologically and linguistically, an influence that Sono elaborates on in great detail (cf. Sono 1993: 34-55; Gerhart 1978: 275-77).[4]

The BCM did not offer a "sophisticated theory of political and cultural domination" (Kavanagh 1981: 157) or a "fully articulated philosophical manifesto" (Steadman 1984: 106) but promoted the "uncompromising application of a few clearly-grasped principles to the full gamut of social relations" (cf. Kavanagh 1985: 157). The movement's central aim was the *conscientisation* of the black population, defined by Paulo Freire as "learning to perceive social, political and economic contradictions, and to take action against the oppressive elements of society" (qtd.

---

[4] The American Black Power Movement is traced by Camichael & Hamilton (1967) and Van Deburg (1992). The concept of Black Theology is also presented by Moore, ed. (1973) and Snail (1993: 252-65).

in Kavanagh 1985: 157).[5] As this theatre was created for the majority of the population, it can be referred to as 'popular theatre.'[6]

The black South African Students Organisation (SASO), one of the leading organisations of the BCM,[7] stated that culture was "tied up with the aspirations of a people." It resolved to create a committee which would deal with "the awakening and heightening of cultural awareness and the involvement of the black people in their struggle for identity, self-respect and liberation" (qtd. in Kavanagh 1985: 149).[8] The BCM recognised drama as an "instrument of conscientization and liberation" and developed a "rudimentary" theory of theatre and art (Kavanagh 1985: 162; cf. Sole 1984: 56). As Steven Biko, the first leader of the BCM, pointed out, black theatre and drama constituted one of the possibilities of black culture's freedom to develop without reference to white values:

> A culture is essentially the society's composite answer to the varied problems of life. We are experiencing new problems every day and whatever we do adds to the richness of our cultural heritage as long as it has man as its centre. The adoption of black theatre and drama is one such important innovation which we need to encourage and to develop. We know that our love of music and rhythm has relevance even in this day. (1978: 96)

To a large extent the theory of the theatre of BC adhered to the same principles as the BCM: "[...] black theatre had created works rooted in Black Consciousness and based on themes of resistance" (Steadman 1984c: 11). The BCM's tenet of freeing blacks from white cultural domination was articulated in its theory of the theatre which proclaimed the "withdrawal from association with whites, the creation of new structures and the conscientization of black people" (Kavanagh 1985: 164). These aims were realised by the formation of all-black theatre groups who had

---

[5] For more details on the South African BCM refer to Adam (1973), Biko (1978), Gerhart (1978, ch. 8), Lodge (1983: 321-62), Kavanagh (1985: 145-68), Pityana (1972), Roux (1964) and Woods (1987).

[6] Critics emphasise the fact that not every performance created for the people actually reached the intended addressees. In this vein some critics put up for discussion whether the appellation 'popular' is appropriate (cf. Orkin 1996: 49; Steadman 1986; 1990b: 209). David Coplan introduced a different notion of 'popular' as "arising out of the community that it serves and organic to the lives, concerns, and aspirations of those who perform and support it" (1986: 174f.; cf. 2000).

[7] SASO was founded in 1969 and presided by Steve Biko during his student years. The Black Peoples Convention (BPC) is considered the other leading organisation of the BCM.

[8] Kavanagh quotes these statements but fails to name his source. However, it can be deduced from his formulation that he refers to a conference communiqué.

complete control over their theatrical activities: acting, directing, technical issues and administration. This control was regarded as the first step towards establishing larger black associations which could be linked to national political and cultural organisations ("new structures") of the BCM. In order to raise the consciousness of the black community, it was deemed necessary to perform before African, coloured and Indian audiences. The presentation and re-examination of their true history and culture was considered an essential step towards achieving psychological and spiritual transformation. This increasingly "radical, militant" and "overtly political" theatre (Mshengu 1979: 34) also addressed the problems which blacks, as the oppressed group, were confronted with in daily life. It also offered preferably revolutionary solutions. The aim of these plays was not to show blacks as "passive bearers of suffering" (Sole 1984: 57) as in 'protest plays' such as *Sizwe Bansi is Dead* but to motivate the audience to accept themselves and fight for their rights (cf. Kavanagh 1985: 162-65; Chapter 3.5). This so-called 'resistance theatre' (cf. Brink 1997: 168; Larlham 1992: 46; Peterson 1990: 237; Steadman 1991: 84) addressed itself directly to the oppressed group and won mass support, despite frequent detentions of its activists and bannings of the plays. It aimed at asserting an "alternative, black South African cultural identity" (cf. Steadman 1994: 27). Its goal was also to mobilise the oppressed to reflect on and rebel against their oppression. In this light it is clearly agitprop, "for it attempted to propagate a message, and agitate for action [...]" (Mda 1996: 201; cf. 1998: 257f.).

Mark Fleishman evaluates these resistance plays by looking at how successful they were in translating the theoretical ideas of BC theatre into practice. He uses Mtuli Shezi's *Shanti* (1973) as an example, a play that Kavanagh rates as "possibly the best known play to emerge from the activities" of the BCM (1985: xx; cf. Steadman 1990b: 222). By contrast, Fleishman argues that *Shanti* was still anchored in the literary theatre tradition and that prior to 1976 the BCM did not succeed in including the mass black audience into its theatre work (cf. 1990: 99; 1991: 59).

The cultural debt BC theatre owes to the theatre of the American Black Arts Movement is also evident. In 1968, Larry Neal described the Black Arts Movement as the "aesthetic and spiritual sister of the Black Power concept ... The Black Arts and the Black Power concept both relate broadly to the Afro-American's desire for self-determination and nationhood" (1968: 29f.). These notions were imported into South Africa by supporters of the BCM, and they "supplemented" similar ideas by

BC leaders in South Africa (Steadman 1998: 60).[9] The Black Arts Movement was initiated and supported by young African-American artists in the 1960s with the goal of creating a revolutionary "art, a literature that that would fight for black people's liberation." In their opinion, black art had to represent black life and the history and legacy of the struggle of resistance, educate and unify African-Americans in their opposition to white America, and reflect the African-American cultural heritage of oral tradition, black music, rhythm and poetry (Baraka 1989: x; cf. x-xii). Black Theatre specifically strove to promote the idea of BC and to replace the negative image of Blacks in literature with a positive one (cf. Williams 1985: 16f.). Prominent plays of the American Black Arts Movement were staged by South African BC groups - for example, *Requiem for Brother X* (1966) about Malcolm X by William Mackey, an African-American playwright, was performed in South Africa in 1972 (cf. *Black Review* 1972: 203; 1973: 109). Plays by Amiri Baraka/Leroi Jones, probably the most prominent representative of black American "revolutionary theatre" (Jones 1966), were also known (cf. Steadman 1990b: 223).[10] The BCM also established its own publication, *Black Review*, imitating the style of African-American journals and magazines such as *Black Dialogue*, *Journal of Black Poetry*, *Liberator* and *Black World* (cf. Steadman 1998: 60).

The black theatre that emerged in South Africa incorporates militant songs and chants as well as direct audience addresses typical of epic theatre.[11] Their didactic quality becomes apparent in the increasingly overt call for revolution that intercepts and concludes these plays and leaves no doubt about their strong tendentious or agitprop thrust. Exchanging class-based arguments for conscientisation, and revolution with race-based ones, BC theatre stands in the tradition of the leftist or worker theatre movement in the Unites States and Germany in the 1930s, represented, among others, by Clifford Odets and Bertolt Brecht.[12]

---

[9] The American Black Arts Movement is presented in detail by Neal (1989). With regard to BC theatre and revolutionary theatre in the United States as well as information on leading playwrights see for example Kaufman (1980), Sanders (1988) and Williams (1985).

[10] In return the South African plays that developed from BC were received with much political interest in the United States. The anthology *Woza Afrika!* ['Come, Africa!'] is composed of hitherto mostly unpublished plays presented at the WOZA AFRIKA! Festival at the Lincoln Center Theatre in New York in 1986. *Woza Afrika!* is edited by Duma Ndlovu from South Africa and carries a foreword by the Nigerian writer Wole Soyinka and a preface by Baraka. Kruger comments on this festival (cf. 1991).

[11] See Goetsch (1977) for a presentation of the characteristics of epic theatre.

[12] Compare the following excerpts: "Workers of the world/In your hands lies the power/To build and rebuild. UNITE AND FIGHT /CLASS AGAINST CLASS" (USA, 1931; qtd. in Goldstein

South Africa in the 1970s witnessed a "cultural revolution" (SASO 1971) or a "new wave of cultural energy" (International Aid and Defence Fund 1977/78: 57) in the black community which was directly related to the renewed political energy initiated through the BCM (cf. Akerman 1977/78: 56).[13] Black theatre functioned as a "consciously articulated cultural counterpart of the movement towards political liberation": "Black Consciousness, in short, gave black theatre an identity" (Steadman 1990b: 222, 212; cf. Gwala 1973). André Brink highlights the plays' political function by calling them "combative strategies" (1997: 169). Some art groups, whose members included BCM activists, explicitly identified with the aims of BC. Their theatre activities were "formally a part" of the BCM (Kavanagh 1985: xx).[14] Contrary to this, other artists and groups adopted some aspects of BC ideology without considering themselves to be political BC activists. Even mixed groups with a non-racial, integrationist agenda (such as Workshop '71, whose inclusion in this chapter is problematic and debatable from the perspective of 'race') adopted some of the BCM's ideas. On the other hand plays by Africans that did not sufficiently create a revolutionary mood or promote black liberation were not considered "Black drama but drama presented by Blacks" (*Black Review* 1973: 105). Wally Mongane Serote went so far as to insult the African members of Workshop '71 as "'non-whites, schizophrenics, guinea-pigs'" (qtd. in Sole 1987b: 257).

1974: 31); "WE GOTTA ORGANIZE! ALL BLACK PEOPLE! [...] POWER IN THE HANDS OF MILLIONS OF BLACK PEOPLE ALL OVER THE WORLD [...] That's the key, you know: BLACK PEOPLE PROUD OF BEING BLACK!" (USA, 1966, *Requiem for Brother X*; King & Milner, eds. 1972: 335f.); "Mother Afrika wake up/And arm yourself,/wipe the tears of your brave/Mother Afrika wake up,/Lest umlungu [the white man] rapes you" (South Africa, 1979, Maishe Maponya's *The Hungry Earth* [8]); and "SONQOBA SIMUNYE [United we will conquer]" (South Africa, 1986, Matsemela Manaka's *Children of Asazi* [151]).

The American theatre of the Great Depression is presented by Goldstein (1974) and Smiley (1972). For a study of the leftist theatre movement in Great Britain see Lehberger (1977).

[13] According to Larlham the formation of black theatre groups in the late 1960s "coincided" with an increased interest in BC (cf. 1985: 75). However, it seems that a causal connection between the two cannot be denied.

[14] These groups include the South African Black Theatre Union (SABTU) in Durban, the Theatre Council of Natal (TECON), the People's Experimental Theatre (PET) in the Transvaal as well as the Johannesburg group Music, Drama, Arts and Literature Institute (MDALI) (cf. International Defence and Aid Fund 1977; Gwala 1984; Kavanagh 1985: 149; 1981: xiv; Larlham 1985: 76; Sole 1987b: 256). Mtuli Shezi, the author of *Shanti*, was Vice-President of the BC organisation BPC.

During a time of firm government action against the strong opposition of the BCM by means of threats, detainment, interrogation, torture and banning orders,[15] many artists involved in black theatre groups were severely effected by persecution and prosecution.[16] This led the International Defence and Aid Fund to state in 1976 that because of the broad banning and arrests of black activist theatre practitioners, "[...] by the end of 1975 there were apparently no black theatre groups directly involved in using drama as a means of spreading the message of Black Consciousness [...]" (1977/78: 62). Steadman argues that this did not signify the end of BC but that a "younger generation of black theatre practitioners in South Africa" emerged after the 1976 Soweto uprising (1984c: 17). In the light of white measures to appropriate black theatre after 1976[17] he maintains that "[...] a small group of black artists, stressing the ideals of Black Consciousness and solidarity in the face of white dominance, have created innovative forms of cultural expression" (1984: 9). Steadman (cf. 1984c: 14) and Fuchs (cf. 1992: 168) consider the work of Matsemela Manaka a prime example (cf. Chapter 4.4).

What the artistically engaged groups of the time had in common was the desire for black conscientisation and liberation through active resistance represented by various dramatic forms, alternative (i.e. non-Western) acting styles and staging techniques (cf. Larlham 1985: 81).[18] These are the criteria used for the plays to be discussed in this chapter: the prison play *Survival* by Workshop '71, Percy Mtwa's *Bopha!*, a family play about black policemen and a student activist, and Matsemela Manaka's *Egoli – City of Gold* about work and life on a Johannesburg gold mine. Despite their common denominator, it is undoubtedly problematic to refer to these plays as 'BC theatre' because this term not only implies that the plays adhere to the ideas of BC but also that they are created by black artists and present the vision of a

---

[15] Banning orders restricted a person's movements, employment, political work and social activities and also prohibited their association with more than one other person at a time. Furthermore, it was considered offensive to quote or publish their writings or speeches (cf. International Defence and Aid Fund 1977: 59).

[16] For an elaborate description of the harassment suffered by black artists see International Defence and Aid Fund (1977: 57f.).

[17] The introduction of broadcast television (SABC) undercut black township theatre and attracted artists "with the promise of secure employment, better wages, technological training – and, above all, media exposure." The opening of the Market Theatre in Johannesburg and other white-owned venues provided "conditions for the appropriation of black theatre" (Steadman 1984c: 11).

[18] The International Defence and Aid Fund claims: "Although not all of the individual artists involved would subscribe to Black Consciousness aims and ideals, the recent explosion of artistic activity [...] from the black community has shared a common desire for black liberation" (1977/78: 57).

black state attained by revolution. Workshop '71's production *Survival* does not fulfil the first demand as the all-black cast was directed by a white. Although all three plays call for black liberation, Workshop '71 and Percy Mtwa both supported the idea of an integrated state.[19]

Many different terms have been coined to signify the theatre that incorporated at least some of the ideals of BC.[20] It has not only been referred to as 'resistance theatre' but also as 'BC theatre,' 'real black theatre' or 'black drama' (cf. *Black Review* 1973: 105; Kavanagh 1985: 163), 'theatre of liberation' (cf. *Black Review* 1972: 201; D.O.C.C. 1973: 43), 'militant theatre' (cf. Mda 1998: 257), 'theatre of criticism and confrontation' (cf. Horn 1986: 221), 'theatre of urgency' (Coplan 1986: 175), 'committed theatre' (cf. Larlham 1992: 81; Steadman 1985: 376; cf. Horn 1986: 220) and 'theatre of anger' (Hauptfleisch 1992: 405).[21] Terms such as 'committed' or 'resistance theatre' emphasise this theatre's strong opposition to apartheid in a general way and are essentially colour-blind terms whereas 'BC theatre' is not. Thus the former names may be better suited to signify the plays under discussion. Notwithstanding, this chapter's title, "Black (Consciousness) Drama," is meant in a provocative way and intended to draw attention to the eclecticism of BC and the varied and partially contradictory use of the term 'BC theatre.' In this study the term 'BC theatre' implies both the impact of BC on theatre as well as the capacity of theatre to raise awareness and promote the ideals of BC ideology.

---

[19] It must be stressed that the cast of *Survival* did not label their play as "black theatre." Actor Themba Ntinga exclaims: "You know there's nothing that makes me so sick as black, white, this, that! *No*, it's African theatre. If black means African, South African, *then* it's black theatre" (Workshop '71 1977: 127). Although Workshop '71 subscribed to an integrationist agenda, the play's call for revolution nonetheless clearly pursues black interests and can thus be called 'black' in the sense propagated by the BCM.

[20] It seems that different factors such as the author's political and ideological position, the author's degree of involvement in the political and cultural activities in the 1970s, the author's position as artist and/or scholar, the author's presence in South Africa and the time of the writing of the respective articles have led to different evaluations of the theatre activity during and after the heyday of BC as a political movement.

[21] A useful summary of the development of the scholarly assessment of African theatre is given by Peterson (1995). Additional reflections on the problems of terminology are offered by Clark (1981) on the "archaeology of black theatre," Kavanagh (1981) on "majority theatre," Kerr (1995), Mooki (1986) and Orkin (1996) on "popular theatre" and Sole (1987b), Steadman (1992b), Tomaselli (1980, 1982) and Tomaselli & Muller (1987) on class-based (working-class) theatre.

4.2. Workshop '71's *Survival*: Surviving the South African prison

> Five years in jail . . . that was bad.
>
> Two days in the outside world . . . that was a nightmare.
>
> Slaska in *Survival*[22]

Workshop '71's *Survival* is a play about the true meaning of "survival" in a prison state. It depicts life in South African prisons and events leading to imprisonment. It also portrays the effects of apartheid on the oppressed (cf. McLaren 1996: 44f.). The play evolves around the juxtaposition "'[...] prison without/prison within.'" If apartheid South Africa is considered a 'prison state,' then society represents "'the prison without'" whereas the prison institutions are the "'prison within.'" The play focuses on how, in the words of director Robert Mshengu McLaren Kavanagh,[23] "[...] for black South Africans, being black in the prison state was already an imposed state of inhumanity, an involuntary involvement in a system that led to the constant likelihood of passage from the prison without into the prison within and back again" (all McLaren 1996: 45). Created in 1976, *Survival*'s performance tour coincided with the brutal police suppression that followed the Soweto uprising of 16 June 1976.[24]

4.2.1. Workshop '71's approach to theatre

Founded in 1971 at the Institute of Race Relations with the goal of establishing multi-racial contact and conducting experimental workshops and performances, Workshop '71 brought together white and black actors and drama teachers. Its original aim was to become a non-racial training ground where artists from

---

22 *SV* 155. References to *Survival* are flagged *SV*.

23 Robert Mshengu McLaren Kavanagh uses variations of his name. Robert Kavanagh, Robert McLaren and Mshengu all signify the same person. To avoid confusion, this director and critic will be referred to as Kavanagh in the text. References to his articles reflect his chosen name.

24 The incentive to create a play about South African prisons came from Barney Simon's production of the Canadian prison play, *Fortune and Men's Eyes*, by John Herbert. Instead of portraying a North American prison setting, the theatre group decided to create a South African play about South African prisons because three of the four actors could draw on first-hand experience. Aiming to evoke various experiences and views on prison life, the actors also drew on their literary knowledge (Baldwin, *Notes of a Native Son*; Koestler, *Darkness at Noon*; Poe, "The Pit and the Pendulum"; Wright, *Native Son*) and newspaper and magazine articles (cf. Workshop '71 1977; McLaren 1996: 44f; Kavanagh 1981: 127).

different groups could meet to learn and share techniques and discuss each other's work (cf. McLaren 1996: 28, 41). Their focus lay on "experimentation and invention" (Mshengu 1977/78: 63). Workshop '71 members James Mthoba and Themba Ntinga explain:

> Experimenting in new exciting ways of making the audience think, that is its role. [...] Our aims and objects are to experiment by examining existing theatre and evolving new theatre methods and techniques. [...] We also provide opportunities for people of different cultures to become familiar with their difference, and create original theatre which depends on artistic co-operation and contact." (1973: 46)

In his 1996 account of Workshop 71's development Kavanagh, one of the white founding members, presents his view of the role and function of the theatre. He believes that theatre recognises and works with the paradoxes of life: "wit in oppression, suffering, resistance and transcendence" (McLaren 1996: 27). Creative theatrical work has the power to highlight the small aspects of daily existence and transform them into an approach to life. Kavanagh shows, for example, how an observation about the ragged teeth of a black man can be transformed into a "perception of black urban life" and a comment on gangsterism (McLaren 1996: 27). The group's artistic exercises to experiment with different themes included "dance, mime, drawing, colouring, rhythm, singing, chanting [...] movements in slow motion, reversed motion, and zoom lens and tableau effects." In order to develop a dialogue, edit and record it, the artists employed techniques such as "Writing, improvisation, tape-recording and group discussion" (Kavanagh 1981: 127).

Kavanagh identifies the four main elements of Workshop 71's ethos: "liberal philanthropy, a political agenda, a dream of livelihood and an immense interest in theatre as art" (McLaren 1996: 28). The group subscribed to liberal multiculturalism:

> Workshop '71 attempts to create South African theatre out of a composite culture of all South Africans at a time when there is not a meeting of cultures but a confrontation of cultures. Interpretative drama must pick its way through a complex web of confusion and misunderstanding when audiences are from very similar, yet very different backgrounds. (Mshengu 1977/78: 66)

Despite this premise, the free use of language advocated by Kavanagh led several white liberals to leave because they failed to master any African tongues. The use on stage of predominantly indigenous languages and slang, adapted to the linguistic preferences of the respective township audiences, was one of Workshop 71's pioneering achievements. However, its reinstatement of racially mixed casts and theatre audiences, which led to the successful multi-lingual production *Crossroads*, clashed with the rise of BC. The BCM's opposition to multi-racial collaboration led many whites and blacks alike to withdraw from Workshop '71. With director Kavanagh remaining the only white among several black actors, the group focused on performing to all-black audiences and toured the townships with *ZZZIP!*, their new play in Zulu and Sotho. However, performances to mixed audiences in towns soon proved to be economically necessary (cf. McLaren 1996: 28-33).

Politically speaking, Workshop '71 regarded popular theatre as a potentially revolutionary medium in South Africa and proposed an agenda that focused its theatrical output at the masses while bypassing the educated élite. In the group's opinion, a play acquired the role of "a hub for organizational and conscientization work involving written literature of different kinds" (McLaren 1996: 34). Workshop '71 did not want theatrical activities to be involved in manifestations of overt political protest such as demonstrations or political rallies. However, its intention to covertly use theatre for mass political organisation became submerged in the political importance of the plays' statements. Their works moved from assertions about African culture, art, religion and history (*uNosilimela* by Credo Mutwa, produced by Workshop '71) to more aggressive racial politics (*uHlanga*, 'The Reed'). *Small Boy* and *Survival*, the group's last two productions, culminated in visions of revolution (cf. McLaren 1996: 33-38; Mshengu 1976).

Workshop '71 was never a theatre group directly related to the BCM. It was, nonetheless, influenced by BC and, to some extent, responded to its mood. The didacticism of its plays concurred with the movement's objective of raising the consciousness of the people (cf. Shava 1989: 136-38; Kerr 1995: 223). However, its ideal of a non-racial democratic South African society with majority rule, which it embodied in its aesthetic and its practice and which revolution was sought to bring about, was diametrically opposed to the goals of the BCM.

In 1971 Workshop '71 had begun as a school or training ground, but when it became a theatre group, producing *Crossroads* and *ZZZIP!*, time for experimental workshops decreased. In 1975 Workshop '71 was turned into a professional theatre company, Workshop '71 Theatre Company. Its first professional production, the one-man play *uHlanga*, lived through two years of successful performances, ending its run in 1977 at London's Royal Court Theatre Upstairs. Encouraged by this success, Cape Town's Space Theatre commissioned a new play from the group.

Survival, which was established in experimental workshops, premiered at the (mixed but predominantly white) Space in May 1976 after a three-month-rehearsal period. After touring Cape Town's black urban areas, it opened in East London's fringe Window Theatre and continued on to the YWCA in Dube, Soweto in July 1976 (just weeks after the Soweto uprising) where soldiers invaded the venue, beat up staff members and closed down the centre (cf. Kavanagh 1981: 127).

Anne Fuchs argues that "*Survival* [...] scarcely seems to have a code of reference other than that shared by the black actors and the black members of the audience in Soweto in 1976" (1985: 60). This view fails to take into account the fact that *Survival* addresses both white *and* black spectators. It appears that Fuchs does not consider the fact that the play targets audiences in areas *not yet* involved in militant struggle in order to galvanise them into action. *Survival* mirrors the potentially violent situation of the months leading to the Soweto uprising on 16 June 1976. As Kavanagh reports, it played to Cape Town audiences in the black urban areas of Langa and Gugulethu and so-called 'coloured townships' after 16 June but *before* the violence of the Soweto uprising had physically spread to the Cape. He concludes that "[...] at that stage the play performed an effective political function" (1981: 126). However, he is convinced that during the times of militant struggle, "[...] conventional performances of a play, no matter how militant, had become anachronistic, impossible, even a little ridiculous." In his opinion, the play's presentation in Dube, Soweto in July 1976 was futile as the revolutionary struggle had rendered theatre and its political and social tasks irrelevant (1981: 127).

After this incident in Dube *Survival* successfully played to large audiences at the (mixed but predominantly white) Box Theatre in Johannesburg for another six weeks before it went on to tour the United States. The play experienced a revival in 1978 when pirate performances were presented by a new cast with director Peter Sephuma, the understudy of *Survival's* US tour. Although the original cast considered this version a "'diluted' travesty of the original," it led to the play's ultimate banning in South Africa (Kavanagh 1981: 126; cf. Fuchs 1985: 55; McLaren 1996: 40; Orkin 1991: 174).

4.2.2. *Survival* – the play

The main body of *Survival* is composed of four stylistically different reports or plays-within-the-play. The characters present different viewpoints of a black man's life in and out of prison in apartheid South Africa and dramatise their growing consciousness of the mechanisms of apartheid. The sketches are arranged in chiasmatic fashion: two episodes about the situation in prison frame two further stories about life outside. The humorous, satirical quality of the first two dramatisations is followed by a "*break*" (*SV* 155), after which the remaining reports become more serious and aggressive.

In the first two reports the actors exhibit witty and satiric verbal play that lays open and criticises the mechanisms of the judicial and penitentiary system as well as the apartheid government's alleged attempts at reform in the early 1970s. In the third report the men present South Africa's prison environment as a metaphor for apartheid society by juxtaposing the story of an intellectual and an urban worker. Finally, the "combined statement" of the reports climaxes in a prison hunger strike. This strike symbolises "total political revolt" and goes further than plays such as *Sizwe Bansi is Dead* or Gibson Kente's popular township musicals. *Survival* does not merely "indict the apartheid system," it openly defies it and imbues the audience with the vision of liberation (all McLaren 1996: 45; cf. Fuchs 1985: 60; Orkin 1991: 174f.). J. Ndukaku Amankulor even characterises *Survival* as "one of the most radical plays from contemporary South Africa" (1993: 166).

These reports are embedded in a frame play in which the actors invade the audience space in the roles of fleeing criminals who are disguised as actors. Caught and imprisoned by a policeman, the actors then introduce each other to the audience with their real names and state which characters they are going to play in the sketches. After each narrative the characters communally evaluate and discuss its bearing on reality. In the end they break the theatrical illusion again and shed their roles to play themselves and discuss the sketches they have presented. Throughout the play the actors/characters engage in assertive and powerful songs[25] calling for revolutionary action.

4.2.2.1. The prison within and the prison without: The dramatisation of apartheid

The first report by the actor David Fana Kekana alias Criminal Vusi dramatises Habbakuk Ngwenya's introduction to prison life. Fana presents his story as an

---

[25] It is not possible to comment on the use of music because this is not documented in the published version of the play. However, actor Ntinga points out: "Music is essential in 'Survival'" (Workshop '71 1977: 125).

authentic and exclusive depiction of the South African penitentiary system. He manoeuvres the audience[26] into the position of eye-witnesses: "I'm going to take you right into the cell with us" (*SV* 135). The spectators are removed from a distant vantage point and placed in the immediacy of the action. While this creates an impression of intimacy and conspiracy, it also forces the spectators to accept a possibly discomforting proximity.

The episode begins with the registration of several criminals in a prison. A warder records their personal information and distributes the khaki prison uniform. The men must perform the 'tausa dance' to prove they are not carrying forbidden objects. The prisoner has to strip naked and perform a dance designed to reveal or dislodge any objects that may be hidden in the anus. A similar apartheid procedure was employed to test migrant workers for venereal disease – another form of humiliation imposed on black men in daily life. The characters present an improvised version of the tausa dance which allows the actors to depict the horror and degradation of this practice "without repeating the humiliation imposed in real life" that their characters symbolically experience (McLaren 1996: 46). The new prisoner, Habbakuk, nervous, confused and ignorant of what is expected of him, performs in a "*compulsively comical*" fashion what the stage directions call a "*travesty*" of the tausa (*SV* 135). This stylised presentation brings to the fore the intensity of apartheid's dehumanising practices. At the same time the prisoner's failure to conform represents a strategy of resistance in that it parodies and subverts prescribed behaviour. It thus establishes subjectivity and functions as a mode of empowerment. While the tausa dance is a site for apartheid's representation of Africans, the travesty constructs an "active, moving body that 'speaks' in own forms of corporeality" (Gilbert & Tompkins 1996: 242; cf. 237-42). This is in complete contrast to the dancing, happy African in black musicals designed for white audiences such as the highly criticised *Ipi-Tombi* (see Chapter 3.2.1), in which dance expresses exotic 'otherness' within a discourse which represents blacks as objects of the gaze, as opposed to the tausa travesty which defines the dancer as a "self-constituting subject" (Gilbert 1992: 137).

Interestingly the dance scene foregrounds the different degrees of awareness of the actors and their characters. For the characters the tausa is a concrete procedure of prison reality. By contrast, the actors are removed from directly experiencing this

---

[26] Since the text can be adapted according to the demographics of the spectators, it is essential to note that the printed version of the text seems to be addressing a white audience.

process and comment on its degrading nature. Hence they imply the need for self-examination and a personal awareness of one's environment. Again, this shows that we can maintain a distance from the roles we adopt so that our identity does not fuse with our roles. This allows us to see ourselves objectively and gives us the wherewithal to try to maintain this healthy balance.

Fana's report specifically focuses on the dehumanising reality of life behind bars: daily experiences such as sleeping in overcrowded cells with not enough blankets for everyone, eating food of terrible quality, etc. Life is reduced to a strict routine in which the prisoners' primary aim is to satisfy their basic needs and avoid additional harassment by the warders, even if this requires obsequious behaviour.

The three occupants of the cell test the integrity of the newcomer, Habbakuk, before they decide to trust him and accept him into their group. The men introduce him to the routine of prison life, but they take advantage of his inexperience and naiveté to play pranks on him which gets him into trouble with the prison authority (cf. *SV* 137). However, these games should also be seen in their didactic function because they warn him against such behaviour in the future. Thus the men are teaching him the mechanisms of survival.

In a scene reminiscent of *Sizwe Bansi* and *The Island*, the prisoners engage in role-play and enact mock trials which allows them to experiment with and display their vitality and role-versatility. They slip into the roles of the magistrate, prosecutor, court constable and an accused. Habbakuk is the accused and takes the stand. He clearly does not know how to behave; so one of the other men replaces him. Yet Habbakuk is not satisfied with this loss of his role and exclaims: "Hayi, wait! Habbakuk's *my* name. Don't call him with *my* name" (*SV* 140). For him his name is an essential part of his identity which cannot be adopted by anyone else in the game. By failing to grasp the metaphoric range, he does not recognise the demonstrative quality of this exchange. Habbakuk is also reluctant to be tried in an imaginary case because he fears that a guard could overhear their game and misuse it as incriminating evidence. Yet he learns in the course of the enactment that role-play is a theatrical activity which enables the men to explore different identities and test the consequences of various strategies of defence. Again, this confirms that behavioural strategies are forms of "self-presentation" (Goffman) that are learnt through socialisation in a particular environment.

In their defence speeches during these mock trials the men portray themselves as the victims of their weaknesses and unfortunate circumstances. They act out the arrest of a man who wishes to pay for an apple, which he has already eaten, only to discovers at the cash register that his few coins have fallen out of his pocket. This story implies and is critical of the fact that economic circumstances catapult the poor into delinquency. The prisoners are able to dramatise these aspects and then take on the roles of state representatives. This shows that they can successfully reflect upon and analyse their own behaviour and that they have come to an understanding of the mechanisms and ideology that inform apartheid's roles.

The one thing that the long-term prisoners do learn from Habbakuk's naiveté and his propensity to take everything literally is his ability to call things by their real name and not by apartheid's redefined words created through language manipulation. For example, the prisoners teach Habbakuk how to behave vis-à-vis the guards: "And say 'dankie, bass' [thank you, boss] when they hit you. [...] Otherwise they'll hit you again" (*SV* 136). The newcomer reacts with indignation. For him 'dankie' expresses gratitude and is thus completely unsuitable in this context, but the word has lost its original meaning for the other prisoners and now only serves to procure an end to corporal punishment. In another situation, when the four prisoners rejoice in song and dance and are subsequently reprimanded by the warder, the prisoners adopt 'apartheid-speak' and excuse themselves obsequiously for "making a noise" while Habbakuk defiantly claims: "We weren't making a noise. We were singing" (*SV* 139). Similarly, the new convict is the only one to complain about the inedible food. One prisoner is actually encouraged by Habbakuk's frankness to start a hunger-strike but this idea is not pursued for lack of followers.

As in *The Island* this first story never visibly stages a prison officer or warder but only suggests their presence. Because of this invisibility, the actions of the guards can only be deciphered by the movements of the prisoners, for example, when they suddenly recoil from imagined blows to the face. This element of surprise serves to highlight the brutality of the guards and depict the prisoners as victims of a powerful system. But the report also celebrates the men's resistance to this violence and humiliation, their solidarity and desire to assert their identities. Anne Fuchs emphasises that their humour – "pungent witticisms and broad farce at the expense of themselves and their surroundings" (1985: 60) - allows them to continue living. It is exactly this attitude that helps them to relate their actions to their environment and recognise the histrionic quality of role behaviour and how it can work to their advantage.

The second report is set in the 'outside' world which is satirically revealed as being just as much a prison experience for the released prisoner as is his incarceration in jail. The actor Dan Selado Maredi alias Criminal Slaska experiences the public world of Johannesburg in 1976 in which the changing face of apartheid manifests itself. Much to his disbelief Slaska encounters racially mixed hotels, acknowledges that the football team has become multi-racial and walks into a desegregated park. However, when he wants to eat in a restaurant or use a public toilet, he soon comes to realise that petty apartheid is as strong as before and that serious reforms have not taken place. He concludes that his allegedly regained freedom is useless because as a black man he is still imprisoned by apartheid's laws. Thus the only solution is to *dream* of a better future with a well-paying job.

Slaska's dream is interrupted by the other actors who force him to take part in the dramatisation of a day in the life of a migrant worker in search of a job in the city. While rushing from the pass office to the employer to the township superintendent, he realises that he is trapped in a vicious circle: without a house permit, proof of a hostel contract or registration in the township, he will not receive the required stamp in his passbook allowing him to apply for a work permit. This scene is not presented as a normal dialogue but as a succession of demands and commands that are barked at him, "Passbook! [...] House permit? [...] Contract," with the understanding that no house permit means no registration and no registration means no work (cf. *SV* 149). Not only is Slaska treated in an inhuman way and reduced to a victim of the laws of apartheid, but the authority figures themselves also appear unable to interact other than in this mechanical way. This not only shows that apartheid dehumanises the oppressed group but suggests that the oppressors' unwillingness to acknowledge the humanity of the blacks indicates the loss of their own human qualities and confirms their degeneration into inhumanity.

Slaska has a similar experience at the police office where a man reports the disappearance of his brother while another man gives an account of a crime. In both cases the duty officer continuously harasses the men by interrupting them and misinterpreting their words to distort their stories. By making fun of them, the policeman shows that he considers these incidents unimportant and that the black men are wasting his time. In the end, however, the policeman is unmasked as the laughable figure. By not attending to the men's requests, the officer is handling his job in a completely unprofessional way. Hence he discredits himself as well as the image of the police force. His failure to treat the black men as equal human beings reveals more about his own racism than about the men's supposed immaturity.

Fleeing from the unexpectedly inhumane atmosphere of the police office, Slaska believes that he was sleep-walking: "I thought I was in a police station. [...] I must be dreaming" (*SV* 153). With these words he questions the police's use of the word 'police station' to denote their institution. He implies that apartheid's police do not fulfil the functions that are normally carried out by the protectors of public order.

Disgusted with the world he experiences, Slaska longs for peace. He is horrified to learn that even cemeteries are segregated and that he could not be laid at rest in the city's burial grounds, but would have to be transferred back to the black townships. Threatened and oppressed by the outside world, he prefers to return to the relative safety of life in prison and hands himself over to a policeman, proving that one can be sent to jail "for nothing" (*SV* 155).

The significance of the second report lies in the fact that it not only shows the effects of apartheid on the oppressed population but also examines its effects on the group in power. Apartheid's representatives degenerate into inhumanity and become increasingly incapable of normal human interaction. They seem caught in the roles that apartheid ascribes to them and identify with them to such an extent that they are no longer able to maintain role distance.

The third and fourth reports are introduced by the stage direction: "*It is as if the play were turning its other face to the audience*" (*SV* 158). After the wit and satire of the first two episodes, the play becomes more serious and emotionally intense. Themba Ntinga's story plays in the outside world and combines narration and dramatisation to juxtapose the autobiographies of the intellectual, Leroi Williams,[27] and the urban black worker, Edward Nkosi. Themba alias Leroi explains that he was born in Sophiatown before being resettled in Dube Village, Soweto. As his parents both have jobs, he describes his family as black bourgeoisie. Although he graduated from secondary school, he only finds a position as a clerk, where he has neither responsibilities nor opportunities: "Slaving away at a dead-end job for their profit. [...] 'Clerk wanted – no brains required'" (*SV* 159). Evaluating these experiences and drawing from the knowledge he received from reading thinkers such as Fanon, Camus, Baldwin and Cleaver, he understands that "little things were only part of big things" and that "unrelated circumstances were in fact just parts of something bigger – a system" (*SV* 159). Leroi argues furthermore that "[...] at obstinate moments, these circumstances come together and trap a human being so

[27] Leroi Williams may have been named after the American Black Power activist Leroi Jones/Amiri Baraka.

tightly that for one moment the parts become the whole" (*SV* 160). The petty injustices and frustrations in daily social life are part of the system of oppression. He summarises the story of a minor character against his theory and shows that violence is sometimes the only logical conclusion: "Injuries in mines. No phones. No electricity. Unreasonable traffic cops. All parts – then suddenly ... a whole. Five years – manslaughter" (*SV* 160). This is one of *Survival*'s strongest messages: the idea that apartheid is a complex system that works on many different levels and affects the whole black population.

Leroi, now working as a theatre practitioner, provokes a shop owner and consequently is arrested. It is interesting to note that the man in Leroi's story quoted above is truly a victim trapped in the system whereas the intellectual's arrest is a consequence of his consciously provocative behaviour. After accidentally dropping a full bottle in the shop, Leroi refuses to clean up and starts threatening the Portuguese owner with political slogans ("Remember Frelimo" [*SV* 161]). His behaviour is not only impolite and provocative, but it is also dangerous to politicise every situation at a politically charged time in South Africa. This scene can be seen as criticism of the intellectual who is so immersed in politics and political theories that he is too removed from reality to react appropriately and set a good example. Instead of making use of his knowledge, he misjudges the original harmlessness of the situation and resorts instantly to violence. At the same time this occurrence also shows that South Africa has reached a stage at which it is no longer possible to react calmly. Every incident, no matter how small, becomes politicised. The inclusion of an intellectual also shows that apartheid is not considered to affect only working class blacks but that its victims come from all levels of society. This approach could be seen as rejecting the interpretation of apartheid as a class conflict rather than a struggle between races.

The dramatisation of the story of the urban black worker, Edward, vividly demonstrates a man's fall into delinquency and suggests that it is an inevitable result of living under apartheid. The strict pass laws do not make it easy for Edward's mother to apply for a work permit for her son. She is blackmailed by the black pass officer, who leaves her no alternative but to prostitute herself. Edward helplessly witnesses his mother's descent into alcoholism and domestic violence. He cannot cope with this situation: "I got a pass. Mama got me a pass. I don't know how. [*suppressed shout*] *Yes, I don't know how*" (*SV* 163). With his mother's and his own integrity violated, he is filled with anger but does not have the knowledge or the means of changing his situation. He attempts to ignore his victimisation by and simultaneous dependence on the system.

Leroi must intervene in Edward's story to prevent the man from breaking down. He teaches Edward to look at the situation rationally: "Brother Edward, learn to see it whole. Don't let it eat out your mind. Break it down. Analyse. Recognize its rules" (*SV* 164). Leroi's role here resembles that of the main representatives of the BCM, who hoped to educate and mobilise the masses. The microcosm mirrors the macrocosm. Whether they are intellectuals or urban workers, the characters' aim is to portray black society in its social variety and political unity so that blacks from different classes and backgrounds all recognise the "lawless criminality of the apartheid system" (Orkin 1991: 175). Martin Orkin asserts that the play promotes awareness of the structure of apartheid before it moves to a call for overt resistance. He claims that " [...] the play argues for a more analytic approach to the social order [...]" and suggests the need for identity construction in terms of "class analysis, worker unity [and] industrial action" (1991: 175f.).

Leroi closes his story by relating how, after a car accident, he rushed to rescue only the black chauffeur, leaving the white passengers in the car to burn to death. By analogy to Leroi's behaviour, Edward murders his mother's violently abusive black customer and ends up in prison. For both Leroi and Edward it was the loss of the family's integrity that produced an anger strong enough to lead to a desire for "*retribution*" (Orkin 1991: 175). The overt manifestation of this desire was an innovative element in the South African drama of the period. It clearly supersedes the protest plays of the early 1970s which culminated in a call for resistance (cf. *ibid.*).

The second and third episodes vividly demonstrate that life under apartheid is confining and that blacks are trapped in an all-encompassing system. The first report shows that imprisonment means degrading treatment. The other stories imply that the real prison is apartheid society itself where the black men are treated as badly as behind bars. In fact, life outside is even worse because there is no escape. This conclusion calls for change.

At the end of the third report the four main characters of the sketches address the audience directly, stating that circumstances have turned them into murderers, strikers and agitators. They proclaim that they are all "Against a system not of our making" and yoked "Under laws not of our framing" (*SV* 166). Thus every common crime becomes a political act and turns these men into political prisoners.

They realise that resistance is the only means of survival because not fighting against apartheid equals living a lie fed to them by the whites. Their movements leave no doubt that this resistance must be physical: "*As they move slowly forward towards the audience they utter a low, slowly rising scream of hatred [...], literally on top of the audience, they reach a crescendo. Blackout*" (*SV* 167).

It is important to recognise that the play's development so far is a "progressive education in the real meaning of 'survival' in South Africa" (Kavanagh 1981: xxviii). The first report focuses on a tendency to make fun and take advantage of others who are less clever than oneself. The second episode emphasises the fact that it is illogical to wait passively for change. The third section sketches the suffering of the oppressed masses as part of a system that reduces all crimes to political acts and all criminals to political prisoners. Now that action is possible, the fourth report can represent the struggle to oppose and alter the system (cf. Kavanagh 1981: xxviii).

Seth Sibanda's story, the fourth report, calls for mass resistance through a prison hunger strike. This scene shows how difficult it is to deny the fulfilment of basic human needs. The prisoners not only suffer from a lack of food but are also subjected to severe beatings by the guards and police, which they enact in mime sequences. When a prisoner is too weak to go on hunger strike and is almost killed by the others, a prisoner intervenes. In a call for solidarity he teaches the strong not to punish the weak but to support them instead. After everyone has rejected the food and taken beatings the next time around, they "*lie on the floor of their cell weakly. Then there is the quiet sound of tears. One by one they cry*" (*SV* 168). This report vividly highlights the fact that numerous hardships have to be overcome before heroes can emerge. However, as Kavanagh stresses, the possibility and act of "heroic creation" is an important and often forgotten part of survival (cf. 1981: xxix).

This final scene of the hunger strike's failure has led to criticism of the play. Director Kavanagh states that the failure can easily be seen as a "damagingly defeatist tendency at a crucial state in the play's depiction of the struggle to resist." While the scene's gentle tone and atmosphere, after the violence of the preceding section, may be sophisticated and theatrically aesthetic, he nonetheless concludes that in this case art compromises the meaning and message of the play (1985: xxix).

In my opinion, it is wrong to dismiss *Survival* because it depicts a failed strike. The play does not compromise its own call for resistance but forces the audience to acknowledge, as Orkin asserts, "the difficulties in achieving unified action" and examine "the existence of differing and conflicting subject positions within the struggle" (1991: 175). This fits in with the play's dramatisation of various characters who have different experiences and react in different ways. *Survival* advocates the need for a rational understanding of the complexities of social existence under apartheid. It is only after this point has been clearly established that the play targets the audience's emotions and, as it were, threateningly raises its fists. It argues for a strategy of resistance that incorporates society's diversity. In this the play differs from BC philosophy that tended to ignore black diversity and created a black unified, homogenous group that worked towards a black revolution. *Survival*, by contrast, suggests that only recognition of different opinions and identities can lead to mutual support and consensus, the prerequisite for unified action on the way to liberation.

4.2.2.2. Actors and characters: The break-down of theatrical illusion

The four reports show that life under apartheid is as imprisoning as life behind bars. Yet *Survival* employs another strategy to criticise apartheid's social and personal confinement: it juxtaposes this system with the theatricality and versatility of the stage. The technique of actors playing themselves before they visibly switch to the roles of prisoners, who proceed to narrate and enact stories about their prison experience, foregrounds the creativity and histrionic quality of human existence and the possibilities of role-play.

Survival begins with the sounds of the triumphal march from *Aïda* to which the four male actors enter successively. The First Actor, dressed in street clothes, runs in from the back of the theatre, hides in the audience and exclaims: "Help, help, how do I get out of this prison?" (*SV* 130). In this still very vague and introductory situation his question is open to interpretation because he does not define his usage of the word 'prison.' Different meanings are possible. The actor may be referring to the stage setting as a prison from which he, an incarcerated criminal, is attempting to escape. If this is the case, he is introducing himself as a person who has failed to adopt a social identity that conforms to society's norms. His privilege of identity construction is revoked, and he is given the title of 'prisoner.' This description immediately places him at the bottom of the social hierarchy and denies him individual development, reducing him to the function that society imposes on him. Deprived of the possibility of normal social interaction and the freedom to contribute to the shaping of his social role, the 'prisoner's' attempt to hide among the spectators is doomed to failure because his social definition stigmatises him and prevents his reintegration into society.

Furthermore, in a broader sense, the actor may be defining current apartheid society as a 'prison.' If this is correct, then the audience members are caught in the same prison environment as the First Actor. He asks how he could escape and includes the audience and, by metonymical extension, society as a whole in his questioning. For a white audience this question can be understood as a call for non-racial co-operation to overcome the racialised prison environment of apartheid South Africa, a country where neither black nor white are completely free. When playing to a black audience, this is an attempt to call for resistance to apartheid.

Thirdly, one must not forget that it is an actor in a theatre venue who is calling out for help to "get out of this prison." From this perspective the theatre and the stage are considered an imprisoning environment that confines the actors during their development of ideas. This might allude to the fact that at a time of the BCM's ascendancy in the 1970s Workshop '71's multi-racial composition and performances to white and black audiences made the group a target for harsh criticism as collaborators with whites.

Thus the play's opening invites several different interpretations of the use of "prison": the term can refer to stage reality. It can also serve as a metaphor for society or the theatre. Accordingly, the man takes on the identity of a character, a social critic and/or an actor. This role confusion is voluntary and leads to a breakdown of clear-cut definitions.

The First Actor is joined by other men who also invade the audience's space and allude to themselves as escaped convicts. Surprisingly, as if to confuse the audience, the men seem lost and inquire which theatre they are located in, explaining that they are "looking for the triumphal march in *Aïda*" (*SV* 130). Are these men lost actors, or are they escaped criminals who want to camouflage their identity by blending in with the choir of *Aïda*? Or are they social critics who emphasise the parallels of tyranny and slavery in *Aïda* and apartheid South Africa? Again, several interpretations exist simultaneously and multiply the men's identities.

Suddenly, one of the actors announces the arrival of the police. The Fourth Actor appears on the scene and introduces himself as the white Constable Visagie. He is looking for three escaped convicts who, as he claims, are disguised as actors. By their very presence the audience find themselves hiding the men from the constable and arousing his distrust: "For some time now the force has been keeping its eye on this place and [*wagging his finger suspiciously*] we've got our suspicions" (*SV* 130). Similar to Styles's classification of the spectators into co-conspirators and representatives of apartheid in *Sizwe Bansi is Dead* (see Chapter 3.4.1), Visagie also suggests the presence of traitors amongst the audience. He forces them to identify with one of the two sides, denying them the possibility of hiding in the anonymity of the dark audience space. Yet in contrast to Styles, Constable Visagie as a state representative threatens the spectators who sympathise with the escaped prisoners.

It is also worth noting how the black actor playing the constable introduces himself to the audience: "[*pointing to his black skin*] do not be deceived by my disguise. I am Constable Visagie, a white police officer" (*SV* 130). Defining his blackness as a camouflage of white skin, the white character foregrounds his manoeuvre of racial disguise. At the same time this allows the black actor to emphasise his black skin and overtly racialise his own body. Thus the actor ridicules his character's belief that he could actually pass as black. Little does Visagie realise that racial passing (cf. Robinson 1994) is not simply mastered by treating skin colour as a stage prop that can easily be donned and discarded. His heavy Afrikaans accent, authoritative tone and condescending speech give him away as white. This confirms what Morris learns in *Blood Knot*. Being white or black does not just apply to skin colour but also to one's language, behaviour and attitudes; it has become a social phenomenon. This scene then shows that blackness is not a shell around an empty core but a socially defined existence and way of life formed by cultural, economic and political circumstances. Thus without recognition of the Other in their black social identity, knowledge or appropriation of blackness is not possible. The black actor who plays the disguised constable not only mocks this character in Bhabhaesque fashion and uncovers his ignorance and chauvinism but also clearly distances himself from white behaviour. In addition, this actor shows that he can convincingly take on the role of this white constable. This proves that he has successfully observed and analysed black and white society and come to an understanding of the mechanisms that govern apartheid.

The play then shifts to a "*dreamlike*" mode in which the convicts, after their failed attempt to escape, are arrested "*ritualistically*" by the constable. Highlighting its own theatricality, this mime-like sequence dispenses with verbal or physical contact: "*Again without touching them he* [the constable] *closes the second actor's eyes, place the first actor's hands over his ears and places the third actor's hand over his mouth*" (all *SV* 131). The movements clearly symbolise arrest, gagging and blindfolding. The prisoners are pushed onto the rostrum on stage where all the prison scenes take place. This mime sequence points to the inhuman and violent prison conditions and a judicial system that denies proper defence. This image of the three men also mirrors the public's lack of awareness about the current situation.

After the initial arrest scene the four actors face the audience and present themselves with their real names (Fana, Themba, Seth and Dan) and then present each other in the roles of their characters. The play's debt to *Sizwe Bansi is Dead* is apparent in its technique of overt role-play and self-referential manifestation of theatricality (cf. Orkin 1991: 174). However, in Brechtian fashion *Survival* goes one step further by allowing the actors to stage themselves. Also, in accordance with epic conventions the dramatic space is directly characterised as a theatrical one. When an actor is not involved in a scene, he recedes to a corner of the stage area and remains visible throughout the whole production.

The actors announce that they have followed, from birth, the careers of both criminals and singers in the "Four Behind Bars Quartet." In their roles as prisoners they claim to be "working on something" (*SV* 133), playing creative, witty word games and charades. Suddenly, the actor Seth slips back into the role of the constable and confronts the prisoners:

> SETH [*heavy Afrikaans accent*]: What's going on here?
>
> FANA/THEMBA: This is a play.
>
> SETH: You call this a play – robbing people of their money? It's against the law.
>
> *He handcuffs Themba to Fana.* (*SV* 133)

Apartheid society, represented again by the constable, identifies these men as convicts and denies them the freedom to define themselves as actors. The official appropriates the right to define the word 'play' and what 'proper' acting is. The officer's behaviour reveals that he cannot overcome his one-sided, prejudiced perspective. For him the men remain criminals ("You're not actors, you're terrorists" [*SV* 132]) and thus continue to deserve stigmatisation (cf. Goffman 1963). He highlights the fact that their police record determines their position in this totalitarian society: their activity cannot be defined as playacting but as that of petty criminals. He merely claims that they are *disguised* as actors and denies the black artists existence in this role. The stage directions then indicate that the actors "*drop this charade*" (*SV* 134) and address the audience:

> DAN: [...] there's a whole lot of people here [*pointing to the audience*] who've paid money to see what goes on *inside* there [*pointing to the rostrum*]. We're going to show them what's happening *out there* [*points in direction of the audience and the outside world*] – right under their noses.
>
> THEMBA: But is that sufficient? Don't you think they ought to know what's happening in there? [*points to the rostrum*]
>
> DAN: [...] And so we decided to act out the viewpoint of each. (*SV* 134)

Again, the significance of this dialogue lies in its overt acknowledgement of the theatrical reality of the situation. The actors behind the characters step forward, and the illusion of the action is interrupted in favour of self-referentiality. By announcing the juxtaposition of different prison experiences, the actors emphasise the exemplary status and the collective implication of their individual viewpoints. In Brechtian fashion they appropriate theatre for social analysis and comment.

When acting as prisoners, the actors slip into different roles to narrate and dramatise their four 'reports' on prison life. However, at the end of each episode the characters discuss what they have just enacted. This technique of re-presenting the episodes shows that identity is socially constituted. By telling each other stories, the prisoners secure for themselves a play-internal audience. Identity is constructed in front of others who act as witnesses and as a social frame. Going one step further, the audience - and by extension society - as witness of the stage action enlarges this social frame. In Orkin's words the subject is socially positioned instead of being privatised. He evaluates the techniques used in *Survival*:

> Importantly, in all four reports, while interiority is not denied to the speakers, their identity as well as their past is presented as socially dependent: what they 'report' to one another is offered, within the framework of the play, for communal evaluation and discussion. [...] By this means, as well as in its awareness of the social context of language and action, the play's links with its audience is [*sic*] underlined. (1991: 175f.)

A close relationship is established with the audience when the men address the spectators. So, instead of waiting for the audience to draw their own conclusions, the characters didactically direct the spectators' interpretations.

After the fourth report the actors take on their own personal identities again and talk about the "joys of life and the fears of death." In Kavanagh's opinion, this points to an important statement, namely, that "[...] for the oppressed, survival is not only a grim endurance but also [...] an act of heroic creation" (1981: xxix). This penultimate scene portrays the humanity and the culture of the blacks and allows them to challenge an inhuman and impoverished oppressor. The director considers *Survival* an original play: firstly, it goes beyond protesting against the system in that it calls on people to act to change it; and secondly, it defines survival exactly as this "act of heroic creation," an aspect of the South African experience that he does not see emphasised enough (cf. 1981: xxviiif.).

In the closing scene the actors directly face the audience and summarise the thesis of their play: if prison destroys and the system is like a prison, then society should disintegrate as well. However, it does not because the "strength lies with the people, who carry with them in their lives the justification for the struggle – the victory that is [...] SURVIVAL!" (*SV* 170). In a dramatically effective final gesture the actors raise their fists and march out of the audience singing "We go for(ward)" (*SV* 171). That this ending has been considered "undeveloped" and lacking sufficient discussion (cf. Shava 1989: 138) is surprising. After all, this final message summarises the idea that the play has been developing throughout: the humanity of the oppressed is the key element that allows them to live and actively fight for survival in the face of the inhuman oppressor.

4.3. *Bopha!* and apartheid's infiltration of the family

> Can you see your job has made you an enemy of your own family.
>
> Zwelakhe to his father in *Bopha!*[28]

Percy Mtwa's 1985 play, *Bopha!* (Zulu for 'arrest'), examines the life under apartheid of three male African family members with differing beliefs. By playing out father against son and brother against brother, Mtwa is not only innovative in confronting the characters with their conflicting familial loyalties but, in addition, places the men against a situation of growing unrest in the townships of 1976. Thus he forces the family members to deal with the consequences of apartheid. Mtwa shows that apartheid is more than the experience of the dichotomous world view of

[28] *BP* 256. References to *Bopha!* are flagged *BP*.

black versus white and that it can blur the fine line which separates the perpetrators from the victims. The family comes to represent the larger issues of society.

4.3.1. Percy Mtwa's views on theatre

Percy Mtwa says that he created his plays for a township audience. He explains that with his group of actors, the Earth Players, his goal was to start a theatre in one of the Johannesburg townships in order to give an impetus to the creation of a theatre industry with proper facilities. He believes that it was necessary to bring theatre to the townships because very few Africans could or wanted to watch a play in an institution such as the Market Theatre. Mtwa emphasises the importance of theatre for society and the necessity for the people to understand "what theatre is all about and what it should look like and what are the conditions [*sic*]" (1988: 168f.). He argues that it is a prerequisite that people recognise what theatre represents in their society before a healthy township theatre can be developed.

> [...] theatre is a social product. It is what we call culture. For that reason it will reflect the values and the viewpoints of that society from which it springs. And, for it to do it successfully, it must also grow with the culture of the people. Even though people would regard theatre as something of an enjoyment, or just entertainment, o.k., that is fine, but that quality of entertainment has to be enriched, it has to be made better so that it improves with the people and the people's consciousness open up [*sic*] so that people can identify good and bad. (1988: 169)

Mtwa asserts that the stagnant quality of Gibson Kente's musicals in the late 1970s did not respond in content or style to the developing consciousness of the people and the increasingly confrontational period: "[...] he did not take the people further, but people wanted to grow" (1988: 170). Kente's fear of harassment and his compliance with apartheid restrictions seem to be the cause. By contrast, Mtwa, who started as a Kente student before moving on to develop his own style, displays a high degree of courage and belief in himself and his ideals:

> Apartheid is an illusion, it is just racism by law. And it is only when we start looking at it as a reality that it can stop us from doing certain things. But if you look at it as an illusion it cannot stop you from doing what you want. You just go and get what you want while it is existing. But you go and get what you want the way you want it. (1988: 168)

Mtwa believes that he and his theatre partner Mbongeni Ngema succeeded in fulfilling this demand and making revolutionary theatre with their successful and highly praised play *Woza Albert!* (with Barney Simon, 1981) because it "began to open up other possibilities that are available for theatre in the townships" (1988: 170).

Christopher Balme considers Mtwa (in co-operation with Ngema in *Woza Albert!*) one of the theatre's prime practitioners who introduced an aesthetic of movement to South African township theatre by adopting a new theatre method: the transformation the body into the dominant sign transmitter of the performance (cf. 1995: 184, 189). Eckhard Breitinger maintains that Mtwa has successfully created a "radical actor's theatre" (2003²: 140) that the dramatist himself proudly identifies as pure township theatre of quality (cf. Mtwa 1988: 166). One such play is *Woza Albert!*. It was revolutionary in that it crossed the barrier between township and city and thus became more effective in reaching a larger black audience than did a play such as *Sizwe Bansi is Dead*. Mtwa confirms that the latter, despite its revolutionary impact, "did not make it in the townships" (1988: 167).[29]

Percy Mtwa's long-term aim has been to profit from black and white collaboration to make a contribution to the development of "a multi-racial theatre in that country which will in those days reflect the values and the viewpoints and the future of that country which will bring us hope as a people" (1988: 174).

4.3.2. *Bopha!* – the play

In *Bopha!*, his first self-authored play, Percy Mtwa experimented with his style of actor's township theatre. It premiered in 1985 at the Market Theatre in Johannesburg. Set in the explosive year of 1976 at the time of the student uprising in Soweto, *Bopha!* looks at the conflict between a father, his son and the father's brother. The father, a successful policeman, enforces the government's strict laws and profits from job security and the promise of retirement benefits. He is aptly named Njandini, which is an "abusive term for black policemen, meaning watchdog or bulldog" (Breitinger 2003²: 147). The numerous Afrikaans expressions that pervade his speech in this English-language play suggest that he identifies with his

---

[29] David Coplan gives a possible explanation for *Sizwe Bansi's* failure to communicate to a township audience: "Black playgoers, however, complain that despite the high quality of *Sizwe* and the strength of its protest against homeland policy, influx control, and the pass laws, it is too complex in structure and expression, too 'talky', and too unmusical – in short, too Western in form – to be worth seeing more than once. As one theatrical promoter in Port Elizabeth told me, Africans might return any number of times to Kente's *Too Long*, but *Sizwe* was not 'a renewable experience'." (1985: 215).

superiors' language. His son, Zwelakhe, is a radical student leader who opposes the Afrikaans education system and fights against his father's ideals. The policeman's brother, Naledi, comes to the city from the homelands to find a job, a hopeless undertaking as his pass lacks the required stamps. The policeman offers his brother 'freedom' and valid documents if he agrees to join the police force. Duma Ndlovu asserts that the growing unrest in the townships forces the three men to take clear positions in the struggle. They must decide between their political and ideological convictions and their family loyalties. The activist son, who refuses to adopt his father's position, is arrested and sent to jail. The father and his brother are ordered to suppress the violent outbursts in the township, but the latter refuses to shoot at "rebels" in his own community. Instead, by arresting whites and questioning racist laws, the brother breaks the behavioural code he is forced to adhere to and is dismissed. When Njandini's house is burnt down by angry black protesters, he realises that his belief and actions have turned him into an "enemy of his own people" (Ndlovu 1986: 227).

What makes *Bopha!* interesting in its portrayal of apartheid and resistance to the system is that it dramatises differing subject positions on both the public and private levels. The three men act according to the social roles they have adopted. However, the demands of these roles are incompatible with the roles they play in family life. This inevitably leads to conflicts on various levels.

Bopha! is composed of seventeen scenes which consist mostly of short dialogues between a total of three main black and twelve minor black and white characters played by three black actors. The scenes are loosely connected and episodic but linked in content to form an evolving story line.[30] In each scene Mtwa introduces a particular tableau or image in photographic style whilst retaining a dramatic presentation (cf. 1988: 174). He emphasises that his ideal is "pure drama" which he contrasts with narration, concluding, "In *Bopha!* I managed to avoid narration a lot, because somewhere I find that sometimes a person can be dragging by giving his

---

[30] In an interview with Percy Mtwa Breitinger calls the structure of *Bopha!* a "sequence of scenes [that] is loosely arranged as on a string," a description that I agree with. Mtwa, however, does not like the term "loosely structured" because to him this refers to a succession of independent images. He insists on the fact that *Bopha!* presents a "sequence that people will follow" (Mtwa 1988: 174).

story as narration. So what I did here, I created the drama, but we have narrations that come across to lead us" (1988: 173).[31]

Structurally the play juxtaposes episodes of apartheid's representatives in action with scenes that dramatise resistance to apartheid. *Bopha!* alternates between implicit criticism in its ironic portrayal of supporters or defenders of the system (Njandini) and overt opposition to apartheid through both a politically radical (Zwelakhe) and more liberal perspective (Naledi).

4.3.2.1. Executing the rules of apartheid

Bopha! opens with a graduation ceremony at the South African Police School. In honour of the occasion an Afrikaner Commissioner, played by one of the three black actors, gives a short speech with "*pride and arrogance*" (*BP* 230). He measures the effectiveness of the South African Police Force by its number of arrests and defines the country's isolation as a result of foreign jealousy over this 'success': "The whole world hates Suid Africa today because of the clever ways in which our policemen know just when to prevent crime and other disturbances from going too far!" (*BP* 230). This speech reveals a highly chauvinistic attitude and clearly defines South Africa as a police state that classifies everyone who does not actively collaborate with the police as a potential criminal or agitator. The police motto "We serve and protect" (*BP* 231) is ironic because the officers offer protection to the white minority group rather than to the people in general.

Njandini, a policeman by conviction, explains to the audience, after a quarrel with his politically active son, his reasons for identifying with his profession: "I'm proud to be a sergeant today. A true gentleman. A man amongst men. A policeman of strength and loyalty" (*BP* 233). His identity construction revolves around his notions of masculinity which include model behaviour, comradeship, strength and respect for his superiors. This attitude can be compared to the concept of masculinity that developed in late nineteenth-century imperial Britain. Alastair Pennycook describes it as "a hardened, militarized, physical games-oriented masculinity that was linked to physical prowess, a spartan existence, a rejection of all that came to be defined as 'feminine' (caring, intellectual pursuits), and patriotism" (1998: 63). He comments that this notion of masculinity included

---

[31] Matsemela Manaka draws a similar distinction when he emphasises the effectiveness of showing over telling (cf. 1997b: 110; Chapter 4.4.1).

"aspects of imperial command" such as courage, endurance, assertion, control and self-control as well as "aspects of imperial 'manliness'," which he identifies as dominance, deference, the ability to follow commands and the ethic of loyalty and obedience (*ibid.*).[32]

It is also interesting to note that Njandini believes that his actions characterise him as a "gentleman." The concept of the 'gentleman' is traditionally class-based and reflects the views of the influential social class that has the power to define this notion. With this self-definition Njandini emphasises the fact that he acts and lives according to the codes of conduct and convictions of that class or group of society that he serves, namely, apartheid society.[33] The police force is identified as an organisation that shares and protects society's value system. It can thus be seen as a microcosm of society. Njandini's identity is firmly rooted in a system which provides all role behaviour and definitions of self for him. He need not negotiate or adapt his identity on a daily basis but is guided and protected by this system. To enjoy this support he must remain loyal and accept the place that he is accorded in the hierarchy.

As mentioned above, a central element of Njandini's self-definition is his emphasis on masculinity. He convinces his brother, Naledi, to join the police force by arguing that he is trying to make a man of him. Njandini also points out that Naledi could then live in an urban environment and would not have to lead a rural life and remain confined to the homelands simply because he does not have a valid work permit. When Naledi refuses to join the force, Njandini exclaims: "Back to Qwaqwa. On top of the mountains and ride those horses until your bum is red like a monkey" (*BP* 234). His words characterise life in the homelands as savage and bestial and suggest that it reduces humans to primates. In his eyes city and country form a clear dichotomy: 'urban' symbolises 'civilised' and 'human,' whereas 'rural' connotes 'uncivil' and 'sub-human.' This view represents what Loren

---

[32] The games ethic that developed in late-Victorian England's public schools and spread to organisations such as the Boy Scouts led to a male education that oriented itself on these qualities and produced "generations of boys ready to take up their positions in the colonial service" (Pennycook 1998: 63). Allen Warren (1987) and John K. MacKenzie (1987) also discuss concepts of masculinity derived from notions of imperialism in late nineteenth-century England. Both critics focus on R. S. S. Baden-Powell. During his involvement in the Anglo-Boer War of 1899-1902 he developed ideas of training for boys on the imperial frontier, published as *Scouting for Boys* in 1908.

[33] This suggests that apartheid is not only a racial structure but is also based on class distinctions (cf. Kavanagh 1985: 7-9, 156-9; Manaka 1997a: 45f.).

Kruger calls the "classic modern paradigm where [...] the city represents progress and the agency of mature citizens against what Marx famously called the 'idiocy of rural life'" (1997: 566). One must bear in mind that Njandini does not want Naledi to merely come to work in the city - he must actively collaborate with the system and subscribe to its ideology. This differentiation fits in with Kruger's assertion that the post-colonial city, of which she considers Johannesburg an example, reversed the city-country-paradigm. It came to signify the "threat of barbarism," represented by the urbanising black masses that influx control could not prevent from assembling in the cities (1997: 566). All these aspects point to the fact that Njandini shows he believes in a system in which a spatial proximity to the ruling group must be supplemented by an ideological proximity before a savage can develop into a true 'man.'

In the private domain Njandini's behaviour towards his son, Zwelakhe, is characterised by his adherence to the same ideals and norms displayed in his public life. He exercises his authority over his son and treats him as a subject that must obey the rules laid down by his superior: "[...] in this house you're going to follow in my footsteps. When I say left, I want your left foot there [...]" (*BP* 233). There is to be no discussion or intellectual reflection under his roof. Njandini accepts without question what the police and official state ideology prescribed for him. Hence he does not understand his son's position as a student leader and political activist. Njandini does not want to listen to his son's arguments; he perceives Zwelakhe to be critical of apartheid's practices and thus a threat to his identity. He distances himself from his rebellious son by calling him a "fucking school boy" (*BP* 233), believing that his son's childish rebellion must be met with strict control and authoritarian rule (cf. Pennycook 1998: 60). Njandini behaves towards his son in his public role as policeman and protector of apartheid. He projects his role norms onto his private role of father: instead of supporting and guiding his son, he is authoritarian and sees his son as an immature dependent with erring political convictions.

In a later discussion with his brother Njandini says that he is proud of his son's education because he believes it will enable him to acquire a good position in the police force: "This boy is educated man. One, two, three, Major!" (*BP* 242). Although he knows that Zwelakhe is a student activist, he naively expects his son to become a policeman.

Njandini fully identifies with the police force and the ideology of apartheid: "The law is the law. [...] The police are the protectors of the law and the law is made by the white man there in Pretoria" (*BP* 233). It is indicative of his total identification that he does not even question the validity of the laws although he is aware of their racial origin. In Dreitzel's terminology Njandini identifies with the "aggressor" and thus is incapable of voicing criticism or maintaining distance to the role senders and role norms. The external pressure is so strong and the norms are so dominant that it becomes impossible for him to develop any form of individual behaviour. Because of the totality of expectations of behaviour in the police force, he is no longer able to exercise the critical role distance which is necessary to actively shape and adapt a role (*Rollenengagement*) and guarantee personal contribution to the role (*Ich-Leistung*). In fact, disturbed role behaviour is inevitable. Dreitzel argues that roles related to organisations (for example, the role of a soldier, a functionary or, in Njandini's case, a policeman) have a repressive structure that derives from the ruling character of these institutions and their constraints of action. Disrupted behaviour that arises in these roles can be characterised as 'forced ritualism.' This term refers to situations in which an individual follows prescribed role behaviour without reflecting on the goal or object of their actions. This seems to be the case with Njandini (cf. Dreitzel 1980[3]: 228; 240-46).

Furthermore, as both son and grandson of policemen Njandini's social origin can be used to explain his lack of role distance. He was raised by men who also closely identified with their profession and, fusing their roles as officer with that of father, educated him according to the role expectations addressed to a policeman. Hence he was taught to value his function in society instead of his identity as an individual.

Percy Mtwa also portrays Njandini on duty in the townships. When rioting breaks out, Njandini and one of his superiors are involved in the township turmoil. Back at the police station he recounts how his boss was hurt and had to go to hospital. The officer at the station, who was not there to witness the events, is prejudiced against Njandini and reproaches him for failing to come to his boss's aid. Njandini stands up for himself: "[...] if I was not there he would be dead. [...] I've got 15 kids in the van and you say I ran away. I'm not a coward" (*BP* 253). By emphasising that his initiative saved his boss's life and that he worked effectively in arresting the children, he defends himself against accusations of failure. It is interesting to note that he also distances himself from character traits that negate his image of masculinity: he refuses to be associated with cowardice and points out that he remained loyal and helped his superior while taking vigorous action against their opponents (thus successfully handling the intra-role conflict[34] he was exposed to). Again, he clearly identifies with the ethos of the police force and insists that he behaved according to his prescribed role in the organisation.

4.3.2.2. Apartheid's powerlessness

In order to put Njandini's behaviour into perspective and to portray the overall position of the police force in South African society, *Bopha!* features several scenes that show police officers in conflict with Africans. In contrast to Njandini's depiction of himself and, by extension, the police as a powerful institution that deploys strong action, Mtwa also offers a very different picture. For example, the dramatist creates a scene with the arrogant Captain van Donder. The Captain is on the phone talking to his wife and reports that there is trouble at the home farm, a small barb that suggests he is not able to keep his personal employees under strict control.[35] This can be read as a sign of impotence on a minor scale which points to a general helplessness of the rulers vis-à-vis the resisting masses.

In the middle of their telephone conversation van Donder is approached by the black intellectual Styles. Styles (his name probably a tribute to *Sizwe Bansi is Dead's* versatile and cunning photographer) has come to inquire about the fate of his missing brother. He uses complex, stylistically elevated language to express his discontent with the police's methods of arresting and incarcerating men without informing the family members of their fate. In his condemnation of the police he implies that many of apartheid's political victims supposedly commit suicide and that everybody knows these deaths are often not voluntary acts. The Captain reacts verbally with hatred and anger not only because Styles's knowledge represents a threat to him but also because he does not know how to defend himself and discuss this matter calmly. He has learnt to take and give orders in the police force but not to discuss and analyse a particular topic: he lacks basic democratic communication skills. In addition, his outburst reveals an inferiority complex: "Die swart engelsman die bliksem! [The Black Englishman, the bastard!]" (*BP* 247). His racism results from his fear of being inferior to a black man. He feels threatened,

---

[34] An intra-role conflict is a conflict arising from the incompatible expectations that exist in the various sectors of one and the same role (cf. Dreitzel 1980[3]: 44).

[35] This aspect contradicts the Afrikaner idealisation of the farm as a *locus* of purity, isolation and tranquillity (cf. Kruger 1997: 566).

his masculinity is challenged. By verbally degrading Styles, he is able to give vent to his frustration and assert himself. It is interesting to note that he uses "Englishman" as a derogatory term. Firstly, this points to the fact that the Afrikaners and the English are also engaged in power struggles and regard each other as rivals. Secondly, the Afrikaner National Party felt threatened by the African urban intellectual élite that chose English as its *lingua franca*. The vibrant urban cultural life, symbolised by the hybrid Sophiatown of the 1950s (see Chapter 5.3), defied apartheid norms, particularly the concept of racial purity and the policy of separate development in rural 'homelands' (cf. Kruger 1997: 566; Coplan 1985: 214). Thirdly, by calling a black man 'English,' he confirms that language and culturally determined behaviour are acquired socially and are not a natural, strategically essential quality (cf. Spivak). This view explains the alleged 'necessity' of separate development which aimed to keep Africans in a subaltern position. By locating blacks at a distance from white society, the ruling group actually admits that because role behaviour is a social phenomenon, blacks could integrate white society by learning and adapting to its norms and roles. This implies that the government recognises the fact that blacks are not essentially inferior but can be considered 'uncivilised' as long as their social norms do not conform to the 'white' normative matrix by which they are judged.

The reduction of police power is also presented in an encounter between the Captain and a woman, Magogo, who protests against the destruction of her township. This scene depicts and heavily criticises the awful conditions in the townships and makes the government responsible for the prevailing situation. Magogo's case illustrates that documents issued by the local government no longer carry validity. Because the mayor and councillors have resigned or fled, the township is left without political representatives. Police patrols have taken over, creating havoc with tear gas bombs. The Captain is incapable of assisting Magogo. He tells her not to come to the police station to complain because the presence of the police vans is "not [her] fucking business" and adds that she is "*maal*" [*sic*, Afrikaans for 'mad'] (*BP* 248). It is revealing that van Donder calls her 'mad.' By denying her the faculty of reason, he stigmatises and marginalises her and asserts both her inferiority and alterity.[36] However, his behaviour shows that he cannot

[36] As Foucault points out in *Madness and Civilization*, by the end of the Enlightenment mad individuals were confined to the asylum and treated according to the equation "Madness is childhood" while the man of reason saw himself as an adult who directed both domination and

control the situation and that he perceives this as a reduction of his authority. Thus he compensates his loss of power with verbal violence. The inherent irony is that by emphasising Magogo's madness, van Donder actually also agrees with her complaints, for, as a literary trope, the madman or the fool traditionally functions as the "guardian of truth" (Foucault 1965 [1961]: 14).

In another scene Mtwa stages the aftermath of a student riot in which the police officer Piet was, as he claims, hit by a stone and in panic opened fire. He relates how he ended up shooting children in the back and wounding them. Zwelakhe's words, voiced in the scene directly prior to Piet's appearance, question the validity of the latter's action: "[...] there is never any violence until the police come. These people are killing us" (*BP* 251).

Back at the station Captain van Donder reproaches Piet for his action and tells him that he must bear the consequences and justify his deed in public. The Captain's reaction shows that the golden rule of the South African Police is to shoot only when attacked. In this context the officer's words of self-defence are illuminating: "It was a matter of life or death Captain. Those kids are treating the situation like a carnival. Burning of our policemen and burning of innocent people is seen as some kind of fire works display. I thought that laughing must come to an end" (*BP* 252). Piet presents himself as a guardian of honour and moral integrity in the face of savage immoral minors who do not recognise, and even go so far as to defy, the value of human life. These remarks are, of course, extremely ironic because the accusation reflects upon those who voice it.

Piet feels threatened by the school children and their actions and characterises the politically active teenagers as irresponsible adventurers. They are, he says, only interested in having fun and creating a spectacle or staging a "carnival." His use of the term 'carnival' is interesting because it evokes a folk culture that has traditionally stood in opposition to official festive acts. Mikhail Bakhtin argues with regard to the European mediaeval carnival:

> As opposed to the official feast, one might say that carnival celebrated temporary liberation from the prevailing truth and from the established order; it marked the suspension of all hierarchical rank, privileges, norms, and prohibitions. Carnival was the true feast of time, the feast of becoming, change, and renewal. It was hostile to all that was immortalized and completed (1984: 10).

---

destination of the mad (1965: 252; cf. 252f.). This parallels the theme of the necessity of colonial dominance over the alleged savage child.

Seen in this light, carnivals as forms of secular, popular festivals invert conventional social hierarchies and offer a critique of the 'high' or official culture. As Peter Stallybrass and Allon White maintain, this approach to the carnivalesque automatically leads to a model of culture that includes a high/low binarism and the idea that an unofficial expression always implies a pre-existing official counterpart (cf. 1986: 16). They point out that 'carnival' is no longer used only as a ritual feature but also as an "epistemological category." They assert that the notion of the Bakhtinian carnivalesque has been applied to "literatures produced in a colonial or neo-colonial context where the political difference between the dominant and the subordinate culture is particularly charged" (1986: 6, 11).[37]

Piet's classification of the children's actions as 'carnival' points to their display of violence as an overt form of political protest against the white establishment. In contrast to Piet's narrated account of the events, the film version of *Bopha*[38] depicts several scenes in which the young adults sing songs of defiance and perform war-dance-like moves in their confrontation with the police. For Piet this group of youngsters cannot be controlled or called to obey what apartheid ideology defines as reason and order. Their assembly appears to him as a Bakhtinian grotesque body: "It is an image of impure corporeal bulk with its orifices (mouth, flared nostrils, anus) yawning wide and its lower regions (belly, legs, feet, buttocks and genitals) given priority over its upper regions (head, 'spirit,' reason)" (Stallybrass & White 1986: 9). The body of Bakhtin's "grotesque realism" is a positive concept that signifies fertility, growth and abundance as well as the collective body of all the ancestral people (cf. Bakhtin, 1984: 18f). In this light it is not surprising that Piet stigmatises the carnivalesque as "the vulgar practices of a superstitious and crude populace, [...] a negative phenomenon" (Stallybrass & White 1986: 9).

---

[37] In their examination of the Carnival as an important influence on post-apartheid drama, Gilbert and Tompkins trace the development of the Trinidadian Carnival as an expression of black culture and a rebellion against colonial authority. They explain that the "spirit of protest was evident not only in the traditional calipso [*sic*] lyrics and the various masquerades which satirised white society but also in a pattern of disorderly behaviour that culminated in riots during the 1881 and 1884 Carnivals" (1996: 79f.). In Trinidad's post-emancipation era ritualised forms of conflict such as the stick fight signified an important element in Carnival. Their performances were in part designed to challenge the repressive forces of law and order. The critics conclude that this form of Carnival in its historical development contains a theatre of anti-colonial resistance (cf. 1996: 81f.).

[38] The film *Bopha!* (1993) was directed by Morgan Freeman. Danny Glover plays the role of Njandini.

The fact that Piet feels threatened by the children's laughter can also be explained by the idea of carnival laughter. Bakhtin asserts that this laughter is "ambivalent: it is gay, triumphant, and at the same time mocking, deriding. It asserts and denies, it buries and revives" (1984: 11f.). This laughter can also be described in terms of Bhabhaesque mimicry. In both cases it represents a denial of authority and thus justifies, in Piet's opinion, his excessively violent reaction as a manifestation of the dominant group's authority and power. However, the fact that the police feel compelled to exert such brutality can again be seen as a sign of its impotence in the face of a strong opposition to the regime.

4.3.2.3. The power of resistance

Mtwa stages the opposition between the ruling group and the oppressed masses by depicting two brothers in a professional conflict brought about by different world views. Njandini is a policeman by conviction and believes in his work whereas Naledi joins the police force despite his moral condemnation of this institution. His passbook is not in order so that joining the force is the only possibility if he is to stay in Johannesburg legally. The irony of this situation is that Naledi was born in Johannesburg as a member of the Sotho ethnic group. According to apartheid legislation, such a person does not 'exist' because each ethnic group is allocated to its homeland. However, his passbook is not legal in his designated homeland because he was neither born there nor has ever lived there (cf. Breitinger 2003[2]: 147). Naledi quotes his police school graduation class: "We all came from the homeland. Some of us were recruited from the mines and we all knew that the only way to beat the influx control was to join the police force" (*BP* 231). This severely criticises the economic implications of the government's homeland policy for the African inhabitants. Lack of jobs in the rural areas forces the men and women to move to the cities in search of work. It was ironic that some men had to take up a profession like joining the police force, that allowed them to support their families while forcing them to work against their own people. For instance, the men learn at the police school that they are to arrest without warrant individuals who are in contravention of the influx control law. Naledi's experience shows that even with a valid pass it is not easy to find a job. In a scene with a potential employer he is refused work because he has no qualifications. The employer explains: "I don't take people with no qualification no more! No more! You people are no good! No good! I give one a job, plus free accomodation [*sic*] tomorrow you tell the police. I get into serious trouble. I pay big money man" (*BP* 235). This speech is critical of the government for preventing the African population from education and thus obtaining job qualifications. The salaries are, in contrast to the employer's claim, exploitatively low. All these measures are implemented to keep blacks at the bottom of the economic ladder. The result of all this is, as Naledi learns, "The law says if you find a black man who does not have qualification '*Bopha*!'" (*BP* 239).

Naledi is also confronted with clichés derived from colonial discourse such as the injunction that black men are promiscuous and licentious. At the police academy the sergeant tells the men: "Welcome to the SAP [South African Police] Training College. This is not Sun City where you dance with the naked women all night long" (*BP* 237).

Naledi's ideological position characterises him as a supporter of a society in which blacks have their rightful place. Much to the dismay of his police academy training officer and later on his superior, Naledi voices opinions that revolve around the topic of equality in the face of the law. He must learn that "the law says do not arrest a white man *finish and klaar*," that "a white peace officer is his senior irrespective of rank" and that despite the revocation of the Immorality Act, the police still arrests its offenders, a practice from which he clearly distances himself (*BP* 238f.). When Naledi is accepted into the police force, he carries a default on his record regarding his 'heretic' ideas. The Captain warns him that his salary depends on his conformity to the prescribed ideology. Njandini confirms: "in this Police Station we speak one language: BOPHA!" (*BP* 241). Apart from pointing to strict police action and increasing brutality, this quotation also emphasises the importance of complete identification with the role of the police force under apartheid. All police officers belong to the same group and identify with "we" and "one language." Deviation from the ideals of the group is not acceptable because it compromises the efficiency of the institution. Naledi represents what Goffman calls an "in-group deviant" which signifies that he is deviant relative to the ideals of a concrete group. However, it also means that to a certain degree his "intensive if ambivalent inclusion" (1963: 142) to the group secures him group support against outside attack. Once his behaviour becomes deviant to an extent where the group cannot maintain its integrity while supporting him, he must be excluded.

Despite all the warnings he receives, Naledi attracts the censure of his superiors. On learning that a black man has been arrested for using a white toilet, Naledi concludes that he can arrest a white man for urinating in public. This makes him the target of his victim's threats of revenge. His brother, Njandini, prefers not to get too involved in such a situation in order to avoid trouble: "when I see a white man committing a crime, [...] I close one eye and dial 99 Squad car" (*BP* 245). This shows again that the police work according to apartheid's double standard and effectively strike against black people while whites enjoy a large degree of freedom to act as they wish. Naledi defies this double standard with his arrest of the white man and fights for equal treatment of the races. He repeatedly distinguishes himself as a policeman who works for and not against his own people. He sincerely wants to help both Magogo and Styles by sending them to the more influential Captain and thus earns additional default points on his behaviour record. He is also reprimanded for inciting policemen to ask for wage increases which the Captain defines as his incentive to "form a trade union" (*BP* 249). Naledi's actions and opinions clearly show that he does not primarily support Black Power as propagated by the Black Consciousness Movement and represented by his nephew Zwelakhe. Yet Naledi does agree with equal political, social and economic treatment of blacks and whites before the law. This seems to suggest that he takes a non-racial view and accepts the co-existence and integration of the different racial groups.

Naledi must come to realise that his attempts at treating all individuals as legally equal fail to influence the Captain's or Njandini's way of thinking. These officers remain, as Naledi says, "obstinate" (*BP* 250). Discussions, arguments and exemplary behaviour on his part are ineffective and end by getting him into trouble. He finally understands that he will not be able to educate and change the men with whom he is working. In the end his fight for black rights leads to his arrest and dismissal from the force. The police force is too firmly rooted in the system of apartheid and its ideology for one individual to initiate change from the inside as an in-group deviant.

In contrast to Naledi, the third main character, Njandini's son Zwelahke, takes an ultimately more successful approach to exercising resistance. Son and father stand in clear opposition. In the family sphere the son revolts against the father; on a general social level the young rebels against the old; and on the political level the activist student challenges the state and its authority which is protected by the police (cf. Breitinger 2003[2]: 147). It is striking that Njandini never really takes his son seriously. Although he admits that he is afraid to walk past Zwelakhe's school, he gives the impression that he does not want to acknowledge how seriously his son is involved in the struggle.

It is only when riots break out in the township and Zwelakhe is arrested for public violence and distributing pamphlets and T-shirts that Njandini must open his eyes to reality and accept the fact that his son is a committed activist. Zwelakhe is arrested for his activism as a "communist" (*BP* 254) and transported to the station where he not only refuses to collaborate with the police but to Njandini's embarrassment openly displays his commitment to the cause: he clenches his fist and salutes, keeping his fist raised even when his father tries to pull his arm down. Although Zwelakhe primarily sees himself as a political fighter, he still recognises Njandini in the personal role of his father, not just in the role of a state representative: "Policemen were waiting outside the church with guns, and also waiting outside the church with a gun was my father. He knew I was inside the Church. And I was singing" (*BP* 251). It is the son who finally manages to "'save'" his father (Breitinger 2003[2]: 148). While Njandini successfully deals with the demonstrators in a strict and authoritative fashion, thus adequately fulfilling his professional role, he has utterly failed to play his private roles as father and member of the black community. The Captain tells Njandini that his house in the township has been set alight, that people are demanding his son's release and that Zwelakhe's mother has been hit by a stray bullet (cf. *BP* 255). Njandini, trapped in his role as protector of apartheid laws and ideology, naively and blindly blames these incidents on his son and his involvement in Black Power. Zwelakhe explains:

> ZWEL: [...] Can you see if they found you at home, you would have been roasted alive. Can you see your job has made you an enemy of your own family. Right now I don't have any home at all because of your job.
>
> NJA: It's your Black Power [...]!
>
> ZWEL: It's your job baba [papa]! (*BP* 256)

Njandini's estrangement from his own family and community makes it hard for him to understand that the violence directed against his home in the township is targeted against him and not his activist son. This violence against Njandini shows that in the heyday of the BCM the African people defined their identity in terms of race, including every black person in their group. However, this identification is not a choice but an obligation. In times of the increasing radicalisation and militarisation of BC, failure to belong leads to the transformation of a brother to an enemy of his people. After his house has been burnt down, Njandini is literally as displaced ideologically as he is dislocated from his community. Zwelakhe and Naledi succeed in making him accept that the white regime is setting him against his own brothers. What is more, the (white) police force will not protect him if his life is in danger.

Naledi points out: "Where's Van Donder? Van Donder doesn't stay in the township. He's got his waterbed in the farm" (*BP* 256).[39] Brother and son finally convince Njandini to join the wave of people – a community councillor in Alexandra, six policemen in Pretoria and teachers nation-wide – who are resigning from their service to the state. Thus Njandini's resignation is defined as an act of solidarity with other opponents of the regime and can be seen as his reintegration into his family and community. *Bopha!* shows, as Andries Oliphant commented about a play by Victor Shingwenyana, that solidarity among the exploited and oppressed is not achieved "simply by virtue of a shared primordial racial identity or unproblematic class position. Unity is something to be struggled for in the context of multiple and divisive subject positions and experiences" (1992: 26f.).

The effectiveness of *Bopha!*, as Orkin explains, lies in the fact that it "portray[s] the subject [...] in the stance of continual anger and readiness to resist" while it still acknowledges the "exploitative and oppressive nature of existing relations from humanist perspectives." The play calls for a "growth in consciousness of political exploitation" and argues for a "unified stance within a situation of virtual civil war." It emphasises the importance of "loyalty to community" and argues for the "value of socially based and considered perceptions" (1991: 228).

4.3.2.4. Playing oneself and the other

Bopha! not only criticises apartheid but also exercises resistance to the system in its theatrical practices. Two strategies that Percy Mtwa employs deserve examination: the use of movement and multiple role-play. Both of these elements emphasise the theatricality of the stage and reflect the theatricality of the play's topic.

Christopher Balme identifies the presence of an aesthetic of movement in South African township theatre. Body language on stage, he argues, can at times develop into a means of communication that is more important than the spoken text. In this case the body is used as an instrument to convey meaning. Elements such as dance, pantomime and song are derived by the black actors from typical township body

[39] The fact that the Afrikaner policeman lives in the country and not in the city is in accordance with the creation of a counter-*civitas* by Afrikaner Nationalists. They feel threatened by the black urban masses - a "monstrosity born of urban hybridization" - and retreat to their alternative 'city' built on purification and isolation on the land. This is reflected in the rhetoric of the National Party that declares the Afrikaner *volk*'s "innate tribal connection" to the land (Kruger 1997: 565f.).

language. The process in which the artists adopt their culture's traditional forms of movement and use them to express cultural belonging is called 'enculturation' (cf. 1995: 184, 189). Balme considers Mtwa one of the prime theatre practitioners to develop and make use of this theatre method which transforms the body into the dominant sign transmitter of the performance. The body becomes the "Signing Body" (1999: 221; cf. 1995: 189; 1996: 80). Mtwa explains:

> [...] to try as an actor to create these images, that you are talking about as an artist, you are using your body as the only instrument that you have, and that body which you have can be anything, can be a piece of sculpture, it can sing, it can be a song, it can be movement, can be sound, can be anything, that body. So that is what he [Grotowski] meant by poor theatre. (1988: 170)[40]

Mtwa translates this theory into practice in *Bopha!*: the use of the body in song and dance is a central element of the play. Balme argues that the movements displayed in township theatre differ largely from the singing and dancing of plays rooted in the folklorist (or pseudo-folklorist) presentation of the 'happy African' in black musicals created for white audiences such as *Ipi-Tombi* (cf. 1995: 159, see Chapter 3.2.1). In these kinds of spectacles the oppressed subject is stereotyped and represented according to the oppressor's image. By contrast, in the vibrant township theatre of the late 1970s and early 1980s the oppressed insist on self-representation through the body.[41] Gilbert and Tompkins assert:

> Part of the project of redefining staged identity is to affix the colonised's choice of signification to the body [...]. This oppositional process of embodiment whereby the colonised creates his/her own subjectivity ascribes more flexible, culturally laden,

---

[40] As Balme has already pointed out, Grotowski's theatre concept really focuses on the actor as the instrument to realise a religious spiritual idea (1995: 189, fn. 64). See Grotowski (1967).

[41] The focus on the dominated or resisting body can quickly lead to claims of the following kind: "[...] questions of who or what is speaking through the body and in what language, of what discourses are inscribed on/in the body, are clearly questions of power relations of the sort excavated by Michel Foucault" (Auslander 1988: 9). Balme points to the danger inherent in employing discourse analysis to lay open hierarchies of oppression because this could lead to the construction of simplistic dichotomies that fail to mirror the complex situation in post-colonial societies (cf. 1995: 156). Keeping this in mind, it is nonetheless important to note that discourse analysis highlights more than the binary construction of oppression and resistance, but allows us to identify strategies of cultural negotiation and reciprocal influence of different subject positions that reveal the constructedness of the binary categories. Difference is thus revealed to be an artificially created concept that can theoretically be imposed because of existing power relations but that in practice begins breaking down as soon as it is introduced. This simultaneous erection and breakdown derive from the fact that categorisation involves a stable inscription of a subject body that in reality can never fully be circumscribed.

and multivalent delineations to the body, rather than circumscribing it within an imposed, imperialist calculation of otherness. (1996: 205)

Self-representation of the oppressed not only poses a threat to those in power because it frees the subject from its representation in a position of alterity, but it also allows the subject to present itself in action. Elizabeth Grosz's argument confirms this: "[...] the body and its energies and capacities exert an uncontrollable, unpredictable threat to a regular, systematic mode of social organisation" (1990: 64). As if to prove this theory, Mtwa explains how young Africans are able to overcome their lack of contact with art and culture in apartheid schools:

> There is literally nothing happening to encourage us [school children] for show business, for art in general. So what we do as kids, we come together and we play, and we play and we play. [...] We started forming a musical band, but we had no instruments. [... A student] started playing a song that was popular at the time [...]. And then he started miming it, playing the bass guitar with his lips and his voice and then another person started coming in [...] and then, all of a sudden, there we were, miming this song and what came out was something very beautiful. (1988: 160)

Through the use of pantomime the young men achieve a performance unhindered by their lack of material props, in this case musical instruments. Symbolically this signifies their triumph over apartheid-imposed constraints. By analogy, Orkin argues that Mtwa and Ngema's engagement in *Woza Albert!* (1981) suggests that these actors are intelligent, creative human beings whose "bodies become signifiers in performance of energy, wit, and intelligence, skill, the capacity for humour and humanity – all that is denied in prevailing discourse" (1991: 226).

Eckhard Breitinger proposes a different approach to pantomime as a representation of South African township life. He asserts that this art form defines the African's position in terms of the state-imposed racial hierarchy. Instead of emphasising the element of self-representation of the oppressed inherent in mime, he argues, it belittles the self in their poverty and deprivation while aggrandising the other in their excess. This is caricature and hence a form of protest in which blacks perform about how they stand in relation to others. They "enact the non-existent, the imaginary, the desired" which leads Breitinger to the conclusion that the "effect of this musical pantomime lies [...] in the discrepancy between the meaning and the means – or rather the lack of means by which it is realised" (2003^2: 140; cf. 138).

The opening scene of *Bopha!* exemplifies this. As part of the ceremony by the graduates of the South African Police Training College the young officers perform a physical training display routine followed by a police drill. At the end, as the stage directions indicate, "*the routines are transformed into a dance*" (*BP* 230). Balme, having seen a live performance of *Bopha!*, describes this initial scene as a syncretic combination of dance, a cappella song and rhythmic, choreographed movement. In the technique of montage it moves from the drill routine to the presentation of a Zulu dance. Thus the image of apartheid as a police state is juxtaposed with elements of black culture such as the influence of traditional movement (the Zulu dance) as well as the presentation of modern, daily forms of rhythmic and musical expression dominant in the townships. Apart from its entertaining qualities this kinetic montage stages the transition from a discursively prescribed form of movement to a strategy of resistance. It thus points to the central conflict in which Sergeant Njandini finds himself (cf. 1995: 190f.). He can either exercise his profession and identify with the apartheid state, which alienates him from his family and community and forces him to betray his own group, or he can embrace and celebrate his traditional social environment while turning his back on the police force. The fact that this first scene imprints the image of the vibrant Zulu dancers on the audience's mind suggests Njandini's resignation from the police force and his dismissal of apartheid at the end of the play.

A further element Mtwa uses in *Bopha!* to oppose apartheid is overt role-play. Here the black actors move from the three main roles into various other white and black characters before the audience's eyes. Anne Fuchs asserts that in *Woza Albert!* "[...] the actor creators or performers of the play keep their own identity throughout, and never attempt to create that theatrical illusion of Western theatre whereby the actor is supposed to have disappeared behind the character he is playing" (1987: 36). This is also true for *Bopha!*. The stage directions in the printed version of the play script do not specify which actor takes on which additional roles. However, Breitinger gives a detailed account of this role switching. He explains that the man who plays Njandini acts, *inter alia*, the role of the police drill-master Buffalo and a priest. The actor in the role of Zwelakhe also impersonates, for example, the white Afrikaner police officer Captain van Donder. The man playing Naledi transforms into Captain Piet. The role change consists of adding one costume element by which the character is to be recognised: a white rubber nose, a blond moustache or a blue or brown police cap. Again, as in *Survival*, when a black actor plays a white role, a white nose or blond moustache on black skin foregrounds his blackness. This shows that blacks can appropriate white roles and thus that they threaten the alleged white inviolability under apartheid. Additionally, distinct accents, gestures or movements are used in *Bopha!* to distinguish one role from another. Breitinger concludes that each character is presented by one single feature that marks her or him as a type in contrast to the three main characters who are psychologically complex. Thus it is possible to read these additional roles as caricature versions that supplement the first roles as is the case with the pair Njandini-Buffalo. A further possibility is what this critic calls a compensatory or contrastive role. For example, the actor of Njandini takes on the role of a funeral priest who condemns the police for the massacre of Soweto's children and thus compensates for Njandini's lack of paternal behaviour. Breitinger concludes that the significance of the secondary roles lies in their task of defining the social framework in which the main role characters function (cf. 2003²: 149f.). And furthermore, from a performative perspective, the "switching of roles on open scene enforces the dynamics of the performance, it adds to the speed, but it also emphasises the character of play acting and theatrality [*sic*], because it is so insistent on the fact that the figures shown on the stage are impersonated by actors" (1994: 149). By effortlessly slipping from one role to another, these actors highlight the fact that it is possible to play different roles and change one's identity. They suggest that identity is not an invariable and challenge apartheid's monologic definition. Furthermore, by explicitly performing the process of role change on stage, the actors prove that even with their small group they can create a vibrancy and vitality that asserts black life while challenging and criticising whiteness. Through this multiplied perspective they show how one can better understand society and its repressive mechanisms and learn to cope with and eventually overcome oppression.

4.4. *Egoli – City of Gold* and the call for black solidarity

> We all have the right to live. And we shall always sing a song with the spear and calabash next to our hearts.
>
> Hamilton in *Egoli*[42]

Egoli – City of Gold (1978) by Matsemela Manaka presents the lives of two mine workers in the depth of a gold mine in Egoli, the City of Gold, namely Johannesburg. *Egoli* depicts the men's current inhuman working and devastating living conditions as well as their past experience with apartheid regulations. The brutal life in the mines becomes a metaphor for the horrible conditions of existence

[42] *EG* 70. References to *Egoli – City of Gold* are flagged *EG*.

under apartheid as a whole. The play makes clear that resistance in the form of revolutionary action is the only effective means with which to change the situation.

4.4.1. "Acting is the language of life":[43] Matsemela Manaka on theatre

According to Geoffrey Davis, Matsemala Manaka never openly identified with any organised political movement. However, he was inspired by the philosophy of BC.[44] The influence of the BCM's basic tenets as defined by Kavanagh – "withdrawal from association with whites, the creation of new structures and the conscientization of blacks" (cf. 1985: 164) - on Matsemela Manaka's work is variously apparent. In accordance with the principle of self-reliance his plays are directed and performed by all-black casts. He was one of the founding members of the Soyikwa[45] Black Theatre Group composed exclusively of black artists.[46] Manaka's theatre activity was characterised by the commitment to arts' education, the training of the black actors, theatre projects in rural areas, playing township venues and an alternative, non-commercial status (cf. Davis 1993: 160f.; 1994: 29; 1997: 12f.). Manaka also supported the BCM's call for conscientisation of the oppressed:

> At this point in time, the dispossessed are destitute. They are very desperate for the realisation of their aspirations. They are in quest of freedom. They need no entertainment that shall make them oblivious of their state of subservience. They need no entertainment that shall make them submissive to their state of poverty and servitude. They need no entertainment that will be irrelevant to the black man's bone of contention. They need no entertainment that shall not respond to the call of freedom's cry. But they need realistic entertainment that will give them courage to

---

[43] Manaka 1984: 33.

[44] Steadman declares: "Clearly, Manaka's conception of theatre is in harmony with the theory of Black Conscious-ness as espoused by Biko." Furthermore, Steadman considers *Egoli* a "demonstration of the same kind of militant Black Consciousness as exhibited in any of the Black Consciousness plays of the early 1970's" (1984c: 14, 13).

[45] The name Soyikwa was intended to pay tribute to the Nigerian writer Wole Soyinka. In Xhosa the word literally means "we shall be feared." As Davis points out, the group often interpreted it as "we shall overcome" and thus emphasised the challenge that their theatre represented as well as the survival situation it was confronted with (1997: 2).

[46] A further principle, the refusal to accept support from externally based cultural brokers in marketing, was difficult to maintain for reasons of practical want: it was impossible to operate without the financial help of white business and funding from white-owned companies. In addition, the Market Theatre in Johannesburg was the only available venue in the city (cf. Davis 1997: 13).

survive and forge ahead. Entertainment that will bring hope for freedom in their lifestyle. (1997a: 37)

Manaka's main theatrical objective is educating the dispossessed, its function being clearly didactic in that it promotes the conscientisation of this underprivileged group. He believes that the aim of the dramatist should be to avoid making the audience submissive to their state of poverty and servitude. Instead, he aims to promote the courage to survive, look ahead and strive for freedom (cf. 1997a: 37; Davis 1993: 161). Manaka believes that his work cannot be classified as protest theatre because it does not focus primarily on apartheid.[47] He claims that his art is about cultural identity.[48] Nonetheless, Davis emphasises that Manaka's plays comprehensively dramatise the socio-economic conditions of black South Africa under apartheid (cf. 1997: 14).

Manaka asserts that it is the social responsibility of all artists to maintain contact with their communities and voice their aspirations. He believes that cultural activities play a central role in preparing people for change because in a cultural revolution plays occupy the function of dealing with the problems of the dispossessed (cf. 1997b: 109). According to T. Philemon Wakashe, the major concern of theatre practitioners who were influenced by BC ideology is "communication with the audience – to be direct, clear, close" (1986: 45). The focus is not on literary values but on theatricality and the message which is conveyed through images, mime and songs (cf. *ibid.*). Manaka also maintains that communication is the central element of theatre. In his opinion, communication with the black audience relies on two aspects: the creative resources of the black community, namely its culture, and the depiction of the depth and scope of black suffering (cf. 1986: 49). In order to do this successfully, the performer must be able to, in Manaka's words, "integrat[e] the audience with the actor" (1997a: 39). The success of a play depends on the effect it has on its spectators. Manaka comments on the work of the actor Joe Rahube who he believes has successfully achieved this integration:

---

47 Wakashe considers Manaka's work to be "true protest theatre" which he identifies by its revolutionary tone and its criticism of government policies (cf. 1986: 41).

48 Manaka stated in an interview with Anne Fuchs that "for a long time I have not had apartheid so much as a theme in my work. What I was always trying to do was to deal with the issue, I have always dealt with the issue of identity, of cultural identity for people to know who they are" (1997c: 119).

> The kind of performance he gives is rooted in the origins of African theatre – which never separates the actor from the audience. An artist becomes an integral part of the experience performed. Acting is not acting for acting's sake. It is a religious act. We all take part when Joe Rahube is on stage. (1997a: 39)

The importance of the connection and communication between the actor and the audience is also expressed in Manaka's assertion that "[...] acting is the language of life; that theatrical drama is drawn from life" (1984: 33). Here, as if he had read Goffman, he not only makes clear that all social behaviour is a form of acting but that stage performances represent life and are an excerpt of life. Similarly, Manaka also emphasises that his plays do not only *represent* the dispossessed but also *present* them (cf. Tomaselli 1980). The actors become, as Steadman puts it, both signifiers and signified: "Manaka reveals ideology from the inside, as it were: his plays show audiences the very relations upon which they are commenting" (1992a: 204).

In his article "The Babalaz People" Manaka talks to two black actors who live in London about the role of black actors in a white society. They come to the following conclusion:

> [...] the pressure of the white world makes us do what we do, [...] the pressure of being black in a white society is what the play is all about. [...] The motivation that makes you write, act and makes you do what you do wouldn't be the same if those white people were not doing what they are doing to you. (1981: 33)

As blacks perceive their identity to be shaped by dominant white ideology or discourse, blacks are represented in a distorted manner not only in white society but, more importantly, also in black society. Black identity exists in a dichotomous relation to white identity and is shaped by its position of alterity. As long as this separation is not overcome, black identity will always remain the negative counterpart of white identity. When Manaka defines the task of theatre to be the "recreation of people and the showing of a people's depth" and the reconstruction of "a people's history and culture" (*ibid.*), he implicitly criticises apartheid (and other colonial regimes) for destroying the African people in their social as well as cultural identity.

By developing plays in workshops with working-class actors, Manaka is able to present various perspectives of the fragmented sectors of black society in terms of class, status and ideology. Despite Manaka's belief that the struggle under apartheid is based on the primacy of race over class,[49] Ian Steadman argues that the playwright's collaboration with lower class actors allows him to give a more realistic presentation of black life than his own position as an emerging intellectual in the black community would otherwise usually. This is why Steadman calls Manaka not the writer of his plays but the "scribe recording group activity" whose plays "signify a dialectic of experience which includes different class and status positions" (1992a: 205, 206).

Manaka distinguishes between conventional theatre and experimental theatre. In his opinion, conventional theatre is determined by the "'colonial life of the past where the white man came into this country and imposes his values, customs and traditions.'" By contrast, experimental theatre "'diffuses this and creates a state of awareness among the people'" (qtd. in Steadman 1992a: 201). With this juxtaposition Manaka succumbed to a dichotomous approach that tried to distance African theatre from its Western counterpart. David Coplan foregrounds the use of traditional African expressive elements in Manaka's work: "dance and music as well as physical and verbal expression" and "the layering of mutually resonant but disjunct, sometimes nonnaturalistic episodes, imagery, rather than narrative" (1986: 172).

Manaka's theatre is considered stylistically eclectic. It is influenced by the European traditions of Grotowski and Brecht and by various media such as Johannesburg theatre, film and television (cf. Steadman 1992a: 200). Manaka's talent as painter, sculptor, musician, poet and dramatist also contributes to the artistic variety displayed in his plays. Davis even calls his work "a synthesis of all the arts, a South African '*Gesamtkunstwerk*'" (1991: 85; cf. 1997). Thus it is not surprising that Manaka aims to create innovative works that do not rely on Western artistic conventions. Manaka describes his approach as non-literary, focusing instead, like all the other dramatists presented here, on actor improvisation and emphasising the physical aspect of theatre, the "physical word" (1984: 33). He alludes to the idea that the playwright must transform his verbal thoughts into physical action because the effectiveness of a performance is measured by what is actually shown, not told (1984: 33f.): "So instead of *telling* about the South African situation, we started thinking of *showing* and this is why when we read plays like *Egoli*, we find nothing in it in terms of reading, but in terms of performing you see

[49] "[...] our understanding of the South African society is that the class struggle is embodied in the race issue. Here, race determines class" (Manaka 1981: 34).

a lot about the struggle inside the country" (1982: 521; 1997b: 110). The images used in *Egoli* are symbols of this struggle. Consequently, this strategy was not only shaped by artistic considerations but also served a political function in that the play script was less likely to be censored by the authorities. Such devices were not sufficient, however, to prevent the play's banning. The published play script was banned as "undesirable" as defined by Section 47(2) (e) of the Publications Act of 1974, which meant that the authorities considered it "'prejudicial to the safety of the state, the general welfare or the peace and good order'" (Davis 1993: 154; 1997: 6; cf. 1999).

Manaka believes that in the quest for freedom art not only bears a social responsibility but also, as "an emotional, spiritual and intellectual expression and aesthetic experience," plays a role in serving the educational, religious, political and economic needs of the people. He defines the artist as "an educator, historian, interpreter and prophet with a vision and a task to integrate the past, present and future" (1987: 18). In his later years his work was increasingly influenced by the principle of pan-African unity. It sought to reconstruct the cultural identity of black South Africans which had been destroyed by apartheid, to uncover South Africa's roots in the culture and history of Africa and to renew African tradition in new forms of theatre in the contemporary urbanised context (cf. Davis 1991: 84; 1993: 163; 1994: 36). He believes, "Our theatre, as the historical embodiment of our cultural past, should become a threshold towards a new society in this country. Our African identity should therefore take the lead in singing such liberation blues" (1981: 34).[50]

4.4.2. *Egoli – City of Gold* – the play

Egoli – City of Gold presents the inhuman conditions experienced by two mine workers in a Johannesburg gold mine. The first production was performed in Soweto in 1978 as a three-hander with John Moalusi Ledwaba, Susan Shabangu and Daniel Stoppa Lekalakala, who was later replaced by Hamilton Mahonga Silwane. When Shabangu left the cast, the play was transformed into a two-hander and performed in the Cape. At first it was directed collectively by members of the Soyikwa Black Theatre Company (later called the Soyikwa Institute of African Theatre), then co-directed by Manaka and Ledwaba. Rob Amato stepped in as

---

[50] Matsemela Manaka died in a car accident in 1998.

director for the 1979 performances at the People's Space Theatre in Cape Town and Upstairs at the Market Theatre in Johannesburg. These productions were revised in workshop and continued to be constantly re-shaped by in-performance improvisation and the addition of new songs. Thus the presentations could be adapted directly to different audiences such as Xhosa spectators from the Cape Flats or a mixed audience from Cape Town or Johannesburg (cf. Davis 1997: 6; *EG* 51).

Egoli depicts the African miners John and Hamilton in their room on the compound where they live during their employment on the mine. They do highly dangerous and physically very strenuous work in the mine shafts. The play does not rely on plot development but presents a series of contrasting scenes that are described as "a heightened poetic image of the workers' experience, past and present" (Larlham 1985: 86). The realistic, everyday scenes are interrupted by flashbacks and mimed underground work sequences that contain little realistic dialogue, achieving their power through movement, chants, songs and slogans. In the central dream scene John and Hamilton enact their escape from prison. After their successful flight from a police helicopter they free each other from the shackles and chains that bind them together, an act that clearly functions as a metaphor for the struggle for liberation, as many critics have stated (cf. Fleishman 1996: 181; Orkin 1991: 216; Steadman 1985: 370). At the end of the play John learns that his son has been killed in an accident in the mines. After a symbolic burial the men sing songs that call for black solidarity and resistance against oppression. The movement from past to present and from mime to dialogue epitomises this play as a "compact and heightened collage" of scenes from the life of these two miners (Larlham 1985: 87).

Loren Kruger points out that like *The Island*, *Egoli* portrays two men engaged in a struggle with each other as well as with their spatial confinement (cf. 1999: 170).[51] The mining system is compared to the prison system as it forces the men to live in similarly inhuman and restricted conditions. The play makes clear that the miners were not only physically bound together in the past but also connected as victims of the system of political and economic oppression.

Egoli depicts the men's present working and living conditions and their past experience. It ends with a call for revolutionary action as the only means to bring

[51] Although the play does not openly follow an existentialist thrust, John and Hamilton almost seem bound to each other like *Waiting for Godot's* Vladimir and Estragon (cf. Steadman 1984c: 12) or *Blood Knot's* Morrie and Zach.

about change. These elements suggest a reading of *Egoli* as a tendentious play that offers a one-sided view of black life as continuous suffering in apartheid South Africa. Despite the unambiguous presentation of the plight of the African population, a closer look at the two mine workers reveals that they are portrayed as, first and foremost, characters who suffer both economically and psychologically from apartheid. Hamilton and John are not simple stock types but complex characters who must learn to analyse their behaviour, hopes and fears in the light of their political, economic and social reality in South Africa.

The men's interactions suggest that the prerequisite for engaging in active resistance to apartheid is a conscious understanding of their personal suffering which is part of the suffering of the black population as a whole. Furthermore, the play makes clear that freedom can only be won if the people come together in a display of solidarity to exercise resistance against the regime.

4.4.2.1. The dream of freedom

The second act of *Egoli* opens with a flash-back presented as a dream sequence. This is the central scene in the play in which the men exchange only a few words. Mime and exaggerated movement convey the content of the scene and highlight the fact that the characters' experience is not a daily one.

The protagonists, John and Hamilton, have managed to escape from prison and are on the run. In their role as convicts and refugees they have to be very careful how they move about in order to avoid being caught by the police. Thus for strategic reasons their freedom of movement is limited. In addition, the men are chained to one another by their necks, a handicap that requires them to act and react in the same manner so that they do not get into each other's way. Considering that the men are forced to act quickly, they must agree on their next movement almost intuitively. This is shown by their spontaneous but synchronised jump into the bush to hide from the approaching police helicopter. Their success shows that the characters can only survive by staying together. Hamilton's exclamation "Into the bush" (*EG* 63) should be evaluated as a cue and not as an order because both characters move at the same time. As soon as the danger is over the refugees can no longer agree on their next move. Hamilton is forced to watch John's attempt to ascertain a successful escape route with the help of a fortune-telling rock game. Against his will Hamilton helps his partner collect stones and discovers a source of water in the process. John anticipates Hamilton's spontaneous run towards this source because, in their moment of suffering, both men simultaneously need to satisfy their basic bodily needs.

A further conflict follows: Hamilton plans to free John and himself from the chains and shackles that bind them by first breaking open John's neck ring. John's words express his lack of trust and fear that Hamilton's hand will slip and kill him in the process. After the first dangerous and painful blow John refuses to co-operate and thus destroys their chance of attaining liberation. However, Hamilton manages to change John's mind by making it clear that they are not only fighting for their physical liberation, but that they must also ideologically free themselves from the "chains that curse your manhood. Chains that rust your brains" (*EG* 63). The long-term goal promises freedom from daily oppression. Even with this powerful argument Hamilton cannot convince John, who is so overwhelmed by his fear that he can no longer react rationally. He defends his feelings by drawing an analogy to Hamilton's criminal past, the rape and murder he committed. John's adoption of the role of the prosecutor prevents the men from acting effectively. In addition, this also shows that he completely fails to recognise the seriousness of their personal dilemma which Hamilton sees as symbolic of the general situation of the African people who are born into poverty and spend their lives "entombed in the dusty streets of Soweto" (*EG* 64). It is only after Hamilton explains the situation in detail that he receives John's consent to smash the chains. Before they start to do this, they sing a militant song that is typical of agitprop or epic theatre. The song expresses their desire for freedom and change in the name of the African people and the audience members. Since they include their fellow-Africans in this song, the breaking of the chain celebrates their own liberation and symbolises the step that all fellow-Africans have to take to acquire freedom. While singing, the men treat the chain "*like a dead snake*" (*EG* 65) that they have killed: the chain becomes a metaphor for apartheid as the evil that must be destroyed.

Significantly the dream sequence concludes exactly at this point. This abrupt ending shows that the wish for change and the movement towards liberation and freedom are still a dream of which the people must become conscious before they can start realising it. And as Hamilton's arguments with John have shown, this can be a long and difficult process.

In a free society the men's confinement in this extreme situation would be considered an exceptional experience. However, *Egoli's* depiction of Hamilton and John's daily routine suggests that the everyday life of black men in apartheid South

Africa is also characterised by such confinement. The situation of the men as prisoners is paralleled by a scene that depicts them at work in the mine. In the depth of the mine their work space is extremely cramped and narrow. Thus the men are figuratively chained to one another in the mine shafts as well.

4.4.2.2. Work and alienation

Hamilton, who was born in Johannesburg, and John, a migrant labourer from one of the homelands, have contracts to work on a Johannesburg gold mine and live in the mine's compounds. By coincidence the two men who escaped from prison together are now assigned to work and live together in the mine. Their task is to drill holes in the stope faces where other men – the blasters - then insert and detonate the dynamite. After the explosion the protagonists collect the rubble and load it into a container that other workers have lowered down from the top of the shaft. This scene is presented as a mime sequence. The characters' gestures and movements show how badly-equipped the miners are and how inadequate or practically non-existent their protection is, given their proximity to the actual placing of the dynamite. The stage directions indicate this. Anticipating the explosion, the "*two men crouch, with the spades at the side of their heads as protection.* [...] *They block their noses, blow out their cheeks and put their free hands over their unprotected ears. There is an explosion. The two men casually get up and start preparing the pile of rubble* [...]" (*EG* 66). These explanations show that the miners' work is to be considered routine. Although the men are experienced in their task and fulfil it "*casually*," this does not mean that they feel comfortable in their job or identify with it. In fact, John explicitly draws an analogy between their fate as prisoners and their life on the mine: "We were chained together by our necks when we escaped. We broke those chains with a rock and now we are chained together here again – Egoli, city of hatred, city of misery" (*EG* 55). The suffering they experience in their role as prisoners corresponds to their suffering in the roles they play in daily working life. Ironically, the substance that gave them freedom – rock – now imprisons them, despite their attempts to tunnel through it.

At night Hamilton comments on the effects that their inhuman condition has on his partner:

> A mineworker from the living grave. Look at his face, glittering with sweat, full of dust. This whirlwind within his muscles is turning Jo'burg into skyscrapers, [...]

> castles and temples. Look at his sweat, If [*sic*] this sweat could quench his thirst! [...] This man is tired of living. He is not enjoying the fruits of his sweat. (*EG* 62)

Hamilton describes their work as alienating. A Marxist interpretation of work as exploitation and alienation is clearly suggested. In his *Economic and Philosophic Manuscripts of 1844* Marx emphasises that the act of labour must be considered in several ways. He describes the "relation of the worker to the *product of labour* as an alien object exercising power over him" (Tucker, ed. 1978[2]: 74). Apart from this estrangement from the product Marx also speaks of self-estrangement which grows out of the relation of labour to the act of production within the labour process: "[...] it is activity as suffering, strength as weakness, begetting as emasculating, the worker's *own* physical and mental energy, his personal life [...] as an activity which [...] neither depends nor belongs to him" (Tucker, ed. 1978[2]: 75). Hamilton's comment alludes to both of these aspects.

Marx argues that estranged labour turns man into a being which is alien to nature, himself, his active functions and his activity. Estranged labour also alienates the species 'man' from the individual and "makes individual life in its abstract form the purpose of the life of the species." A free human being can consciously shape their life-activity and turn it into the *object* of their own will. In this case human activity is free activity. However, estranged labour reverses this relationship and makes a person's life-activity the *means* to their existence. As a final consequence of man's estrangement from the product of his labour, his life-activity and his species as a whole, man is also estranged from man (Tucker, ed. 1978[2]: 75, cf. 76f.).

It seems that Hamilton is aware of Marx's arguments when he calls for the need to raise the consciousness of the black people in regard to the reality of their situation. In apartheid society labour is the means by which African workers maintain their meagre physical existence. Their activity is not free and does not allow them to contribute to the conscious creation of a self-defined objective world which would appear as their work and their reality. Marx argues that man duplicates himself not only intellectually but also actively, contemplating himself in a world he has created (cf. Tucker, ed. 1978[2]: 76). In apartheid society the black population is forced to create the world in which whites live but in which they are offered no participation. From a Marxist perspective it is the regime's strategy of economic exploitation that prevents the oppressed from being able to realise themselves both as self-reflexive and as social beings.

Given that an individual can no longer consciously shape their life, it automatically follows that they will not be able to exhibit healthy role behaviour. They will not be able to influence their behaviour intentionally so that it is no longer possible to contribute personally to role behaviour. The individual cannot maintain the necessary distance to their role. Thus the roles they play appear as inflexible codes of conduct which do not allow individual self-realisation. The social role loses its function of satisfying personal needs in the frame of the normative regulation of these needs. These aspects lead Dreitzel to the conclusion that by analogy to Marx's concept of a worker's alienation from his labour in a capitalist society, all role-play that lacks distance to the normative catalogue of behavioural expectations may cause the individual's self-alienation (cf. 1980^3: 246f.). This explains why Hamilton and John suffer in their role as miners.

Hamilton criticises the apartheid regime for the suffering it inflicts on the African population. He slips into the role of the white mine *baas* who gives John the message of his son's death. With the help of this role game Hamilton places the whites in a position of alterity and holds them directly accountable for his general desolate circumstances and the death of his son. He stresses that blacks, in their roles as mine workers, carry no responsibility for this catastrophe. Each racial group or class takes on roles that are socially distributed but clearly defined and limiting. To use Goffman's terminology, *Egoli* shows in this scene that role change is only possible if one has mastered the required techniques of impression management. Hamilton's case proves that knowledge of society's hierarchies and structures is the requirement for destabilising them. Hamilton's lucidity and heightened state of consciousness are, however, not sufficient for him to overcome apartheid's powerful laws alone.

4.4.2.3. The private sphere

Egoli's initial scene introduces the audience to John and Hamilton's compound room on the mine. The room is characterised by its overwhelming bareness. Folded blankets serve as beds, and two wooden crates are used as chairs. In addition to the mining equipment the men have a plastic bath and some buckets of water at their disposal. Their personal belongings consist of a battery-operated radiogram, records and beer, which all belong to John. Some bread, a knife, candles and a mine newspaper lie on Hamilton's side of the room. These objects reflect the men's different personalities (see below). The emptiness of the room that the men are required to consider their 'home' is striking. In fact, it strongly resembles the bareness of the prison cell in *The Island* or *Survival*. Thus prison, work and the private sphere are linked. The men's suffering is emphasised no matter which role they play. There is no escape from the starkness and confinement that affects black life under apartheid.

John and Hamilton are already on stage as the audience enter the seating area. The two men are shown "*smoking, drinking, reading, dreaming, listening to the F.M. radio*" (*EG* 53). The characters' presence suggests that this is their routine, their daily life, their reality. In fact, these are all actions that one would consider 'normal' relaxing activities at home at the end of the work-day. However, the audience soon realise that something is unusual and different. These men are alone, they have no families with them, they are denied the freedom to move about in the outside world. Their situation is characterised by a deprivation of both their material circumstances as well as their freedom of movement.

In the midst of this bareness, as in *Blood Knot* or *Sizwe Bansi is Dead*, we encounter two very different men caught in the same dilemma. Although both characters are dissatisfied with the quality of their lives in South Africa under apartheid and give various, sometimes contradictory, explanations for their situation and solutions for change, their opinions on how to lead their lives and challenge apartheid differ noticeably. Bearing the characters' differences in mind, we can describe the friends and co-miners, Hamilton and John, as contrasting figures set in an asymmetrical relationship of teacher and pupil. Hamilton is the teacher whose past experience leads him to believe that political activism is the only effective strategy against apartheid. John represents the emotional counterpart whose hedonistic life-style and desire for instant gratification are his only therapy against his daily suffering. He needs Hamilton's support to escape his personal destruction and reach the understanding that he can play a role in changing the situation of his people. By communicating past experiences and the conclusions the men have drawn for their present lives, *Egoli* explains the men's attitudes and evaluates their ability to contribute to future change. The play thus comments on the three phases of time - past, present and future.

4.4.2.3.1. John and the lack of self-awareness

John can be characterised as a hedonist whose life revolves around the evenings he spends listening to music, drinking alcohol and meeting with prostitutes. He is not a carefree party animal who lives like this because it represents a life-style. Instead, he feels resignation in the light of all the suffering he has experienced in his life. He wants to be a hero who his children can look up to, a desire that he reveals when he speaks about his memories of Oupa Phalaborwa. This old respected man from John's African community is his source of hope and comfort. John presents Oupa as a supporter of indigenous traditions and customs, as an African story-teller and historian who passes down the cultural memory[52] of the people: "[...] the tone of his voice always blending with the ancestors. Telling stories that taught us how to live. How to survive the grips of Piet Retief[53] and fight for our liberation. He used to tell us how they fought battles of resistance against the settlers" (*EG* 54). The idealisation of a glorious past is one of the BCM's strategies for achieving a unified positive black self-image. However, as the following interpretation shows, turning to the past is only effective if one knows how to adapt the acquired knowledge to one's current situation and link past and present.

John mentions stories of Oupa's own involvement in World War II, an event that qualifies as historical in the dramatic present of the late 1970s. Oupa, like the Africans who were victorious over Retief, survived immense suffering and brutality in his successful fight against the enemy. Hamilton adds that his own father served in the war and that "[...] he got his share from the gun. That is why he had something to tell us" (*EG* 55). Despite the fact that the men consider these two military operations comparable, John contributes to a more differentiated perspective by criticising Hamilton's evaluation of his father's involvement as "serving the State" (*EG* 54). Similar to Styles's condemnation of his own father's treatment after the end of the World War II in *Sizwe Bansi is Dead*,[54] John implicitly denounces both the fact that Hamilton boasts of his father's achievements and that the state failed to recognise the patriotic service of its subjects.

John wishes to be the kind of hero that Oupa's tales bring to life: "I will tell stories to my children. [...] And I'll tell them about myself. Tell them how the honey went

---

[52] 'Cultural memory' is used as defined by Assman & Assman (cf. 1988).

[53] Piet Retief was a Voortrekker leader during the Great Trek by the Boers out of the Cape Colony which was under British rule. He led his followers into Natal in 1837 and was murdered a year later by the Zulus under Dingane.

[54] Styles comments on his father's treatment: "[...] they stripped him at the docks – his gun, his uniform, the dignity they'd allowed him to have for a few mad years because the world needed men to fight and sacrifice themselves for something called Freedom" (*SB* 17). See Chapter 3.3.1.1.

bitter. How I survived cold winter nights without food. How they arrested me under the Terrorism Act when I was only sixteen" (*EG* 55). These words express John's desperate search for his identity in the frame of his family and community. He obviously longs for recognition from others to confirm not only his identity but, on a more basic level, his existence as well. This wish conforms to Lothar Krappmann's assertion that the constitution of identity relies on social recognition (cf. 1982^6: 8). Because he craves attention from his own children, John reveals a longing to act out his role as their father. And by adding his own experience to the stories he learnt from Oupa, John hopes to secure his place in his community's genealogy. This need to establish a connection with the past and define himself as an extension of his ancestors also becomes apparent in Hamilton's behaviour. Although Hamilton is severely opposed to apartheid and denounces everyone who, like John, does not actively take part in resistance, he nonetheless identifies with his own father despite his service to the state in World War II. On the one hand, this can be condemned as inconsistent and contradictory behaviour. On the other, these inconsistencies make the characters all the more human and psychologically complex and emphasise the fact that a common opposition to apartheid will have to incorporate people with different opinions.

Hamilton deflates John's image of being a popular hero and of fulfilling his role of father by pointing out the weaknesses in John's character and the inconsistencies in his behaviour. In Hamilton's opinion, John does not qualify as a hero because he fails to exhibit the courage to openly fight for his rights, preferring to follow others. Although John defends himself and demands Hamilton's recognition for his organisation of a hunger strike, of starting a protest and leading a resistance song during his time in prison, Hamilton heavily criticises his character and behaviour beneath a friendly and "*mocking camaraderie*" (*EG* 54). John is "too easy-going. Not prepared to make a stand, to fight for [his] freedom. [...] he could hardly raise one finger when something really happened" (*EG* 53f.). In Hamilton's opinion, John's life shows that he was too immoral and cowardly to be a good example to his children. Hamilton believes that John is only deluding himself if he thinks he is a good father: "Hey man, you can't teach your children anything. They never see you. And even if they did all they would see would be the records, the beer, and the women who come in here every day" (*EG* 55). In the light of John's life-style it is ironic that he fails even to stitch his torn trousers, a repair which would make him respectable enough to pick up a prostitute. Howard Barrell suggests that this could be read as a symbol of his emasculation (cf. 1997 [1979]: 202).

Hamilton clearly holds the system of separate development and economic deprivation of the African people as well as the resulting labour migrancy responsible for the break-down of traditional family structures and the loss of the traditional role system that underpins them. However, he is critical of John's behaviour because he believes it is important to recognise the present-day situation instead of dreaming of heroic events of the past. Hamilton sees that John's current life-style would not allow him to realise his dreams, but more importantly, it also prevents him from fulfilling his obligations to his family. This gap between reality and ideals places John under such pressure that he can no longer act sensibly and turns to deviant forms of behaviour as compensation for his frustration (cf. Dreitzel 1980[3]: 193; Goffman 1963). Music, alcohol and women are thus no longer simply signifiers for a carefree evening but become icons for John's compensatory adoption of the role of the hedonist. Although this seems to be the solution to his immediate problems, he realises that it forces him to adopt an identity from which he distances himself. This creates new problems: "The beer is no part of the true story of my life" (*EG* 55). His attempt at differentiating between a presentable public identity and a private identity shows several things. Firstly, John admits that he cannot fulfil the socially prescribed norms. Secondly, he lives in self-delusion. He believes that he can develop a positive public image by simply denying his private behaviour. Hamilton tries to make him aware that his drinking leaves him without money to send to his family. Hamilton's point is that John has developed a secret private identity from which he publicly distances himself. This kind of behaviour leads to self-denial. John must leave this life-style behind if he wants to prevent his destruction (see below).

A look at John's past and his experiences with apartheid is necessary in order to understand his current behaviour. He recounts scenes from his life that define him as a fighter against and victim of apartheid. He tells Hamilton about his employment with the Johannesburg City Council as a scavenger, a job of cleaning streets and collecting rubbish. Forced to work under barbaric conditions, he was caught taking an unauthorised break. He dared to challenge the Afrikaner inspector and was consequently beaten up by the officials. He was then accused of having undermined the dignity of the white boss and penalised. He refused to carry out his punishment of cleaning toilets, preferring instead to be expelled to the homelands, thus accepting the poverty and hunger that this choice would inflict on him. He reproaches his African colleagues for not coming to his aid: "The others did not warn me about the inspector. There is no brotherly love, that is what is wrong with this country" (*EG* 58). This statement fails to lay the blame on apartheid's policy of racial separation and economic exploitation and becomes a one-sided explanation for the suffering of Africans in their own country. However, John's complaint can be seen to allude to a different strategy of apartheid policy: the separation of the Africans from each other. Just as the regime plays off one African group against another, John deplores the fact that the state has been so effective in creating fear among the black workers to the extent that they refuse to act in solidarity against the common enemy. In contrast to John's belief, the problem is not the lack of mutual compassion and help but a feeling of fear brought about by the black population's lack of awareness of the political reality. This prevents the people from defending each other against the common enemy. The loss of "brotherly love" must be recognised as a consequence of this lack of consciousness, not as the reason for the implementation of apartheid. John describes his life as a vicious cycle: "We run. We escape. We go back to the women and the children. We watch them starve. We come back again to breathe dust for them" (*EG* 55). His words leave no doubt that this cycle knows only one way out: death. He sums up his past experience:

> When I was young I fought. And this time I think it's despair. [...] People live on false hope! The train to Egoli. [...] They sang, shouted, screamed, as if they were to meet God at their destination. And my heart started to bleed when I saw the happy faces of my people heading for what they thought was a brighter future. [...] When we arrived in Jo'burg our eyes were kissed by the flickering lights of the big city. The train disappeared into darkness. (*EG* 57)

According to John, not only did the train disappear into darkness but so did his hopes. Life on the mine is equivalent to being "in the living graves" (*EG* 60). Here he presents himself as disillusioned and no longer affected by the false consciousness from which his fellow-Africans suffer. He speaks of the men who believed that after working in the mines they would have "Stinking gold in their bodies, vomiting gold coins" (*EG* 57). John's brutal definition of gold mining as 'vomiting' expresses his disgust and his awareness of the miners' exploitation. In the light of Julia Kristeva's assertion that vomiting is a form of self-protection from the abject, this experience of the abject is necessary for the manifestation of self. The feeling arises in someone when they recognise that an identity, a system or an order is disturbed by a transgression of limits and rules (cf. 1980: 10-12).[55] Thus John's image of gold-vomiting miners expresses his rejection of apartheid's mining industry and the economic exploitation of the African people that the system requires for it to be successful.

Although John has experienced the evils of apartheid, he cannot translate this knowledge into anti-apartheid action. Instead, he feels powerless in the face of the new mining recruits' powerful illusion and blind hope. This inability to act has a negative effect on his personal behaviour. Hamilton comments: "I would not escape from prison to imprison myself in another poison like liquor" (*EG* 69). John's main fault, according to Hamilton, does not lie in his inability to become a public leader but in his failure to develop a strong personality in order to support his family.

At the end of the play John is informed about the death of his son who had worked in the mines to support his mother and sisters. In a reversal of roles his son was forced to nourish the starving family while John ends up as the weeping child and immature adult who now literally falls into his own vomit: "Not my son! Oupa, Oupa don't come. Oupa, stay at home, my son! Oupa, Oupa. (*He is collapsing into the vomit and the horror.*)" (*EG* 69). This reaction is important for John because his vomiting expresses his self-disgust and self-pity and, as a ritual of self-cleansing, offers him a second chance. He finally accepts his own mistakes and distances himself from this irresponsible behaviour. He realises that it was his own negligence and failure to take responsibility that drove his son into the "living graves" which literally became his son's real grave.

4.4.2.3.2. Hamilton and the struggle against apartheid

Hamilton, by contrast, is the more "level-headed" character (Kruger 1999: 170). He reproaches John for his life-style and the poor role model he is for his children. It almost seems as if the childless bachelor Hamilton envies John for having a family: "You are lucky to be blessed with a son. I haven't a cat to give milk to" (*EG* 57). However, when he realises that John has five children, he considers a large family irresponsible given their material poverty: "The more we give birth the heavier the

---

[55] Kristeva asserts, "Dans ce trajet où 'je' deviens, j'accouche de moi dans la violence du sanglot, du vomi" (1980: 11) which I translate as "in this passage where 'I' become, I am born of myself in the violence of pain and vomit" (H.F.).

burden" (*ibid.*). He believes that John should be saving money to send home to his family in the homelands.

Hamilton reveals a fact from his past which explains his present rigorous adherence to a moral life: he committed rape and murder and is now haunted by the brutality of his deed and his memory of his victim. John does not believe that Hamilton suffers from a troubled conscience or sincerely regrets his misdeed. When John defends himself against Hamilton's heavy criticism, he retorts by reminding Hamilton of the rape but does not expect to be physically threatened by his outraged friend. John thinks that Hamilton needs to overcome this event in his life and encourages his friend to join him in his drinking and womanising: "Be like other men! Enjoy life!" (*EG* 56). Hamilton's reflections on the rape and murder have made him realise that violence against his community is not the way to solve problems. His refusal to go with a prostitute is a sign of his newly-acquired respect for the dignity of human life. He prefers to save his money instead of letting prostitutes take advantage of him: "She is one of them. Those who prowl through men's pockets. Come one, *oho!* come all! Gates are wide open for everyone to come in" (*EG* 61). His statement implies criticism of the system of migrant labour which separates families so that the partners are no longer able to take care of each others' physical and mental needs. Furthermore, Hamilton has realised that prostitution is all the more dangerous because it causes the dispossessed - in addition to their rigorous exploitation by the state - to exploit each other instead of joining together in solidarity to protest against apartheid's economic policies. In the course of this discussion Hamilton, in his self-imposed role as teacher and counsellor, does not succeed in opening John's eyes to this reality. He realises that John's behaviour is an indication of his helplessness and inability to cope with the degradation that apartheid imposes on them: "This man is tired of living. He is not enjoying the fruits of his sweat. He is praying for death to come his way" (*EG* 62). He feels the only way to successfully overcome this situation is to eradicate the whole system of exploitation that treats the black population as sub-human: a robot-like entity that need not be compensated for their labour. All Hamilton's suggestions on how to lead a moral life under these dire circumstances are finally no more than cosmetic attempts at temporarily covering up the problem without actually solving it. However, his proposals are important because they aim at raising John's consciousness about the world in which he lives.

Hamilton also undergoes a process of conscientisation and believes that he can successfully contribute to changing the plight of the Africans. He sees this as a process consisting of two steps, both of which must be fulfilled: large-scale political conscientisation of the black population which must be complemented by the support of family and friends on a private scale. The political activist in Hamilton leads him to join a mine organisation that supports the interests of the workers. At the same time he continues to take great pains in making John understand his own situation - that John must first become conscious of his personal fate before dealing with more general political ideas on an abstract level. Hamilton, the self-confessed rapist and murderer, demonstrates his conscientisation by affectionately caring for his friend John when he receives the news of his son's death.

It is only after this final gesture of compassion and solidarity that John reaches self-awareness. He gives his son a spiritual burial and spontaneously joins Hamilton in a call for overt and militant resistance to apartheid. The men voice a militant chant that is again typical of agitprop or epic theatre in which they express the necessity to fight for change and, in the long run, their liberation: "We shall all have to worship the spear and drink blood from the calabash until we all sing the same song – *Uhuru – Azania Uhuru Azania*"[56] (*EG* 71). John and Hamilton now represent the conscientised African people who must join in this struggle. These two individual characters transform into freedom fighters as well as Brechtian commentators. Thus with this call every individual is requested to show solidarity with their people to improve both their individual fate as well as the situation of the blacks as a whole.

4.4.2.4. Representing apartheid

Egoli was originally designed for a stage completely surrounded by a maximum of 200 spectators (cf. Larlham 1985: 87; Shava 1989: 157). John and Hamilton are already on stage as the spectators enter the seating area, an arrangement which leads to a feeling of intimacy and immediacy and gives the impression that the audience members are witnessing their own reality on stage. Shava goes so far as to suggest that this may even enable the audience "to feel that they are *acting out* the experiences of their daily lives" (1989: 157, emphasis added). The play is clearly rooted in the socio-historical situation of its time.

Because a depiction of reality can never be more than a subjective representation, the aim of a play like *Egoli* must be to convince its audience that the reality

[56] 'Uhuru' is Swahili for 'freedom.' 'Azania' was the name for South Africa used by the BCM.

presented corresponds to their own perception. Such is the situation in the case of black audiences or audiences that share the play's ideological or discursive position. By contrast, as Keyan Tomaselli suggests, white audiences must be convinced that the stage is not only a metaphor for the world but that metonymically the world is the stage. In this case social reality is seen as a type of performance, with performance and reality becoming indivisible. Or as Schechner and Turner would say, social drama and stage drama engage in a reciprocal relationship. Tomaselli emphasises the importance of analysing a play like *Egoli* against the development of the gold mining industry and its effects on black society. The play aims to expose the plight of the exploited group and make public their inhuman living conditions known, which have been brought about by capitalist interests and racial discrimination (cf. 1980: 56f.).

According to Tomaselli, white spectators who remain at a metaphorical distance to the stage will perceive *Egoli* as a representation of the consequences of urbanisation compared to tribal, rural life. However, whites who approach the play metonymically will perceive the segregation between capital and labour that results in apartheid policies which treat Africans as exploitable labour entities. Tomaselli concludes that in this case whites will no longer be able to avoid the reality of how blacks are affected by apartheid. By contrast, black audiences see the actors as communicators of their plight and fuse with the performers to form a single entity to declare their dissatisfaction with their situation and raise their consciousness through the presentation and analysis of their opposing ideology (cf. 1980: 57).

4.5. Conclusion

Survival by Workshop '71 Theatre Company, *Bopha!* by Percy Mtwa with the Earth Players' and *Egoli – City of Gold* by Matsemela Manaka with the Soyikwa Black Theatre Company are South African resistance plays that reach beyond the depiction of black suffering to include a call for conscientisation of the oppressed masses and the vision of liberation through revolution. Each drama group makes use of different strategies, varying degrees of comedy and overt militancy to deliver their message to the audience.

All three works stress the confinement of life under apartheid. They suggest that the limitations imposed on the roles that blacks are allowed to play in South African society result from the general pathological quality of apartheid society, represented by the prison and mine metaphors. The increasing brutality of the whites, who are presented in overt role-play by the black characters, gives proof of this loss of humanity. Healthy identity construction and role development are not possible for blacks as all three plays make a point of showing. However, with the help of lucid and intelligent teachers such as *Egoli*'s Hamilton, the experienced prisoners in *Survival* or Zwelakhe in *Bopha!*, weaker and more confused characters are educated and learn to recognise and analyse the evils of apartheid. The mentor figures exhibit a strong personality that allows them to act in the face of role degeneration. These characters are important because they succeed in constructing an identity which, to a large extent, evades apartheid's definition of black existence. The teachers construct their identity by negating and inverting white norms and rules. They clearly place the oppressors in a position of alterity. For example, mimicry is no longer a strategy with which black characters show that they are at least as versatile and human as a white (as suggested in *Sizwe Bansi is Dead*). Instead, mimicry has developed into a manifestation of distance between black and white.

The mentors' task of conscientising the other characters on the plays' level of reality is mirrored on the play-external level by the actors' direct audience addresses and their overt call for resistance to apartheid. This element from the epic theatre tradition characterises the works as didactic and agitprop theatre. However, the three theatre groups made use of this method to reach the spectators in varying degrees. To what extent they were successful remains debatable. *Survival*'s sketch structure allows several interruptions in the action for militant chants and songs, thereby imprinting the message on the spectators' minds. But perhaps the effectiveness of mixing a failed prison hunger strike with a call for revolution can be questioned (cf. Kavanagh 1985: xxix). Furthermore, despite *Bopha!*'s powerful message, newspaper reviewers criticised the play for not mobilising its audience into action. The high degree of theatricality exhibited in role-switching, pantomime, singing and dancing were said to "defuse much of the anger and frustration in the story-line," a quality that made the play "enormously disturbing at an ideological level" (August 1986: 7; cf. Fairbairn 1986). And in *Egoli* the powerful image of the breaking of the chain is clearly the play's strongest element. This is supported throughout the play by political chants directed at the audience. In the end Hamilton succeeds in helping John to rise from the ground and transcend the barriers imposed on black life by apartheid.

5. Multi-racial Workshop Productions and the Quest for Co-existence

> The workshop space in South Africa is a space where South Africans can momentarily leave the monster of apartheid behind them and meet as equals, without prejudice, to work together creatively.
>
> Malcolm Purkey[57]

5.1. Workshop theatre and its development

Like so many of the labels used to describe specific trends and developments in South African theatre, the term 'workshop theatre' is difficult to define. Mark Fleishman suggests, "It is unclear where the boundaries between what is and what is not workshop theatre begin and end" (1990: 88). South African theatre has been created in workshop from as early as the 1950s, and the collaboration of Fugard, Kani and Ntshona or the groups discussed in Chapter 4 marked important achievements in this tradition. Multi-racial workshop theatre grew during the late 1970s in opposition to the revolutionary theatre of the Black Consciousness Movement (BCM). These new groups of both black and white actors presented a different type of theatre by offering South African audiences a vision of multi-racial co-existence.

In 1976 Mshengu (Robert McLaren Kavanagh) had already noted the emergence of "corporate playwrights," which he defined as "a group of actors and a director who draw on combined memories and insights of the South African experience to improvise plays of shattering force, subtlety and eloquence" (1976: 44). Malcolm Purkey emphasises that the workshop situation provides an "environment where people meet and confront each other, and create out of such encounters" (1984: 66). However, it is important to note that such groups or teams do not constitute "totally homogenous" entities (Fleishman 1991: 70). This form of theatre production is now referred to as 'workshop theatre.' The term encompasses a wide spectrum: from Gibson Kente's township musical productions to plays created by multi-racial casts in co-operation with white "'culture brokers'" (Fuchs 1990: 19) such as Barney Simon at the Market Theatre or Malcolm Purkey from Junction Avenue Theatre

[57] 1996: 156.

Company. Critics agree that apart from the "poorly documented improvisational efforts of Esau Mthethwa's Lucky Stars" in the 1920s (Holloway 1993a: 18; cf. Coplan 1985: 125) the first traces of the workshop principle can be located during the late 1950s in Sophiatown, the "centre of much of the country's intellectual activity, a multiracial wellspring" (Schwartz 1988: vi). Athol and Sheila Fugard together with the writers Bloke Modisane, Zakes Mokae, Nat Nakasa and Lewis Nkosi formed the African Theatre Workshop Company. Their co-operation led to a play about township life and gangsterism, *No-Good Friday* (1958), which has been analysed as an "expression of [...] liberal multiracialism" (Walder 1992, 348; cf. Holloway 1993a: 18; Kavanagh 1985: 59-83; Walder 1993: xviiif.; Wertheim 2000: 2). David Coplan describes Athol Fugard's success as "due in part to his innovate composing and directing methods. Drawing on African tradition, he developed scripts through actors' extemporaneous performing, or by giving them skeletal scenes to work up through their own improvisational treatment" (1985: 206).

In the late 1960s Gibson Kente's musicals introduced a "broad, physical acting style" which later became typical of workshop theatre (Fleishman 1990: 97). These productions were characterised by a non-naturalistic, physical and musical style, combining music, narrative and dance in a single performance. Kente's musicals displayed "an ironic comic vision which is both regenerative in the face of the essential tragedy of the South African situation, and transformative in its ability to estrange power structures through grotesque parody." It was the ironic and carnivalesque elements of his plays that were to appear time and again in workshop productions by other groups (Fleishman 1990: 89; cf. 97).

Fleishman asserts that the episodic structure of Kente's musicals, which also found its way into many workshop plays, draws on traditional oral forms such as the storytelling technique (cf. 1990: 97).[58] David Coplan traces the "plotless, episodic and improvisational" and "discontinuous" form of, for instance, Matsemela Manaka's *Egoli* to traditional African theatre (1985: 221; 1986: 171; see Chapter 4.4). Anne Fuchs comments, "The whole point, surely, is that this new type of theatre has adopted the structures of a certain type of oral performance, without trying to imitate the unity of action of Western drama. The episodic structure

[58] Mzo Sirayi (1996) even identifies activities such as hunting, the circumcision ceremony and telling folk-tales (storytelling) among the Xhosa people as indigenous oral drama forms. These activities can be considered forms of drama because elements such as actors, song, music, dance, poetry, narrative, dialogue, mime, improvisation, action, plot, role-playing, etc, are incorporated into them.

corresponds very closely to that of the Zulu folk-tale [*inganekwane*] and the Xhosa intsomi" (1987: 34).[59] Walter Ong assesses episodic structure in terms of the dichotomy of orality and literacy. He reinforces this by saying that the Ancient Greek oral narrative, the epic, is based on episodes which are strung together not in a "chronological" or "climactic linear" order but in a pattern based on themes, formulas and stanzas (1988: 144). Ong asserts that this method of structuring also applies to "other forms of narrative in oral cultures" to which in this case he assimilates drama. A clear linear plot only became possible with the advent of writing (1988: 146, cf. 139-47). Furthermore, the formal structure of the indigenous folk-tale combines "verbal narrative, body movement, vocal dramatics, and song" (Scheub 1975: 171), or in Coplan's words, "interconnections that move traditional performance into the realm of the theatre, an inherently multimedia art form" (1986: 153).

In the 1970s many workshop groups subscribed to the ideology of Black Consciousness (BC) and represented the movement's aims of black hegemony on a cultural level (cf. Fleishman 1990: 89, 97f.; 1991: 115f.; see Chapter 4.1). Yet Fleishman argues that workshop theatre emerged as a "cogent form" *parallel* to the rise of the BCM. This can be seen in the works from groups such as Workshop '71, Athol Fugard with the Serpent Players[60] and Barney Simon with the Phoenix Players.[61] However, because these groups were multi-racial, they were heavily criticised at a time when BC was the leading ideology challenging apartheid (cf. 1990: 99).

After the Soweto riots of 1976 workshop theatre became the "dominant form of play production" amongst apartheid's opponents. A performance form focusing on

---

[59] Similar to Vladimir Propp's analysis of Russian folk-tales Fuchs offers an analysis of the sequences, their combinations and their functions in Mtwa, Ngema and Simon's play *Woza Albert!* (cf. 1987: 34-36). Fleishman exemplifies the same approach on *Wathint' Abafazi, Wathint' Imbokodo* (*You Strike the Women, You Strike the Rock*) by Phyllis Klotz and the Vusisizwe Players (cf. 1990: 114-16; see Chapter 6.2 of this study).

[60] Apart from *Sizwe Bansi is Dead* and *The Island* with the two members of the Serpent Players John Kani and Winston Ntshona, Fugard and the Serpent Players also created *The Coat* (1967) as well as plays such as *The Last Bus* (1969) and *Friday's Bread on Monday* (1970) which have remained unpublished to date (cf. Gray 1991: 35, 39f.).

[61] The Phoenix Players were initially founded at Dorkay House in Johannesburg to present Fugard's play *Hello and Goodbye* to a black audience. In 1972 the Phoenix Players performed *Phiri*, an African jazz musical for which Simon adapted Ben Jonson's *Volpone* to a township setting. They also sponsored the first Johannesburg performances of *Sizwe Bansi is Dead* (cf. Coplan 1985: 209, 219f.).

the urban experience, it was, according to Fleishman, practised by "all sectors of the population" and "could be made by anyone regardless of education, regardless of an ability to write well or to speak English well" (1990: 99). In theory this was possible, but in practice many sectors of the population were excluded. For example, the number of women involved in theatre was still very small, and the rural population rarely participated (nor received much attention) in traditional workshop plays. It was not until the workshop technique was adopted for the educational theatre-for-development that the rural population was included in the creation process more often. This criticism notwithstanding, it appears justified that workshop theatre was considered to be democratic because it was a multi-racial and a multi-class development. These aspects of workshop theatre were anathema to the BCM – even though their own creative methods had apparently failed to rouse the working classes. It was therefore this period after the Soweto uprising that marked the change in resistance politics. In 1983 the formation of the United Democratic Front, an alliance across class and race, followed principles similar in essence to those of workshop theatre. Most of the 1980s was marked by waves of mass protest spreading across the country and underpinned by a growing armed resistance and an increasingly organised and unionised working class (cf. Fleishman 1990: 110). Commenting on and reacting to these developments, the multi-racial workshop play was necessarily political and openly displayed this aspect. Ian Steadman even claims that in this decade "'...the preponderance of plays made through 'workshop' theatre can be seen as analogous to the emergence of progressive action based on a mass-democratic movement in South African politics'" (qtd. in Fleishman 1991: 62f.). This leads Fleishman to consider what he (perhaps somewhat inappropriately) calls the "rise" of workshop theatre in the 1980s as a confirmation of Victor Turner's claim that the social dramas and stage dramas of societies engage in a dialectic relationship (see Chapter 1.5.2). In this way multi-racial workshop drama, by striving to overcome racial barriers, logically distances itself from polarising ideologies such as BC. Miles Holloway argues that these workshop plays also "bluntly contradict the racist, segregationist ethos of the day, and signify a communality of human endeavour in defiance of state intention" (1993a: 18; cf. Peck 1997: 156). The plays under discussion in this section, *Born in the RSA* and *Sophiatown*, clearly illustrate this return to creative collaboration and co-existence of different races in the hope for a peaceful and integrated future.

Fleishman identifies three functions that workshop theatre fulfils in the social process. Firstly, by documenting the history of the struggle, it shows that the contemporary protest movements are part of a long tradition in the fight against oppression. Secondly, workshop theatre functions as popular memory by presenting current events but revealing them as a consequence of events from history. Finally, workshop theatre also aims at educating and mobilising both the actors and the audience (cf. 1990: 110-13). A few of the plays that are acknowledged as a documentation of contemporary struggle during the 1970s and 80s are *Imfuduso* by the women of the Crossroads squatter camp in Cape Town; the workers' theatre productions *Ilanga Se Lo Phonela Abasabeni* ("The Sun Will Rise for the Workers") by members of the Metal and Allied Workers' Union employed in a Johannesburg iron foundry; *The Dunlop Play* by workers of the Dunlop factory; and *The Long March* by the Sarmcol Workers' Co-Operative (cf. Kerr 1995: 227-31; Tomaselli 1981a; 1981b; 1982). The plots in these plays can be described as "collective autobiography" (Gordimer 1990: 39; cf. Gready 1994).[62] The plays *You Strike the Woman, You Strike the Rock* (*Wathint' Abafazi, Wathint' Imbokotho*) by the Vusisizwe Players with Phyllis Klotz (see Chapter 6.2) and *Sophiatown* by Junction Avenue Theatre Company (see Chapter 5.3) focus on the non-racial politics of the ANC prior to 1960. *The Native Who Caused all the Trouble* by Vanessa Cooke, Danny Keogh and Fink Haysom comments on the development of racial segregation during the 1930s and deals with the conflict between the colonial and African value systems (cf. Botha & Blignaut 1992: 162; cf. Botha & Van Aswegen 1992: 98).[63] Developments such as workers' theatre (or trade union theatre)[64] and theatre for development (environmental, health and sex education, etc)[65] endeavour to educate and mobilise (cf. Fleishman 1990: 110-13; Holloway 1993a: 21-27; Orkin 1991: 190-202).

---

[62] These plays can be described as what Nadine Gordimer calls "People's Literature," i.e. written by the black workers who in their role as "worker-actor-playmakers are in total, immediate interaction with the roles they play in real life. There is unity of experience in the actuality of dramatized events [...]" (1990: 39).

[63] *The Native Who Caused all the Trouble* has received little academic attention. It was turned into a film (1989) directed by Manie Van Rensburg starring John Kani as Tselilo the "Native" (cf. Botha & Blingnaut 1992: 162-5; Botha & Van Aswegen 1992: 98-103; Williams 1990).

[64] For detailed accounts of workers' theatre productions see Gready (1994), Hlongwane (1994), Holloway (1993), Kerr (1995: 225-31), Orkin (1991: 190-7), Sitas (1996) and von Kotze (1984; 1988). Kerr considers workers' theatre as a type of theatre for development (1995: 227).

[65] See Zakes Mda's accounts of the Marotholi Travelling Theatre (n.d.; 1994) and his more general reflections on the practice, form and function of theatre for development (1993) as well as on its development (1998).

The process of creating a workshop play is essentially composed of three steps that Fleishman describes as "observation," "improvisation" and "selection." Observation consists of various forms of research: reading, conducting interviews, observing one's environment and personal experience. In the improvisation phase, which Fleishman calls the "major element of the playmaking process" (1991: 74), characters are created with the help of information acquired during the observation phase; individual episodes are then developed. In the third phase, that of selection, episodes are chosen and combined to form a frame against which a performance is set. This process of selection can take place in a collective participatory fashion, at the desk of an individual or in other ways. Fleishman claims that the respective method of selection chosen for a production will give each play either a more oral or more literary quality. Nonetheless, he emphasises that regardless of the process of selection the improvisational and physical form of character creation leads to a more physical performance (1990: 102). He describes improvisation as "a physical process in which gesture exists before and alongside words as an independent sign system."[66] He adds, "The physical body in South African theatre is a source of primary meaning which constantly challenges the hegemony of the written word in the meaning-making system" (1996: 175). Ong also points out that oral memory displays a large "somatic" element and that consequently, "Spoken words are always modifications of a total, existential situation, which always engages the body" (1988: 67; cf. Fleishman 1996: 175).

There are many different ways in which the processes of observation, improvisation and selection can be combined. It must be kept in mind that no two plays were created in exactly the same manner. This accounts for the large variety of methods for creating workshop plays and for the many different forms of performances that emerged. For instance, the cast of *Born in the RSA* did not rely on the improvisational phase, but each actor began developing characters after the phase of observation (cf. Fleishman 1991: 113). And the script of *Sophiatown* was composed by Malcolm Purkey in isolation after six months of group work. This leads Fleishman to detect a "dominance of the literary" in the text and to classify *Sophiatown* as a well-made play (1991: 154, cf. 152).

---

[66] In a recent interview Fleishman talks about "'physical theatre'" and "'dance theatre,'" a contemporary development that originated in avant-garde theatre (Ionesco and Brechts's portrayal of the absurdity of language and Artaud's "body-centred theatre") and contemporary dance (Laban's focus on the "body-space nexus"). This development is not linked to the physical acting style that Fleishman detects in the workshop productions discussed here (cf. Abrahamse et al. 2000: 199-201).

Based on collective decision-making and consensus, the production process of workshop theatre is democratic and also constitutes a political act.[67] As a "communal and participatory" undertaking it is similar to the practice of oral tradition, a further parallel that leads Fleishman to regard workshop theatre as an "essentially oral form of cultural expression" (1990: 102, 90). By contrast, Coplan emphasises that the improvisational techniques employed in workshop derive from Western drama theory (cf. 1985: 220). Anne Fuchs argues, for example, that *Born in the RSA* and *Sophiatown* are not only "non-racial and anti-apartheid" but "synthesize European, Western-inspired forms with traditional story-telling techniques and music" (1991: 78). These different evaluations show that workshop productions constituted a new development that could not be explained in conventional terms. Temple Hauptfleisch calls this new kind of theatre an "'indigenous, hybrid'" performance form (1997: 60; see Chapter 1.3.2.). Holloway notes that these plays permit "a fusion of cultural and social knowledge that would probably have been inaccessible to the individual playwright and unavailable to the average white South African" (1993a: 18). Similarly, Hauptfleisch emphasises that improvisational and workshop techniques are well suited to groups which struggle to bring together and to communicate across the gulfs that divide the South African people:

> [...] since it is not merely a matter of matching differing concepts of society but also of matching different concepts of theatre, they [workshop groups] began to utilize the improvisational format in order to create texts which married the 'non-theatrical' performance elements contained in indigenous (traditional and contemporary) communal performance with the more conventional forms of Western tradition. [...] The best of the hybrid work is a complex fusion of a variety of traditions, conventions and performance techniques drawn from various times and cultures. (Hauptfleisch 1997: 61)

---

[67] This quality is more pronounced in non-professional productions than in professional ones. Fleishman attributes this discrepancy to the fact that in non-professional productions the workshop group are responsible for their collective idea and also responsible to the community which they represent. By contrast, in professional productions, apart from the fact that professional actors can be hired to embody certain characters, the director occupies a more central role in the final creation of the script (cf. 1990: 103). Holloway confirms that these plays often exhibit more "narrative coherence" (1993: 21).

A technique that is typical of Barney Simon's productions at the Market is a mixture of narrative from the Xhosa oral tradition of storytelling[68] and dramatic interchanges in style of vaudeville. This is particularly predominant in *Woza Albert!* (cf. 1997: 61). *Born in the RSA* also makes use of the strong narrative element but uses dramatic passages to a lesser extent. It is interesting to note that the Xhosa storyteller of *iintsomi* is traditionally female (cf. Scheub 1975, 1977; Zenani 1992) whereas storytelling is normally considered a male domain – as suggested in Walter Ong's seminal study of exclusively male oral traditions (cf. 1988). As in the Xhosa storytelling tradition, the majority of characters in *Born in the RSA* are female.

5.2. *Born in the RSA* and life in a "country on fire"[69]

> [...] the struggle would always continue [...] through our government's special genius for creating black political activists by the thousand.
>
> Mia Steinman in *Born in the RSA*[70]

5.2.1. Barney Simon on theatre

In 1976 Barney Simon, Mannie Manim and other members of their young independent acting group, The Company, opened the Market Theatre in Johannesburg's old Indian fruit market.[71] Since its foundation the Market Theatre subscribed to a non-racial policy, encouraging black, white and mixed theatre groups to play to multi-racial audiences, even at a time when such practices were very limited: "[...] the kind of space it provided from the start, remains rare, one of the few places where people have been able, to an extent at least, to share a non-apartheid space and to glimpse within the space of the theatre itself, intimations of an alternative South Africa" (Orkin 1991: 185; cf. Schwartz 1988: 43).

---

[68] Storytelling is an ancient oral form of art, a tradition which had developed historically to a communal activity and occupied a firm place in the daily life of older societies. On the topic of storytelling in Africa see also Ruth Finnegan (1970: 373-78 and 501f.).

[69] Cf. Barber 1999: 243.

[70] *RSA* 94. References to *Born in the RSA* are flagged *RSA*.

[71] According to the Group Areas Act, which restricted all residential, commercial and industrial land use to a specific race group, the premises on which the Indian market was located would have only been allowed to be used by Indians. However, because the market had been frequented by people from all race groups, it was possible to consider racial mixing in the Market Theatre as legal (cf. Schwartz 1985: 43).

The Market has hosted "some of the most successful indigenous works of South African theatrical history" (Hauptfleisch & Steadman 1984: 168) both by individual dramatists and workshop groups. Barney Simon became known not only as the artistic director of the Market but also as the director of many workshop productions in the 1980s and early 1990s. Often (but not exclusively) working with racially mixed groups, he and his actors created productions such as *Cincinatti* [*sic*] – *Scenes from City Life* (1979), *Black Dog/Inj'emnyama* (1984) and *Born in the RSA* (1985). They are referred to as "by Barney Simon and the cast" which shows Simon's great contribution to their making. The internationally successful *Woza Albert!* is attributed to Percy Mtwa, Mbongeni Ngema and Barney Simon. The latter played a central role in the creation of these plays. He not only directed them but also guided the actors in developing and writing their roles. Manim, the Market's manager, asserted that Simon "'gave workshop a good name ... The best actors of our time loved working with Barney because he challenged them and took them higher, faster, further, deeper than the other work they were involved in [...]'" (qtd. in Schwartz 1997: xvi). Despite the actors' strong involvement in creating the plays, they nonetheless clearly carry Simon's signature.

Involved in health education in the Transkei and Zululand before the foundation of the Market Theatre, Simon had worked with a group called Mirror One. The name signified "a reflecting surface in which we might find an image of ourselves [...] a mirror in which our community can see itself and watch each other." He described this project as his "personal commitment" (Simon 1996: 225; cf. 1995a: 91f.; 1995b: 20). At the Market Simon also attempted to create plays that would "go on holding the mirror to the society that we have" (1995a: 93).

Simon's creative involvement with actors at the Market Theatre Laboratory was based on the explorations of their biographies and the biographies of the characters that they embodied, for he saw himself as a storyteller:

> For me there's something fantastic about theatre as a communication. It's people getting together to tell a story on a theme that matters to them, and forming a community to tell that story, and using the greatest treasure house available, which is, by my standards, their own biographies, with which they inform the text that they value. (Anon. 1978: 8)

Simon sent the members of the cast to observe life on the streets of Johannesburg and Soweto and to "hunt among the people for the feelings that were there [...]" (1995b: 19). The actors collected impressions of urban 'reality' in cafés, parks, train stations and public institutions by watching and interviewing people. The actors then chose characters they wanted to present and developed roles under Simon's guidance.[72] This "theatre from the street concept" led to a unique form of theatrical expression, a new South African theatre which Simon called "'Azanian theatre'"[73] (qtd. in Sichel 1984: 10).

Simon's workshop process consisted not only of a phase of creation, but he insisted on the importance of "a time of meditation, of digestion, of perspective" (1996: 228). The artists' aim was to give birth to characters that were as genuine as possible: "gritty and real, [...] authentic characters drawn from the South African landscape and shaped by events, large and small, which shaped their country and their lives." Schwartz attributes this success not only to the group's observation of people but also to Simon's sensitivity to "the biography of his country and the time in which he was living" (Schwartz 1997: xv, xix). Simon explained:

> We work for discovery not display and that usually involved the elimination of lies and cliches. And to me there's something stunningly beautiful about people coming together and discovering the gestures, the sounds and silences, the spaces that are going to best make the story real to people who are going to witness it. (Anon. 1978: 8)

Schwartz argues that Simon's method of working included "elements of danger, of challenge and of struggle." Simon considered it "a constant quest for knowledge, for deeper understanding, for new ways of approaching both the work and the reality it reflected." He hoped that not only the actors but also his audience recognised this quest (Schwartz 1997: xvi). Simon had to realise that the search for knowledge of 'reality' and the presentation of this 'reality' remained subjective. Nonetheless, he was convinced that what all people had in common was the need to be recognised as human:

> '...sometimes I have been accused of giving greater value to the black experience than the white. I find that an astounding judgement. I can't begin to choose, to say that one life decision is more valuable than another. All that I can begin to be witness to and more often than not be astonished by, is the struggle for dignity, for visibility within each person.' (qtd. in Schwartz 1997: xvii)

---

[72] The intellectual co-operation of many artists in the creation of one play did not always end harmoniously. Arguments around credits and royalties as well as allegations of intellectual theft had to be dealt with (cf. Schwartz 1997: xvf.).

[73] 'Azania' is the name for South Africa preferred by the BCM.

Simon's work was of a socio-political nature although he himself was never involved in politics, rejecting its "'interference of ideas, concepts'" (qtd. in Schwartz 1997: xvii). Simon refused to let his work be pigeonholed as 'protest' or 'political' theatre:

> 'If you want to reflect a community you want to reflect as much of it as possible, and if you start to reflect a black reality it can be very painful for whites to confront – for them it becomes protest theatre. What they call protest or political theatre is a black man's everyday.' [...] 'Every adult South African sitting in this auditorium was born into an insane world. Insane because it denied and confused mankind's greatest gift, the equality of our humanity. We were forced to behave as if cultural differences between human beings were stigmas, separations, that curiosity and passion could be crimes; and we were denied that dignity of even comprehending the lives being lived beside us.' (qtd. in Schwartz 1997: xviif.)

Realities such as these led Simon to create plays about "the consciousness of our time" (1995a: 85): "What we were doing was strongly committed theatre reminding the people of freedom and reminding the people of heroes and reminding the people of what was happening in our lives and in our streets" (1995b: 19).

One of Simon's aims was the representation of the "'Others'" of society, from Africans to gays, from political activists to informers (qtd. in Sichel 1984: 10). He wanted to confront his spectators with their fears and prejudice, hoping that eventually they would overcome their ignorance and recognise the humanity of these 'Others.' One play which attempted to realise this goal is *Black Dog/Inj'emnyama* which stages "a patchwork of cultures and identities" (Sichel 1984: 10). It tells the story of an ANC freedom fighter who is forced into exile after the student revolt in Soweto in 1976 and is later killed by a white paratrooper. The play thematises the disrespect that human life in South Africa is accorded. Simon explained: "It's how we are taken, by the systems around us, from ourselves and what we can be. Our most precious asset is our potential as human beings" (Sichel 1984: 10). The play received a sensational comment in the pro-government newspaper *Die Burger*: "'After this play [...] it will be difficult to look in the same discriminating way at people on the street. It was [...] fascinating, multi-racial drama which rouses compassion for people from every race group'" (qtd. in Schwartz 1997: xx).

In his last public speech before his death in 1995[74] Simon expressed his conviction that in the course of the past two decades the Market had not only witnessed changes in South Africa but played an active role in caring and providing for South African society (cf. Schwartz 1997: xvii). In 1984 the run of *Black Dog/Inj'emnyama* preceded a time of political unrest and violence. Simon believed this to be purely coincidental: "'We didn't cause them [riots], but merely smelled them coming. It's there in the whole tone of the play and I think that's an extraordinary indication of theatre as a sensor'" (qtd. in Schwartz 1997: xix). Seen in this light, the role and function of theatre can be determined as both a reflection of and an influence on society in Schechner and Turner's sense.

5.2.2. *Born in the RSA* – the play

Born in the RSA premiered in August 1985 in the midst of a time of violent unrest that *Black Dog* had prophesied. A state of emergency was declared. Charles Barber says about the period: "By early 1985 'unrest' had become a euphemism for a land in turmoil. Black resistance reached unprecedented levels of intensity. The country was on fire" (1999: 243).[75] *Born in the RSA* presents this fire on stage not only in the unfolding story line but also by using a backdrop of powerful video images from township streets. Marianne Thamm describes this video material as "film footage of township violence – flames, smoke, angry children and strutting policemen" (1986: 6). It is not surprising that the play is hailed as the first one "that confronts head-on the violence and horror of what is now happening in the townships" (Jacobs 1985: 6). The creators of *Born in the RSA* regard it as a combination of journalism and theatre, a hybrid form. Schwartz argues that Simon conceived the play as "'a living newspaper'" (qtd. in Schwartz 1997: xxii). The term 'living newspaper' had been coined in the United States in the 1930s to signify a division of the Federal Theatre Project. This organisation was initiated by the Roosevelt government but set up on a federal basis to create the maximum number of jobs for unemployed theatre personnel during the time of the Great Depression. The 'living newspaper' division was headed by director Hallie

---

[74] Barney Simon, in his early sixties, died in 1995 after a multiple bypass operation.

[75] At a time of strong international pressure and hopes for reform President P.W. Botha, in his famous 'Rubicon address,' refused to make concessions, repeating instead past principles and rejecting any form of majority rule. This led to an increase of violence in South Africa and the declaration of a state of emergency (cf. Schwartz 1997: xxiii; Worden 1994: 135).

Flanagan, whose idea it was to "'[...] dramatize the news with living actors, light, music, movement'" (Flanagan 1973: vii; cf. Bigsby 1982: 211-36).[76]

Born in the RSA's journalistic touch is also reflected in its presentation in the playbill (cf. *ibid.*) and in the latest published version (1997): "A docu-drama by Barney Simon *with* Vanessa Cooke, Timmy Kwebulana, Neil McCarthy, Gcina Mhlophe, Terry Norton, Thoko Ntshinga, Fiona Ramsay" (*RSA* 91). This stresses both its journalistic quality and its creation through the collaboration of individual artists and suggests that multiple perspectives will be presented (cf. Fuchs 1990: 75).[77] At the same time Simon also aimed to raise the awareness of his audience about other sectors of society. According to Loren Kruger, *Born in the RSA* surpassed earlier Simon productions which also "drew on immediate experience and research on actual people." It successfully combined "the display of these testimonies with their collective and individual enactment, by working the gaps as well as links between nationhood and selfhood, agitation and restoration, agency and being" (1999: 178). In contrast to *Black Dog/Inj'emnyama*, which followed the model of *Survival* in contrasting the lives of "unrelated individuals," *Born in the RSA* succeeded in "integrat[ing] black and white spaces or public and private action [...] to portray characters as protagonists of national as well as personal dramas of contact and conflict" (*ibid.*).

Born in the RSA is a play about political activists who are betrayed by their friend, a police informer. Seven characters tell the audience their story in the first person and only occasionally acknowledge each other's presence or interact with one another directly. Because of this technique, Fleishman calls *Born in the RSA* a "monologue play[...]" (1991: 144). The characters also play minor roles in each other's stories and present short dialogue scenes with the main character. Strong emphasis is placed on the characters' development in the face of apartheid. This allows the cast to present individuals who go far beyond being simple stereotypes. The informer,

---

[76] Flanagan describes the objective the 'living newspaper' project as the dramatisation of a new kind of struggle that no longer looked at psychological character traits or class arguments but that revolves around "the search of the average American today for knowledge about his [*sic*] country and his world; to dramatize his struggle to turn the great natural and economic and social forces of our time toward a better life for more people" (qtd. in Bigsby 1982: 218). A group of famous federal theatre plays (*Ethiopia*, *Triple A Ploughed Under*, *Injunction Granted* and *One Third of a Nat*ion) was written by Arthur Arent between 1936 and 1938.

[77] By contrast, Duma Ndlovu introduces *Born in the RSA* as a "collaborative effort by Barney Simon and the Cast" before listing the actors' names (1986: 129). He thus places more emphasis on the group-production process in workshop under Simon's lead.

the betrayed lover, the activist, the human rights lawyer, etc, are all human beings with their own personal histories and different motivations and emotions.

The play presents seven characters whose stories are closely linked to one another. Hence they talk not only about themselves but also about each other. Some of them are mentioned in the monologues of the other characters before they address the audience directly for the first time. This technique of external characterisation not only builds dramatic tension and arouses the audience's interest in the characters, but it also allows for the presentation of multiple perspectives and gives the play a democratic feel – everyone is allowed to voice their opinion about everyone and everything.

The characters can be grouped into three categories. The first is Glen, the student spy and police informer, who works for the apartheid system by betraying political activists including his friends and even his lover, Susan. Three very strong women fall into the second category: Mia, the Afrikaans human rights lawyer; Thenjiwe, the black activist; and Susan, the white activist. They represent different ways of and reasons for actively fighting against apartheid. Finally, Thenjiwe's boarder Zach, her sister Sindiswa and Glen's wife Nicky are to different degrees and for varying reasons all victims of apartheid. The large number of different stories and perspectives allows for the presentation of what Anne Fuchs calls a "visible swiftly-changing situation" (1990: 72). Multiple *loci*, understood as places referred to in speech and created on stage, and as physical and moral spaces, allow for the presentation of a broad spectrum. The "spaces" staged in *Born in the RSA* are the "'space of the law'," the "[...] 'party scene'," meetings, arrests, the police station and the "landscape of detention, Diepkloof prison" (1990: 73). While parties become the basis for betrayal, the prison is characterised as a space of resistance and hope for change.

By portraying the involvement of black and white characters, Simon comments on a reality that is easily forgotten or denied. He asserts that "'[...] it was not to the converted that I was preaching, but to those who weren't aware of the fact that there were blacks and whites who had struggled together against apartheid'" (qtd. in Schwartz 1997: xxiv). John Kani suggests that the play "shocked the complacent white community into realising that their offspring would not necessarily accept the status quo in this country as God-given and never to be questioned" (1994: 7f.). While these comments point to the major issues that the play addresses, they both omit the important aspect that *Born in the RSA* is one of the first plays to accord a central position to the role of women in the fight against oppression.

5.2.2.1. Obsessed with power: Supporting apartheid

Glen Donahue is the only white male among the play's main characters. He explains that his interest in things and people came from "simple fascination" and inquisitiveness (*RSA* 95) such as his curiosity for Africans which allowed him to get along well with them. His wife, Nicky, claims that she was drawn to him because she found his "strange kind of privacy" attractive (*RSA* 95). He had quickly learnt how to attract the interest of others: "Privacy intrigues people, so on the whole, people find me quite intriguing – especially women" (*RSA* 95). He seems to have always been a mysterious person and has been able to profit from this character trait.

Glen describes himself as a man who was fairly uninterested in politics in his younger years. He explains that he performed his national service in the police force not because he wanted to support the state or protect the white population but because it allowed him to continue living at home: "The reasons I do things are usually very simple" (*RSA* 95). He considered the police force a multi-racial institution, which of course it was because it opportunistically employed white and black policemen. However, it cannot be denied that the main task of the police was to protect the white population by brutally suppressing militant black resistance, as is also shown in Percy Mtwa's play *Bopha!*. Content with his life and not wanting anything to change, Glen felt no need to question state policies, justifying this with his observation that he had "seen shit happening on both sides of the Police Force" (*RSA* 96). However, at the University of the Witwatersrand in Johannesburg his political science tutorials on Marxism have, as he says, "put me off it for life" (*RSA* 96). Whether this was for political reasons is debatable because he makes a point of expressing his dislike for his tutor Feigle, one of the "bullshitters who are so goddamn sure of themselves" (*RSA* 96). This hatred was not based on differing political opinions but on different temperaments and personalities. When Glen was asked by the Police to keep an eye on the dissident tutor, he declined at first but then realised what immense power he could thereby acquire over another person: "There was this strange double feeling, you know, this feeling of my own power, and of Feigle as ... innocent" (*RSA* 97). And a while later he says: "I discovered how easy it is to manipulate people – to get to know what you want to know.

There's no two ways about it, I started to enjoy it" (*RSA* 99). As suggested above, Glen not only likes exercising power over people but also enjoys being admired by women. He explains that shortly after he had met Susan at one of these multi-racial political parties, they began an affair. Where his wife, Nicky, had not been able to relate to his sudden 'interest' in politics and his new group of 'friends,' Susan accepted Glen. Although Glen initially wanted to use Susan to spy on her friends in the Black Women Workers' Rights group, he could not help getting close to her: "It became a very complicated situation" (*RSA* 101). Thus when he found brochures from Umkhonto We Sizwe, the armed wing of the ANC, he realised that he could not play the roles of the spy and the lover at the same time. Caught in an inter-role conflict,[78] he was forced to choose: "I really cared for Susan, but I felt this crazy kind of high; it was like standing on the top board, waiting to jump. I decided to hand it [the brochure] in" (*RSA* 102). Glen was obsessed with power. In fact, his power over Susan gave him more satisfaction than his sexual affair with her. Glen's information allowed the police to raid a Black Women Workers' Rights meeting and to arrest Susan and other activist women including Thenjiwe. His political betrayal of Susan even took on sexual overtones. Frank Rich comments on Glen's behaviour: "As his betrayal of women mirrors his betrayal of blacks, so his exercise of power becomes a kinky sexual escapade" (1986: C3).

Glen justifies the state's action against apartheid's opponents by arguing that racism is an international phenomenon that is handled brutally everywhere. It accords immense power to all those who belong to the group of the oppressors and allows them to demonstrate their superiority. Again, political and racial dominance gives sexual satisfaction: "Racism is a problem everywhere, it's primal, man! And deep down that goes for the Feigles too. They need us to be like this, it's the new pornography! We're the stars of the world. They watch us like voyeurs in some sleazy leather bar" (*RSA* 113). Glen eventually accepted a full-time position in the police force, executing apartheid ideology as a means of acquiring power over individuals. His thirst for power forced him into a role that alienated him from his peers. Having betrayed his 'friends' and grown apart from his wife and child, he is now branded as an informer and socially excluded, allowed to play no other role than that of the police spy: "[...] people avoid me in the streets, they don't wave back. [...] Only cops love me now" (*RSA* 124). In the end his appreciation of his

[78] An inter-role conflict arises when the behavioural expectations addressed to two different roles that a person plays at the same time are not compatible (cf. Dreitzel 1980[3]: 44).

fellow police officers does not give him satisfaction either. Despite his personal victories over the tutor, his lover and her group, he comes to recognise that apartheid as a system is on the verge of becoming powerless. And since his own power relies on the structures of apartheid, he will soon be powerless, too. He has realised that the real power lies in the hands of the young black generation: "You must go to Soweto, you must look at these kids, you must look into their eyes. They stink, man! They stink of victory! It looks like we're all going to have our houses burned down pretty soon [...]" (*RSA* 124). When the task of talking to the imprisoned Thenjiwe, who has so far refused to make a statement, falls to Glen, he knows that his mission is futile. She tells him that he is not worth the match that she and her supporters would need to necklace him,[79] thereby threatening his only role identity by refusing to recognise him as the dangerous informer. In the end he leads a pathetic, lonesome existence and feels sorry for himself. His role as the informer no longer gives him power because nobody fears him or takes him seriously. Glen is left feeling that the roles of perpetrator and victim have become reversed. He regards escape from society and its norms as his only chance of survival: "I've often thought about becoming a game ranger or a forester" to be "in a place with no houses" (*RSA* 124). He clearly suffers from the identity that his roles have forced upon him.

5.2.2.2. Keeping up the fight: Apartheid's opponents

Mia Steinman is an Afrikaans attorney committed to helping the oppressed. Having grown up in a liberal, multi-racial environment, her childhood is reminiscent to Rosa Burger's, the main character in Nadine Gordimer's *Burger's Daughter*. The deconstruction of the opposition between the private and the public that Nicole Cujai detects in this novel is also present in Mia's story (cf. 2001: 64). Liberalism and multi-racialism in her family are not only political programmes but represent their way of life.[80] Following in her father's lead, Mia has always regarded the struggle against apartheid for peaceful co-existence and political equality as a part of her life: "[...] although times have changed, and faces have changed, I still feel

---

[79] Necklacing was a practice used in the townships to murder opponents. A tyre filled with petrol was placed around the victim's body and set aflame.

[80] Mia remembers her parents taking in the children of their white and black detained political friends. She also recalls well-known oppositional leaders at her family dinner table (*RSA* 94). This mirrors the Burgers' raising of their friend's son Zwelinzima ('Baasie'), who becomes a brother to young Rosa. Political guests are also common at the Burger's house.

privileged to be part of a community that is mine – it's a group of really wonderful people, some are clients, a lot are potential clients" (*RSA* 94). As a human rights activist Mia strongly identifies with the plight of the directly persecuted, accused and victimised: "We all have one basic thing in common – it's a desperate need to change the world we live in" (*RSA* 94). Her personal happiness is secondary to the struggle and to society's general well-being. Not having had "time to look" (*RSA* 94) for a new partner since her husband's death two years previously, she can be described as very much a political and a public person who, like her father, has made the political personal. It seems as if large parts of her identity have fused with the collective identity of apartheid's opponents.

Nonetheless, Mia still remains an individual human being who reacts to her experiences in a very personal way. She tells the audience about her experience as a lawyer acting on behalf of black dissidents who were involved in township riots. Rather than immediate legal attention, which she would have been able to give them, many of the wounded fighters needed medical assistance. However, they refused to go to hospital for fear of being arrested by the police. Mia had to slip into the role of the first-aid helper, washing and dressing the wounded and taking them to doctors. This additional role is one that is forced upon her, that does not come naturally to her. It is not surprising that she does not feel comfortable playing it: "I came home feeling just sick to the stomach – I mean obviously about what was happening, but about myself as well. I mean I was so relieved to get away from it all – and it was so easy to do" (*RSA* 103). Mia's nausea suggests that she is helpless and cannot intervene in the brutal suppression of the rioters. She strongly senses, maybe even fears, the power of the state. Not being able to cope with this situation, she leaves the scene of the action. Her guilt about being relieved to return home makes her feel even worse about herself because she knows that in the end, these feelings will reduce her ability to work efficiently. This incident characterises Mia as a person who can cope better with rational problems than with emotional situations, as someone who wishes to erase her personal and private reactions. Her occupation as a lawyer requires this talent when analysing and interpreting the language of the law. Although she may be able to fulfil the theoretical, objective expectations of her professional role, the explosive South African context forces her to accept a role with a larger scope and meet additional expectations that traditionally belong to other roles.

Mia does not begin her monologue with stories about the personal experiences she has had as a lawyer but quotes the Internal Security Act that prohibited legal proceedings against the state or its representatives.[81] She defines herself as a witness to all atrocities committed in the name of apartheid from the 1950s treason trial, the Sophiatown removals, the Sharpville massacre to the first state of emergency. This explicitly links the current state of unrest in the mid-80s to other events of apartheid history. Kruger argues that "[...] by embedding both [past and current crises] in the memory of an Afrikaans woman [...], the play challenges the iconic dominance of the male activist, black or white" (1999: 179).

Thenjiwe Bona is the play's other major and politically active character. Fighting for female rights, she supports black women workers who suffer from 'triple' oppression (race, class and gender). Thenjiwe can be considered the most powerful and "most explicitly political" character of the play (Kruger 1999: 180). She is also an important character from a structural point of view because her story functions as the link between all the characters. Before she speaks for the first time, she is described by several other characters in whose lives she has played an important role. She has made a strong impression on Mia, who sees in her the first female president of a free South Africa, and on Zachariah, her boarder. He characterises her as an "amazing woman" who is "famous for her courage" (*RSA* 98). Her power derives not only from the fact that she has many friends and supporters but also from the fact that she is a thorn in the flesh of the police who have continuously kept her in detention or under house-arrest. She can be considered a role-model for political activists. Her strength and will to survive, not only as an individual but also as a political leader, are exemplified in her story about her imprisonment and torture.

Thenjiwe's behaviour behind bars shows that she is an experienced prisoner and that she has a strong character. Instead of crying and not eating, she digs into the food that is brought to her, knowing that hard times are yet to come. When she refuses to confess in writing the details of her involvement in the black women workers' movement, she is tortured. Forced to stand for first eighteen and then twenty-four hours a day, suffering from physical and psychic abuse, Thenjiwe does not give up and dreams about escaping from prison with the help of her friends. She also draws strength from closely observing the prison warders. When she believes that one of the white men might make a pass at her, she realises that "[...] for a moment I pitied him. At least I was doing something I believed in, but what was his

[81] The regime used this act to justify the state of emergency declared in July 1985 shortly before the play's premiere.

life? Locked up in a cell with a swaying, swelling kaffir-girl with rolling eyes" (*RSA* 114). Thenjiwe also demands recognition from the warders. She refuses to be humiliated when they talk about her as if she were invisible. Instead, she insists that they acknowledge her existence by forcing them to look her in the eyes. Thenjiwe is also lucky and gets the opportunity of communicating with the outside world. By chance she hears Zach calling her from outside the prison walls and asks him how her children are, in which prison she is being held and what day of the week it is. Thus she is able to let her family know that she is still alive. Zach's answers also allow her to regain her temporal and spatial perception and resituate herself in the same time and place scale that is valid in the outside world.

In the end it is not surprising that the police do not succeed in forcing Thenjiwe to make a statement. When Glen is sent in to work on her, he knows from the start that his undertaking is useless because he has been exposed as the informer. Thenjiwe does not take him seriously, she is full of contempt and spits in his face. After this cathartic moment she lets him know that it is beneath her dignity to take revenge. By refusing to threaten his life, she does not recognise him in his role as her oppressor and therefore asserts her superiority. On a larger scale Thenjiwe's ability to defend herself against her tormentors symbolises her general involvement and strength in the struggle against apartheid.

Susan Lang, an art teacher, is also politically involved in the resistance movement. She is the only white member at the meetings that Glen attends and thus becomes both his object of desire and his source of information. Throughout their affair she never suspects him of being an informer. She is devastated when she finds out at her own trial after weeks of imprisonment that he is responsible for the arrest of her group.

After the raid on the Black Women Workers' Rights meeting Susan had already accepted the idea that she would be arrested and is not at all surprised when the police come for her in the middle of the night. She is, however, offended by the way she is treated as a person:

> SUSAN: [...] They're here for me.
>
> There was this blonde lieutenant woman. She kept touching all my clothes.
>
> COP (*played by* MIA): Ag shame, you're going to miss yoga tonight. (*RSA* 104)

Susan differentiates between her different private and public identities or roles. As an activist she plays a public role and thus offers no resistance to her arrest by the police (a public institution) for her political engagement in the struggle. However, she perceives the lieutenant's touching of her clothes as a physical invasion of her privacy. Apart from official gestures such as handshakes, bodily contact is an element reserved for role behaviour in the private encounter between friends or family members. It requires mutual consent which is not given in this situation. Susan also realises that every minute of her life has been observed, not only her political involvement in Botswana but also her private activities such as her yoga classes or her affair with Glen. In the eyes of the police every move a suspect makes could be part of the struggle and thus justifies complete surveillance. That is why her whole identity is reduced to the role identity of a dissident. Susan must present herself in this identity and also find a way to assert her personal identity. She must play the role of the dissident who does not betray her comrades when tortured. At the same time, in order to preserve her sanity and individuality, she must find a way to regain a sense of privacy. When she moves her mats in the prison cell out of the camera's view, she is reprimanded by the warders. Yet she counters, "That's your problem. This is my cell, I'll sit where I like" and "You told me this is my space" (*RSA* 106, 112). These retorts show that as a dissident she accepts the institution's definition of herself as their prisoner. However, as an individual she thinks in categories associated with subjectivity and liberty: possession, space and freedom of movement. She also gathers strength by reversing the order of surveillance: "They kept me busy but I watched them like a hawk" (*RSA* 108). In addition, she starts a pin collection, stealing a pin off the desk of the interrogation room every time she is questioned there. It represents her scheme for exercising revenge: "They take lots of things away from you [...]. So you start to think of ways of getting back at them" (*RSA* 109). A further strategy of resistance that she develops concerns the interpretation of the Bible. She challenges the Afrikaner appropriation of the Holy Word and exposes it as a false, even blasphemous reading: "I have studied the Bible and there is no sin in opposing a state that disobeys the word of God" (*RSA* 112). She also denies the authority of the apartheid regime with this argument.

Susan remains true to the cause and to her role as an activist for a long time by refusing to reveal any information about the group's secret activities to the police. However, when the police tell her that this strategy will determine Thenjiwe's torture, she is not able to hold on to the idea of resistance at all cost and confesses in order to save her friend: "Ja, they got to me. I began to do a lot of screaming. I'm not sure if it was while I was sleeping or awake. All I know is that one day they showed me a statement I had signed" (*RSA* 117). When she learns at her trial that Glen betrayed the group, her world falls apart. In his role as police informer he betrayed her as an activist and as an individual human being by misusing her affection and her trust.

5.2.2.3. Trying to survive: Living with apartheid

Nicky Donahue can be characterised as a woman who has never learnt to live as an independent human being. She defines herself through Glen, first her boy-friend, then her husband and father of her child. She is apolitical and fairly self-absorbed and cannot or refuses to cope with the social and political realities of life in South Africa under apartheid. She relates how she insisted on joining Glen at university but quickly lost interest in her classes. Pregnancy became the ideal excuse for dropping out of university and getting married. Yet she was soon forced to realise that she was placed second to his interest in politics and political parties. They separated without her knowing about his affair with Susan. Nicky's life now revolves around her role of mother. She relates how one day while shopping downtown, she and her son witnessed a bomb explosion in a restaurant. Apart from being scared for their lives, she is generally also annoyed by acts of violence because they disturb her daily routine. She does not reflect on the reasons for such violence or place them in the South African context. She tries to ignore (or even deny) the political situation: "Look, I'm a single parent. I'm trying to bring up a child, a boy, without a father, I just can't afford to get depressed" (*RSA* 119). When she reads a newspaper article about the trial that mentions Glen's affair with Susan, her world collapses. She still defines herself through her former relationship with him and has not been able to develop an identity independent of his existence.

In contrast to the other women in the play, Nicky lives in her own personal world that revolves around her private tragedy. She doesn't allow apartheid to affect her daily life. Because she is white, many of the hardships that afflict black women such as Sindiswa are not part of her reality; she is hardly even aware of the daily problems they encounter because of their skin colour. In summary, she is quite unlike the other female characters.

Sindiswa introduces herself as Thenjiwe's sister. She gives the impression that she largely defines herself only in relation to her well-known sibling. She sees herself as standing in her sister's shadow, a position about which she feels both comfortable and uncomfortable. On the one hand she is clearly proud and in awe of her sister's achievements. On the other hand she also seems jealous of Thenjiwe's ability to play so many roles successfully and master both her political 'career' and private life: "I'm not famous, I'm not too clever, and I'm not so beautiful either" (*RSA* 100). Yet Sindiswa depends on her sister's help. As a school teacher she lives in a woman's hostel near the school and leaves her son, Dumisani, with Thenjiwe. Nonetheless, Sindiswa is critical of her sister's activism and her inability to relax: "Ag sure I understand about using your time well, and being responsible, but you must also know how to waste it! Otherwise what kind of a person are you?" (*RSA* 100). Sindiswa's outlook on life is radically different to her sister's. Not actively involved in politics, her maxim is to avoid trouble with the police so that she can lead a tranquil and balanced life. She suffers from apartheid and the restrictions that it imposes on her life, yet she finds herself in a defensive position. She does not act but can only react. Receiving the news of Thenjiwe's arrest, she comments: "Now it was not the first time I'd received a message like that - it's become part of our lives, now, so I packed my bag, got a taxi across to Soweto" (*RSA* 105). She also explains: "Mostly there are more soldiers and policemen at our schools than children. [...] Usually there are too few of them to teach. [...] So mostly we just sit and worry – worry about those who could be arrested, those who could be shot" (*RSA* 105). She does not join the students in their fight against the police, preferring to hide in her room: "I ran back to the hostel and watched from a window, high up" (*RSA* 108). She sees the students setting houses on fire. The surveying gaze from above - a symbol for power and possession in colonial fiction that Mary Louise Pratt has described as the "monarch-of-all-I-survey" (1992: 201) - has ironically become a sign of Sindiswa's impotence and fear. When her ten-year-old son does not return in the evening, she goes to look for him at the police station. She is faced with bureaucratic hurdles and uncooperative policemen. She does not find her son among the many arrested students who are being brought to the police headquarters in overcrowded vans. When she is summoned to the station, she learns that Dumisani has made a statement and confessed his involvement in the street violence. As a mother Sindiswa recognises him as her victimised little boy whom she wants to protect. However, the police imprison him because they do not see him as a child but as a potential freedom fighter who could escape to Botswana for guerrilla training. Dumisani's skin colour and age automatically qualify him as a 'street fighter,' a role that the police determine for him by making him sign a false testimony and lie under oath. Despite the injustice inflicted upon her son by the police, Sindiswa still speaks in categories of innocence or guilt. Had her son been involved in the street fighting, she would have considered him guilty. She does not justify all action against apartheid as innocent, heroic behaviour. This is typical of her character: she is not prepared to fight the system and hopes to make the best of the life that apartheid accords her.

Zachariah Melani, a "gentle musician" (Kruger 1999: 180), is another character who, given the circumstances, fights for survival and a 'normal' life. He lives in Thenjiwe's garage, the former living quarter of a friend who he had once helped out of trouble. He does not want to get involved in Thenjiwe's political activities but is too scared to admit this because he admires her work and feels obliged to help her in return for her support. The fact that Thenjiwe keeps stacks of Umkhonto We Sizwe pamphlets in a secret hiding place under his bed makes him uneasy. When he hears of her arrest, he is terrified that the police will come for him as her accomplice. Therefore he is adamant about destroying the political pamphlets:

> So I found myself running with the box through yards, over fences, past barking dogs, to the football field. I dropped the box behind the goal posts, and ran back home. I looked back and I saw Thenjiwe's pamphlets moving like ghosts across the field. In thirty seconds flat I was back in bed, with the door locked behind me. (*RSA* 104)

The image of the leaflets floating around like ghosts expresses Zach's genuine fear. He felt that the pamphlets were following him to prove his involvement in the struggle. These "ghosts" can be seen as a gothic element. A psychoanalytic approach to gothic literature focuses, for example, on Freud's theory of the uncanny (*das Unheimliche*). The idea that the home is familiar and comforting is reversed. The home becomes the place of the uncanny and must be freed from the element of evil before it can return to its original position as haven. In Zach's case the pamphlets are the first sign of danger and foreshadow the arrival of the evil force in the form of the police. Zach cannot relax until the police fail to find any evidence.

Zach is fond of Dumisani and teaches him to play Thenjiwe's favourite blues song on the recorder, Mackay Davashi's *Lovely Lies*.[82] Zach sees his own children in Dumisani and cares for him as if he were his own son, taking him to jazz performances and making music with him. It is a fate typical of African families under apartheid that Zach has never been able to live with his own children. When

---

[82] Mackay Davashe, bandleader, composer and saxophonist, was one of the most talented African performers in Johannesburg in the 1940s and 50s. He was also involved in the musical *King Kong* (1959) as the leader of the Jazz Dazzlers Orchestra (cf. Coplan 1985: 150, 174).

Dumisani is released from prison into Mia's custody, Zach goes to see him in the white suburb. This visit makes a strong impression on him because it shows the injustices of apartheid so clearly. He sees how African women work as nannies for white children and care for them as if they were their own. He also sees how poverty is forcing them to earn money to support their own families. Because of this they are compelled to neglect or abandon their own children and leave their upbringing to other family members. Apartheid deprives the African people of playing their natural roles, the roles of mother and father, and forces them to play such roles for the children of strangers. While the black women look after white children in the well-off suburbs, the white men shoot black children in the streets of the townships. Zach's anger and frustration build up when he sees the heavily sedated Dumisani in Mia's house, a stark contrast to the happy, carefree white children playing in the school yard. He is taunted by his feelings of revenge for Dumisani and for all general injustices inflicted upon the African population by apartheid:

> Suddenly, I moved through the gates to the middle of the playground. I started to swing the baseball bat. Skulls cracked, brains and baby teeth flew. I splintered arms and legs and spines. There was blood everywhere. I went on swinging, left and right. I was a panther, I was a tiger, I was everything they wanted me to be. I was their black King Kong. A bell started to ring. I found myself on the pavement. The bell was calling the children to go inside. I continued to watch them play. I couldn't breathe. I turned and walked up Oxford Road. I heard myself yelling 'Fuck you! Fuck you for what you have done to Dumisani, and fuck you, fuck you, fuck you for what you are doing to me!' (*RSA* 125)

At that moment Zach is completely dazed. He does not control his thoughts but lets his mind run wild. The scene leaves him breathless as if he actually had enacted the gruesome deed that he imagined. This experience is cathartic as it allows him to express his emotions. From the way Zach tells his story it becomes clear that he sees himself not as attacking his opponents but considers himself to be a victim acting in self-defence. It is apartheid's treatment of Africans that makes them turn into or adopt the roles of the animals or monsters they are said to be, rather than the other way round. This idea is also suggested in Buntu and Sizwe's discussion in *Sizwe Bansi is Dead* about the latter's use of the dead man's passbook and Native Identification number[83] (cf. Chapter 3.3.1.2).

---

[83] "All I'm saying is be a real ghost, if that is what they want, what they've turned us into" (*SB* 38).

It is interesting to note that Zach experiences this playground scene as if he had a split or double identity and could observe himself acting out what was actually only going on in his mind. The comment "I heard myself yelling 'Fuck you![...]" emphasises the idea of Zach's simultaneously objective and subjective perspective. However, there is no doubt that Zach did not attack the children. There is an echo in this scene of the motif of the *Doppelgänger* in Victorian novels such as Robert Louis Stevenson's *The Strange Case of Dr. Jekyll and Mr. Hyde.* Zach experiences a personality-split that in a way is comparable to the case of Jekyll and Hyde. Yet while Jekyll actively creates his *alter ego* to cope with his double nature,[84] Zach turns into the "black King Kong," a transformation that he does not consciously pursue and is only able to analyse afterwards. Nonetheless, both texts express social criticism. Stevenson's novel is often seen as a condemnation of society's hypocrisy and double-standards, an evaluation which could also be attributed to the scene in *Born in the RSA.* Zach's story criticises apartheid's double-standards that have pushed the black population into the role of 'inhuman savages' while it is actually the brutal, inhuman system of oppression that is responsible for creating a country in turmoil and initiating black resistance.

5.2.2.4. Storytelling as confession

The predominant technique employed in *Born in the RSA* is that of personal storytelling through which the characters relate their own experiences. In contrast to the male storytelling tradition of traditional African peoples, the Xhosa women combine ancient traditional and mythical elements in their stories (*iintsomi*) with images from the contemporary milieu to reflect and comment on society (cf. Scheub 1977: 346; Zenani 1992: 3). *Born in the RSA* is best described as a dramatic version of the narrative genre of life-writing, a form popular in Western literature in the late twentieth century.[85] The use of the first person narrative style gives the anecdotes a strong self-reflexive and confessional quality. The characters describe

---

[84] Jekyll relates: "It was the curse of mankind that these incongruous faggots were thus bound together – that in the agonized womb of consciousness these polar twins should be continuously struggling. How then, were they dissociated?" (Stevenson 1994: 71). Having developed a magic potion, Jekyll is able to transform into Hyde, the personification of evil, to follow his socially non-acceptable pleasures which soon turned into monstrous activities.

[85] 'Life-writing' is a term that exceeds the confinements of autobiography to include memoirs, diaries, journals, letters and all other personally inflected fictional texts such as the *bildungsroman*, confessional novels, *romans à clef*, biomythography and autofiction (cf. Henke 1998: xiii).

their experience from their own point of view with everyone telling their own story. However, it is the sum of the seven different accounts that gives a comprehensive picture of life in South Africa in the early 1980s.

The characters tell the stories of their lives under apartheid and include not just facts but also their thoughts, emotions and evaluations of events. At times their storytelling produces a confessional tone. The confession as a method of producing knowledge and truth and as an exercise of civil and religious powers was derived in Western thinking from Christian practices of confessing one's sins (cf. Foucault 1990: 53-73). There are three kinds of confession detectable in *Born in the RSA*.

One particular style of confession used in this play operates on the personal level between the character and the audience: the characters admit to (or confess) what they believe are their own faulty character traits. Examples of this style are Mia's story about her revulsion to administer first-aid to wounded street fighters; Glen's recognition of his hunger for power over others; Sindiswa's story of her emotional relationship with her sister, Thenjiwe; and Zach's unsettling imaginary encounter with the white schoolchildren. These so-called 'faults' make it easier for the spectator to recognise these characters as humans with individual personalities.

Another form of confession is the type institutionalised by the apartheid system - the police confession – where arrest, imprisonment and torture were techniques used by the police to extract confessions from political activists. Foucault describes the nature of forced confession:

> One confesses – or is forced to confess. When it is not spontaneous or dictated by some internal imperative, the confession is wrung from a person by violence or threat; it is driven from its hiding place in the soul, or extracted from the body. Since the Middle Ages, torture has accompanied it like a shadow, and supported it when it could go no further: the dark twins. (1990: 59)

As happens in *Statements after an Arrest under the Immorality Act*, Susan is eventually broken by psychological torture and makes a statement. Thenjiwe, by contrast, is pressured by psychological and physical torture but refrains from revealing herself. The police try to force her confession by making her write down her life-story. In Thenjiwe's own words, "I took the pen and started writing. How I found my opening lines, Jesus only knows; but I kept on writing. Where I was born, where I was schooled, my family and my work. I didn't care about sense, I just kept writing. My pen stopped at the eleventh page" (*RSA* 106). The cop's reaction shows that this is not the story that the police wanted to read: "Eleven pages? No, no, my girlie, you've got another eighty-nine pages to go" (*ibid.*). Foucault's ideas explain why Thenjiwe's text is not considered a sufficient account of her life story. A "'political history of truth' [...] show[s] that truth is not by nature free - not error servile - but that its production is thoroughly imbued with relations of power. The confession is an example of this" (1990: 60). Dumisani's experience is comparable to Thenjiwe's. The police do not believe that he did not participate in the street battle and intimidate him until he signs a false testimony that confirms his involvement. The system has appropriated the power to define what does and does not constitute the truth. The police do not grant Thenjiwe and Dumisani the right to tell their own story. Obviously the system's 'others' are not accorded the rights of individuality, self-representation and self-possession, rights associated with the ability to engage in autobiographical exercises.[86]

Glen's story can be regarded as a third form of confession. Psychologically confused and without a stable place in society, his whole account is one large confession, a self-recognition of his downfall and isolation. Cast out from civil society and unable to identify with the system any longer, who is to pardon him and accept him into a group environment? The audience as the representatives of civil society would probably not accept the role of confessor that Glen is trying to impose upon them. As the spectators do not sympathise with him, he has nobody who can 'free' him from his sins. Like Thenjiwe, who refuses to affirm Glen in his role as informer and thus subverts his identity construction, the audience choose not to sympathise with Glen. Once again he is denied the possibility of creating a new role identity.

The seven life stories can also be regarded as first-hand testimonies. The characters then become witnesses to life under apartheid. Indeed, five of them, when introducing themselves to the audience, raise their right hand,[87] say their name and announce that they were "born in the RSA" (cf. Fuchs 1990: 73). It is almost as if they were testifying at a hearing of the Truth and Reconciliation Commission after the demise of apartheid. In this way the play projects hope for change and looks to the future.[88]

---

[86] See Leigh Gilmore's arguments about exclusion from autobiography due to race and gender (2001: 20f.).

[87] This gesture is indicated in the version edited by Ndlovu (1986).

[88] Loren Kruger also argues that *Born in the RSA* uses the "format of the courtroom testimony." The bare stage, except for chairs and microphones, suggests that this courtroom is "stripped of the naturalistic box that might hem it in." In contrast to my reading, she believes that the

With its emphasis on confession and testimony the reading presented here supports *Born in the RSA*'s reception in the national media which focused on the play's mimetical qualities. While Garalt MacLiam argued in his review that the "play doesn't provide any answers. It simply holds 'a mirror up to nature' and allows the audience to come to their own conclusions" (1985: 9), Jean Fairbairn went one step further in her evaluation:

> If theatre is meant to imitate reality, then in South Africa something quite odd happens when it does. Depending, of course, on who you are, what happens on stage can seem more real than life itself. Perhaps this is a result of apartheid; perhaps it is a result of the distorted reality presented in the media; perhaps we just don't want to know. More likely it is a combination of all these evils. Whatever, *Born in the RSA* carries the stamp of truth, and it is a clearer truth than the one we experience or acknowledge outside the theatre. (1986: 8)

It is possible that Fairbairn was led to this conclusion by the play's strong personal, confessional quality and by Foucault's notion of confession as a method for producing the truth. Be that as it may, her evaluation confirms Schechner and Turner's assertion that social drama and stage drama engage in mutual reception and influence. In addition, MacLiam claims that the

> play is a strong political statement which moves it into the social arena and it demands recognition as such. If it was descriptive of events in another country, it would be easier to apply to it words such as brilliantly perceptive [...]. But its content is of such personal relevance to all in this country that it would be facile to observe it merely as a play in the theatre. (1985: 9)

These evaluations seemed to suggest that the play's success in communicating with the audience lay in its convincing presentation of the topic and its achievement of spectator identification with the characters. The personal quality of this play distanced it from other works which relied on the presentation of types to agitate and mobilise its (black) spectators such as Percy Mtwa's *Bopha!*. Yet reviewers also criticised *Born in the RSA*'s mimetic aspect as insufficient: "We have to move from protest theatre to resistance theatre. Perhaps that was what left me most uncomfortable about *Born in the RSA*. It shows us life in South Africa; it does not urge us to act on what it shows us" (Jacobs 1985: 6).

---

repetition of "born in the RSA" is ironic and foregrounds the fact that the characters are "separated by acts of disenfranchisement as well as private disavowal" (1999: 178).

5.2.2.5. Presentation and role-play

The narrative element in *Born in the RSA* is an important part of the play. However, it would be wrong to deny the play's dramatic quality. Like so many of the other plays discussed in this study, *Born in the RSA* makes use of role-play, song and dance to present and vividly comment on the content of the stories in epic manner. In contrast to *Survival*, for example, the actors here do not keep their own names but completely slip into the roles of the characters who alternately narrate their stories. Although they often speak in the past tense, the characters also employ, as Fuchs points out, "the historical present to give scenes more urgency and occasionally a present tense with a phatic function, to convince and persuade the audience" (1990: 71f.) and to state what they consider general truths. This is apparent in Glen's monologues. At one point, for example, he says: "Listen, no one in the world has any right to judge anyone else" (*RSA* 113). The audience become the immediate addressee. As in Styles's opening monologue in *Sizwe Bansi is Dead*, the spectators are forced to judge the characters. It seems almost impossible to stay unaffected by these direct addresses.

The narrative voices of *Born in the RSA* all participate in dramatic dialogues and play the roles of friends, policemen, prison warders, cell inmates, etc. In contrast to plays such as *Survival*, *Bopha!* and *Egoli*, in which black actors take on white roles to voice criticism with interracial mimicry, the actors in *Born in the RSA* do not transform their race on stage. The white actors slip into the roles of cops and warders, a strategy of "contrastive" role-play (Breitinger 2003^2: 149) that foregrounds their primary role as activists and emphasises white participation in the struggle against apartheid. Unlike in the other plays mentioned, these scenes are neither plays-within-the-play, nor do they function as scenes of education in which the teacher raises his pupil's consciousness. Anne Fuchs suggests that the dramatic dialogues "heighten[...] the impact" of the play on the audience (1990: 72). They undoubtedly create a sense of immediacy and reality.

Fuchs asserts that the use of song and dance in the play imitates its use in 'total theatre,' a term that Wole Soyinka coined to signify daily events of real life in South Africa (cf. 1990: 73). There are three examples for this in the play: the song that Thenjiwe, Susan and Sindiswa sing for Mia at her birthday party; the song of the children in prison, which Susan translates for the audience ("The Boers can't sleep because they are afraid of the children" [*RSA* 121]); and finally a militant song that the characters sing when Thenjiwe describes how she was reunited with her former friends from the struggle in Diepkloof Prison. She accompanies the song with a wild, passionate dance, whistling and ululating. By calling out to the other actors, who stand in the dark behind her, while a film of a clash between street fighters and the police is projected in the background, she emphasises the activists' joint commitment in the fight for freedom.[89]

5.3. *Sophiatown*: The search for identity in the face of alterity

> I don't know what the hell I am.
>
> Ruth Golden in *Sophiatown*[90]

5.3.1. The work of Junction Avenue Theatre Company

Junction Avenue Theatre Company (JATC) was founded in 1976 at the University of the Witwatersrand by a group of white students and graduates including Malcolm Purkey, William Kentridge, Pippa Stein, Astrid von Kotze, Ari Sitas and Patrick Fitzgerald. Their agenda was to "reveal apartheid's brutality, engage with the hidden history of struggle, and make a theatre that conscientised and polemicised" (Purkey & Steinberg 2001: viii). Purkey explains:

> An obsession to reclaim and popularize the hidden history of struggle in our country is part of Junction Avenue Theatre Company's self-appointed task. This history has been wiped off the map by the State in its oppression of the majority of South Africans. The powerful flourishing of the contemporary theatre in South Africa, against all odds, indicates the hunger that all South Africans have, to have their world interpreted. We need an informed and articulate new generation, steeped in the past and carefully theorizing about the future, who have shaken off the blanket of silence and are committed in the deepest way to liberation. (1993: xi)

JATC believes that theatre in the sense of a "living theatrical encounter" is "one of the most effective ways to communicate ideas, information and feelings." Their first play, *The Fantastical History of a Useless Man* (1976), attempted to "evaluate the possible role of white, English-speaking South Africans in the context of the

---

[89] Loren Kruger points out that the resistance songs sung in the play stem mostly from the Soweto uprising and address topics such as "martyrdom as well as solidarity, lament as well as struggle." She argues that since the songs are performed mostly by the female characters, they emphasise the women's contribution to the struggle (1999: 181). The song that Thenjiwe, Susan and Sindiswa sing in honour of Mia's birthday, "I never loved a man, the way that I loved you" (*RSA* 100), can then be seen as a "moving expression of female solidarity as well as a testament to the difficult necessity of non-racial collaboration" (1999: 182).

[90] *ST* 27. References to *Sophiatown* are flagged *ST*.

'76 Soweto uprisings." They believed that as an all-white group their reflection of the nature of conflicts remained "entirely unsatisfactory," a conviction which gave rise to the wish to develop into a non-racial workshop group. This goal was realised in co-operation with the actors Ramolao Makhene, Siphiwe Khumalo and Arthur Molepo, former members of the dissolved theatre group Workshop '71, which JATC looked up to as a "working model of non-racial democracy" (all Purkey 1993: xi; cf. Orkin 2001: 2; see Chapter 4.2). JATC thus became "one of the first multi-racial theatre companies in the country" (Perdekamp 2003[2]: 161) whose members were both "dissident ruling-class as well as oppressed subjects" (Orkin 1991: 198).

JATC created plays that Malcolm Purkey describes as "militantly oppositional" and "critically reflect[ing] the mad world of apartheid in all of its manifestations" (1996: 158, 156). The main subjects have been "life in colonial segregation and apartheid Johannesburg" (Purkey & Steinberg 2001: x). In 1978 the Company explored the "relationship between labour and liquor" on the Johannesburg goldmines around 1900 in *Randlords and Rotgut* (Purkey 1993: xi).[91] One year later they produced *Will of a Rebel*, a play about Breyten Breytenbach. Two popular plays toured both the townships and white areas: *Security* (1979) about an unemployed man who, in an exploitative society, is transformed into a 'dog,' and *Dikitsheneng* ('In the kitchen,' 1980), which dealt with the madam-maid relationship. Both of these plays explored how power and resistance could be exercised through roles.[92] Several of JATC's members including Ari Sitas and Astrid von Kotze turned to worker plays in the light of the trade union movement in 1982 (cf. Orkin 2001: 3; Sitas 1996b; von Kotze 1984; 1988). The urban removals in Doornfontein in the 1930s and 1940s constituted the focus of *Marabi* (1982), a play based on *The Marabi Dance*, a popular novel by Modikwe Dikobe (cf. Purkey 1993: xiif.; Orkin 2001: 3f.). The theme of forced removals was taken up again in *Sophiatown*. Martin Orkin emphasises that all the plays concentrate on "processes of domination and exploitation" (2001: 3), typical Marxist themes which reflect JATC's

[91] The play is named after an article by the historian Charles van Onselen (cf. Purkey 1993: xii; Orkin 2001: 2f.).

[92] Personal discussion between Ari Sitas and the author on 11 June, 2002 at Freiburg University, Germany.

> attempts to draw on Marxist/socialist discourse as a more reliable means of articulating or narrating history than that dominant in the apartheid state. And, in accord with Marxist/socialist belief in the dialectic of history, the Company defines as part of its endeavour to understand its present world, an urgent need to recover particularly marginalised or suppressed narratives of the past. (Orkin 2001: 12)

This revelation of hidden history and the telling of stories from the perspective of the voiceless is based on a model for theatre making that heavily employs character development and narrative structure. For Orkin there is a connection between the rise of the anti-apartheid novel from the 1970s onwards and the narrative focus of *Sophiatown*. Both the new novel and the play concentrate on the "act of writing to create 'reality'" (1991: 199).

JATC followed Brechtian theatre theories. Despite the serious subject matter, the group took Brecht's saying to heart that "'A theatre that can't be laughed in, is a theatre to be laughed at'" and strove to create "theatre that gave pleasure" by including "Song, dance, humour, wit and crudity" (Purkey & Steinberg 2001: viii).

Purkey explains that JATC based its work on a model of creating theatre that relied on a "strong concept of character development and narrative structure" and that, somewhat contradictorily, is "indebted in part to a kind of social realism and in part to the theories of Brecht." *Sophiatown*, for instance, stages a set of relatively realistic characters interacting in a domestic drama on the one hand, on the other, however, songs, slogans and shouts intervene "almost arbitrarily" in the action (1996: 158). This description corresponds to C.W.E. Bigsby's characterisation of the American playwright Clifford Odets' *Waiting for Lefty* (1935) as a "play which negotiated a middle ground between extended agit-prop sketch and realistic play" (1982: 200). Similarities between anti-apartheid plays and the American left-wing theatre movement again become apparent.

All of JATC's plays have been created in theatre workshops. "Research, oral testimony, yoga and theatre games, exercises and African dance, music workshops and the study of sociology are some of the strands that have made up the eclectic whole designed to unleash the creative energies needed to forge a workshopped play" (Purkey 1996: 156).

5.3.2. *Sophiatown* - the play

Sophiatown, which premiered in 1986, deals with the destruction of the last mixed township in the Johannesburg area in the late 1950s.[93] This idea followed from the group's play *The Marabi Dance* and their conviction that the subject of forced removals had a bearing on the present: "The current struggle [in the 1980s], with its roots firmly in the Freedom Charter, had its first seeds in the momentous political events of the fifties, events which the official culture and history have attempted to hide" (Purkey 1993: xii). Purkey describes the atmosphere in which *Sophiatown* was created:

> When Junction Avenue Theatre Company embarked on the making of *Sophiatown* in July 1985, there was a sense of deep-rooted optimism in the company about South Africa's future. This was not a calculated or well thought-out position, but rather an emotional response to the period just proceeding. The general insurrection of the period 1983 to 1985 had shaken the very foundations of the state. At last it seemed that it was possible to overthrow apartheid. A spirit of revolutionary optimism was in the air. [...] a sense of euphoria was generated from this most palpable evidence of the emergence of people's power. [...] *Sophiatown* was created in this spirit. (1996: 158)

This hopeful spirit found its way into the play in the form of "a positive, joyful and forward-looking energy" (Purkey 1996: 159).

JATC was intrigued by a story in *Drum*, a popular black magazine of the 1950s, about Nat Nakasa and Lewis Nkosi's successful search for a Jewish house-mate. The group decided to reconstruct the event and convey an idea of the "spirit of the times" (1993: xiii). Loren Kruger asserts that

> [...] the play revived what might be called the myth of Sophiatown. Part ghetto, part cultural bazaar, a meeting place of black radicals, bohemians of all colors, and organized and disorganized criminals, Sophiatown was an actual but thoroughly imaginary place that came to symbolize a fragile moment of racial tolerance and cultural diversity, crushed by the apartheid juggernaut and later buried under the weight of more militant times. (1995c: 60)

The representation of the social, cultural and racial diversity of Sophiatown is mirrored in the play's use of various performance elements. Anne Fuchs believes

---

[93] For accounts on the historical development of Sophiatown and its destruction see Gready (1990), Hannerz (1994) and Lodge (1981). Gready and Hannerz also discuss the resident Sophiatown writers, journalists and artists of the 1950s such as Don Mattera, Es'kia Mphahlele, Hugh Matshikiza, Bloke Modisane, Casey Motsisi, Nat Nakasa, Lewis Nkosi, Henry Nxumalo and Can Themba.

that *Sophiatown* "is probably an example of theatrical syncretism at its best, with its mixture of South African languages, traditional and contemporary music and dance forms, storytelling, intimate family scenes, and the hard politics of the outside world" (1999: 133).

JATC's source material was composed of films from the 1950s, *Drum* magazine and interviews the group members conducted with well-known Sophiatown figures. Published in *Sophiatown Speaks*, the interviews included accounts by Father Huddleston, gangster and poet Don Mattera, the leader of the American Gang Kort Boy, schoolteacher and property owner Jane Dakile, and black and white intellectuals such as Nadine Gordimer, Arthur Maimane, Es'kia Mphahlele and Anthony Sampson (cf. Stein & Jacobson 1986, Purkey 1993: xiii; 1995). The use of these sources allowed the theatre group to incorporate many historically documented details about the political, social, cultural and economic development of Sophiatown in the late 1950s and thus to mirror the reality of the time. For instance, the interviews given by Mattera and Kort Boy most likely led to the creation of the gangster figure Mingus and the reflection on the activities of the *tsotsi* ('gangster') gangs thematised in the play.

In the creation process of *Sophiatown* the group used narrative workshops to develop an effective structure that placed Sophiatown's destruction central to the story, thus preventing any one of the characters from becoming too dominant. The artists also engaged in workshops focussing on rites of passage to "explore [...] common life experiences" (Purkey 1993: xiv). Victor Turner argues that ritual and the performance arts derive from what he calls the subjunctive and liminal "redressive phase" of social drama, that is, the phase in which group experiences are foregrounded and given meaning. By offering heightened experiences based on ritual, a performance can create a general feeling of *communitas* by uniting people beyond their formal social bounds (see Chapter 1.5.2). Several of the characters (for instance, Jakes, Ruth and Mamariti) strive to create this feeling of *communitas* among the Sophiatown inhabitants as does JATC among the audience.

Sophiatown tells the story of the destruction of the township from the perspective of the members of Mamariti's household. Mamariti runs a local shebeen. Her daughter Lulu is a sixteen-year-old school-girl who is dissatisfied with the deficient system of Bantu education. Her son Mingus is a successful and respected gangster and leader of the "Americans." He is accompanied by his girl-friend Princess and his coloured side-kick Charlie. Mamariti's boarder Jakes, a journalist with *Drum* magazine, has advertised in a newspaper for a Jewish woman to live with them in the township. Jakes's friend, the ANC member and illegal gambling leader Mr Fahfee (named after a game of chance),[94] completes the group. The play opens as Ruth arrives at Mamariti's house, willing to give this illegal multi-racial co-habitation a try. The government's plan to knock down Sophiatown and resettle its black population in Meadowlands, twenty kilometres outside 'white' Johannesburg, is reflected in the characters' conversations and interaction. At the end of the play they are forced to part – Ruth must go back to the white world while the others set out for the black township.

5.3.2.1. Identity and roles: Surviving in Sophiatown

Ruth, the English-speaking Jewish girl from the white Johannesburg suburb Yeoville, comes from a part of South African society that regards all non-white members ideologically, politically, economically and culturally as a collective 'other.' The alterity of the Africans is the necessary prerequisite for the successful development of a racist white identity and view of the world based on notions of superiority and exclusivity. Apartheid discourse is supported by a politically powerful, dominant minority that is present in the play only as the ominous 'they' who issue evictions and execute forced removals.

By moving to the black township of Sophiatown, Ruth believes that she can develop her own identity. She refuses to play the role of a supporter of apartheid and thus defines herself as an individual 'other' to the state. She has, as Yvonne Banning argues, "set out as a solitary 'I' in search of herself" (1989a: 23). From Ruth's point of view her otherness is not constituted by her difference to the native population of Sophiatown but by her spatial and ideological distance from her

---

[94] The following information about Fahfee is available on the internet: "Nobody knows much about the secret game of Fahfee except that it was brought here by chinese [*sic*] immigrants to this country [South Africa] and has been passed down from parents to children...and those people who know anything about the game are not prepared to speak about it. Tens of thousands of mostly black South Africans play every day - giving money to runners who in turn give their money to runners who give the money to The Chinaman - a mysterious figure who each day will select a number for their area. If his number coincides with yours, you will win money - the odds are 24 to one - (the runner gets 4 to 1 commission) and if it doesn't you will try to catch him again tomorrow. Run entirely on trust and in secret, Fahfee amounts to a million rand industry run by a number of families who control different areas. Undocumented and unregulated, it provides an income and a social life to the unemployed, to domestic workers, the marginalised and the poor who support it with enthusiasm" ("Mail & Guardian Television: Completed Projects").

'own' population group. This allows her to "claim difference from the white political oppressors and to assert her belief in the liberal concepts of individuality, personal freedom and private moral conscience" (Banning 1989a: 23, cf. 1989b: 97f.). She has come to Sophiatown in search of her identity: "I don't know what the hell I am. I'm Jewish on Mondays, I'm White on Tuesdays, I'm South African on Wednesdays, I'm a Democrat on Thursdays, and I'm confused on all the other days. Mostly I'm just confused" (*ST* 27). The fact that Ruth links the various elements of her identity to different days of the week instead of seeing herself as simultaneously being a white Jewish South African democrat is a comment on apartheid's attempt to create clear - especially racial and ethnic - boundaries between the different groups in South Africa. The fact that she defines herself and "is distinguished by the blacks as white, but Jewish" points to the "growing, deep splits in the white community at large" (Fuchs 1999: 132f.). Because Ruth does not fit the ideal of a white Christian Nationalist, she cannot express and develop her identity in a society defined by apartheid. She does not identify with the milieu she lives in and thus cannot execute the roles that she is expected to play. Dreitzel describes this as an imbalance between role engagement and role distance. Ruth flees to the township, a new environment with different roles and expectations, where she hopes to escape from this form of state-enforced identity construction. Jakes understands her problem of being unable to fit into a given category: "The Boere [Boers] want us in separate locations, but what am I? I speak Zulu, Xhosa, Sotho, English, Afrikaans, and in moments of weakness I even speak Tsotsitaal ['gangster speak']. [...] So who the hell am I?" (*ST* 28). He concludes: "These native reserves that Verwoerd[95] wants, what have they got to do with Sophiatown? Here we listen to Bach and Beethoven. We listen to great American jazz. We read great Russian novels. We are a brand-new generation" (*ST* 53). As is the case with Ruth, the identity of the intellectual group to which Jakes belongs does not correspond to the state-given definition and thus represents a threat to the system.

While Ruth feels displaced in her own community, she is displaced once more in Sophiatown, where she is a solitary white liberal in a culturally and ethnically diverse society. From the perspective of the township's inhabitants she also constitutes an 'other.' Banning emphasises that although Ruth is welcomed by the African household members, "[...] both they and she conspire to sustain her

[95] Hendrik Verwoerd was Minister of Native Affairs from 1950-58, issuing a number of acts that introduced both petty and grand apartheid (see Chapter 1.1). He became Prime Minister after Strijdom's death in 1958 (cf. Barber 1999: 41, 161).

otherness as a necessary condition for comfortable exchange between them" (1989a: 23). Mamariti earns good money from the rent that Ruth is asked to pay and gains access to "Spirits from town" (*ST* 14) for her shebeen. Ruth can help Lulu with her schoolwork and teach her things from her English background that are not components of Bantu education. Mingus can secure his high status in the American gang by claiming possession over the white woman and by protecting her, in his own self-interest, from sexual advances by other gang members. Jakes needs her because she is a "hot story" and because she will make them "the talk of the town" (*ST* 17, 19). Although he values Ruth for being unlike the typical apartheid-supporting white, he sees her more in economic terms as a rare commodity than as an individual. "You write about me, but you never look at me properly," she accuses the journalist (*ST* 58). She is instrumentalised by all the household members who like Jakes barely identify her as ideologically or politically oppositional but take advantage of her to profit from her racial otherness. "For them the difference of racial identity is an all-encompassing one because is [*sic*] enables Ruth to do things that they cannot, to acquire goods to which they have no access" (Banning 1989a: 24). Seen from this perspective, it seems doubtful that the African characters would ever want to overlook her racial identity and help her to integrate into Sophiatown. Therefore if Ruth's identity as an 'other' is preserved, she can always function as a scapegoat in times of conflict because traditionally, "European girls mean trouble" (*ST* 11), as Princess exclaims.

Although Ruth hopes to find her own identity in Sophiatown, she realises that despite the fact that the township is a "freehold suburb – no fences, no superintendent" (*ST* 17), it is a functioning social community with its own conceptions of identity and social role behaviour. Ruth wants to move about more freely. She takes 'lessons' from Jakes, Fahfee and Mingus on how to survive in the township. She must learn to play a new role that only exists in Sophiatown society. The men do not only teach her basic *tsotsitaal* expressions, including greetings and small talk, but also modes of behaviour with which she is supposed to defend herself against unwanted male advances:

> MINGUS: [...] And if the majietas [young men] kom [come], and go for you, what do you say?
>
> RUTH: I'm a virtuous well-bred girl, I'm a nylon.
>
> MINGUS: And if they don't leave you alone, they really go for you...?
>
> RUTH: Julle moenie baaiza nie? [Don't put a foot wrong]

> MINGUS: Ag! Nee man!
>
> RUTH: I don't know – I'll never learn.
>
> JAKES: Look, it's in the eyes, it's a warning signal which says, 'Leave me alone.' It's because you're white. White flesh, it's a fatal attraction. They get you into bed – it's a fart in the face for this Prime Minister Strijdom. (*ST* 25)

The men instruct Ruth in Goffmanean manner on how to develop a plausible performance. She must learn to play her new role convincingly if she wants to present a credible new identity. She must therefore convey a complete and consistent picture of herself by polishing not only her verbal expressions but also her facial and body gestures.

Furthermore, Jakes explains to Ruth that white women are considered to be an effective tool for breaking the colour-coded rules legislated by the government. Mingus adds that the Sophiatown gangsters consider the women in their territory as commodities: "I see something, I go for it. Look at me and Princess. I klapped her till she loved me." White women are a strong attraction for Mingus and his gang: "They see white girls and they're over the back of the moon. And white girls living in Softown! It's our territory man" (*ST* 25). Ruth cannot relate to these attitudes and outlook on life. Although she came of her own free will to live in Sophiatown, she did not expect to have to "change [her] whole life!": "You want me to learn a whole new language," she exclaims, "and you want me to have a special look in my eye, and you want to klap me until I love you. I think I must be mad to even try" (*ST* 26). Her outburst shows that she is unhappy with the new role behaviour that the men have introduced her to. She thought she could use her new life in Sophiatown to explore her own identity and develop individually. She had not understood that this was impossible in a setting where every socially organised group had its own rules and codes of conduct that determined the co-existence of its members.

If Jakes's "hot story" is to be successful, it is important that Ruth should stay and not be chased away by Mingus. Therefore Jakes must mediate between the two of them in order to find a compromise: "[...] we want life easy for the lady but not so easy that she leaves" (*ST* 26). On the one hand he must create an environment in which Ruth feels that the others respect her and that she is an individual who can pursue her own wishes. He knows that the white suburb of Yeoville will always remain her anchor, especially in moments when she laments her lack of privacy in Sophiatown. On the other hand Jakes must give the household members the impression that Ruth's presence as their guest does not cause any problems, that she can be integrated into township society without threatening their own positions. However, when Ruth rejects Mingus' advances, Mingus becomes angry and refuses to comply with Jakes's request that Ruth should receive special treatment. He threatens to withdraw his protection:

> MINGUS: Shaddup, Jakes, man. She's got to learn, man. This is not Yeoville here, man. It's rough here. You can't be a larnie ['white'] and live here. You think your sweet polite words will save you? You think your sweet white words will protect you? [...] Here it's bicycle spokes, and jungles [knives] [...].you think Sophiatown is just jazz and clubs and the bright lights! It's a war, man – and you want to make this your war! Well, you've got lots to learn. You can't pretend it's not happening because it will never go away. If you want to live here, white girl, you must learn or pack up! Voetsak! [Fuck off] Go back to Yeoville! (*ST* 29)

In this tirade Mingus understands 'white' and 'black' as ways of life. He warns Ruth that she cannot live in Sophiatown as a "larnie," a white who speaks white English. "Sweet polite," white English and the Sophiatown variety of English, (a mix of indigenous languages, Afrikaans, *tsotsitaal* and English words), are two sociolects that mirror different lifestyles and outlooks on life. It is not Ruth's white skin that prevents her from being accepted but her white attitude. *Blood Knot*'s fair-skinned but coloured brother Morris learns from experience that successful passing for white is determined by skin tone, clothing, etiquette and that "something inside you" (*BK* 103). Although he can *play* a white man, he fails to integrate into white society because he lacks the 'real' white attitude (see Chapter 2.2.3). In contrast, Mingus' comments suggest that Ruth can, despite her skin colour, survive in Sophiatown and integrate into bohemian society if she is willing to recognise the township as both a cultural meeting place and gangster territory. She also has to accept the township's rules of conduct and play the roles that are required of her. For instance, Mingus forbids her to acknowledge Charlie as an individual. His reasons for this are gang-related and based on the power hierarchy in such gangs: "Never, never apologize to Charlie. Understand? He does everything I say. Just keep your damn nose clean" (*ST* 22). Ruth must also learn to respect Mingus because he is a powerful and dangerous figure in Sophiatown. When he offers Ruth a necklace of pearls as a present, she declines because she knows that they are stolen and does not want to get involved. However, Mingus feels that she is rejecting him personally. He points out that she has known about his activities and consequently has always implicitly been involved because she has never attempted to stop him. It is only when Princess remarks that Ruth will not take the pearls because she is "too clean, too holy, too white" (*ST* 46), again implicitly defining 'white' and 'black' as a way of life and not skin colour, that she suddenly insists on accepting the gift. It is Ruth's refusal to be stigmatised as white which causes her to change her mind.

A further element that Ruth must learn concerns Mingus' treatment of Princess. Ruth defines this as "plain bullying" and a reason why Princess should leave him, yet his violence is considered normal in the township (*ST* 57).[96] Jakes warns her not to challenge Mingus' attitude towards women. However, she is personally drawn into the problem. One of Mingus' conditions for accepting Ruth as a member of Sophiatown society is that she, too, must comply with his view of women as commodities. By adamantly rejecting his renewed advances, she challenges his power and deflates his pride. (He emphasises: "[...] nobody says no to Mingus" [*ST* 62]). Mingus believes that she is turning him down because she feels racially superior. He uses a racist argument in his accusation: "You bloody nylons, you're all the same, man. You try and you try but once a nylon, always a nylon!" (*ST* 62). In this exclamation it becomes clear that identity always depends on recognition by the partners of the interaction (cf. Goffman 1959; Krappmann 1982[6]). Here Mingus is denying Ruth the ability to learn and adapt to the norms and expectations of Sophiatown society. Identity suddenly becomes fixed and essentialist.

While Ruth is learning about the attitudes, views and traditions of Sophiatown, she introduces the household to some of her own customs. To celebrate the publication of the first part of Jakes's articles about Ruth, she offers the household a bottle of "special home-made Jewish Friday-night wine" (*ST* 41). Jakes proposes a traditional toast whereas Mamariti wants to follow the Jewish custom of saying a prayer. The fact that she knows about this custom and wishes to practice it shows that she is open-minded and that she respects Ruth. Mamariti also addresses Ruth with an indigenised version of her name, "Ruthiwe" (*ST* 43), a gesture with which she offers the young woman access to her own traditions and customs. Fahfee sprinkles some drops of wine on the ground to demonstrate to Ruth the African tradition of paying homage to the ancestors. Ruth points out similarities between Jewish and indigenous traditions: "We do the same! On Passover we leave the door open, and the ghost of Elijah's supposed to come in and drink the wine. I suppose it's the same thing really" (*ST* 42). In this way Ruth shows that she can think

---

[96] Anne Fuchs believes that the fact that JATC was male-dominated at the time of *Sophiatown*'s creation is responsible for the "stereotyping and passivity of the black women characters" (1999: 133).

laterally and that she is trying to achieve consensus and understanding by comparing rituals. She takes comments by the others seriously and attempts to bridge the gap between them and herself. This scene is characterised by mutual interest and cultural exchange. It opposes apartheid's method of classification according to colour and ethnic background. In a multi-cultural society Jakes and Ruth wouldn't have to define their identity as the sum of mutually exclusive terms but as a multifaceted and organic whole.

The peaceful multi-cultural and multi-racial co-existence of all the members of Mamariti's house is disrupted by the news of the government's plan to destroy Sophiatown by forcibly removing its inhabitants. Fahfee, a member of the African National Congress, supports a secret plan of resistance. When Ruth wants to know the details, he suddenly becomes suspicious, seeing in her the cliché white - an informer, not an opponent of the state. Fahfee believes that she must earn their trust by actively engaging in the struggle. However, his demand that she "stop all this shit" (*ST* 36) is emotionally charged, unrealistic and contra-productive because it causes distrust amongst people, all of whom oppose apartheid for the same reasons. In this tense and emotional situation the men vent their anger on the woman:

> FAHFEE: [...] Petitions, letters, committees – it's rubbish! I'm telling you, it's rubbish. There must be blood. Then things will happen.
>
> MINGUS: (*To* RUTH *in a moment of great anger*.) And it will be your blood! (*ST* 36)

Fahfee and Mingus turn on Ruth, identifying her as being representative of all whites, and hold her responsible for their suffering. She becomes their scapegoat because she is within their reach whereas their letters and petitions to halt the removals are too abstract and ineffective to achieve results. However, Ruth is not willing to play this role and appeals to Jakes who doubts the strategic usefulness of a fight between Africans and the police. Nonetheless, it is revealing that Jakes, the objective journalist and onlooker, remains passive and does not defend Ruth in front of the increasingly emotional Fahfee and Mingus. Although Ruth is the target of the men's anger, she sympathises with their conviction that only an armed fight could prevent the pending removals. And although she feels emotionally drawn to Jakes and needs him for protection, she also confronts him with his weaknesses. Critical of the effectiveness of his intellectual work (JAKES: "I don't know [what to do]. Write the story. What else can I do?" [*ST* 35]), she blames him for his failure to actively participate in and contribute to the struggle: "Well, why don't you join Fahfee? He needs you. You can't watch forever, you know" (*ST* 58). She reproaches him for living in a world of intellectual "fictions" and failing to understand the reality around him: "Well, you're in your own kind of laager, aren't you Jakes? Buried in this new journalism, and the African short story" (*ST* 58).[97] The fact that this criticism of the black intellectual in favour of both political and militant resistance stems from a white woman is all the more interesting as she implicitly characterises her own liberal belief as also being ineffective. Ruth decides to leave Sophiatown as the forced removals set in, deploring the fact that she and Jakes did not begin a relationship. Banning argues that she still "does not fully recognise the connection between her personal relations with the household and the legislated categories of identity that isolate and confine her within the all-encompassing difference of race" (1989b: 98). Ruth believed that she could develop a new role identity and become Jakes's lover. She failed to realise that social norms and attitudes were formed in relation to the strict political system of oppression and would not accommodate her new role definitions. Jakes's reaction confirms this. Caught in fixed racial categories, he admits that he has always felt threatened by her and that she has remained "some white girl" or the 'other' to him: "You want to ride me over like a bulldozer and leave me here for dust. [...] Truth is, all the time you've been with us, we've both known you have a back door to Yeoville" (*ST* 70f.). It is only then that Ruth really understands the power of the apartheid system over society. Like the coloured Charlie, she is excluded from the new all-black community in Meadowlands and has no home: "Right now I don't know where I'm going, but the door to Yeoville is shut. [...] I'm the one who's closing it" (*ST* 71). Her experience, however, makes it impossible for her to reintegrate into a white society whose beliefs and values she does not share. In the 1950s both Ruth and her Sophiatown friends are left suffering from their roles in Dreitzel's sense. However, in the context of the play's performance in the 1980s the necessity for interracial co-operation becomes all the more apparent. *Sophiatown* implies that although Ruth may have been reduced to a "solitary, deracinated ghost," the opportunities for "mutual social and political interchange" between whites and other ethnic groups remain "viable and necessary" (Foley 1991: 25).

---

[97] *Drum* magazine, publishing both works of journalism and creative writing, has been considered as representing South African black literature in English, promoting especially the short story. Gready explains, "Although this fictional style was encouraged by *Drum*'s white management and protected its authors from censorship for some time, it is also undoubtedly the case that it intentionally enhanced a myth surrounding the unreality of the writers' projected urban world" (1990: 145).

5.3.2.2. Fiction, multiple truths and the construction of reality

Martin Orkin argues that one of the central elements in *Sophiatown* is its "consciousness of its reliance upon the narrative in order to construct its world" (1991: 199). As suggested above, the discussion between fiction and truth is accorded a central meaning in the play. Jakes constructs his fictional reality through the stories he writes for *Drum*. Articles similar to his by the historical Sophiatown journalists are now considered source material for reconstructing life in the township. Orkin points out that Fahfee's interpretation of reality - with the help of his gambling numbers and the meaning accorded each in the game - as well as Mingus's attempts to live his life through fictions extracted from American gangster films are "further means whereby the text suggests its own strategy of representation" (1999: 199; cf. 199f.). The play is highly self-reflexive of its own goal which is "to move by means of the making of these fictions of different kinds towards an understanding of some kind of 'truth' about Sophiatown" (Orkin 1999: 200).

Despite the plausibility and importance of Orkin's argument, *Sophiatown* does not only comment on its own methodology, but it could be argued that it also uses the discussions about fiction, truth and reality to comment on apartheid discourse. This can be seen in Ruth's discussion with the sixteen-year-old Lulu when they talk about the meaning of truthful representation. Lulu's homework assignment is to write an essay about her family, and Ruth makes Lulu understand that there are "different sorts of truth" about the same topic (*ST* 33). These different truths are realised by approaching the subject from a variety of perspectives. For example, Ruth suggests that Lulu should not portray Mingus as a ruthless gangster in her essay. "It's true to say your brother steals from the railways, but it's also true to say that he gives your mother money to run the house, and money for your school" (*ST* 31). Ruth is advocating the necessity of keeping an open mind in order to respect both sides and judge each situation on its merit rather than reverting to pre-conceived notions. This is diametrically opposed to apartheid's monolithic method of fixing meaning from above without allowing for flexible definitions in individual contexts.

Ruth is convinced that there are always multiple truths. She is disappointed and dissatisfied with Jakes's article about her. She confronts him with the fact that he is making statements about her without even having interviewed her. He markets her as a "Sophiatown phenomenon." The journalist feels that he is now "dealing with socialites" (*ST* 38), a category into which his former stories on boxing and gangsters do not fit. The article is filled with speculations and invented comments, a stretched version of the truth that is manipulated to make a good story. Lulu also recognises that the truth has been reshaped and functionalised to meet the magazine's sensationalist tone. Lulu, however, does not see this manipulation to be a problem as she believes that in this case the end justifies the means and that therefore Jakes's article "doesn't have to be true" (*ST* 39). This scene again confirms Orkin's assertion that *Sophiatown* comments on its own methods.

In summary, these scenes show that the extraction and reconstruction of knowledge and truth can be effective in opposing apartheid discourse and in attempting to "constitute or develop views of the oppressed subject that draw on [...] a discourse of resistance" (Orkin 1991: 201). The call for resistance to apartheid is embedded in the tradition of strikes and boycotts as far back as the 1940s. Orkin goes so far as to suggest that the play posits a "national culture of liberation" (*ibid.*) in its appeal for co-operation from all oppressed groups, "the Berliners, and the Americans and the Vultures and the school children, and the journalists to fight" (*ST* 55). This call for a common national identity is prepared in several places during the play when various characters experience difficulty in defining their own identity because they identify with many different groups: Ruth as the white Jewish South African Democrat, Jakes as a speaker of many of South Africa's indigenous languages and Sophiatown itself as a multi-cultural township cohabited by coloureds, Indians, Chinese and Zulus (cf. *ST* 27f., 44). The call for multi-culturalism mirrors the goal of the United Democratic Front in the 1980s and thus creates a link between the politics of the 1950s and the present at the time of the play's creation (cf. Orkin 1991: 202).

5.3.2.3. Language as a mirror of racial, social and cultural diversity

Sophiatown's characters claim that there is a 'white' and a 'black' way of speaking that expresses different attitudes and ways of life but is not an essentialism linked to race. In this aspect the play has often been examined as one that places a variety of different languages, sociolects and ideolects on stage to represent South Africa's cultural diversity (cf. Combrink 1990). Hauptfleisch explains, "The assumption that different languages also imply different – and perhaps irreconcilable – differences between peoples, their customs, and their aspirations, has been fundamental to what has come to be known as the Apartheid society." This has created the "impression that language (and cultural) diversity is a fixed, unchanging and uniform phenomenon." He continues, "Yet this neat theoretical construct is refuted daily by the reality of the society itself, for despite politically and ideologically inspired attempts to persuade people to the contrary, contact and interaction between language [and racial] groups [...] has always existed, and quite widely so" (1990: 103).

Hauptfleisch considers *Sophiatown* to be "Multilingual theatre." He argues that this kind of theatre, which arose in the mid-1970s, was regarded as "ideologically 'confused and confusing' art work (i.e. multilingual and therefore culturally unspecific), until the 'confusion' itself became a very specific ideological position" (1990: 104f.). It symbolised the new political coalitions formed from the 1970s onwards. The redefinition of 'culture' in a changing South African society led to a redefinition of the role of language and theatre. It had become "necessary to experience and work one's way through" (1990: 105) society's issues instead of merely talking about them. This demand led to new forms of theatrical activity which attempted to create a political awareness, communicate across the constructed racial barriers and develop an African theatre. Hauptfleisch identifies the emergence of a new paradigm for South African theatre. This includes a shift in the nature and function of language and the development of a new concept of theatre making in workshops (cf. 1990: 105). The different dramatic purposes that language fulfils in Sophiatown can be seen in the following excerpt:

> JAKES: What the hell am I? The Boere want us in separate locations, but what am I? I speak Zulu, Xhosa, Sotho, English, Afrikaans, and in moments of weakness I even speak Tsotsitaal.
>
> FAHFEE: Hey! Tsotsitaal! Dis die taal van die ouens. It's a sophisticated taal.
>
> JAKES: So who the hell am I?
>
> FAHFEE: Vra jou ma, man!
>
> JAKES: I'm a would-be intellectual, living in a wasteland, with no power to change anything except words – and a fat lot of good they do!
>
> MINGUS: (*Suddenly aggressive, jumps up and moves in on* RUTH.) Come on, we must teach you lang-arm dancing for the Ritz. Arm uit! Daai kant! Ga my skouer. (RUTH does not understand.) Ga my skouer, man! (RUTH *hesitates, then takes his shoulder. They take up a position for a waltz.*) And – one, two, three, one, two, three...
>
> RUTH: (*Laughing.*) I can do this! This is just a European waltz.
>
> MINGUS: (*Offended.*) Nee man. This is for the Ritz, Sophiatown style. [...]. (*ST* 28)

This use of a variety of languages has a mimetic function. For example, Mingus's use of Afrikaans, *tsotsitaal* and American slang (in other conversations) reflects how a Sophiatown gangster might have spoken. Hauptfleisch believes that the presentation of a multi-lingual conversation allows for a "'mirroring' of reality" that is more realistic than in other contemporary plays (1997: 98). At the same time, however, their language mix clearly remains "theatretalk," a functionalised form of dialogue (cf. 1997: 98; cf. Banning 1990: 14). In addition, Mingus and Jakes's different sociolects show that they come from different social backgrounds with contrasting levels of education and cultural values. Furthermore, the distinctive idiolects help to characterise each Sophiatown inhabitant as an individual. The men and women present themselves as vibrant, lively characters whose creative, sometimes even comic use of language contrasts with the bleak "tragic reality" of apartheid (Hauptfleisch 1990: 107).

Language also plays an important role at the symbolic level. It becomes an indicator of social status and political views. The township's population, with the exception of the intellectuals, speaks Afrikaans. Notwithstanding, the government's language teaching policies (which culminated in an attempt to enforce the use of Afrikaans in black education in 1976 and led to mass student revolts) are heavily criticised. "The play points both to the divisive role played by language patterns, attitudes and policy in the country [...], and to its communicative role, as symbolized by Tsotsitaal – with its Afrikaans base and English, Zulu, Sotho and Xhosa vocabulary" (Hauptfleisch 1990: 108; cf. 107f.; cf. 1997: 97-100). The play also uses language poetically. The use of songs in the background in combination with the characters' voicing their lamentations or anger creates a "seriousness" which the songs do not express in the streets (1990: 107).

In contrast to this focus on the multi-lingual aspects of *Sophiatown*, other interpretations have been advanced. For example, Banning argues that the play "speaks from an essentially English South African perspective and is inscribed with English cultural values, English cultural history and English education" (1989b: 101). Banning regards the emphasis on English as a means of conserving its "hegemonic effects" (*ibid.*),[98] instead of seeing it as both a black *lingua franca* and, as Lulu observes, a way of escaping a constricting and limited apartheid education

[98] Consequently, Banning argues that the play's popularity lies in its "appeal to South Africans who participate in or aspire to such dominance." This leads her to claim that "If the politics of the play are oppositional, the ideology is not" (1989b: 101).

in Afrikaans that is equivalent to being "illiterate" (cf. *ST* 51f.). Consequently, the discussion about education, language and the plans for school boycotts can be placed in a tradition of resistance to Afrikaans as the education policy which culminated in the 1976 Soweto uprising. Again, this connection evokes that the long tradition of black resistance to apartheid policies is still relevant in the 1980s.

5.3.2.4. Epic conventions and the use of role-play

In *Sophiatown* JATC effectively combines elements of realism with epic conventions. Fairly realistic characters engage in a "domestic drama" while *a capella* songs, political slogans, commentaries, shouts and audience addresses interrupt the narrative flow of the action. In general this serves to distance the audience from the action in a Brechtian manner and create a different awareness of what is happening on stage (cf. Purkey 1996: 158).

The performance and entertainment characteristics of the play are emphasised through its many songs. However, the *a capella* interludes must also be seen as important comments on the course of the action. These songs include energetic celebrations of individual characters or events (Scenes I,2; I,7), ranging from accusatory to sad laments about the fate of Sophiatown (Scenes I,3; II,3; II,7) and from melancholic to lively expressions of defiance (Scenes I,1; I,6). Included are also calls for liberation in an almost revolutionary mode similar to many of the plays influenced by the Black Consciousness Movement. At the beginning of the second act the characters, who are singing a revolutionary song, storm on stage and shout threats of defiance addressed to Prime Minister Strijdom. The stage directions indicate that the characters should take up their positions for the upcoming scene as the song reaches its climax (cf. *ST* 49). The defiant atmosphere of the performance is thus carried over into the play's action. It is also reflected in Fahfee's announcement that Congress should call for a unified fight against apartheid. In situations like this the song and shouts support the action although they are epic elements which also prevent the spectator from becoming too immersed in the action.

Sophiatown is one of the few plays analysed in this study in which the actors do not slip from one role to the next but play only one role. However, it is in epic elements such as direct narrative address to the audience that the play's theatricality is articulated. Jakes introduces the setting by turning to the spectators to give them information about Sophiatown whilst the rest of the cast sing a song of resistance.

Similar narrative methods are used to link the scenes to one another. Furthermore, in the final scene the characters talk to the audience about their forced removal and relocation to Meadowlands. By addressing the spectators in a first person narrative, the characters reconstruct their own memory and subjective version of the events, reinforcing the endeavours of Junction Avenue Theatre Company to bring Sophiatown back to life on stage. Therefore this last scene can be structurally understood more as an expression of JATC's own reflections on its theatrical venture than as a comment on the representation of truth, fiction and reality.

5.4. Conclusion

Of the various plays examined in this study, *Born in the RSA* and *Sophiatown* make minimal use of overtly theatrical role-play. Yet with the help of epic conventions the actors alternately draw the spectators into the action and distance them from it, thus emphasising the play's nature as performance or representation of reality.

These two dramatic works are of fundamental importance to this study because they show that to a large extent the individual's identity is shaped according to society's predominant interests, attitudes and norms. These plays clearly illustrate that identity and roles are not defined by the individual alone but always require social recognition. The story of Glen, the white police informer in *Born in the RSA*, shows that the power of social opinion is so strong that his failure to achieve public acknowledgement of his identity eventually deprives him of his place in society. The stories of the activists that he betrays, Thenjiwe and Susan, suggest that a strong personal identity can persist in the face of adversity but that this requires a psychological triumph over the refusal by others to recognise one's identity. By contrast, Sindiswa is intimidated by the system so that she accepts state-conferred definitions of identity without any resistance.

In apartheid society the pathological behaviour of individuals is clearly a reflection and result of society's pathological state. Zach's story shows that monstrosity is not innate but that a monstrous system can turn its subjects into evil creatures. What is more, when traditional role behaviour is no longer possible, some individuals are deprived of their roles whereas others must take on new roles. This places a strain on all affected individuals: Sindiswa cannot afford to raise Dumisani, her son, and has Thenjiwe look after him; Zach, who has been forced to leave his children and work in the city, acts in a caring fatherly way towards Dumisani; and Mia takes the boy in after his release from police custody. In addition, Mia's professional role clearly expands when the growing confrontation between freedom fighters and the state forces her to become involved beyond the limits of her legal training and render medical assistance.

Sophiatown stages characters who challenge the state-imposed separation of the races. However, the play's thesis is that in the end the pressure emanating from an inflexible and racially divided society prevents the characters from bridging the gap across the colour bar. Interracial co-habitation seems possible, yet it remains only an experiment during which their racial differences, institutionalised by the apartheid state, cannot be overcome. With both the Sophiatown inhabitants and Ruth relying on the certainty that she could always return to her white suburb, racial privilege and discrimination remain largely unchallenged. It is only when the removals leave Ruth homeless and make her realise that she also has no place in white society that she begins to understand the scope of the given definitions of racial identity. She recognises that like her Sophiatown friends she cannot develop an identity that is not recognised by the society in which she lives. As Dreitzel argues and this play substantiates, role behaviour in a pathological society itself becomes pathological. The final farewell between Ruth and Jakes demonstrates that in a repressive society individuals are deprived of the ability to actively shape their roles to accommodate their own personal attitudes and beliefs. Suffering from one's roles is the inevitable consequence.

What distinguishes the multi-racial workshop plays *Born in the RSA* and *Sophiatown* from the other plays discussed in earlier chapters in this study is the fact that they portray an interaction between black and white characters which is based on the attempt to achieve tolerance and acceptance of diversity. Instead of relying on the construction of a utopian state of peaceful co-existence, the plays show very clearly that political and social attitudes are responsible for the breakdown of multi-racial co-operation. Full of hope the characters look to a brighter future by suggesting that a change of politics can lead to a change of social attitudes and vice versa.

6. Theatre by Women and the Focus on Women's Lives under Apartheid

> How many have died under this law? [...] What has it caused us – pain – sorrow – destruction. We carry a heavy burden that defeats men but won't defeat us women.
>
> Sdudla in *You Strike the Woman, You Strike the Rock*[1]

This introductory quotation from one of the plays discussed in this chapter suggests that although black men and women both suffered under the oppressive system of apartheid, they reacted differently to their state of oppression. In *You Strike the Woman, You Strike the Rock* Sdudla, a character informed by the time of the play's publication (1986), expressed her belief that men had been overpowered in their struggle against apartheid whereas women still had the strength to bring about change. *You Strike the Woman, You Strike the Rock* was the first published play to focus on the involvement of black South African women in the struggle.

It was only from the mid-1980s that plays by women featuring all-female casts began to appear on the anti-apartheid theatre scene. These plays presented the lives of women under apartheid, thus allowing an examination of the roles that women occupied in the society at that time. Before turning to the plays in question, a brief overview of the political and artistic involvement of women in twentieth century South Africa is given. Although the focus in the following sections is gender-specific, the approach taken for the actual interpretations of the plays by women playwrights is not feminist but, in keeping with the general approach of this study, based on role theory, albeit from a gendered perspective.

6.1. The role of women and female concerns under apartheid

At a conference on South African literature in Bad Boll, Germany in 1986, Rebecca Matlou addressed the importance of the black South African female writer to express the "needs of the woman" and to support the "woman in her struggle against exploitation and oppression, injustice and discrimination" (1987: 74). A poet and ANC activist, Matlou supported the political participation of black women and emphasised their right to poetic self-representation: "'What kind of

---

[1] *SW* 199. References to *You Strike the Woman, You Strike the Rock* are flagged *SW*.

consciousness as women do we look forward to? Are we going to continue to be projected through the eyes of men? Or a political system that tends to reject or devalue women? That is where our role is. We should take part in transforming society'" (qtd. in DeShazer 1994: 182). DeShazer describes Matlou as a forerunner of the public discourse on gender and feminist issues that came about in the early 1990s (cf. 1994: 182). Matlou criticised prominent African women writers for rejecting the label 'feminist': "It would seem men have successfully intimidated women over issues of women's liberation" (Matlou 1987: 77). This does not mean that she argued for a critique of sexism in preference to a struggle against racism and apartheid. In her opinion, both elements carried equal importance in the work of a committed artist (cf. 1987: 76).

Such clear statements in favour of a feminist position were rare at the time. The prevailing attitude had been expressed by an ANC spokeswoman at the Nairobi Women's Conference in 1986: "'It would be suicide for us to adopt feminist ideas. Our enemy is the system and we cannot exhaust our energies on women's issues'" (qtd. in Seidman 1993: 297), or "[...] we are opposed to activities which obscure the identity of the real enemy" (Rivkin 1985: 215). An examination of the conditions of women's lives in twentieth century South Africa and their involvement in the women's struggle explains why this was so.

6.1.1. The position of women and the women's struggle: A historical overview

Apartheid oppressed its population on the basis of race and class. However, the fact that black men and women seem to have experienced and reacted to their oppression in different ways appears to be due to the manner in which the sexes were often forced to lead separate lives under the apartheid regime.[2]

From the late nineteenth and early twentieth century the rapid escalation of the mining and associated industrial economy needed vast numbers of labourers to support its growth. It was this development that brought about the introduction of various restrictive land-ownership acts and selective taxes which forced blacks from the rural areas into the mining towns in search of work to support themselves

[2] A very detailed representation of the development of the politicisation of women in the twentieth century is offered by Cherryl Walker (1982). See also the collection of essays edited by Walker on women and gender in Southern Africa up to 1945 (1990).

and their families. Mostly it was the males who made the journey to the towns, leaving the women to take over as the head of the household, traditionally the male role. The various negative factors – the lack of access to arable land, the difficulties of subsistence farming, the lack of money coming from the menfolk now based in the towns - forced some of the women also to leave the homelands in search of work. They were faced, however, with limited opportunities and access generally only to low-paid work, often as domestic servants, farm labourers or factory workers. The alternative was in the better-paid but far more dangerous illegal sector of brewing beer and prostitution.

Despite these traumatic experiences, the discussion about the sufferings of black women under apartheid, even up to the late 1980s, focused only on the breakdown of the traditional African household and the additional strain that this placed on the black woman (cf. Seidman 1993: 295). Lapchick explains that women joined the struggle once their "family structure and with it the basic fabric of their respective societies" were put in jeopardy (1985: 256). Social reformers, politicians and anti-apartheid women's organisations such as the Federation of South African Women (FSAW) in the 1950s and the ANC up to the 1980s did not address gender-based inequality within these households or challenge domestic patterns. Instead, they predominantly regarded women only in their roles as mothers and wives (cf. Seidman 1993: 296).

The increased numbers of women living in urban areas did lead to a more stable urban population in the first half of the twentieth century. As they constituted only a small minority of the industrial workforce, these women were exempt from official regulations such as influx control (pass laws), a situation which changed with the advent of apartheid in 1948. The Nationalist government's intention in the early 1950s to introduce passes for women was met by large demonstrations and protest movements from African women.[3] Women who were involved in anti-apartheid organisations decided to establish a non-racial women's organisation which would not only work towards majority rule (and the end of apartheid) but at the same time advance women's rights (cf. Lapchick 1985: 236). It was out of this

[3] Tom Lodge argues that the women's political assertiveness (or even militancy) derived from their experience as trade unionists in the 1930s and their work in protest committees linked to trade unions and the Communist Party in the 1940s (both non-racial institutions). He comments on the reason for the women's psychological strength: "Confronted with the threat of pass laws they could compare their present degree of independence from official restriction with the position of men and perceive they had something worth fighting for" (Lodge 1983: 141).

coalition that the Federation of South African Women (FSAW) was formed in 1954.[4] The 'Women's Charter' drew attention to discrimination against women in law while committing women to participate in the struggle for national liberation. The FSAW fought particularly against the pass laws for black women right up to the late 1950s. It organised many protest marches, but the most strident was a march in 1956 which culminated in the singing of their protest song "'Strydom[5] you have tampered with the women, you have struck a rock'" (qtd. in Lodge 1983: 145; Walker 1982: 195, cf. 153-282), the slogan after which *You Strike the Woman, You Strike the Rock* is named.[6] But in the end the protests did not contribute to any improvement in the living conditions of women in the country or the city. According to Tom Lodge's evaluation, the 1950s women's protest movement was "not a feminist movement."[7] Instead of fighting for an extension of rights and a change in their domestic responsibilities and relationships, the black women wished to conserve their rights and status in their role as wives and mothers (1983: 150; cf. 142-51; cf. Lapchick 1985: 236-43; Rivkin 1985: 224).[8]

Industrial expansion throughout the 1960s led to increased demand for cheap African labour. But with the male workers' eventual incorporation into the permanent workforce they were often allowed, after many years of separation, to have their families join them.[9] Because the men did not earn enough to support their

---

[4] The 1952 co-operation of trade unionists, members of the ANC Women's League and white women involved in the foundation of the Congress of Democrats was expanded when women from the Indian Congresses and the South African Coloured People's Organisation joined to found the FSAW (cf. Lapchick 1985: 235f.; Lodge 1983: 142).

[5] J. G. Strijdom was South Africa's Prime Minister from 1954-58.

[6] Thirty years later the Vusisizwe Players created *You Strike the Woman, You Strike the Rock* as a "theatrical homage to the courage of our mothers" and as a "celebration of the spirit of the millions of black women in South Africa who refused to give in to an oppressive system" (*SW* 164). The play is dedicated to three founding members of the Federation of South African Women (1954),[6] Lilian Ngoyi, the major player of the 1954 protest against passes (her biography is offered in Qunta 1987: 112-14), Doro Tamana, a black activist and poet, and Annie Slinga, an active ANC member and leader of the 1956 anti-pass campaign (cf. *SW* 165, 189; DeShazer 1994: 40, 148, 192; Lipman 1984: 50f., 113f.).

[7] For a discussion of the meaning of "feminist" in the South African context see Chapters 6.1.3 and 6.1.4.

[8] By the late 1950s most of the leaders had been arrested and charged with treason. Additional laws had been issued that made legal protest more difficult, and the lack of ANC support for the women's cause – due to ANC-internal conflicts and financial reasons - eventually put an end to the women's struggle (cf. Lodge 1983: 146).

[9] Growing poverty, government limitations on cattle and land possession, and new tax laws continued to make survival through subsistence farming impossible.

families, the women increasingly participated in the (urban or rural) labour market[10] but still remained solely responsible for the household. African families often lived illegally in informal townships near urban centres. These squatter camps were without infrastructure or services and were constantly under threat from police raids to check passes or forcibly remove inhabitants from the area. By 1986, when the pass laws were removed, at least half of South Africa's population lived in or around urban areas (cf. Seidman 1993: 298). Many of these aspects and their consequences for the reality of black life are explored in the plays discussed in this chapter.

With the rise of the Black Consciousness Movement (BCM) in the 1970s a new attempt was made to cater to what were considered the needs of African women. Some of the wide-spread black community programmes included a Women's Division which focused on work and skills attributed to the female domain: "'spheres such as nutrition, child care, basic skills such as knitting, sewing, crocheting, cookery and gardening'." The Black Women's Federation, which was formed in 1975, stated in its manifesto that it was striving to support black women in presenting a "'united front'" while defining the role of women as securing the "'survival and maintenance of their families and largely the socialization of the youth for the transmission of the Black Cultural Heritage'." The primary role of the black woman as mother was expanded to support the "'Black people's social, cultural, economic and political aspirations'" (all qtd. in Driver 1990: 235; cf. Lapchick 1985: 247f.). Black men felt that the white patriarchal system had symbolically "emasculated" (Manganyi 1973: 11) them and turned them into children. They depended on the black women to restore their masculinity and thus their self-esteem as men (cf. Driver 1990: 236). In the BCM the image of the woman as mother occupies a central position.[11] Seidman remarks that anti-apartheid organisations employed the term 'woman' interchangeably with 'wife' and

[10] In rural areas the pattern of African women's employment also changed. The mechanisation of white agriculture reduced the number of farm workers but led to an increase of women working as seasonal labourers during harvest times. And the government offered incentives to industries willing to relocate in non-metropolitan areas in order to reduce the speed of black urbanisation. Especially the textile industry was attracted by low labour costs and increasingly employed women (cf. Seidman 1993: 299f.).

[11] Driver explains the reasoning of the time: When boys have grown to men, they leave their mothers and thus assert their own masculinity. Then, in taking a wife, they (re)possess the woman's body that will bear their children and hence confirm their masculinity. The strength of women derives from the strength of motherhood, and consequently, it is not surprising that African feminist ideas emerge through the notion of motherhood (cf. 1990: 237).

'mother' up to the 1980s. The FSAW and then later on the women involved in the ANC preferred to support national liberation over challenges to specific gender ideologies. Even in the mid-1980s, when leaders in nationalist organisations began to realise that black working-class women encountered very specific problems, their calls were for equal wages or day-care facilities and did not address the issue of male dominance within the household. Attempts to analyse gender and family relationships from a political perspective were regarded as being derived from 'bourgeois' or 'Western' feminism and were thus rejected (cf. 1993: 297).

However, during the last decade of apartheid rule the speed of political mobilisation led to an intensification of female involvement in the labour movement (trade unions), street committees and localised community groups, community-based women's organisations and political campaigns.[12] They placed the focus on gender-specific needs and women's autonomy. The attempt to raise the consciousness of the oppressed black women and convince them of the need to distinguish between gender and race (class) oppression was increasingly successful.[13]

6.1.2. Women in South African theatre: A historical overview

In one of the few published articles which focuses specifically on the involvement of women in modern English-language South African theatre, Stephen Gray explains:[14]

---

[12] In the late 1980s challenges to gender discrimination were no longer considered dangerous to the unity of the labour movement. Demands such as equal pay, maternity leave, health care facilities, day-care centres and protection for pregnant women were addressed in union negotiations in 1983. The involvement of women in community groups that dealt with issues such as bus fare, rent increases, education or the legalisation of squatter communities resulted from the need to address growing family concerns such as their children's education or their inability to sustain their family with their low income. Women also began to create their own separate organisations and introduced a gendered view to the nationalist liberation movement by discussing domestic issues in terms of gender as well as racial and class oppression. For the first time topics such as job opportunities for women, day-care facilities and the political basis of problems of household maintenance were viewed from the perspective of family relationships. The involvement of women in political campaigns also had a consciousness-raising effect and convinced women of the need to distinguish between gender and race oppression (cf. Seidman 1993: 302-6).

[13] Shamim Meer offers an overview of the situation of women in the 1990s which shows that especially rural African women still suffer from race, class and gender domination and are often victims of the gender division of labour (cf. 1997).

[14] Gray does not focus on the role of women in traditional African performance forms but takes for granted that 'theatre' automatically refers to a Western-style art form. However, he

> Although it is probably as true of South African theatre as of any other postcolonial English-language theatre that women in the past have been excluded from the centres of its power, women have nevertheless at various times been crucial to its development. By today, in 1990, their influence is no longer peripheral, but essential to the theatre's maintenance and viability. Theatre as professional career is a longstanding part of the stake that women of all kinds hold in South Africa's cultural life and, of all the arts, theatre is the one in which women have come to flourish most visibly. Traditional notions of women as culture-carriers ensures [*sic*] that this continues to be so. (1990: 75)

Despite Gray's positive evaluation of the contribution of women of all races to South African theatre, it must be emphasised that their participation, especially that of black women, is far less frequent and of a much more recent date than that of men.[15]

Athol Fugard contributed to the involvement of women on stage in the sense that many of his plays feature women as the central characters - from the poor coloured woman to the eccentric white artist – who to varying degrees all suffer from either institutionalised racism, sexism and/or class constraints (cf. Gray 1990: 81).[16] Orkin praises Fugard's plays as especially subversive because "[...] contestation against prevailing discourse is almost always expressed through women and this in a social order the ruling class of which is dominated by strongly patriarchal and Afrikaner Calvinist discourse" (1991: 230).

---

acknowledges the incorporation of traditional elements such as song into 'black drama' and thus only implicitly refers to its distinct quality in contrast to more European styles (cf. 1990: 82).

[15] A few plays about female characters appeared in the eighteenth and nineteenth century and led to the creation of prototypical female characters (cf. Hauptfleisch 1997: 37).[15] However, it was not until the early twentieth century that Stephen Black wrote two plays about strong and independent female characters, *Love and the Hyphen* (1908) and *Helena's Hope, Ltd.* (1909). The first South African woman dramatist, the British emigrant Bertha Goudvis, wrote one-act plays in the early twentieth century about local urban life and introduced amateur drama (in contrast to performances by touring companies) as a stable element of South Africa's theatre scene. The short-story writer Pauline Smith and the well-known prose author Nadine Gordimer each wrote a play that focused on the entrapment of the white woman in a patriarchal society (Smith, *The Last Voyage* [1929], Gordimer *The First Circle* [1949]). Working-class black women were not represented on stage until the 1970s, when Elsa Joubert's novel *Poppie Ngema* was dramatised and turned them into "the central symbol and great money-earners of South African showbiz" (Gray 1990: 78, cf. 76-8).

[16] Fugard's strong female characters are Hester, the poor Afrikaner in *Hello and Goodbye* (1965), Lena, the dispossessed coloured in *Boesman and Lena* (1969), the slowly ageing Milli whose life passively passes by in *People Are Living There* (1969), Frieda, the white lover of a coloured man in *Statements After An Arrest Under the Immorality Act* (1974), the English woman who suffers in the oppressive Afrikaner society in *A Lesson From Aloes* (1978) and Miss Helen, the white eccentric artist in *The Road to Mecca* (1985). Fugard developed many of these roles in collaboration with South Africa's leading actress during apartheid, the late Yvonne Bryceland.

However, it was not until the emergence of 'alternative' theatre at the Space in Cape Town and the Market in Johannesburg in the 1970s that women began to enter the theatre scene as playwrights, actresses and directors. One of the most important and currently still active playwrights to emerge was Fatima Dike, a Xhosa, who concentrated on black history in *The Sacrifice of Kreli* (1976). The play tells of the final resistance to colonial forces by Africans under King Kreli in the late nineteenth century. It allegorically focuses on "what vulnerabilities in the black social structure rendered it collapsible and open to white exploitation: fragmentation, disunity – in short, the lack of a mass democratic base." The interesting and unusual element of this play, which Gray classifies as typical "'black drama'," is that the central character is an old woman whilst "black liberation theatre is often a fiercely male-dominated and chauvinistic affair" (1990: 82).

In 1979 the all-woman show *Call Me Woman* devised by Barney Simon and the Company for the Market Theatre was based on the lives of women in South Africa and made what Gray calls the "strongest mixed-race feminist statement yet seen on the South African stage" (1990: 83). The increasing focus on women's issues and women's liberation was reflected by the first South African Women's Festival of the Arts at the Market in 1985. Clare Stopford's *The Patchers* looked at the reality of both black and white women's lives on the Rand as a result of men's wars and the mining industry. Her next play, *Ulovane Jive* (1986), focused on the common base of the women's struggle regardless of race. During a state of emergency in 1986 the Durban-based dramatist Saira Essa staged *The Inquest* about the detention and death of Steven Biko, the first leader of the BCM, a daring undertaking at the time. In the same year Gcina Mhlophe's *Have you Seen Zandile?* introduced "the most oppressed of all South African stage characters – black, female, working-class and a school-child as well" (Gray 1990: 84, cf. 83f.; see Chapter 6.3). *You Strike the Woman, You Strike the Rock* by the Vusisizwe Players with Phyllis Klotz exposed the oppression of uneducated black working women in South Africa and commented upon the history of the women's struggle under apartheid (see Chapter 6.2).

The strong theatrical activity at the time, especially the contribution made by women, leads Gray to describe 1986 as the year in which

> [...] the arts finally seem to have broken with the system entirely, declaring their firm democratic independence beyond racism, classism, and sexism. The truth is that alternative theatre in the country had by then moved as a whole into becoming

> mainstream, the core of all the people's common cultural life, and long before the old guard knew that it had been usurped. (1990: 84)

The emergence of women onto the theatre scene signified both their participation in the anti-apartheid struggle and their specific emphasis of the reality of women's lives. Therefore Gray concludes that women should be regarded as "distinct as a pressure-group from the powers that be in the theatre" (1990: 86).

6.1.3. South African theatre by women as feminist theatre?

Gray's conclusion implies that theatre by women in South Africa can be read as feminist theatre to the extent that it is theatre produced by women who automatically constitute a 'distinct pressure-group.' This suggests that women either pursued a specific agenda or at least offered new representations of socially topical issues. This reading is one way of defining 'feminist theatre,' yet as is the case with so many abstract concepts, other definitions are possible depending on one's point of view (cf. Aston 1995; Case 1988; Goodman 1993; Keysaar 1984). One concept that all critics seem to agree on is that not every play created by women playwrights can be considered feminist, although every play, independent of the sex of its playwright, director or actors, can be examined from a critical feminist perspective.[17] For example, feminist criticism of so-called 'male plays' in South Africa became prominent in the course of the early 1990s (cf. Steinberg 1996 [1992]; Ojo-Ade 1996; Sher 1987).

Lizbeth Goodman gives a very general definition of 'feminist theatre': "political theatre oriented toward change, produced by women with feminist concerns" (1993: 1). Helen Keysaar offers a variety of definitions of 'feminist theatre' that help to understand what could be subsumed under "feminist concerns":

> productions and scripts characterised by consciousness of women as women; dramaturgy in which art is inseparable from the condition of women as women; performance (written and acted) that deconstructs sexual difference and thus undermines patriarchal power; scripting and production that present transformation as

[17] Sue-Ellen Case points out that the development of feminist thought and practice in the Western world in the 1970s led to a distinction between the two aspects "'women' in theatre" and "feminism and theatre": "Feminism began to be perceived as a specific political practice and analysis, committed to radical change and direct political action. Some women began to distinguish between their interest in the work of women in the theatre and feminist politics" (1988: 62f.).

> a structural and ideological replacement for recognition; and the creation of women characters in the 'subject position.' (1996: 1)

These definitions remain very general because the term 'women' is not a homogenous category and ideas of 'womanhood' vary according to area and cultural backgrounds. In the South African context the self-enforced and culturally specific idea of the African women as 'mothers' in their private, domestic role was still prevalent in the 1980s. In fact, this notion of the woman as first and foremost 'mother' prominently figures in the plays discussed in this chapter and represents the source of self-empowerment of the female characters. This concept differed considerably from the strongly political Western feminist demands of economical and social equality which were voiced from the early 1970s (cf. Chapter 6.1.1).

The discrepancy between African and Western approaches also raises the issue of race.[18] As Goodman remarks, "Can some contemporary theatres made by black women be called feminist? If so, which ones, and by whose standards?" (1993: 149). The idea that a deconstruction of sexual difference is an effective weapon to undermine patriarchal power is clearly present in South African theatre by women. However, it seems that the gender struggle had been subordinated to the more urgently felt need for the struggle against racial oppression. At least this appears to have been the case until a mood of transition to a democratic state started to set in. An increase in the focus on gender-specific problems during the political transitional period is explored in the analysis of Susan Pam-Grant's 1989 play *Curl Up and Dye* (cf. Chapter 6.4). Keysaar's claim that feminist theatre is characterised by the creation of women in the 'subject position' has limited application to South African theatre. In spite of the increasing emergence of women playwrights and actresses claiming agency for themselves, the main female characters in the plays written by South African women were only slowly becoming conscious of themselves as gender-oppressed subjects under the double patriarchal hegemony of the state and African tradition.

This brief discussion of notions of 'feminist theatre' concentrated on a few problems which can arise when Western concepts, created in a specific political and ideological moment in history, are generalised and used to denote developments in other political and cultural situations. The intention was to show that existing

[18] The African-American activist bell hooks [*sic*] criticised the white middle-class orientation of feminism as early as the first half of the 1980s and called for a reformulation of the aims of the feminist movement to include the women in the 'margins' (cf. 1982; 1984).

concepts can be employed as aids for orientation but are not a proper substitute for the creation of new theories and concepts about women's theatre specifically suited to the South African context.

6.1.4. South African approaches to feminism

In her introduction to *South African Feminisms* Margaret Daymond argues that

> [...] cultural feminism in South Africa does not form a single, coherent movement. After the simplistic (and ultimately exclusionary) assumptions of sisterhood that were made in the early days of a revived feminist movement here in the 1970s, the present need to accommodate social diversity has largely been matched by an acceptance of a plurality of theoretical positions. (1996: xivf.)

In spite of this diversity many critics are agreed that one cannot speak of a homogenous 'sisterhood.' In the apartheid context the discussion evolved around the ways in which race also determined women's power: "What is now replacing 'sisterhood' is necessarily complex: a challenge to its universalism and its hidden power relations has to be pursued simultaneously with efforts to establish a community of purpose within the recognition of 'difference.'" Questions of "how knowledge of the Other is produced, who produces it and who owns the understanding of relations of power" have become central to scholarship (Daymond 1996: xix). Western notions of 'feminism'[19] are not automatically suited for answering these questions in the South African context and thus should be, as Cecily Lockett demands, examined for their appropriateness and effectiveness before they are adopted by Western (white) critics operating in the country (cf. 1990: 3). Western feminism has been reproached by African-American and Third World feminists for its view of Third World women as an "already constituted, coherent group with identical interests and desires, regardless of class, ethnic or racial location, or contradictions" (Mohanty 1991: 55). In South Africa the strategy of viewing female solidarity as an essential political weapon (cf. Daymond 1996 [1990]: xlvii) is not successful because, as Dabi Nkululeko points out, it "fails to understand sexism in the more complex situation of the Third World, where class and sex oppression are joined by colonial and racial oppression" (1987: 99) or

[19] Feminism is obviously not a homogenous category and - in addition to the culture-based distinction between French and Anglo-American feminism - it exists in a variety of forms based on different political and ideological ideas, for example, liberal-humanist, Marxist, structural, post-structural, psychoanalytic and post-modern influences.

where women are said to suffer from triple oppression (race, class and gender).[20] According to Albie Sachs, gender inequality in South Africa has an apartheid-specific character: "[...] there is inequality within inequality, or, put another way, some are more unequal than others" (1990: 53). Nkululeko even prefers to speak of "quadruple" oppression, including colonialism as the "primary manifestation of imperialism" in South Africa (1987: 99). Because of these deficits in Western feminism, South African feminists have rejected this very broad approach in favour of an emphasis on what Lockett describes as "gender politics within the framework of a struggle for a more equitable society" (1990: 1). Referring to articles by Isabel Hofmeyer and Shireen Hassim, Jo Metelerkamp and Alison Todes, Michael Chapman concludes:

> [...] the material bases of poverty and economic marginalisation that in the African situation give substance to the categories woman, mother, children, and home, may enable us to view the trajectory of struggle in terms other than the well-established 'reactive' BC versus woman model: the primacy of the male revolutionary hero; the domestic support role of wife and mother. Rather, sociological modifications require us to see a gendered campaign, in which women outside their depictions in the novel, outside the reception of their texts in literary studies, were drawn into conflict because they were mothers and because the conflict had moved into the area they regarded as their own responsibility: the area in which they had to defend their children and their homes. In justifying motivations and principles rooted in localisms, women's struggles are not a 'bit on the side' but, in character, plot, theme and symbolism, are central to the narrative of any society that espouses non-oppression. (1996: 422)

Zoë Wicomb agrees that the South African woman's participation in the struggle foregrounds her involvement as a gendered being, a mother who defends her children and her home. She concludes that the "politicization of women's domestic role is indeed a departure from the Euro-feminist view of motherhood as a condition of passivity and confinement [...]" (1996 [1990]: 47).

Lockett argues that in the light of the South African women's movement and the nationalist liberation struggle "[...] the major challenge facing feminist critics in South Africa is to find a method that goes beyond the limits of the white middle-

[20] One of the early uses of the term 'triple oppression' goes back to Amiri Baraka/Leroi Jones, who referred to the situation of African-American women in the United States: "Third World women in this country suffer a triple oppression, if they are working women, as workers under capitalism – class oppression, national oppression and oppression because of their sex" (1980: 12).

class text" (1990: 14). The question which then arises is if white women "have the right to speak for or about black women" and if this act consolidates white women as the agents of oppression of black women (*ibid.*). Gayatri Spivak warns First World feminist critics not to impose their own theories on Third World women but suggests that they should speak to and listen to black women (cf. Lockett 1990: 15).[21] Much of the discussion about white and black feminism has revolved around the question of who can rightfully speak on behalf of whom.[22] It was during the 1980s that the African-American writer and critic Alice Walker and the Nigerian critic Chikwenye Okonjo Ogunyemi simultaneously (but independently) developed a concept of 'womanism.' Their ideas allowed a more appropriate critical approach in the examination of works by black women who focussed particularly on their oppression. Walker defines a 'womanist' as a "black feminist or feminist of color [...]. A woman who loves other women, sexually and/or non-sexually [...]. Committed to survival and wholeness of entire people, male and female. Not a separatist, except periodically, for health" (1984: xif.). The acknowledgement of the fact that black men and women share the experience of racial oppression is also central to Ogunyemi's approach. Ogunyemi believes that a black womanist is not only conscious of "sexual issues" but also "must incorporate racial, cultural, national, economic, and political considerations into her philosophy" in order to emphasise the "positive aspects of black life" (1985: 64, 68). In the African context this means:

> The intelligent black woman writer, conscious of black impotence in the context of white patriarchal culture, empowers the black man. She believes in him; [...]. Given this commitment, she can hardly become a strong ally of the white feminist until (perhaps) the political and economic fortunes of the black race improve. (1985: 68f.)

Black womanism strives for "black unity" in its celebration of "black roots, the ideals of black life, while giving a balanced presentation of black womandom." It addresses both the "black sexual power tussle" as well as the "world power structure that subjugates blacks" (1985: 72). Thus, according to Ogunyemi, the womanist writer has become a "spokeswoman for black women and the black race"

---

21 Variations of this idea have been voiced by many other so-called 'Third-World critics' such as Trinh Minh-ha (1989).

22 Lockett believes that white women, who must first recognise that they belong to a privileged class, should discuss the work of black women and develop ways of "talking about it" in order to try to understand the experience of the black woman (1996: 15). By contrast, Sisi Maqagi claims that privilege always widens that gap between the experience of black and white women (cf. 1996 [1990]: 28).

by distancing herself from both "black male chauvinism and the iconoclastic tendencies of feminism to embrace the relative conservatism of womanism" (1985: 79).[23] It was the South African BCM which attributed a similar 'womanist' role to women in the nationalist struggle for liberation during the 1970s.

In 1988 at a conference held by the Congress of South African Writers in Johannesburg the major focus was on the problems and aspirations of black women writers. Boitumelo Mofokeng, Nise Malange and Roseline Naapo addressed the cultural and educational difficulties which a black woman writer was confronted with. They highlighted the problems encountered by the increasing need for women to work to secure their family's economic survival and how this had drastically changed a woman's social position within her family and traditional culture. These increased demands had destroyed her role as "the first teacher in the home, the mentor and custodian of our culture" (n.d.: 8). It was the double shift of working women (job and household), patriarchal notions of the woman's inferiority and a lack of education which made it difficult for women to tell the stories of their lives. However, the few texts that had been produced certainly functioned as "an important social documentation of their lives [...] and their role in the whole struggle" (Mofokeng, Malange & Naapo, n.d.: 8; cf. Lockett 1990: 18f.). Thus Lockett calls for the need to "view black women's writing from this perspective, to recognise that their work is primarily socio-historical and that its purpose is to record the experiences of black people in South Africa under apartheid" (1990: 19). It is precisely this idea which underpins the overall approach in this chapter. The following interpretations of *You Strike the Woman, You Strike the Rock, Have You Seen Zandile?* and *Curl Up and Dye* concentrate on the role of women in a male-dominated society.

---

[23] Susan Arndt (cf. 2000) discusses the plurality of feminism in Africa.

6.2. *You Strike the Woman, You Strike the Rock* (*Wathint' Abafazi, Wathint' Imbokotho*) and the political voice of black South African women

> [...] for years now we black women have been fighting for our rights. It is a long hard struggle.
>
> Sdudla in *You Strike the Woman, You Strike the Rock* [24]

6.2.1. The collaboration of Phyllis Klotz and the Vusisizwe Players

In 1984 an all-female black cast supported by the Community Arts Project (CAP) in Cape Town performed *Telling Tales*, a production featuring English and Xhosa stories adapted from Western folk-tales which attacked socio-political oppression. The actresses Itumeleng Wa-Lehulere and Andile Nyembezi felt that the elements which made up *Telling Tales*, "'stinging attacks', the 'humour', the Xhosa 'dance, music and mime'" (Fuchs 1990: 93), needed to be placed in a more particular and militant context. Together with other young Xhosa women involved in the CAP they began developing a play in workshop about the lives of migrant Xhosa women who were driven from the homelands to the city by economic necessity. It was through this collaboration that the idea for *You Strike the Woman, You Strike the Rock (Wathint' Abafazi, Wathint' Imbokotho)*[25] was born.[26] By employing methods typical of workshop theatre, the actresses researched the lives of women selling their various products in and around Cape Town and incorporated these and their own experiences into the play. Thobeka Maqhutyana, Nomvula Qosha and Poppy Tsira were joined by Phyllis Klotz, a white theatre director working with the University of Cape Town's Drama Department and the Community Arts Project in the 1980s. Xolani September supported the group as stage-manager. Klotz had previously been working in a project called the Young Peoples Theatre[27] which was involved in "touring townships schools, both to improve a staggeringly inept education system, as well as exploring social wrongs, particularly the oppression of women" (cf. Barker 1997: 45). She felt that this new project about the reality of

---

[24] *SW* 188.

[25] Loren Kruger points out that the correct translation of 'wathin' abafazi' should be 'you strike the women' because 'abafazi' is plural. She argues that the use of the plural would also make more sense as the slogan (after which the play is named) stresses the collective action of women (cf. 1999: 238 fn. 40).

[26] The published version of this play features Itumeleng Wa-Lehulere as one of the creators while Andile Nyembezi is not mentioned (cf. *W/S* 163).

[27] The Young Peoples Theatre was a non-profit theatre trust financially supported by "the Klotz business connections" (Fuchs 1990: 94).

black women's lives represented an opportunity to achieve "something important from a social and from a theatrical point of view" (Fuchs 1990: 94). "My mother was progressive and as a child it never occurred to me that women were disadvantaged," Klotz explains. "When I was older, I realised that women are at a distinct disadvantage but that combined with being semi-literate and unskilled, some were even more disadvantaged than others" (Kennedy 2000: 25). In addition to the socially progressive focus of the play, its physical acting style and energetic humour, reminiscent of the highly successful *Woza Albert!*, made the play very powerful. *You Strike the Woman* premiered at UCT's Arena Theatre in 1986 with financial support from both CAP and the Young Peoples Theatre Educational Trust. It then went to the Grahamstown Arts Festival where Mannie Manim invited the company, who now called themselves the Vusisizwe Players, to perform at Johannesburg's Market Theatre (cf. Fuchs 1990: 93f.; *SW* 165).[28]

6.2.2. *You Strike the Woman, You Strike the Rock* - the play

"In the dead of the night there comes a plague bird. [...] That runs above the location, the whistle blows, the people fear [...]" (*SW* 166). The prologue to You Strike the Woman, You Strike the Rock takes this "plague bird" - the police helicopter - as its central image, an image of power. Thus the audience is introduced to the play's theme of victimised black versus white oppressor which places the play firmly in the tradition of South African resistance theatre. However, the opening scene goes one decisive step further in that it draws attention to the "weeping mothers [who] protect their children as chickens protect their chicks from the hawk" (*SW* 166). The main victim of apartheid from the perspective of this play is now specified as the black woman. Its militant title, You Strike the Woman, You Strike the Rock (a slogan from the 1956 march by women to Pretoria to protest against pass laws for women), has already suggested that this play focuses on

[28] Together with Smal Ndaba, Phyllis Klotz is one of the founding members of the Sibikwa Community Project (1989). Located in the township of Benoni on the East Rand, Sibikwa aims to "promote theatre and performance arts education with the aim of integrating the growth of life skills, vocational training and cultural awareness through the creation of a school which will render classes for children and adults in a multi lingual approach to the full spectrum of performance disciplines" (Sibikwa n.d.: n.p.). As artistic director, apart from directing and devising performances with Ndaba, Klotz is in charge of implementing and providing funding for all educational programmes and is involved in the development of new arts policy (cf. Barker 1997: 45; Kennedy 2000: 25).

female empowerment. However, Strike's emphasis on the black woman's plight and the explicit call for female resistance challenge not only apartheid but also the male-dominated struggle of the BCM that silenced the female voice in the name of resistance against racial oppression. In addition, from the point of view of theatre history, Strike challenges the black resistance play which had hitherto been predominantly workshopped by men and had also focused almost exclusively on the male perspective. In fact, Strike remains even today one of the few published plays by black women within a male-dominated theatre scene (cf. Loots 1997: 148). Lliane Loots posits that the play's "uniqueness" lies in the fact that it "challenges any monolithic understanding of power relations by looking at how issues of race, class and gender interact in positioning the subject in South African theatrical and performance history" (1997: 145).

Strike presents three female vendors, Mampompo, Mambhele and Sdudla, who sell their produce at a market in Crossroads, a formal township surrounded by squatter camps on the Cape Flats.[29] Each woman has experienced a family tragedy that has forced her into securing her economic survival. Approximately half of the fourteen scenes portray the women at their market stalls; the other scenes replay key moments from their past and the long road taken to reach their current predicament. Instead of presenting characters who merely narrate their experiences to each other in storytelling fashion, the actresses directly re-enact these scenes for the audience. Each protagonist is supported by the other two actresses who play the roles of minor characters in order better to convey the atmosphere of their stories.

---

[29] Crossroads represents African women's resistance to the policy of forced migration. What began as an "emergency camp" in the mid 1970s turned into an organised community with committees and support groups (cf. Lipman 1984: 38-41). The government's plan to demolish the township and send the inhabitants to the Transkei in 1977 was met with such resistance from the Crossroads Women's Movement that the government announced in 1978 under international pressure that there would be no forced removals (cf. Lapchick 1985: 250-52).

This setting also bears significance in South Africa's tradition of resistance theatre. The women of the Crossroads squatter camp created the play *Imfuduso* in the late 1970s as a documentation of their experiences (cf. Orkin 1991: 191, 230). And a few years earlier Workshop 71's play *Crossroads* (1972) had drawn attention to the suffering of blacks (men) from the perspective of a gang leader and functioned as a "document of urban moral anarchy in an apartheid situation" (Mshengu 1976: 41). In 1983 the Squatter Players from Crossroads created a play called *How long, Crossroads?* in which they dramatised daily aspects of their lives. Their play was conceived as "a strategy for social action" (cf. Steadman 1990: 311). Thus in the South African oppositional theatre tradition the township Crossroads is associated with a site of the suffering of not only black men but especially also black women.

6.2.2.1. The triple oppression of the black South African woman

Mampompo, Mambhele and Sdudla sell chickens, oranges and vetkoeks (deep-fried cakes) at the market in Crossroads. The three women compete for the small number of paying customers in the poverty-stricken township. They employ various strategies to make their few sales such as selling on credit or flirting with their male customers. They tease each other and also criticise each other's sales' strategies so that they can show off their own self-declared professional or moral superiority. They are always on the lookout for cheeky children who steal their goods. Another problem is that they all work illegally as not one of them has a licence to trade, so they are also constantly forced to protect themselves against police raids. But despite their squabbles and competitiveness it is the regular police patrols which force them to unite against a common enemy and share their experiences of oppression and exploitation.

Mampompo has left her four children in the rural Transkei and come to the Cape area in search of her husband. He is a migrant worker in Cape Town but had stopped sending her any money. She finds her husband hospitalised with tuberculosis and has to take on any work that is available in order to support herself. She labours on a Boer farm, works as a domestic servant for a Muslim family and sells chickens for the African lady Mrs. Ntlebi. When he has recovered, Mampompo's husband is employed once again, and the couple can live together in Crossroads. However, they are still not able to earn enough to provide for themselves, let alone for their children in the homeland.

Mambhele has grown up in the Cape Town area. She is the mother of four children and has an unemployed husband who is an alcoholic. He drinks away the money she has been earning as a domestic servant, a laundry woman and a self-employed market woman. While her co-vendor Mampompo is full of hope and dreams of a better future, Mambhele's outlook on life is much bleaker. She is caught between an oppressive state and an abusive husband and resigned to the fact that she can do nothing to improve her situation.

Sdudla is the only politically-minded character in the play. She is involved in the women's struggle and took part in the 1956 pass law protest march to Pretoria. Mambhele believes that Sdudla was a member of Poqo, the armed wing of the PAC (cf. *SW* 191). Sdudla is a widow, her husband died while serving a sentence on Robben Island. Her sons have left her, possibly fleeing the country. She considers it her task to raise the consciousness of her two co-workers and make them aware of their state of oppression as black women.

Through their stories the women explore and challenge various pairs of binary oppositions that have been constructed and appropriated by apartheid ideology (such as race, class, gender). Their tales illustrate how other social groups that are also oppressed to varying degrees by the white patriarchal system appropriate these oppositions for themselves in order to keep the poor, uneducated African woman at the bottom of the hierarchy. The characters depict the black woman and her family as victims of the apartheid system in general. They also explore ways in which the black woman is oppressed by the white man and woman in particular.

Mampompo tells her colleagues about the hardships she endured as a woman living in the rural areas and how she was victimised by apartheid's policy of separate homelands. Just as Matsemela Manaka's play *Egoli* concentrates on the plight of migrant workers on the Johannesburg gold mines, Strike analyses the effect of this labour system on the wives and children left behind in the poverty-stricken homelands. Mampompo was forced to leave the Transkei out of economic necessity. Her husband, who had already left to find work in Cape Town, had not fulfilled his role as bread-winner and had not sent money to his family. She never blames him for his lack of support and thus leaves no doubt that she regards his illness with tuberculosis, his inability to provide for his family and her consequent suffering as directly resulting from apartheid. In contrast to John in *Egoli*, who suffers from the effects of the apartheid system but is still held personally responsible by his friend and co-miner Hamilton for spending his money on alcohol and prostitutes instead of supporting his family, Mampompo exclusively defines her family as a victim of institutionalised racism.

Mampompo has experienced with her own body that she is not just racially oppressed. In her stories she relates how she has been abused as a black woman. When she arrived in the Cape, she found employment on the farm of a Boer who sexually molested her. He not only exercised dominance over his female victim but also manifested his power over her husband, the black man, by denying him the right to a monogamous relationship with his wife. Both the black woman and the black man are oppressed by a racist patriarchal system that degrades women to the role of sex objects and reduces men to minors. The fact that a Boer land owner is revealed as sexually violent criticises colonial practices in that it reflects colonial discourse's descriptions of the so-called 'uncivilised' African land as a female body that can be (sexually) conquered. Gilbert and Tompkins emphasise that interracial rape is a symbol for the "colonisers' violation of the land" and also stands for "related forms of economic and political exploitation" (1996: 213). In addition, in Afrikaans writing the farm represents a sacral and secluded haven of freedom for the Afrikaner (cf. Coetzee 1988: 175) but is now exposed as an immoral place where one of the most brutal forms of the colonial encounter is practised. However, Mampompo's defiance and her mockery of the Boer show that she is not prepared to suffer passively.

Mampompo's experience of molestation and through this act her exposure to the white patriarchal system is contrasted with yet another story she has to tell about forced sexual intercourse. This time it is about her own African (Xhosa) tradition, another patriarchal system: "Ya, the man is the head of the house, you must do what he says – it is our tradition" (*SW* 188). At the male hostel in Cape Town her husband insists on having sex with her in an overcrowded dormitory which provides no form of privacy (and where female visitors are illegal): "How can I do such as thing, while people are eating and drinking, playing cards, moving around, not even a curtain to cover the bed?" His dismissal of her sense of shame and embarrassment forces her to realise that she must accept her role as his wife and perform the duties that are expected of her: "I had no choice, he was demanding" (*SW* 192). Although this scene is not associated with rape, the parallel with her violent encounter with the Boer farmer is nonetheless present. In both cases the woman is turned into an object of male pleasure. She then relates how another man in the hostel room asked her for sex, which as a married woman shocked and disgusted her. She refused him, realising at the same time that he too had been suffering from a long separation from his wife. Thus she implicitly redefines her husband's sexual possession of her as a consequence of the dehumanising practices of apartheid, not as a natural form of dominant male sexual role behaviour. In the end she forgives the man for offending her and thus implicitly also pardons her husband. While her reaction may be regarded as problematic from a feminist perspective because it 'justifies' the sexual oppression of women by the victims themselves, Mampompo clearly singles out apartheid as the threat against the African couple rather than focusing on possible internal conflicts between men and women.

Eventually Mampompo finds a low wage job in Crossroads selling chickens for the African woman Mrs. Ntlebi. After having been racially exploited as a domestic servant and sexually exploited on the farm, she is now victimised because of her class. The women in the market criticise Mrs. Ntlebi who is middle-class, owns a car and has a house in the township which is "beautiful – just like a white person" (*SW* 186). Although Mambhele and Sdudla urge their friend to defend herself against this form of black-on-black class exploitation, Mampompo is "proud" of her job because "I'm sure of my R2,00 a day selling or not selling" (*SW* 168). However, she also has to acknowledge that her employer is exploiting her and takes advantage of the fact that she is illegally employed: "This Mrs Ntlebi doesn't want to pay a licence for me; if these police can come and take these chickens away, she will deduct my money" (*SW* 172). Consequently, her job becomes more and more dangerous. The increased police brutality makes Mampompo realise: "I can be shot by a stray bullet, while Mrs Ntlebi is sitting in her house" (*SW* 193). This is the first time that she questions her job.

The play shows that black women are also victimised by white women despite the fact that they often both occupy the same role, that of mother. Apartheid, to which the white woman is an accomplice, prevents the black woman from playing this role. Often driven by economic necessity, a black urban woman like Mambhele typically works as a maid and nanny for a white family. This job is accompanied by all kinds of hardships which prevent the black women from maintaining a reasonably stable family life. The time it takes to commute from the townships to the white suburbs forces the women to leave their homes very early each morning, returning only many hours later. The relationship with their husbands suffers, and the lack of time does not allow them to properly raise or supervise their own children who are then susceptible to gangs and other bad influences in the townships. Ironically, those women who are prevented from playing their natural role as mothers for their own children are forced to enact this role for white children. The madam says to her domestic: "You must understand that I work as well and I simply can't have someone who is unreliable. Who will be here when the children come home from school?" (*SW* 183). The fact that nobody is home to greet the black children after school does not occur to the white employer who regards the black woman as her employee only but fails to recognise her in her own private roles as wife, mother and housewife. Jacklyn Cock calls this type of behaviour on the part of white 'madams' "'a technique of depersonalisation'" (qtd. in Lenta 1989: 242, cf. 238f.). The black employees are silenced about the reality of their lives. The female employers, in their "need at the conscious level to believe that blacks are different, with different needs and lesser rights," thus become "accessories to the white males who possess the political power" (Lenta 1989:

243). Strike shows that the maids are helpless in the face of their madams because they cannot afford to be fired. For many the only solution for this exploitation is to pray together and ask God to look after their children during their absence (cf. *SW* 183). This allows them to express their common plight and draw strength and hope from their solidarity. But at the same time it also shows that the black women are trapped by their position.

6.2.2.2. Women as wives, mothers and activists: The road to female empowerment

Mampompo chooses to accept her Xhosa traditions and respect her husband in his role as head of the family. This decision is based on the fact that he fulfils her expectations. He takes his traditional role as bread-winner and provider for his wife and children seriously and thus demonstrates to her that he respects her and the family: "Nozulu is a very good man. He is earning R30 a week. R2 for bus fare, and he give [sic] me R24, that is something" (*SW* 191). She proudly defines herself through him: "Yes, I know myself, I'm Nozulu's wife [...]." Although Mampompo is forced to admit that she and her husband do not earn enough money to survive, let alone support their children in the Transkei, she is convinced that her knowledge of "how to make money, like selling the chickens" will allow her eventually to realise her dream for the future: "When I've got money I'm going back to Transkei [sic], build myself a big house, educate my children, buy myself a farm with a tractor, and be my own boss" (*SW* 199). This dream is interesting and contradicts her earlier self-definition when, just a few seconds after describing herself as "Nozulu's wife" and praising him for his support, Mampompo desires to be her "own boss" (ibid.). Her husband does not seem to figure in her future life or at least does not play a prominent role. Her goal is to educate her children and provide them with a better future which shows that she primarily sees herself in her role as mother. Part of her function will also be to take over the responsibility as head of the household. Influenced by Sdudla's feminist conviction that women need not listen to their husbands, Mampompo imagines herself as economically independent from male support. Motherhood is her main motivation, it strengthens her identity and allows her to be forward-looking in her support of the next generation. Mampompo does not conflate motherhood with victimhood as feminist theory has done. Obioma Nnaemeka argues that in the African context motherhood is defended because it is considered to be a woman's experience ("'mothering'") including both “pains and rewards” (1997: 5). She bases this insight on Adrienne Rich’s distinction between patriarchy’s construction of motherhood as an institution and women’s experience of motherhood (cf. Nnaemeka 1997: 5; Rich 1997).

Another reason why Mampompo believes that her dream will come true is that she thinks she is free to work in whatever job she chooses: “[...] Botha has taken the passes away, so that I can go wherever I want to” (*SW* 180).[1] However, Mambhele and Sdudla make her accept reality: “Since you come from the Transkei you think you are clever and your eyes are wide open. If you think your eyes are wide open, why don’t you see things that are happening around you?” (*SW* 181). They also make her aware of the fact that she cannot improve her situation: “Have you forgotten that you can’t read or write?” (*SW* 199) and “What job can you get? [...] You see you are qualified for nothing and you will do what others tell you your whole life” (*SW* 188f.). Sdudla is convinced that Prime Minister Botha’s reform plans are all just part of a political strategy because ultimately the “system hasn’t changed, [...] we are forced to obey laws in which we have no part or say in the making” (*SW* 199).

Compared to Mampompo, Mambhele perceives her life very differently. She suffers from her husband’s behaviour and describes the family’s situation to her daughter:

> Oh! He is going to spend all my money on drink. All day I’m working hard selling chickens, smiling if I don’t want to smile, laughing even if I don’t want to, men are touching me and I am still laughing. I’m working for you and your brothers. I come home tired, and I must cook, your father is demanding a plate of food from me. Work all day and work all night. I must look after the house, clean, wash, iron, while your father is drinking my money at Madlamini place. I can’t tolerate this any more. Uyandiyela. He is shitting on my head. (*SW* 195f.)

Mambhele feels exploited by her unemployed husband who makes her work outside the home and take on his traditional role as bread-winner. In addition, he demands that she must fulfil her traditional role as housewife and mother by doing all the household chores. Yet she does not have the power to change her situation: “Yaw, men think we are toys for them to play with. No, no that’s why I told my husband to go but he doesn’t want to.” Mampompo sympathises with Mambhele and advises her to “chuck” her unemployed, lazy and alcoholic husband “out of the

[1] By early 1986 the government had lifted the state of emergency and had announced the abolition of the pass laws (cf. Barber 1999: 262).

house" (*SW* 192). This shows that Mampompo does not accept men who clearly misuse their role as head of the household and harm their own families. Mambhele believes that as women are forced to take all the responsibility and care for their family they certainly deserve to have their say: "[...] aren't we working hard, earning the money to support our children, must we still do what they [the men] say?" (*SW* 188). With an abusive husband at home and increasing police harassment in the townships affecting all three women from making enough money to support their families, Mambhele has little to hope for: "Trouble here, troubles at home" (*SW* 197). She defines herself both as a victim of apartheid and of her husband. Although she describes his unemployment as a result of an accident, a broken leg, after which he could not return to his old position, she also criticises him for not putting enough effort into his job search. In the end, however, despite the fact that she feels used and abandoned by her husband, she ultimately blames the apartheid system for transforming him from a "good husband" (*SW* 196) into a burden on her and the direct source of the family's suffering. She shouts at the police helicopter, a symbol of apartheid's power: "You are a monster which separates us" (*SW* 197). Unlike Mampompo, she regards Botha's promises to abolish the pass laws as "fairytales" pacifying the oppressed group like children with stories of make-believe (*SW* 180). Even though Mambhele is more aware of political reality, she, too, fails to defend herself against oppression:

> SDUDLA [to MAMPOMPO]: You spend your time worrying about money and chickens – money and chickens. That is all that is on your mind.
>
> MAMBHELE: You always talk to us about politics. I can't worry with politics – I must look after my children and I want to live quietly.
>
> SDUDLA: Don't talk nonsense, politics comes into everything. What you want is peace, but what you get in another thing. (*SW* 198)

Mampompo and Mambhele do not comprehend that their personal troubles are a result of politics. In the lives of the dispossessed, especially poor, uneducated black women, the combination of race, class and gender oppression in the name of apartheid and African tradition is at the same time a political and a private phenomenon. It is exactly because the opposition between the private and the political does not hold that Sdudla calls upon her friends to join her in the struggle. She is convinced that only political protest and resistance can change the situation of the dispossessed whereas individual efforts to improve one's living conditions equal subjugation to the system.

Sdudla is the only character in the play who has been involved in the women's struggle against apartheid. In 1956 at the age of eighteen and with her small baby strapped to her back, she eagerly joined other women in the protest march on Pretoria. Sdudla's political consciousness is expressed in her sales slogan: "Buy an orange and suck it: the juice of this orange will open your eyes, you will know right from wrong" (*SW* 167). As is the case with the protagonists in other plays influenced by the BCM, she sees herself in the role of the teacher raising the awareness of her pupils. She tells her friends from the market that some of the African men feared that the regime's implementation of passes for women would interfere with their own patriarchal traditions: "I remember attending meetings long time ago where men stood up and said that the government cannot give us black women passes because the woman is under the control of a man. Some men are frightened by the passes we had to carry, they thought we would not listen to them anymore" (*SW* 188).[2] The women's struggle in South Africa historically aimed to empower the black woman in her traditional roles as mother and housewife and certainly did not address the question of gender equality. It was only in the late 1980s that women increasingly claimed their political voice to call attention to gender concerns. Sdudla's opinions were clearly progressive at the time of the play's creation:

> [...] for years now we black women have been fighting for our rights. It is a long hard struggle. We are treated like children by everyone, but as wives and mothers, it falls upon us to make small wages stretch a long way. It is we who feel the cries of our children when they are sick and hungry. It suits the men to keep us like fools. (*SW* 188)

At the same time Sdudla points out that the apartheid regime has managed to defeat the black man in the struggle, killing the husbands and sons, causing "pain – sorrow – destruction." Although apartheid's laws are "made by a human being for another human being" (both *SW* 199), there is no humanity left. Brutality fosters brutality, and apartheid's soldiers, who have become merciless killers in the name of an oppressive state, turn the black children into freedom fighters of equal ruthlessness: "These my children, who spill blood as easy as saying voetsek [fuck off], created by the system, and the men in blue who protect it. These are not the children who we laboured to give birth to, [...], but the monsters created by the system of oppression" (*SW* 200f.). The African woman is not recognised in her role as mother and nanny to white children. Her own children have "no mothers to look after them.

---

[2] This is historically documented by Lodge (cf. 1983: 151).

Growing up with no laws" while the white children have "forgotten [their] black mothers" who cared for them when their own "white mother was too busy, playing tennis, or shopping." In the end the men on both sides of the fight "kill without respect for a human life" (all *SW* 200). Sdudla believes that the black women must take over because it is only they who have retained a moral sense of right and wrong, human dignity and respect for others and are thus the only group who can achieve liberation for their people: "We carry a heavy burden that defeats men but won't defeat us women" (*SW* 199). Typically, Sdudla defines women in their role as mothers but decries apartheid and the African patriarchal system for not allowing women to develop this role. She says that unwittingly the opposing sides have become collaborators in the oppression of black women. Thus Sdudla believes that if women are strong enough to free themselves, they will be able to free the black man (and thus the entire black people) from the yoke of oppression. The common goal is still the nationalist struggle for freedom. Yet instead of waiting for the breakdown of apartheid to then include gender-issues in the negotiations for a new democratic state, *Strike* reverses the order of priority. The concept of 'motherhood' is central to this play as a source of empowerment for the African women. In fact, *Strike* also suggests that 'motherhood' is the central, even essential, element in the identity construction of African women (in contrast to white or Western women). And it is this focus on the mother role which places this play in a tradition of female 'writing.' Deirde Byrne's observation that black South African women's writing is so powerful because of the authors' "enlistment of maternity in a political cause" can be extended to include the three characters in this play:[3] "Their desire to give their children a better life than they had becomes a motive for resistance and agitation for change" (1994: 24).[4]

At the end of the play the three women slip into the role of activist students who manifest their resistance to the state in a protest song and a "*toi toi action*" (toyi toyi dance).[5] The women honour the commitment of the children, yet they also

---

[3] At this point I abstain from discussing Phyllis Klotz as a 'white culture-broker' and the impact of white capital on the production of *Strike*, well aware of the fact that critics have regarded this element as a form of consolidation of the black women's oppression.

[4] See Driver (1992) for an analysis of other forms of representation and functions of femininity/womanhood in South African writing by men and women. In contrast to *Strike*'s call for revolution by women/mothers, Driver mentions two novels by men (Mongane Serote, *To Every Birth Its Blood*; Enver Carim, *A Dream Deferred*) that suggest that motherhood outlives the revolution instead of supporting it (cf. 1992: 471).

[5] 'Toyi toyi' is a contemporary type of anti-apartheid protest march that includes chanting and dancing (cf. Henry 2002: n.p.).

believe that the confrontation between the Casspirs[6] and the students will only lead to more and more violence. When the women see a soldier shoot a very young girl right before their eyes, Mampompo and Mambhele realise that they cannot longer passively watch the bloodshed. Because it is a small child who dies, they are touched as mothers: "Bloodshed all around me and I have done nothing, today is somebody else's child, tomorrow mine" (*SW* 203). Motherhood finally empowers them.

The three women unite in their common grief and with new determination (cf. Fuchs 1990: 95) and immediately also start protesting, shouting "The sun will rise for all the working women of the world" (*SW* 204). This call appears to be initially a statement about the class struggle. However, as discussed previously, apartheid was a racist system which promoted the breakdown of traditional African gender-based family structures, and it can be held responsible for the increasing need for women to work to support their families. The women warn Botha with the protest slogan: "When you strike the woman/You strike the rock" (*SW* 204). The traditional stick fight performed at the end of the play suggests that they no longer wish to resist peacefully but even as women are willing to use more powerful means to confront the apartheid state. The stick fight is an African ritual reserved for men and therefore can be regarded as a symbol of the women's struggle against apartheid and equally against their domination by African patriarchy.[7] It could at the same time also be regarded as the women's appropriation of a typically male weapon which is no longer useful to the weakened men. In this sense the female stick fight symbolises the liberation struggle carried out by women in the name of the oppressed population as a whole. However, as Loots argues, this element could also be read as the play's "final weakness" in that it represents an "ideological falling back on gender stereotyping, where 'true' resistance to any oppressive system of rule is seen as violent, proactive and therefore masculine" (1997: 150). In a more general way Loren Kruger suggests that the women's political agency turns them into "vehicles for social forces deemed more compelling than gender" (1995b: 48). Despite these considerations, this indeterminacy does not weaken the play's

[6] 'Casspirs' are armoured, mine-proofed military vehicles used to police the townships during the 1980s.

[7] The general term 'African patriarchy' is problematic since it fails to convey the fact that historically African patriarchy did not represent a single power relationship but what Belinda Bozzoli called a "'patchwork quilt' of patriarchies" (1995: 126). Different societies knew different forms of patriarchy that changed due to the influence of colonial conquest and trade (cf. 1995: 126f.).

message but rather points once more to the many different reasons why women could and did become engaged in the struggle for their 'triple' liberation. This strong agitprop finale was severely condemned by an American critic after the play's run in New York in 1988. It was considered to be no more than a "commotion of consciousness raising and message mongering" and "stamping about with raised fists and menacing poles," which "comes close to defeating a noble endeavour" (Goodman 1988: C3). However, as a resistance play created in South Africa *Strike* was not intended to please the artistic expectations of white or Western audiences but to entertain, educate and mobilise national white and black audiences.

In summary, *You Strike the Woman, You Strike the Rock* does not attempt to deny the binary opposition between black and white, rich and poor, man and woman, but uses these clear-cut differences to argue for political empowerment of poor, uneducated African women. The play characterises these categories as constructions by powerful discourses that strongly limit an individual's role repertoire. However, the women show that they have learnt to analyse the reality of their oppression and defend themselves by arriving at a new interpretation of their traditional roles. Thus *Strike* both stands in and criticises the (male) tradition of the resistance play.

6.2.2.3. Resisting oppression through theatre

You Strike the Woman, You Strike the Rock begins with the three actresses "rotating their arms above their heads making the sound of the helicopter," - the 'plague bird' police helicopter which harasses the township in the middle of the night (Fuchs 1990: 94). The actresses switch from miming machines to playing the roles of township women who fear for the lives of their children. Then, in the first scene they change roles once more and become Mampompo, Mambhele and Sdudla. This, as Fuchs remarks, is Grotowskian poor theatre at its best (1990: 94). With this series of transformations the actresses have introduced the play as being openly theatrical, clearly identifying it as a South African resistance play of the 1970s and 1980s. Like *Survival*, *Bopha!* and *Egoli* (see Chapter 4), *Strike* not only criticises apartheid through the characters' dialogues but also effectively employs theatrical practices to express resistance. At the same time the play clearly strives to entertain its audience with its "infectious explosive humour [...] channelled along *Woza Albert!* lines" (*ibid.*).

Of the plays discussed in this study so far, *Strike* most resembles *Bopha!* in its detailed employment of dramatic means (see Chapter 4.2.2.4). The use of movement through the body and role-play occupy a central position and emphasise the theatricality of the stage and of life under apartheid in epic fashion. Both movement (mime, song, dance) and role-play capitalise on the body's characteristic as the dominant vehicle of the performance (cf. Balme 1995: 189; 1999: 221) which frees itself from being degraded to an "inscribed object of knowledge" (Gilbert & Tompkins 1996: 204) in favour of self-representation from a subject position. This strategy is also apparent is *Strike*. However, in contrast to the focus on the deconstruction of essentialising white/black oppositions in male plays and ignoring gender, *Strike* as a race *and* gender-oriented play by women attempts to "recuperate female subjectivities while showing that gender is an ideology mapped across the body in and through representation." With the help of mime and role-play the actresses demonstrate how "[...] women's bodies are not only exploited by the colonisers but also reappropriated by the colonised patriarchy as part of a political agenda which may not fully serve the interests of the women in question" (Gilbert & Tompkins 1996: 212, 213). For example, the sexual violation of Mampompo by the Boer farmer (played by Sdudla) is explicitly re-enacted and openly criticised not only in the victim's verbal protest but also in a song and dance of defiance. Mampompo and a co-worker mock or subversively mimic him by "*lift*[ing] *their skirts to match his uncouth behaviour*" (*SW* 188). By contrast, Mampompo represents her involuntary sexual encounter with her husband in the overcrowded hostel with hand gestures and plays out the scene herself. In both cases she conveys her feeling of degradation by the men through mime.

As mentioned above, the play begins with the actresses miming police helicopters, the dominant symbol of oppression. Directly after this scene the actresses in the roles of the three vendors imitate the sounds of the chickens they are selling. Then the stage directions indicate for Mampompo to mime a "*chicken running away from her. She runs after it clucking like a chicken and shouting; she grabs the chicken by the neck, it wriggles in her hand*" (*SW* 167). During the encounter with the helicopter one of the women had explained to the audience that the "weeping mothers protect their children as chickens protect their chicks from the hawk (*SW* 166). The parallel established between the mothers and the hens suggests that the women are as defenceless towards state measures of oppression as the chickens are towards their slaughtering by these women. While the market women may appear to be helpless against attacks at this early stage in the play, the actresses demonstrate that they are most certainly in control. The representation of apartheid through a machine emphasises the inhumanity of the system. By contrast, the women's acting points to their own versatility and flexibility. The actresses create a similar effect when they mime the work they had to do on a farm and in a laundry service. They represent these activities in stylised form, following a regular rhythm which they speed up as the scene continues. The stage directions for their mime of laundry work read: "*It has a regular rhythm to the count of four. Sdudla is ironing sheets. Mampompo sorting washing into trolleys to be weighed and washed. Mambhele is working with a heavy pressing machine.* [...] *They make a sound which expels air to co-ordinate with downward movement*" (*SW* 184). With this mime sequence the three characters are able to convey the impression that they are subjugated by the machines just as they are subjugated by the oppressive laws of the state. This stylised representation of the typical work day of an African woman allows the actresses to severely criticise the system which enforces such conditions.

Role-play is used in many scenes to show how a large part of the South African population is affected by apartheid. At their stalls in the market the women tell each other about their past experiences and perform various scenes for the audience. For example, Mampompo talks about her long walks every week to the homeland post office in the hope of receiving money from her husband and re-enacts one of these futile journeys. She is assisted by the other two actresses, who take on the roles of other needy people and the postmistress who struggles to keep her excitable customers under control. The actresses recreate sufficient commotion on stage to convey the impression of a large crowd. Thus they show that a life story such as Mampompo's does not represent an individual fate but one which is shared by many others as well. They also help to free the dispossessed from their anonymity by bringing them to life in front of an audience. A similar effect is achieved with the re-enactment of Mampompo's bus ride to Cape Town. Not only do the actresses people the stage as the numerous passengers on the hot overcrowded bus, but they also take on the roles of friends and family left behind in the reserves. Again, a voice is given to the otherwise silenced population. This scene on the bus is also clearly funny: the passengers' reactions to a smelly nappy, a loud transistor radio and a snoring passenger all cause laughter among the audience. However, despite this comic quality, the spectators are reminded of the seriousness of the situation. At the end of the scene a clearly nervous Mampompo prays that she will arrive in

Cape Town safely so that she can search for her husband and earn money for the family.

Another element of resistance theatre found in *Strike* is its use, in epic fashion, of slogans, chants and songs which are dispersed throughout the play. They are predominantly political in content and derived from the struggle. Scene 7 offers an example of how role-play and slogans/songs can be used to make a political statement. Sdudla has been telling the other two market women about women's involvement in the struggle against male domination. When she evokes her part in the 1956 Pretoria march, the actresses playing Mambhele and Mampompo become co-protesters and eye-witnesses who underline Sdudla's account with protest songs and comments. They create a powerful atmosphere of collective resistance while preparing the audience for the final scene with the stick fight and the legendary shouting of "Wathint' abafazi? wathint' [*sic*] imbokotho" (*SW* 204). This scene fulfils several functions. By creating the impression of a crowd of protestors on stage, the women are able to define the struggle as a mass movement - they represent the voices of thousands of people and thus mock apartheid's idea of (black) voicelessness. Sdudla emphasises the multi-racial quality of the Pretoria march, and the three women are seen as representative of all women, regardless of race. The point made here is not so much that the characters transgress racial boundaries (in the sense of switching from black to white) but that they represent all racial categories simultaneously and constitute hybrids. By contrast, the categories male and female are deconstructed neither here nor in any other scene of the play. However, the binary concept that the woman is a passive being occupying the private sphere and the man is an active being occupying the public sphere (the domain of politics) is challenged throughout the play. Gilbert and Tompkins consider *Strike* a typical post-colonial play with an emphasis on gender, a play which attempts to "intervene in the discourses that naturalise gender hierarchies" (1996: 212). Yet another important element of Scene 7 is that the actresses playing Mambhele and Mampompo suddenly turn into ardent protesters, foreshadowing their raised awareness and willingness to join Sdudla in the struggle at the end of the play.

There are many examples of mime, role-play and the use of song, chant and dance throughout *You Strike the Woman, You Strike the Rock*. It is this overt theatrical quality of the play which characterises the actresses and their major roles as versatile human beings. Through their histrionic abilities they flout apartheid's concept of the subservient black and the patriarchal notion of the obedient woman, dismissing both as identity constructs which deny the humanity of the oppressed.

This play is an example of women successfully establishing themselves in a predominantly male theatre scene. *Strike* is also a case in point of the reciprocal relationship between theatre and society in that it not only took its impetus from the women's struggle but also inspired political incentives in late 1986 when various women from theatre joined gender-conscious political groups to work towards political change. This new call for action in the political sphere is, as a critic suggests, "nothing new [but] the fact that it has been taken up in direct response to a performance certainly is" (Friedman 1987: 23). Schechner and Turner's notion of the reciprocal influence of theatre and society is confirmed once again (cf. Chapter 1.5.2).

6.3. *Have You Seen Zandile?* and the woman's quest for her role in society

> Human relations are on par with the political relations we give so much priority to.
>
> Gcina Mhlophe[8]

6.3.1. Gcina Mhlophe's views on theatre and women

Today Gcina Mhlophe is probably South Africa's most celebrated storyteller. She started her career through solo performances and then founded the storytelling group Zanendaba ('Bring me a story') in the early 1990s. The group specialised in retelling (South) African folktales, myths, histories, traditions and the personal stories of an otherwise silenced people. Storytelling does not only empower the (often) female performer in claiming a voice but also her audience, who regain knowledge and pride in their own people's cultural values in an oppressive society. The importance of storytelling for Mhlophe is strongly reflected in her play *Have You Seen Zandile*?

Mhlophe began writing poetry and short fiction during her high-school years in the late 1970s. She discovered the stage in the early 1980s while working professionally as a journalist. With no formal training she acted in Maishe Maponya's play *Umongikazi* ('The Nurse') and appeared in Barney Simon's productions *Black Dog/Inj'Emnyama* and *Born in the RSA* (where she played the

---

[8] 1999b: 35.

role of Sindiswa, see Chapter 5.2.2). By 1986 she had created her first play, *Have You Seen Zandile?*, which is clearly based on incidents from her life.[9] After writing the first draft, she workshopped the play with actress Thembi Mtshali and director Maralyn van Reenen (cf. Mhlophe 1999b: 36). The published version of the play refers to all three as co-authors. It carries the subtitle "A play originated by Gcina Mhlophe, based on her childhood."[10] With this play Mhlophe wanted to create a script featuring a more intimate personal story:

> [...] in *Zandile* I was trying to sort out my own life. It was a therapeutic thing. I was being criticised for that. [...] 'How can you do a play like this?' 'It's not the right time'. [...] I argue that if I am allowed to talk about the rest of South Africa, I'm more than allowed to talk about myself. I am one of those masses we talk about all the time [...]. (Mhlophe 1999b: 34)

Mhlophe considered the typical protest and resistance literature and theatre of the time to be important because it allowed people to tell their story and find strength through talking about these problems. Nonetheless, she chose to express herself in a different fashion. She emphasises that her "writing centres around people more than the movements" (Mhlophe 1999b: 34). In another of her plays, *Somdaka* ('Untidy One'), which she directed at the Market Theatre, she focused on a young man who wanted to stay in the countryside and thus strove to create a play that "honour[ed] his manhood" (*ibid.*). Mhlophe consciously avoided presenting a male character who had been stripped of his manhood as this had been seen so often in resistance plays written by men such as *The Hungry Earth* by Maishe Maponya. She based her character on her childhood memories of a young man from her home district. Mhlophe created a "very warm, very strong [...] self-assured" protagonist who refused to join the migrant labour system. She believes that *Somdaka* is not an overtly political play as she was trying to "get to the heart of the man" (*ibid.*). There was no "marching and singing revolutionary songs and 'Amandla!'[11]. I took out the mob and looked at how things affect us personally" (1999b: 35). Mhlophe understands *Zandile* in the same way and asserts that both plays are political in a special sense. In contrast to the majority of South African plays, *Zandile* focuses on relationships, both between men and women and among women. It also looks at the

[9] Mhlophe recounts her life story in detail in an interview with Dennis Walder (cf. 1999b).

[10] *HZ* 83. References to *Have You Seen Zandile?* are flagged *HZ*.

[11] 'Amandla' means 'power' or 'strength.' It is a slogan of the nationalist liberation movement (cf. Manaka 1982: 520).

school system and the fate of illegitimate children such as Mhlophe herself. She says about her parents:

> Their story is not only personal; it is shared, in that it happens a lot in South Africa; these extra-marital relationships bear children, and of course the children are affected by the relationship of the parents. But often this is not seen as political, or at least not so important as 'the struggle', the growth towards freedom. I cannot imagine attaining freedom while pretending we don't fall in love. Human relations are on par with the political relations we give so much priority to. (1999b: 35)

With her focus on the personal rather than the overtly political and revolutionary, Mhlophe is following a strategy which Njabulo Ndebele referred to as the "rediscovery of the ordinary" (1994). Instead of representing the struggle in spectacular fashion, Ndebele called for the need to engage with the "ordinary daily lives of people [...] because they constitute the *very content* of the struggle, for the struggle involves people not abstractions" (1994: 57). Mhlophe also anticipates Albie Sachs's criticism in 1990 of the artist's exclusive focus on the politics of liberation and the resulting (mis)use of culture as a "weapon of struggle" (1990: 175).

Mhlophe's emphasis on the importance of paying attention to both "the personal and the political" (1989: 277) can also be seen in her views on feminism. She differentiates between feminism as a Western term and the "different kind of feminism" of African women (1994: 31). In her opinion, the latter is based on the self-awareness of women being quintessential to the South African struggle, yet "[...] they don't have to shout about it. They have to work. They have to make sure that their children are taken care of, that their families don't break down. [...] We've upheld each other as well as holding up the Struggle [...]" (*ibid.*). Mhlophe deplores the fact that while men were "revered and praised and even celebrated" for leaving the family in the name of the struggle, the women involved were seldom known even though they carried the double burden of fighting for their family's survival as well as for the liberation of the people (1994: 32). She emphasises the need for women's stories of racial and sexual domination to be told (cf. Fitz-Patrick 1987: 77). Mhlophe believes that women's lives are comprised of both private and public tasks and actions. Nonetheless, it also becomes clear in her reflections that this private, personal life is automatically political because it is strongly confined, shaped and directed by apartheid and anti-apartheid discourses and power relations. Although *Have You Seen Zandile?* is often hailed as an autobiographical play (cf. Orkin 1991: 231), it still reflects the impact of politics on the life of individuals, even children (cf. Blumberg 1999: 140f.). Lisbeth Goodman, who works with Western notions of feminism, argues:

> [...] while Mhlophe's work is not explicitly feminist in that it is neither a product of the 'Women's Movement' as such, nor immediately influenced by contemporary feminist theory, it is a political play based on the personal, and one which focuses on women and urges social change on a large scale. In that, it can be seen as a form of feminist theatre. (1993: 178)

Mhlophe distinguishes between obviously political plays such as *You Strike the Woman, You Strike the Rock* and more personal plays such as *Zandile*. In her opinion, resistance theatre generally does not focus on private issues but talks about events on a national scale while women's resistance theatre allows women to speak for themselves without being represented by men. Mhlophe's private theatre, however, allows her to "give priority" to the individual (1994: 277). She explains:

> I'm not a unique person. There's got to be somebody who's gone through it before and that gives it another point of view altogether. And because people go through the same kinds of things for different reasons, I think they've got something to share in my life. [...] Politics changes every day, but the fundamental things that are important to human beings last a long, long time. (*ibid.*)

In *Zandile* Mhlophe reflects on these fundamental questions of life and touches on universal topics frequently neglected in South African political plays.

6.3.2. *Have You Seen Zandile*? – the play

Have You Seen Zandile? is a coming of age story of the young African girl Zandile who gradually learns what it means to grow up in a country where women are dominated on the basis of race, class and gender. By weaving political, economic, social and cultural issues into an intimate story, Mhlophe illustrates how the personal fate of women is affected and influenced by outside factors. The play uses English, Zulu and Xhosa, a mixture which emphasises not only Zandile's cultural heritage but also symbolises that of South Africa (cf. Blumberg 1999: 141). At the same time the language of this multi-lingual play takes on a mimetic function (cf. Hauptfleisch 1997: 98).

Have You Seen Zandile? comprises fourteen scenes spanning a decade from the mid-1960s to 1976. It focuses on key incidents during Zandile's childhood and teenage years or what Miki Flockemann calls "significant moment[s] in the central character's 'rites of passage' from childhood to young womanhood" (1991: 46; cf.

Loots 1996: 65). Zandile is the illegitimate child of Lulama, a young married Xhosa woman from the Transkei, and her lover Tom, a Zulu living in the Durban area. Because Lulama could not return to her husband with another man's child, Zandile went to live with her father and his wife and children in Durban. She grew up speaking Zulu. Her paternal grandmother, Gogo, was afraid that should Tom's family ever be short of money, Zandile would be the first to be neglected as she was not considered to be part of the family. Gogo decided to raise her granddaughter herself and provide her with the necessary schooling. The play opens with the portrayal of the close relationship between the eight-year-old girl and her beloved grandmother ('Gogo' is a term of endearment for 'granny' in Xhosa). Suddenly, the young Zandile is forcefully removed by her mother to live with her in the Transkei where she must now learn the unfamiliar language of Xhosa. The second half of the play shows how Zandile tries to understand and come to terms with her new environment and the customs and traditions of the Xhosa people. At the same time her best friend Lindiwe represents the "new" generation of young people who dream of a sophisticated life in the city. The play features only female characters and concentrates on the models supplied by the four central women in Zandile's life - her school teacher(s), Gogo, Lulama and Lindiwe.[12] Although neither her teacher in the city, Miss Dlamini, nor her instructor in the country, Miss Maduma, actually appear as characters in the play, Zandile repeatedly refers to them as her idols. The girl is forced to develop her own identity and role behaviour, influenced by the life-styles represented by her apartheid-approved teacher, her traditional mother, her partly traditional yet also progressive grandmother and her 'modern' friend.

6.3.2.1. Zandile's search for identity

In the first half of the play Zandile occupies two roles, that of a schoolgirl and a granddaughter. She is educated through both roles and according to two very different ideological concepts, Bantu education versus African tradition.

In one scene where Zandile slips into the role of her teacher Miss Dlamini, whom she greatly admires, she uses her grandmother's flowers as pupils to demonstrate

[12] Miki Flockemann has already pointed out that the grandmother, mother and friend offer Zandile models in her efforts to develop her own identity (cf. 1991: 46), yet she does not include the teachers. I believe that especially the primary school teacher Miss Dlamini is one of the most important role models because it is in Zandile's mimicry of the teacher and her re-enactment of the events at school that the girl learns to think critically (see below).

what she had learnt at school. Discipline is obviously an important element of her schooling, and the first thing she does is threaten to beat her flower 'pupils' if they misbehave. She intimidates them by suggesting that they may even be taken away by the ominous "white car" (at first a general symbol of white power and political menace) of which Zandile herself is clearly afraid (cf. *HZ* 88; Goodman 1993: 176). Another lesson she has learnt in class is that the white inspector who visits the black schools neither speaks Zulu, her mother tongue, nor is willing to remember the children's indigenous names. Therefore in preparation for his visit the students receive "white names," a process which Zandile imitates with her flower children. Her memory of this incident causes her great amusement. She asks her pupils: "Do you know what name the inspector gave me in class today? Elsie. And I don't even look like an Elsie! Don't laugh! [...] And do you know what he called Bongi? [her make-believe friend] Moses! He couldn't even tell that she was a girl" (*HZ* 88). Zandile's laughter over this memory represents a subversive reaction. By not taking the inspector seriously, she questions his power and authority. Flockemann asserts that the girl's "subversion of the very education that she aspires to is indicative of her refusal to see herself as victim" or as the lesser half in apartheid's binary ideological system (1991: 49).

It is interesting that although Zandile laughs at this renaming, she also clearly feels degraded by it and refuses to accept this new name of Elsie at school. However, she forces her flower pupils to undergo the same degrading process. So in her role as the teacher she is prepared to act as an accomplice to the state and adopt the values of Bantu education. As Dennis Walder suggests, this shows how even after the demise of apartheid "[...] inherited structures of power remain [...]" (1998: 185). Notwithstanding, Zandile's own attempt at renaming is more successful because the names she gives her make-believe students are the names of flowers: "Petunia. Daisy. Sunflower and Innocentia ... I don't know what that means" (*HZ* 88). Names obviously do carry meaning for Zandile as she presents herself as conscious of language. Mhlophe explains that the meaning of names is important in traditional culture because they provide a genealogy. Insisting on one's own family-given name becomes a form of self-assertion and thus constitutes political resistance to the state's attempts at erasing black identity (cf. 1990: 122; cf. Blumberg 1999: 143). While Zandile clearly rejects 'Elsie' and 'Moses' for herself and Bongi, she hesitates to name a pupil 'Innocentia' as the word does not mean anything to her. This is insightful because she herself is still too innocent to really understand the extent of her oppression at school despite the fact that she has begun to voice her first criticism. By the end of the scene she gets carried away in her role as a strict teacher and beats her students for not singing properly, ruining Gogo's flower garden in the process. It can only be speculated as to why Zandile imagines her pupils to be poor singers, but most likely she is re-enacting another incident which actually happened at school. It may be that she is imitating an angry teacher and giving vent to her own dissatisfaction with her classmates because she is a good singer herself, well-taught by her loving grandmother. Gogo intervenes and reproaches Zandile for beating her students, explaining that "You must remember one thing, everything that grows has feelings" and must be respected (*HZ* 89). This is obviously something the children do not learn at school, and Zandile excuses herself, "I didn't know that they could feel" (*HZ* 88). With this exclamation she reveals how she believes that the teachers and inspectors see her, namely as a non-human or less-than-human who does not feel pain and can therefore be punished by violence. In this regard the school system has become a mirror-image of apartheid in that both encourage violence as an appropriate, if not the only appropriate, form of problem-solving. In a larger sense this scene might even suggest that militant student uprisings and violent state suppression are the logical consequence of such an educational system in which human beings are reduced to brutes by an inhuman system.

Despite Zandile's mishap, Gogo repeatedly emphasises that her granddaughter is a "clever little girl" with a promising future (*HZ* 89). Gogo justifies her decision to raise Zandile: "Tom thinks education is not important for a girl. Ha! Even if I have to die doing it, I'm keeping Zandile at school" (*HZ* 85). The older woman stresses that education is very important for Zandile's future. This is why she helps the girl with her homework and encourages her to do well in school, spoiling her with treats and presents for her achievements. Devarakshanam Betty Govinden points out that it is ironic that Gogo is prepared to die for her granddaughter's education in apartheid schools in the 1960s whereas ten years later, the Soweto students were more willing to die in the struggle than to accept Bantu education (cf. 1998: 74).

Gogo also educates Zandile with stories from the past and oral poetry that teach her about the communal values, traditions and beliefs of her people. For Gogo these stories are as important as schoolwork, for although she raises Zandile in an urban and industrialised environment, she makes sure that her granddaughter knows about her roots. Storytelling is not only a "formative influence" but also constitutes an "integral component of their tradition" (cf. Blumberg 1999: 143). Story-telling has clearly made a large impression on Zandile, and she grows up to be a very imaginative and creative young girl, entertaining herself with her own stories and learning to tell her grandmother's tales to her friends. Despite Gogo's very progressive dreams that her granddaughter could become professionally successful as a "doctor, or a lawyer or an accountant" (*HZ* 89), the older woman nonetheless believes in the traditional values of patriarchal society. She imagines Zandile "wearing a white dress, walking slowly out of church with her husband and smiling [...]" (*HZ* 89). Apparently, if a woman is to fulfil the role expectations of African society, she must get married and bear children. It is interesting to note that Gogo does not imagine Zandile's own reaction to her wedding but becomes excited at the thought of her neighbours watching the ceremony "with envy" (*HZ* 89). This comment shows that marriage is socially prestigious and that a good marriage even serves as a status symbol for the whole family. Zandile's marriage would also function as a kind of proof that Gogo raised her granddaughter adequately and prepared her for her future roles in society.

All in all, Zandile lives the life of a happy city girl who grows up in relative comfort. Shopping trips to town, a summer holiday at the beach, new dresses, sweets and, above all, her grandmother's love characterise her childhood years. While Zandile aspires to become a teacher, she imagines that her make-believe friend Bongi wants to become a "white lady" with long hair, nice clothes, high heels and make-up, the implication being that white women do not need to perform hard labour. She also realises that if Bongi were a white woman, she would have a car and thus acquire a degree of mobility that black people normally do not have. One of the most important elements of being white is identified by Zandile as being able to speak English which she cannot. Yet despite all the advantages that she knows white people have, she holds on to her own dream of becoming a teacher. Zandile's analysis of 'whiteness' reveals her belief that it is not an essential characteristic but a social quality or behavioural pattern which a person acquires in the course of their life. On this point her opinion differs to that of Athol Fugard's character Morrie in *Blood Knot*. Morrie is convinced that 'whiteness' is a social quality that cannot be adopted easily (cf. Chapter 2.2.3). Zandile, however, is certain that Bongi could learn to behave like a white women and thus become 'white.'

'Whiteness' is again thematised in Zandile's remark about her new toy: "I love this doll but why do they always make them pink?" (*HZ* 85). She accepts the doll as a toy, yet perceives its skin colour to be disconcerting because it makes her aware of her own difference. Suddenly, she defines herself through what Fanon calls the "racial epidermal schema." According to this theorist, a colonised individual becomes aware of their oppressed state when they can only see themself in terms of skin colour (1967: 112, cf. 110-13). Zandile also acknowledges the white world as a distant and anonymous force ("they") that determines and even controls her life by defining 'whiteness' as an ideal that she does not fulfil (cf. Govinden 1998: 73). The irony of this is that apartheid ideology accords a lifeless white doll more value than a real black girl.

Zandile learns from Gogo to value herself. Granddaughter and grandmother enjoy each other's company and love each other very much. Lisbeth Goodman even suggests that they "see the world through each other's eyes," a closeness and mutuality that is conveyed through their "shared phrases, glances, gestures and bits of song" (1993: 175). Yet when the threat of the "white car" becomes real and the frightened Zandile is kidnapped and taken to live with her mother in the rural Transkei, Gogo's world breaks down. The old woman starts saving Zandile's presents in a suitcase to await the young woman's return, an action she continues up to her death ten years later. This allows her to keep alive both the memory of her granddaughter and the hope of their reunion (which never takes place). The suitcase with Zandile's childhood possessions and gifts represents a "personal memory-bank and a cultural treasure-trove" (Blumberg 1999: 140).

Zandile, for her part, is unhappy with her new life and tries desperately to contact Gogo. She writes letters of despair in the sand, hoping that the birds will take the messages to her grandmother. The only thing which links her new life to the past and gives her joy and comfort is her schoolwork and her new teacher - another woman whom she can respect. However, intellectual learning is not of great importance in the rural Transkei. Her mother Lulama makes it clear that the values to which Zandile must now aspire are no longer intelligence and education but hard work, obedience and fertility:

> LULAMA I want you to grow up and be a strong woman and ...
>
> ZANDILE I'm going to be a teacher.
>
> LULAMA Not here. You have to work outside here where the men can see you.
>
> ZANDILE Men can still see me if I teach.
>
> LULAMA Where are you going to teach here? Are you going to teach the goats. [...] Who do you think you are going to marry if you can't do a woman's work? (*HZ* 92)

Zandile's retort that she does not want to marry is problematic as women only receive recognition through their husbands in the patriarchal Xhosa society. "All you have to be is a good wife and have good children," her mother explains (*HZ* 92). An independent, single woman does not exist as a possible role model in this rural society. Hardened by her own life story, Lulama forces Zandile to get used to the hard work - back pains, scratched legs and blistered hands included. Xhosa tradition calls for the fathers of young boys to choose the future wives for their sons. If Zandile does not want to become a social outcast, she must bend to this patriarchal tradition. Although the young girl is angry with her mother for insisting on tradition and custom, she realises that her mother's support of the courtship by a man from a wealthy family is meant to save her from the same fate as her mother. It was Lulama's marriage to a man who was unable to adequately support his family which forced her to look for work in Durban. Her husband had not agreed with this decision because it meant that his wife had taken over his traditional male role. In Durban Lulama joined a new band as a singer and invested hard work into building up the group's success. Yet before she profited financially from the band's growing popularity, she had fallen pregnant with Zandile and lost her job:

> They wanted me replaced. My friends stood for me but the organizers said they wouldn't have a pregnant woman on stage – as if it was such a disgrace, or as if I had made myself pregnant.
>
> You know at times I so wish that men could get pregnant too. All my hopes of improving my life and the lives of my children were finished. (*HZ* 96f.)

Lulama is victimised because she is a woman. When she realised that she had to also leave Zandile, her love-child, with the father's family, she felt she was being forced to give up everything she valued. She returned to her husband who she had married at a very young age, in accordance with Xhosa tradition. When he, in turn, left her, she was determined to reclaim Zandile. "Wait till you have a child, you'll know what I've been through all the years. How do you think it feels, to know that your child doesn't even know you exist?" (*HZ* 92). Zandile's presence satisfies her feelings of motherhood and is a reminder of her love affair with Zandile's father. This is important for Lulama because it represents her (momentary) break-out from the confining boundaries of patriarchal tradition and apartheid. The irony of this situation is that because apartheid kept the income of African men to a minimum and deprived them of their traditional sense of masculinity, Lulama had been forced to embark on a career of her own in the city. At first her story is stereotypical: her papers are not in order, she has difficulty in finding a job and when she does find one, she is hugely exploited, earning almost nothing. Restricted by the multiple handicaps of being poor, uneducated and a black woman, she is unable to earn enough to support herself or her family so she is more than willing to join her friend's band and escape the direct control of the apartheid state into the black entertainment scene. What began as her apparent worthlessness and inhumanity in the eyes of the (white) urban population turns into an opportunity to develop her identity according to her own desires and needs. She rises from a manual worker to an artist, from an oppressed and battered housewife to a lover. Tragically, in the end she is thrown off the band because 'mother' and 'singer' are not considered compatible roles in the music industry – an industry which capitalises on the combination of music and sexuality. Lulama painfully learns that she is not valued as a singer but as a sex object in a male-dominated world. She is also objectified in the name of profit and becomes easily replaceable. Govinden asserts that this is the key experience which robs Lulama of her creativity and imagination and hardens her. Instead of leading Zandile to believe in a romantic picture of the future, Lulama teaches her that hard manual labour is the key to survival ("I have learnt not to live on hopes, that is why I am teaching you to work" [*HZ* 93]). Govinden concludes that Lulama's life is "emotionally denuded, without dream and story" (1998: 75). That is why the only stories she can tell are not the imaginative tales and poems that Gogo taught Zandile but stories which focus on the stark reality of exploitation and the fight for survival.

In the Transkei Zandile learns about her mother's "double oppression" (Kruger 1995b: 49) under apartheid and African patriarchal traditions and also begins to understand that she herself is oppressed by the same two systems. In contrast to her immediate identification with her teacher in her early school years, she has now become critical of the school system. Zandile realises that her history lessons focus only on apartheid's official version of the past: the "great trek, great trek, every year it is the same, the great trek. Nothing else ever happened here or anywhere, just the great trek" (*HZ* 95). Her ironic remarks about the Great Trek reveal both her knowledge about and her frustration with apartheid's deliberate distortion of the past. Zandile and her friend Lindiwe plan to hide *Bona* and *Drum*, two popular South African American-style magazines, in their history books to "discover everything" about life (*HZ* 95). This prank expresses both their naiveté and credulity as well as their discontent with a curriculum which does not teach them about puberty, sexuality and procreation. Their embarrassed parents either evade their questions on these topics or deliberately give wrong answers, so the teenagers are left speculating as to why Lindiwe's breasts are growing, where babies come from and why one of the other girls had blood running down her legs (cf. Scene 9). This lack of sex education ensures that the young women do not understand, let alone control, their own sexuality. Traditions and the state have become accomplices in keeping the girls emotionally and sexually dominated by men.

By the time the girls are in their late teens Lindiwe has matured earlier than Zandile. Lindiwe's trip to a cousin's wedding in Johannesburg is to be her first encounter with the "big city" (*HZ* 97). While Zandile is worried about her friend ("You must be careful ne? All those boys from town are dangerous" [*HZ* 97]), Lindiwe dreams of meeting "sophisticated men" so that she need no longer fuss with the now uninteresting, merely "nice boys" in the village (*HZ* 98, 97). She convinces Zandile to accompany her to the train station but lays down the dress code for her less than fashionable friend: "Don't wear your terylene skirt, please. [...] Terylene skirts are too old fashioned now. It's 1976, you must look sharp." (*HZ* 98). In the course of this scene Zandile tries to tell Lindiwe that she has been chosen to perform a praise poem for a teacher at school, a task traditionally reserved for men.[13] Yet Lindiwe is too preoccupied with her trip to understand what this personally means to her friend and the weight it carries in the larger cultural context. This scene clearly shows that the two girls have different interests and goals in their lives. Lindiwe looks forward to her own marriage and family life, reads novels about love and sex by Barbara Cartland[14] and sings American pop songs such as "Sugar, sugar, honey, honey, you are my candy girl" that show, according to Govinden, "the way women are possessed by men" (1998: 77). Zandile, by contrast, listens to local music (Letta Mbuli's "I'll Never be the Same") and prepares for her praise performance. The song's title already suggests that Zandile is maturing into a young woman who, as a female praise poet, is able to locate her identity somewhere between tradition and change. Govinden also points out other differences between Zandile and Lindiwe: "Zandile [...] does not see fulfilment in her life necessarily culminating in love and marriage, and this is confirmed by the promise of a different kind, as suggested in the concluding scene" (1988: 77). When Zandile realises that Lindiwe's new boyfriend from the city is in

[13] Elizabeth Gunnar explains that the Zulu praise poem (*izibongo*) "celebrates the identity of its owner. To own a praise poem, to be known by it, is to strengthen one's sense of belonging to a particular community and to a particular cultural group" (1989: 37). Praise poetry is usually regarded as a male domain although a few praise poems of famous women exist (cf. Gunnar 1989).

[14] Cartland (1901-2000) is an English writer of several hundred escapist novels set in the nineteenth century dealing with romantic love.

fact her half-brother, she hopes to be able to track down her grandmother. However, when she eventually arrives at the house, she learns from an old woman that Gogo has passed away. She receives a photograph and a suitcase full of presents that her grandmother had been saving for her since her abduction by her mother. Zandile, who is now eighteen-years old, holds several of her childhood dresses up against her body. This can be read to symbolise "a longing to encapsulate her world in the beauty of childhood, of not losing one's innocence with the passage into adulthood." The dresses also "signify the timeless gift of storytelling which is the grandmother's real gift to Zandile" (Govinden 1998: 77, cf. Blumberg 1999: 145). And, as Goodman remarks, the use of women's clothing as a symbol of life's journey is a theme that can be found in other plays by women (cf. 1993: 177). Loots argues that with this emphasis Goodman gives the gender critique precedence over the racial critique of the play. Yet Loots adds:

> It is vital to ensure, however, that oppositional narratives to a social and historical situation like apartheid not simply be hierarchically swapped around (i.e. gender for race) but that emphasis is placed on how the gender ideology behind a play like *Have You Seen Zandile?* challenges the construction of reducing apartheid to simply a race based ideology. (cf. 1996: 65)

In a similar vein Flockemann takes up Orkin's classification of anti-apartheid theatre as either counter-identifying or as disidentifying with the dominant ideology. In the case of disidentification an alternative discourse constructs the subject in a different way to the prevailing discourse. Flockemann asserts that this is the case in *Zandile*. Mhlophe's alternative constitution of subjectivity for a black woman who is traditionally defined as a voiceless and marginal other can even be considered as a manifestation of black feminism (cf. Flockemann 1991: 47; Orkin 1991: 18).

6.3.2.2 Song, dance and role-play

Mhlophe points out that the use of song and dance in her productions has a function that is different from the way it is used in resistance theatre where it presented an energetic and revolutionary atmosphere. Once again, she confirms that her intention is to focus on the private aspects of the life of individuals. For example, the scene in which Gogo teaches Zandile to sing the lullaby 'Ulele na, ulele na' (cf. *HZ* 89) articulates the "intimacy between the girl and the grandmother" (Mhlophe 1999b: 33). Similarly, Gogo's storytelling not only teaches Zandile about her traditions and history but also draws her closer to her grandmother. She is able to draw strength from these stories when she feels miserable and lonely in the Transkei. In addition, when Zandile is asked to perform a praise poem for her teacher, an honour that in the Xhosa tradition is normally accorded to men, she has not only succeeded in crossing a barrier into a traditionally male world but can also revive her private memory of her grandmother in a public domain usually reserved for men.

The scene in which Lindiwe teaches Zandile how to dance and shake her body to the hit "Sugar sugar" in preparation for her farewell party focuses on, in Mhlophe's words, the two girls "being conscious of their bodies, something very rare in our drama" (Mhlophe 1999b: 33). Similarly, the earlier moment when the two younger girls, swimming in the river, inspect and compare their bodies foregrounds this interest in what Walder calls "self-image, self-recognition" (*ibid.*). Flockemann points out the irony of the girls' situation. Although they know nothing about sexuality, a taboo, and are unable to read their bodily changes as signals of puberty and maturity, their parents are already planning their marriages. Flockemann makes another interesting observation. This play ends in 1976 without referring to the Soweto Uprising. Instead, it focuses on the development of female consciousness via the body. Thus *Zandile* can be read as a gender-oriented play that challenges the gender-bias of the BCM and defines 'gender' as a valid and important political topic (cf. Mhlophe 1999a: 46).

As is typical of the protest and resistance play, Mhlophe uses only a few actresses to portray a large number of characters on stage. However, it is interesting that the actress playing Zandile (Mhlophe herself in the original production) never changes her role whereas the other actress embodies all the other exclusively female characters in the play – Gogo, Luluma, Lindiwe and the old woman who gives Zandile Gogo's suitcase in the last scene. By contrast, Zandile is the only *character* to perform a role game – she plays her teacher – and through this presents the spectators with a play-within-the-play. This clear distinction between an actress playing several roles on the performance level and an actress playing one character who plays other roles on the play-internal level suggests to the audience that role-play and histrionic versatility are not only reserved for actors but are social characteristics of human beings (Goffman). However, unlike the characters of agitprop theatre, Zandile never directly encounters representatives (or anti-role models) of the oppressive patriarchal apartheid society or patriarchal African society. Instead, the female characters she interacts with (Gogo, Luluma, Lindiwe) embody potential role models for her future identity as a mature woman.

Commenting on the metaphor of protean transformation, Gray observes that *Zandile* "literally enacts the continuities of black family life in South Africa today" and is able to convince the audience that the otherwise voiceless members (victims) of society are human beings. He concludes, "This is the conquest of inhumanity by warmth" and not by confrontation (1990: 85). A look at the development of the main character leads to the same conclusion. Whereas most of the 'heroes' of resistance theatre are types, Zandile can be considered an individual character. She does not display conventional attitudes or shout militant slogans but forms her own opinions. Although this play stages particular incidents in the life of the protagonist, as does agitprop theatre, its focus clearly lies on the girl's gradual *development* through experience. In contrast to the types presented in plays such as *Bopha!* (the policeman Njandini and the student activist Zwelakhe), Zandile is a three-dimensional character, and Lulama is much more than a melodramatic villain (cf. Kerr 1996: 23; Minervini 1987: 15).

Another element to be found in *Have You Seen Zandile?* is direct audience address. During the enactment of Zandile's desperate attempts to contact her grandmother from the Transkei Gogo walks across the stage showing photographs of her granddaughter and asks the audience, "Have you seen Zandile?" (*HZ* 91). This question automatically defines the spectators as accomplices to the girl's kidnapping because theatrical conventions prevent the audience from communicating with Gogo. Blumberg suggests that this incident stands for the complicity of many South Africans who remained silent and passive despite their knowledge of the injustice of apartheid (cf. 1999: 144). Without rejecting this interpretation it can be argued that the play alludes less to the silence of those in the know than to the identity construction and self-assertion of Zandile, who represents an otherwise silenced and oppressed population. This means that although Gogo's plea for help in her search is central to the play (it also functions as the title), it could be regarded more as a rhetorical question which emphasises the close bonding between the two rather than functioning as an appeal to the audience which was typical of a militant resistance play.

By employing methods other than resistance theatre or giving those elements a different function, *Have You Seen Zandile?* criticises apartheid as a patriarchal and racist system and reveals the complicity of African customs in female domination. The play also challenges the sexism in the dominant tradition of oppositional theatre.

6.4. *Curl Up and Dye* and the power of prejudice and racism over new forms of solidarity

> a desert island play – the play that lumps together different kinds of people and watches how they like or don't like each other
>
> Robert Greig on *Curl Up and Dye*[1]

6.4.1. Susan Pam-Grant's theatre project

As a trained actress with a performer's diploma from the University of Cape Town, Susan (Sue) Pam-Grant had worked as a freelance actress, acting in several fringe productions. Facing unemployment in 1988, Pam-Grant decided to develop her own theatre project which would deal with people, especially women, living in a "'grey area'"[2] (Schwartz 1989a: 27). The idea came to her on a visit to a friend who resided near Joubert Park, a transitional area in central Johannesburg. Observing life in that area, Pam-Grant commented, "Joubert Park makes one realise the extent of the changing urban scenario in South Africa" (Gray 1993: 81). She recognised that "'There are so many textures in the idea of grey areas'" (qtd. in Van Rooyen 1989: 8). Conducting research in Joubert Park, Hillbrow, Boksburg and Benoni, Pam-Grant spoke to the inhabitants, studied them, frequented their shops and was sometimes even invited into their flats. Once she had decided to set her play in a hairdressing salon, she spoke with many hair stylists and their clients, even working in a salon herself for a while. Pam-Grant was supported by producer Michael Hunt and director Lucille Gillwald, both of whom had worked with new South African scripts before. The draft version of the play was revised in workshop by the all-female cast, each actress shaping and perfecting her own role[3] (cf. Gray 1993a: 81; Schwartz 1989a: 27; Van Rooyen 1989: 8). Gray remarks:

> As in many of Gillwald's previous productions of new South African scripts, the team displayed a commitment to engaging social commentary that far outgrew its simple sitcom origins. Five feisty women fighting unemployment, none of whom had been considered prominent or influential in the theatre world before, became one of the hit shows of the late 80s. (1993a: 81)

---

[1] 1991: 6.

[2] A 'grey area' was a residential or business area in which racial segregation was not officially enforced.

[3] Susan Pam-Grant played Rolene; Val Donald-Bell celebrated her comeback in the role of Mrs Dubois; the casting agent Lillian Dube played Miriam; Debra Watson, a newcomer to acting, took the role of Charmaine; and in one of her first acting roles Nandi Nyembe played Dudu (cf. Gray 1993a: 81).

Curl Up and Dye premiered at the Black Sun nightclub in Johannesburg in 1989 before moving on to the Market Theatre. It also played at the Edinburgh Festival and then enjoyed a run at the Tricycle Theatre in London. It was revised and revived in 1991. The following interpretation is based on this newer version.

6.4.2. *Curl Up and Dye* – the play

Susan Pam-Grant's *Curl Up and Dye* takes place in the last years of the apartheid regime. It examines the social, economic and cultural problems that accompanied South Africa's transition from an apartheid state into a young democracy. The play "foreground[s] societal flux in a complex linkage of gender, race and class" (Blumberg 1993: 61). It portrays a transitional Johannesburg through the interaction of women at a hairdressing salon in Joubert Park, a slowly decaying hitherto Afrikaner working class and poor white neighbourhood that is now racially mixed and infested with racism, drug problems, prostitution and street violence. The play "explores the internal dynamics of this racial mixing" (Loots 1996: 66) while also addressing class- and gender-based issues. In the vein of a comedy of manners (cf. Greig 1991: 6) the play highlights the opinions, prejudices and behaviour of different groups in South African society by presenting five women from different racial and class backgrounds. Although it focuses on women, *Curl Up and Dye* is not an "orthodox, unambiguously feminist statement." However, as Stephen Gray observes, "[...] there could hardly be a play in which the power of the white Afrikaner nationalist patriarchy is felt so threateningly" (1993b: 69).

Curl Up and Dye consists of two acts. It combines techniques of realism/naturalism with elements from the television genre of situation comedy. Five women meet in the hair salon 'Curl Up and Dye International' in Joubert Park on a Saturday morning. The characters are Rolene, in her mid-twenties and the working manager of the hair salon Curl Up and Dye International; Mrs Dubois, in her late fifties, caretaker of the block of flats euphemistically called Freda Mansions and the salon's most regular customer over the last twenty years; Charmaine, drug addict and friend of Rolene's; Miriam, now in her late fifties who has been a domestic helper at the salon for the past twenty years; and Dudu Dlamini, a nurse in her late thirties who has recently moved to Joubert Park.

6.4.2.1. Life in Joubert Park: Existing alliances

Rolene is the manager and hairdresser at the shabbily decorated salon 'Curl Up and Dye International,' a business that has "fallen behind the times."[4] Married to Denzil, a Fidelity Guard[5] who abuses her, Rolene takes great care in the salon to hide the fact that she is a battered woman, emphasising her 'happy marriage' and 'kind husband.' She also tries to protect her young daughter from witnessing their fights. The frequent telephone calls from a possessive Denzil to the salon reveal both Rolene's anger towards as well as her dependence on her husband, which always causes her to forgive him in the end. It is clear that the couple's problems are a result of their financial difficulties, not helped by Denzil's additional squandering which is driving them deeper and deeper into debt. Rolene needs the salon not only for the income but also because it represents a refuge from her abusive husband. Although Denzil repeatedly calls her on the phone, the spatial distance from him and the diversion that her job and customers offer allow her to repress and forget her personal problems to some extent. In the end, however, she does not possess the strength to accept her friends' help and leave her husband.

Rolene's need to be accepted in the role of the salon's boss becomes apparent in her squabbles with Mrs Dubois over her (Rolene's) treatment of her domestic helper Miriam and her best friend Charmaine, a drug-addict, prostitute and occasional thief. The crudely racist Mrs Dubois believes that Rolene is giving Miriam too much freedom which the latter shamelessly misuses: "You let her get away with murder, my girl – you soft as butter [*sic*]. I'm telling you - you give them enough rope and they'll hang you" (*CD* 86). Although Rolene curses and threatens Miriam in her absence for not being punctual, when the domestic finally does arrive, Rolene defends her employee in front of Mrs Dubois:

> MRS DUBOIS. And where were you Miriam? What's this coming in at the time you arrive! For Pete's sake man, you must come on time!
>
> ROLENE. Miriam knows she's late, hey Miriam. Morning Miriam. So put your things down Miriam and when you ready, get going, all right. (*CD* 91)

Rolene stands up for Miriam because she depends on her as an employee and as a friend and confident – Miriam is the only person apart from Charmaine who knows

[4] *CD* 83. References to *Curl Up and Dye* are flagged *CD*.

[5] Fidelity Guards is a company employing men to act as armed guards, normally on vehicles carrying cash to banks etc. (Stephen Gray defines a Fidelity Guard as "a member of one of South Africa's paramilitary security organisations" [1993b: 69]).

about Denzil's abuse. She also defends her helper because this gesture allows her to regain control of her shop when Mrs Dubois undermines her authority over her staff. The discussion between Mrs Dubois and Rolene about Charmaine follows the same pattern:

> MRS DUBOIS. [...] she's the one that comes and causes all the trouble and Rolene still calls her a friend! Good God Rolene, I've said my say but really you got to choose your friends man. That's what...
>
> ROLENE. Charmaine is my friend. She's always been good to me and my kid hey – so I'm going to treat her the way I want to treat her. It's got nothing to do with you - right? And second of all, Miriam works for me hey, not you. (*CD* 93)

Mrs Dubois warns Rolene that Charmaine is taking advantage of her loyalty and friendship by continuously asking for money that she never pays back. Rolene defends Charmaine because she has helped her in the past, especially when recovering from fights with Denzil. Mrs Dubois believes that her daily patronage of the salon for over twenty years gives her some say and even allows her to take over the role of the boss. Rolene, however, is not only the comparatively new employer but also the manager and thus a "tacit power broker" (Blumberg 1993: 64). The reasons for this fight for control between the two white women are both class- and race-based. Both women clearly belong to the Afrikaner working class and suffer from the fact that despite their hard work they remain at the bottom of (white) society. Their lack of education, which surfaces in their pathetic attempts to solve crossword puzzles, prevents them from climbing the social ladder (cf. Frank 2003). In addition, the racist Mrs Dubois sees the arrival of blacks and coloureds in their previously white neighbourhood as being responsible for the growing violence and depreciation of the area. Mrs Dubois represents the typical fears of the economically disadvantaged Afrikaners who voted for apartheid in the 1948 election. Demonstration of her power over the black woman Miriam is her personal way of exacting revenge for the plight of her social group.

Once Mrs Dubois has left the salon, Rolene questions Miriam about her late arrival for work. Miriam's insistence that she has "got problems" is not taken seriously by Rolene: "Listen – Miriam - it's always another excuse hey?" (*CD* 99). Notwithstanding, Rolene accepts Miriam's explanation that she had to talk to the headmaster about her late payment of the school fees for her youngest child. Yet when Rolene remembers that Miriam had not swept the floor the previous evening because she (Miriam) had been allowed to leave early, she decides to play the boss and assert her power:

> ROLENE. [...] I think you taking a bit of a [*sic*] advantage here with me – I give you a hand and you grab my whole bladdy foot! Just remember who's boss around here.
>
> MIRIAM. Yes Madame – does Madame want some coffee? (*CD* 100)

Miriam takes Rolene's cue and falls back into apartheid rhetoric. She knows that she can only appease Rolene if she plays along and submits to her employer's need to assert her power. Rolene obviously feels respected when she is approached with the official apartheid form of address by black workers. Her sense of self-worth depends on the belief that her white skin makes her better than Miriam. At the same time, by calling Rolene "Madame," Miriam mimics (in Bhabha's sense) apartheid-supporting whites by appropriating the "'technique of depersonalisation'" that madams typically used to ignore the individuality of their black maids (Cock qtd. in Lenta 1990: 242). This allows Miriam to place distance between herself and her boss. She now only acts out the role of the servant, refusing to play the role of Rolene's friend and confident any longer. With this gesture Miriam shows Rolene that she also has power to decide on the nature of their relationship.

Rolene's dependence on Miriam becomes apparent when she quickly calms down and goes back to calling Miriam "sweetheart" and asks her for help with her crossword puzzles (*CD* 100). With this move she places herself on the same intellectual level as the black woman who has received even less education than her employer. Imagining that Rolene has won the crossword competition and been awarded a large cheque, both women dream of what they would buy with the prize money. They clearly aspire to the same middle-class goal of owning a comfortable home with modern electric appliances, paid in cash without taking out a loan. It is in these situations that Rolene accepts Miriam as her equal instead of seeing her on racially-based terms as inferior. Their body language confirms this. Excited and carried away by their dream, "ROLENE *and* MIRIAM *grab hold of one another.*" It is only Mrs Dubois' arrival that makes them "*snap out of it and resume their habitual roles*" (*CD* 102). By falling back into her traditional role as boss and overtly defining Miriam as her helper, Rolene can assert her power in front of Mrs Dubois and prevent her regular from meddling in her affairs.

At the same time Rolene creates a new alliance with Mrs Dubois. She appeases the older woman by gossiping with her "*confidentially*" (*CD* 107) so that Miriam cannot overhear her strongly racist remarks. As Patricia Meyer Spacks explains, "Gossip occurs at the [...] intersection [of the social and the individual], serving social purposes, defining social opinion, embodying social power (the power of opinion), but issuing from individual mouths and tracing psychic agendas as well" (1986: 8). In this play gossip allows Rolene and Mrs Dubois to give vent to their mutual dissatisfaction and blame the loss of their quality of life on the racial mixing in their neighbourhood, uniting them in a common plight. Rolene and Mrs Dubois do not know how to defend themselves other than by badmouthing others, and the function of gossip here is that it transforms their words into powerful weapons (cf. Spacks 1986: 11, 22). Rolene exclaims, "But now everybody says Joubert Park, Joubert Park – it's a grey area. My arse, this isn't grey, it's black!" (*CD* 106f.). She adds, "[...] I really wish they would blow that block up – for once and for all now" (*CD* 98). Rolene is convinced that the regime is no longer protecting the poor white working class areas: "[...] the fault is on the government. You know, at least they could have given us a fair warning that this was going to happen here. But they don't come clear!" (*CD* 106). Full of prejudice and racism Rolene is not prepared to support the integration of the newcomers to the area. For her the violence, drugs, alcohol, dirt and noise that dominate the street scene are typical of 'black behaviour.' She refuses to accept the fact that Charmaine is part of the street scene which causes the majority of the unrest in the area. She demands of blacks that "[...] if they want to live in a white people's area, then they must behave like a white people [...]" (*CD* 98). Notwithstanding, it is hard to imagine that Rolene would ever judge any kind of behaviour by a black person as acceptable or, in her terminology, 'white,' no matter how impeccable and exemplary. Gossip is important for both Rolene and Mrs Dubois because it allows the women to assert their self-defined superiority, a relic of the long-gone bloom of apartheid.

The gradually changing situation in Joubert Park has turned the otherwise calm and private atmosphere of the slowly decaying hair salon into an increasingly political arena, or, in Pam-Grant's own words, "'a marshmallow haven turns into a battlefield'" (qtd. in Blumberg 1993: 66). Rolene, Mrs Dubois and Miriam, who can forget their racial differences during their daily gossip sessions about their favourite TV soap operas, see each other in race-based terms again now that apartheid is slowly coming to an end and power is to be reallocated.

6.4.2.2. Intrusion by a stranger: The formation of new alliances

The second act begins with the arrival of a new customer, the middle-class African woman Dudu Dlamini. Dudu's "catalytic intrusion" into the very fragile status quo at the salon "polarizes already shifting alliances" (Blumberg 1993: 64). The explosive atmosphere in the neighbourhood brings the true feelings and opinions of the characters, especially Rolene's, to the surface, no longer allowing them to hide behind their masks of hair-dos, facials and make-up.

Miriam, who is watching the salon while Rolene is out, receives Dudu and begins discussing hair care treatments until the manager returns. Although Rolene has served black customers before, she is not used to their presence in the salon and believes that Dudu is Miriam's friend who has stopped by for a chat and is wrongfully sitting in a customer's chair. Once she realises her mistake, she does not apologise but attempts to cover it up by adopting a professional tone and ordering Miriam back to work. Rolene clearly feels inferior to Dudu, whose last name she cannot pronounce properly, calling her "Lamene" (*CD* 114). In addition, Dudu does not let Rolene sell her the hairstyle "Whitney Touch" that is "popular with all black customers" (*CD* 114) but insists on receiving a care treatment that suits her individual needs. Rolene is put off by Dudu's self-confidence, straightforward manner and her superior knowledge and language competence. The new customer notices Rolene's apprehension and comments to Miriam in Zulu: "Madoda liyadelela leligxagxa! [This white trash is spiteful.]" (*CD* 114). While Miriam aligns herself with Dudu on the basis of race and their common mother tongue, she turns back to Rolene with whom she shares her working class background after noticing that Dudu is dressed in smart clothing and clearly enjoys a higher social standing than either of them. Miriam becomes suspicious of Dudu when she learns that the newcomer lives in Joubert Park instead of Soweto, exclaiming: "You are black, you belong to Soweto and la bantu [...]" (*CD* 115). Miriam also accuses Dudu of living as a "larney" (*CD* 115), a posh white person, and suspects her of earning money as a prostitute who goes with white men. When she learns that Dudu is in fact a nurse at a white hospital and not the big Soweto hospital, Baragwanath, she feels that Dudu is betraying the black people: "But sis, you are not helping us. We are short of nurses in Soweto" (*CD* 116).

This triangular relationship is rendered more complex by the arrival of Mrs Dubois for her regular appointment. New and shifting alliances are formed in the course of the morning at Curl Up and Dye International. At first the four women discuss their relationships with their husbands and, by choosing a topic they can all relate to, they create a common base. All the women admit to marital problems except for Rolene, who singles herself out by falsely insisting on her husband's caring qualities. Having had five partners, Mrs Dubois now prefers to stay single. Miriam suffers because of her husband's addiction which makes him drink away her earnings. And Dudu is embittered by her husband's frequent escapades and has left him to earn her own living and support her children. As with the female protagonists in the other plays by women discussed in this study, Miriam and Dudu adhere to the African feminist view when they agree that their role as mother is more important than their role as wife: "It is our children who give us our happiness" (*CD* 120). Dudu especially distances herself from the ideology of Black Consciousness or womanism in denying her responsibility to care for a husband who neglects his own family. Dudu's education and profession have given her the personal strength to leave her husband and earn a financially comfortable living ("five star pay" [*CD* 116]) - a move more easily made by the intellectually independent Dudu than would be possible for the working class women in the salon or the lower class women in, for example, *You Strike the Woman, You Strike the Rock*.

Influenced by Dudu's economic success, Miriam turns small talk between herself and Mrs Dubois into a serious conversation in which she complains about her low wages and lack of increases despite her loyal hard work over twenty years. Although this criticism is reasonable from an objective perspective, Miriam makes two major mistakes. First, she does not respect the rules of conversation by choosing a topic which is inappropriate for superficial small talk. Mrs Dubois exclaims, "[...] what am I listening to here today? I ask you how your child is and all I get it snot and trane..." (*CD* 133). And second, she addresses the wrong person with her plea. As a racist Mrs Dubois would never use her influence and power over Rolene to fight for Miriam's cause. In fact, she even threatens to stop frequenting the salon if Rolene cannot maintain order and keep her employee under control. Because of these errors in judgement, Miriam also loses sympathy points with her boss.

Dudu displays black solidarity and intervenes in Mrs Dubois' racist tirade by encouraging Miriam to defend herself in front of Rolene and the condescending customer. However, Miriam is afraid of being fired and interrupts the heated discussion between Dudu and Mrs Dubois by favouring the white woman:

> MIRIAM. Please sisi [sister] – Mrs Dubois has been here – she is our longest customer.
>
> MRS DUBOIS. Yes thank you Miriam.
>
> DUDU. So you jump on her side now? You want me to come back to Soweto and as soon as they begin to shout it's yes madam, no madam – it's because of your type that we'll always be slaves!

> MIRIAM. Don't you think those smart Brunno Marley shoes and that smart handbag make you a white madam. Haai suka, mind your manners! [...] (*CD* 136)

Miriam adopts the role of the black servant whenever she feels the need to appease Rolene or Mrs Dubois. This shows that she considers her submissive, acquiescent behaviour as part of her required role behaviour whereas Dudu defines her "yes madam, no madam" as a betrayal of the dignity of Africans. Believing that Dudu feels superior to her and that she is treating her in a condescending manner, Miriam accuses the new customer of being just as bad as whites by virtue of her economic independence. 'White behaviour' is seen as a social characteristic that can be adopted by anyone who possesses the means to mix with the corresponding social groups. Thus for the salon helper 'whiteness' is not necessarily linked to skin colour but to social class.

Miriam and Dudu continue their heated discussion in Zulu, the translation of which is only given in the printed version of the play script. This means that their conversation remains incomprehensible not only to many audience members but certainly to the two white women in the salon. Mrs Dubois clearly feels insecure when she does not understand the two African women and defensively accuses them of being "subversive" (*CD* 134). Spurred on by Mrs Dubois' continuous racist remarks about the women ("screaming baboons," not "civilised"), Rolene loses her temper and calls Miriam a "kaffir" (*CD* 136). This time Rolene has crossed the line of what Miriam is willing to accept. Enlightened by her talk with Dudu, the salon helper tells the white women off: "I'm not a stupid. You found me here and I teach you everything you know [...]! I can leave this job at any time, [...] – then you will call – 'Miriam where's this, Miriam where's that' because you can't do nothing without Miriam!" She adds, "As for you, Mrs Dubois – you pretend you are my friend, then when it suits you - you just shout at me" (*CD* 137). It is only when Rolene threatens to fire her that she calms down, and the fragile status quo is momentarily restored.

Rolene's relationship to Dudu also oscillates, in this case between artificial empathy and strong racially-based antipathy. At first the hairdresser strikes a conversation with Dudu in which she goes to great pains to demonstrate acceptance of her new customer. Nonetheless, she still reveals her racist streak, suggesting to Dudu that the interracial areas of Hillbrow and Joubert Park are no longer acceptable for whites but perfect for blacks:

> ROLENE. [...] you can classify the people that's living here – doesn't matter if it's Coloured, Indian, Asian or Black – you know – you get the people that's larney [posh, 'white'] – and you get the people that's rubbish! – in every nation – lift – in whites as well. Ag, you can see by the looks of a person what type of a person that person is – like you can just tell that you a decent, respectable type of a woman. If there was more people like you staying here – no problems – you know what I mean? (*CD* 122)

Rolene's overt demonstration of sympathy must be explained as a result of her feeling racially superior to Dudu. The hairdresser believes that life in new "grey areas" is well-suited for black needs "[...] cause you got restaurants and the shops and you can live here like civilised people. Cos in the locations and that there's all the burnings and the necklaces and the tsotsis.[6] [...] you people must really appreciate grey areas" (*CD* 122). Little does Rolene understand what it means for Dudu to only be allowed to be in her own apartment from ten-thirty at night to six in the morning in order not to be seen by the other inhabitants of the formerly all-white flats (cf. *CD* 105). Rolene obviously associates the townships with disorder and violence while she defines the city neighbourhoods as spaces of order and civilisation. The irony of this is that a large amount of the disorder in Joubert Park is caused by the racially-mixed drug dealing and prostitution scene to which Charmaine belongs. Yet just as she denies her husband's abuse, she also refuses to accept Charmaine's drug-addiction until her friend faints in the salon and is diagnosed by Dudu.

In the course of their discussion Dudu realises that Rolene is her neighbour and that she has been witnessing Rolene's daily beatings by her husband Denzil. Rolene's perfect world of lies and self-deception breaks down under Dudu's revelations. The hairdresser is too weak to accept either Dudu's sympathy or her offers of help and guidance. She feels inferior to Dudu and is jealous of her relative success, freedom and self-confidence and thus falls back onto her racist world view for self-protection. Rolene is further pressured by Mrs Dubois, who forces her to make a choice between two mutually excluding categories, a "bladdy kaffir boetie" ['bloody nigger lover'] or a "white woman" (*CD* 139). Under such pressure she can only react with a "harsh emotional response" (MacLiam 1989: 14) and defend herself by verbally assaulting Dudu: "How dare you come and tell me ... You a

[6] A 'necklace' is a tyre filled with petrol that is placed around a victim's body and set aflame. Necklacing was a practice used in the townships to murder opponents and those suspected of breaking liberation strategies such as boycotts. 'Tsotsi' is the slang term for 'township gangster.' See also Chapter 5.

witch ... that's what you are – you a witch! My problems has got nothing to do with you. [...] You got no right to come and talk about my husband like that" (*CD* 139f.). Racism proves to be Rolene's "very fragile backbone" (Loots 1996: 67). The last words she shouts at Dudu as she leaves the salon sum up her racist opinion: "Black bitch!" (*CD* 140).

6.4.2.3. The victory of racism

The final image of the play presents an insecure and self-deluding Rolene addressing a menacing Denzil on the telephone with a term of endearment, "Bokkie? ... Bokkie?" (*CD* 140). This ending shows that Rolene's character has not developed throughout the play and that she still remains "trapped in [her] fears and prejudices" (Thamm 1989: 22). She does everything to confirm that she is what Garalt MacLiam calls a "product of her society and its built in prejudice. [...] her personal troubles are of an all-consuming nature, leaving her little time to examine the iniquities of life around her" (1989: 14). Rolene is paralysed, preferring to 'curl up' to Denzil and racism, deny or 'dye' the truth and let any opportunities for a fresh start 'die.' In this sense her work place turns into a metaphor for her outlook on life (cf. Schwartz 1989b: 25).

Loots examines Rolene's refusal to "overcome the meta-discourses of race division" and the consequent failure to recognise that both she and Dudu suffer from domestic violence. Rolene's racism has made her adopt the "gendered and social understanding that personal tragedy is 'private'" and that it has nothing to do with politics. In this sense *Curl Up and Dye* shows that the hairdresser's obsession with racial separation prevents her from seeing how "race and gender intersect in patriarchal and racist oppression" (1996: 66). At the same time Loots also questions the interpretation of Rolene and Dudu's suffering from abuse as a "shared experience." This view represents a "'globalizing of sisterhood'" that is clearly "problematic" (1996: 67) because it unites analyses of race and gender in the political situation of South Africa. As feminist theorists such as Chandra Mohanty have shown (cf. 1991a, 1991b), the simple method of rendering the lives of black and white women equivalent in a political system based on race (and consequently also class) leads to a "reductive and essentialist" theory that fails to "include historically specific systems of analyses and criticism" (Loots 1996: 67). Loots concludes that "[...] it is precisely this ellipses of difference in terms of lived experience that causes the continuation of race analysis to be articulated as the final and meta-discourse of opposition to an apartheid society" (*ibid.*).

Pam-Grant stages a protagonist whose life experiences represent a microcosm of the gendered and racial politics of South African society. She follows a similar strategy to Mhlophe in *Have You Seen Zandile?* by also writing "from a personal to a political context" and thus showing that the personal is political (Loots 1996: 66). Loots defines the salon as a "'private' environment" that represents a "clearly articulated 'women's space.'" In the course of the play it becomes apparent that this private setting has turned into a "gendered and racial battle ground of South Africa caught between the 'grey area' progression of its own politics" (*ibid.*). It should not be overlooked, however, that the conflicts carried out in the salon are also class-based. Notwithstanding, Thamm's evaluation that the play explores a "class rather than a race issue - in that it throws together women from different ethnic and class backgrounds" (1989: 22) is also too one-sided because it neglects gender issues. More appropriately, Rolene's rejection of Dudu's sympathy and advice should be read as a white working-class woman's envy of a black middle-class woman's success. It is only the combination of the elements of race, class and gender that allows the play to address the multiple facets of apartheid and the problems that arise in the process of abolishing institutionalised racism.

6.4.2.4. Theatrical techniques

Although *Curl Up and Dye* is not an agitprop play and does not contain music, it has much in common with *Sophiatown*. Both plays, with their linear plot structure, can be characterised as well-written or well-made although the individual roles were shaped in workshop by the actors.

In contrast to the 'poor theatre' quality of the typical protest and resistance plays discussed here, the large number of props meticulously described in *Curl Up and Dye*'s long introductory stage directions as well as the importance of the strict spatial arrangement of the setting is conspicuous for the audience (and the reader). It is important for the play's message that the atmosphere of a salon "fallen behind the times" with an "*overall appearance* [that] *is tacky and somewhat out of touch*" (*CD* 83, 85) is conveyed. The setting reflects Rolene and Mrs Dubois' characters in that their out-dated opinions are as "out of touch" as the salon's decor.

At the same time the spatial arrangement of the stage places *Curl Up and Dye* in the tradition of plays that consciously strive to raise the consciousness of the audience. Blumberg points out that the placing of the stools on which the clients sit is central to this play. The chairs are located in front of an imaginary mirror directly facing the audience. This means that the characters do not only confront their appearance in the mirror, but simultaneously speak to the spectators directly and thus draw them into the conflict. The audience become the mirror of the women in the salon, and simultaneously, see the activities on stage as a reflection of the changes in society (cf. Blumberg 1993: 66). Although the spectators are not verbally defined as characters of the stage action as in *The Island* or *Survival*, this more implicit form of direct audience address nonetheless partly places *Curl Up and Dye* in the tradition of the South African protest and resistance play. At the same time Pam-Grant's choice to have the characters directly facing the audience is, compared to the other plays under review, an innovative staging technique which derives from situation comedies on television. *Curl Up and Dye* points forward to the emerging tradition of post-apartheid imitation of popular television culture in the theatre, a prominent example of which is *So What's New* (1991) by Fatima Dike. The quality of *Curl Up and Dye* as a play about transitional South Africa is thus reflected both in its content and its form.

Dudu and Miriam's use of Zulu as a secret code excludes whites who have not made the effort to learn the African language. This means that the audience are no longer invited to take part in that particular conversation and are alienated from Dudu and Miriam's complaints about white behaviour. This echoes scenes in other plays where rebellious black characters could exclude white figures of authority (officers and guards) by resorting to an indigenous language. The technique also means that the audience is left only with the option of identifying with Rolene and Mrs Dubois. But as the enlightened audience members would probably want to distance themselves from the crude racist remarks of these white women, they are left suspended between two incomprehensible diatribes. The play is effective at emphasising the necessity for new spaces in which blacks and whites can meet as equals who are willing to accept each other and co-operate.

6.5. Conclusion

You Strike the Woman, You Strike the Rock, *Have You Seen Zandile?* and *Curl Up and Dye* are plays by South African women about the reality of women's lives in

South Africa. In the late 1980s, at a time when the South African theatre scene was still controlled by male practitioners, the Vusisizwe Players with Phyllis Klotz, Gcina Mhlope and Susan Pam-Grant raised specifically female issues and focused on the influence of the male-dominated, patriarchal world on women from different racial and class backgrounds.

Strike is a typical South African resistance play that stands in the tradition of revolutionary, agitprop-style theatre. It depicts the process of consciousness-raising of politically ignorant characters by an enlightened activist. Similar to the black plays discussed in Chapter 4, the teacher figure offers an alternative role model to her pupils and thus frees the African women from the confining and submissive roles that the patriarchal and apartheid society prescribes. The women are able to construct a new and empowering identity for themselves that challenges both white and male norms and role expectations. In this play the biggest hurdle on the way to the women's new identity construction is defined as their insecurity and lack of self-confidence as individuals with their own rights and desires. This shows how powerful society's role expectations are and that it is difficult but not impossible to develop new role concepts in the face of a pathological society.

Gcina Mhlophe takes a completely different approach to the question of female empowerment in *Have You Seen Zandile?* By focusing on Zandile's coming of age and looking at ten years of her childhood, Mhlophe foregrounds incidents which impact on the girl's life, clearly showing the effect they have on her development. As Zandile is influenced by women who have each gained their own experiences through oppression, Zandile is forced to incorporate these conflicting role models into the construction of her own identity. In this play mimicry and role-play by Zandile represent her attempt at understanding the roles which are available to her despite society's expectations. *Zandile* suggests that a person who learns to challenge the politically and culturally imposed definitions of identity can develop a strong sense of self and mature into an individual. By focusing on a girl's development into a young woman, this play looks to the future and suggests that a self-confident and enlightened new generation, which has learnt from their parents' fate, may pave the way towards a better future.

By contrast, Susan Pam-Grant challenges such an optimistic message in her play *Curl Up and Dye*. It demonstrates how entrenched and dangerous the powerful apartheid-constructed clichés and prejudices still remain, especially at the time of the country's transition to a democratic state. The poor, working-class white population, protected by apartheid's racist labour laws for decades, is now threatened by an educated black middle-class and a black working-class filled with new confidence in the face of the upcoming abolition of legalised race discrimination. Pam-Grant shows how the insecure Rolene, who adopted apartheid's strategy of lies and deception to define her own private world, cannot accept a black woman's help to escape her problems and develop a new identity for herself. She is trapped in the role repertoire defined by a racist, patriarchal system.

7. Outlook: The Development of Theatre in the Post-apartheid Era

> [...] on the one hand there is the search for a proper reckoning with the past evils of apartheid and on the other there is the project of designing a future which reflects a more just and harmonious society. Post-apartheid theatre has engaged in these competing but not necessarily conflicting perspectives.
>
> Cathy Maree[7]

After the official end of apartheid in 1990 a transition phase prepared the country for the first democratic elections in 1994. In the 'new' South Africa discrimination on the basis of race was officially abolished. While laws were altered fairly quickly on paper, changes in the economic and social fields occurred, and still occur, slowly.[8] Similarly, the attitudes of individuals towards those who used to belong to different groups changed only slowly. The prejudice and stereotypical thinking, on which the ideology of apartheid had largely been based, had to be overcome – a psychologically difficult but necessary task. Consequently, it was equally difficult to revise apartheid's fixed role repertoire for blacks and whites, which had been rooted in the regime's perception of the world.

Temple Hauptfleisch describes the first half of the 1990s as a difficult time for playwrights and practitioners. With South Africa's development from an apartheid state to a democratic country, anti-apartheid theatre lost its common enemy.[9] Loren Kruger comments, "The conviction that sustained several generations of theatre activists and cultural workers and that produced such memorable events as *Sizwe Banzi is Dead* [*sic*], *Woza Albert!*, and *Born in the RSA*, gave way to a variety of not quite compatible political persuasions and cultural practices" (1999: 191). It was no longer possible to call for a unified national culture because economic and social discrepancies among the population were becoming increasingly apparent. However, the political re-orientation allowed theatre practitioners to address new

[7] 1998: 26.

[8] Economic changes were slow to come about. In fact, some of the changes are for the worse with increasing poverty and unemployment among the black sectors of the population (cf. Hauptfleisch 1997: 160).

[9] Discussion between Temple Hauptfleisch and the author on 25 July, 2001 at Stellenbosch University, South Africa.

topics and audiences. They also had to create a new institutional framework for theatre as the various venues and the professional stature of the performers underwent radical changes. The focus of the new themes fixed on social problems arising out of displacement, urbanisation, poverty and AIDS as well as the lives of sexual and ethnic minorities. A growing diversity of forms ranging from "naturalism to forum theatre" replaced the "testimonial and agitprop" typical of anti-apartheid theatre (*ibid.*; cf. Hauptfleisch 1997: 159).[10]

Post-apartheid theatre addressed another important topical theme: truth and reconciliation. One of the self-imposed tasks of the theatre of the 'new' South Africa was to prepare and support the process of uncovering the truth about the past and supporting the process of reconciliation and healing in the country (cf. Hauptfleisch 1997: 161). This mirrored the political aim of the newly elected government under President Nelson Mandela to prepare the country for national reconciliation (cf. Gevisser 1994/95: 10f.). Early in 1996 the Truth and Reconciliation Commission (TRC) took up its work. The TRC's mandate was to encourage the agents, victims or survivors of human rights infringements committed between 1960 and 1993 to testify before a national forum. The TRC pursued several goals: to make lost histories heard, to offer reparation to those who had suffered and to provide amnesty for (exclusively) political acts. Autobiographical stories of loss and pain, violation and triumph came to the fore that "now stand as an account of South Africa's recent past" (Taylor 1998: ii).

To conclude this study, two plays that focus on the importance and difficulty of the search for truth and the process of reconciliation are briefly presented, *Playland* (1992) by Athol Fugard and *Ubu and the Truth Commission* (1997) by Jane Taylor, William Kentridge and the Handspring Puppet Company.

In Athol Fugard's *Playland* Martinus Zoeloe, a black watchman at a small travelling funfair, and Gideon le Roux, a visitor to the amusement park, confess their past crimes to each other on New Year's Eve, 1989. Martinus killed his white *baas* for having raped his fiancée. Although he served a long prison sentence, he confirms that he would repeat his deed. Obsessed with Judgement Day and convinced that eternal punishment awaits him, he has condemned himself to life in a self-made hell. Gideon, who visits the 'Playland' fair in order to forget his

[10] An overview of the development of theatre in South Africa is given by Hauptfleisch (1997: 159-67) and Kruger (1999: 191-216). Comments on the development of post-apartheid theatre are made, *inter alia*, by Brink (1998), Davis (2000a; 2000b), Gevisser (1994/95), Kruger (1995a), Steadman (1991) and Walder (1998b).

troubles, is not diverted for long and pours out his heart to the watchman. A former soldier in the South African army stationed on the Namibian border, Gideon killed at least twenty-seven freedom fighters of the South West African People's Organisation (SWAPO). He suffers from pangs of guilt, is full of despair and lacks a future perspective. His tirades becomes so emotionally intense that he almost attacks Martinus before challenging him to either kill a white man again or forgive him. Gideon needs Martinus' forgiveness to overcome his feelings of hatred and self-loathing, but the black man does not comply because he believes that it is too late to begin forgiving. The men cannot free each other from the guilt with which they are forced to live. However, the break of dawn allows them to physically and metaphorically "see" each other for the first time (*PL* 298) and acknowledge, as Paul Goetsch points out, both "their failings and their humanity" (1996: 77). The men now help each other to face the future: Martinus encourages Gideon to pursue his childhood memory of raising pigeons and Gideon imbues Martinus with a new sense of being alive. In an existentialist sense *Playland* suggests that, unlike *Blood Knot*'s Zachariah and Morris, who are forced to succumb to the world of apartheid, Gideon and Martinus can make a new start. However, Gideon has the especially difficult task of freeing himself from his destructive self-obsession and self-hatred - emotional states derived from his past (cf. Goetsch 1996: 78).

The play ends on the first morning of 1990, the year of Mandela's release from prison, following the unbanning of oppositional parties in November 1989. In this sense the play is a political statement on the coming changes in South Africa and thus "goes beyond an appeal to break out of the country's cycle of destruction and self-destruction" (Goetsch 1996: 78). This reading is close to Fugard's own intentions: "[...] South Africa's political miracle. I saw it coming and I knew that the extraordinary opportunity to build a just and decent society would depend on our capacity for Truth and Forgiveness. *Playland* is my recognition of that" (1998: viii). The play is essentially a call for the citizens of South Africa to open up to the world around them. Yet it recognises that this is a difficult process in which the people must be ready to confront not only their own dark secrets but those of others as well. While some critics have hailed *Playland* as the celebration of a "negotiated and happy-ended future – an [*sic*] utopian fiction" (Maree 1995: 26; cf. Holloway 1993), it is more appropriately seen as a play which addresses the psychological "obstacles in the way of racial reconciliation and national reconstruction" and shows that the "reconstruction of South Africa will be a slow and painful learning process" (Goetsch 1996: 74, 79).

Ubu and the Truth Commission also focuses on the "challenge of reconciliation with the perpetrators of state violence" during apartheid (Kruger 1999: 195). The simultaneous staging of a live actor playing Pa Ubu and animated puppets representing the other characters, against a backdrop of William Kentridge's sketches and animated cartoons, characterises *Ubu* as a multi-media performance typical of productions by the Handspring Puppet Company.[11] The play was inspired by the work of the TRC and the play *Ubu Roi* (Paris, 1896) by surrealist Alfred Jarry about the power-obsessed political and military criminal Ubu. While many anti-apartheid protest plays dramatised the suffering of the oppressed, *Ubu and the Truth Commission* places an executor of state violence at the centre of attention. Pa Ubu and his wife Ma Ubu find themselves in an environment in which they no longer enjoy absolute power. The play shows Pa Ubu desperately trying to keep his secrets from surfacing while he rids himself of all proof of his crimes against humanity. Ubu feeds incriminating evidence to his confidant and advisor Niles, a crocodile puppet with a suitcase stomach. Ubu's beliefs and behaviour are contrasted with his victims' submissions to the TRC until the inescapable moment when he is forced to account for his activities. Yet it is neither guilt nor remorse which makes him confess but Ma Ubu's betrayal of his dark past in an attempt to assert her own power over him. Desperation motivates Ubu to confess and appeal for amnesty to save himself: "[...] we'll blame all on politics and beguile the Commission" (*UTC* 57). When his generals, a three-headed dog puppet named Brutus, threaten to confess all the atrocities they committed with Ubu in order to save their own skin, Ubu brutally murders Brutus. Ubu's appearance before the TRC is fraught with lies and false obsequiousness: "These things, they were done by those above me; those below me; those beside me. I too have been betrayed! I knew nothing" (*UTC* 67). Yet he gives away his true nature: "THIS IS MY COUNTRY. And I won't give it away without a damn good fight" (*UTC* 69). His final, rehearsed statement at the TRC proclaiming that he feels "Remorse, [...] a hell of a lot" (*UTC* 71) is grotesque. Ubu's performance before the TRC oscillates between the emotional exclamation of his actual beliefs, and the irony and incredibility of the behaviour he adopted in order to pacify the committee and the public. The last scene of the play shows Pa and Ma Ubu as the "self seeking and utterly reprehensible figures they always were, locked in a relationship of mutual abuse and betrayal" (Whisson 1997: 7).

[11] Yvette Coetzee describes the relationship between the puppets and their puppeteers in this play (cf. 1998).

Ubu and the Truth Commission does not intend to present "[...] 'art as an instrument of reconciliation, at the expense of truth,'" Jane Taylor comments, because that would turn it into a form of agitprop. Instead art should be used as a "'means of reinvention, and through that, transformation'" (qtd. in Friedman 1997: 2). In this sense Ubu examines the ability of art to work within the spheres of tragedy and trauma. Its powers of reinvention can help a "brutalised society still enmeshed in the humdrum of horror to emerge with a sense of hope" (Friedman 1997: 2). As Mark Gevisser argues, a positive, forward-looking way of understanding the dialectic of truth and reconciliation in both the world of the theatre and politics is possible only if one accepts that "[...] we have to live forever with our past, and that rather than trying to abandon it, we should learn to understand it and integrate it into our present-day lives" (1994/95: 18).[12]

Both *Playland* and *Ubu and the Truth Commission* show that the quest for truth and reconciliation largely influences the interaction between individuals and their view of the world. This search forces individuals to take a critical look at their own deeds and beliefs. However, the process of finding out the truth and reconciling perpetrators and victims requires a positive social environment. This means that not only must the perpetrators and victims directly involved in the violation of human rights acknowledge each other, but, more importantly, society must create an atmosphere in which the executors and the oppressed are not reduced to their apartheid roles. As an individual can only be confirmed in their identity through the recognition of others, so must these others rid themselves of former prejudices and fixed role identities in favour of an open society in which every individual can construct and be accepted in their new roles and new, healthy identity.

[12] The role of the past in post-apartheid theatre is also discussed, for example, by Brink (1998), Steadman (1991) and Walder (1998b).

8. Conclusion: Role Theory, Role-play and South African Theatre

Hans-Peter Dreitzel ends his analysis of the disrupted behaviour of individuals interacting in a social framework with reflections on the applicability of his ideas to modern societies. It must be kept in mind that Dreitzel developed his theory based on his observations of Western industrial (especially German) society of the mid-twentieth century. He points out that one's catalogue of social roles as well as one's classification of behaviour as typical, untypical, healthy or disrupted must always consider the historical and social evolution of a society. As a society develops and changes historically and socially, its norms of behaviour also change. Not only do new social roles emerge while others disappear, and role types become attributed to different social classes, but the typology of social roles itself evolves as well. This means that the typical relation between role norms and the socially expected personal contribution by the individuals to role-play varies, as does the individuals' typical degree of identification with their roles. Consequently, the notions of the repression or the overtaxing of the individuals' personal engagement during role-play are not fixed or generalised categories, but need to be applied and analysed in specific cases. Dreitzel admits that his typology of social roles and his role-analytical examination of disrupted behaviour are only applicable to modern industrial societies. He calls for the need to adapt his theory before employing it to analyse other forms of society or different regional variations of a society (cf. 1980[3]: 299).

How does Dreitzel's call for the examination of role behaviour in the context of the historical and social characteristics of a society affect the approach of analysing apartheid society by looking at how the interaction of individuals from different 'racial' groups is presented in the theatre?

Apartheid society is seen as a 'stable' system in this study, as a society based on the political constant of racial classification. At the same time, however, it must be kept in mind that the conflict between 'blacks' and 'whites' grew in intensity over the decades and led to an increase of the rift between the racial groups of society. Such an evolution then, according to Dreitzel, automatically leads to changes in the standing and prestige of different groups in a social system and induces alterations in the behaviour of individuals and their interaction with each other. This means that the system of social roles also changes gradually and that individuals must react to this evolution in some way, either by adapting or rebelling.

Dreitzel's main thesis on disrupted behaviour is that psychic disruptions have social causes and that pathological aspects of society are mirrored in disrupted or pathological behaviour. He claims that it is possible to deduce the structure of society by analysing individual behaviour, and vice versa, that it is possible to name social aspects which have a pathological influence on the members of society by looking at the social structure (cf. 1980^3: 14-17). In the context of apartheid society it is possible to name political, social, economic and cultural changes implemented by the government and then predict the effects of these developments on the country's population – the rulers as well as the oppressed groups. Such an approach requires a socio-historical reading of texts. By contrast, an analysis of behaviour and interaction with the help of role theory allows for the drawing of conclusions about the nature of society in a deductive manner. For this particular study this means that the examination of the behaviour of individuals from the oppressed groups of apartheid society also gives us information about the ruling group who implemented the political system and thus defined the rules and norms of society. Furthermore, the continuing shift in the characters' role behaviour and role-play points to their gradually changing understanding of their position in society and their possibility of challenging the status-quo. Role-play thus becomes an indicator of the way in which individuals see themselves and the social groups they represent.

In some of the South African plays under review, role-play is employed in a documentary and realist fashion. It is used as a theatrical technique to portray and comment on the fate of the characters under apartheid and on what apartheid means to their lives. The general thesis which can be extracted from these plays is that the oppressed groups' suffering from their social roles will continue if the system of social roles, as it has been shaped under apartheid rule, is not subverted. The dramatists employ the technique of role-play in several different ways to emphasise this. Firstly, there is theatrical role-play. Presenting plays-within-the plays to shift the emphasis on the act of role-playing itself, the characters attempt to conscientise their stage audience by pointing to the evils of the system. Not every play suggests that this form of conscientisation will automatically lead to successful resistance to the regime. In a further step, almost all the plays examined here make use of metatheatrical role-play in epic fashion. In contrast to the separation of the audience space from the stage by the proscenium arch in much of Western-style theatre, most of the South African plays self-referentially comment on their status as theatre by foregrounding the fact that the actors on stage only slip into the role of their characters. This is a first comment on the fact that "All the world's a stage" or that all individuals engage in the "presentation of self in everyday life." Looking again at the characters' behaviour and their attitudes on resistance and change, we can draw conclusions about how absolute the power of the system was felt at specific periods of apartheid reign.

Blood Knot's coloured brothers Morris and Zachariah, living in the early 1960s, realise that their existence is controlled by relations of domination and subordination. Through racially transgressive role-play they have understood that their social identity is defined and fixed by apartheid discourse and that in the eyes of the political regime they exist only as racialised bodies. Their categorisation as 'coloured' leaves them without a meaning in their life and without dreams of a happy future. They continue to break-down racial barriers in their role-playing, but instead of deluding themselves with the hope of escape, they decide to pursue their game as an end in itself. Morrie and Zach perceive the status-quo as omnipotent and unchangeable. Their games show that, on the one hand, the brothers are able to redefine their social roles and create different role identities for themselves in their private world. On the other hand, their games make clear that social norms and pressures are so strong that they paralyse all attempts at publicly engaging in the re-shaping of the social roles system. As Athol Fugard's play makes the audience aware of the deficiencies of the apartheid system and society, the play can be described as a negative parable.

While Fugard emphasises the confining nature of the apartheid system in *Blood Knot*, his plays *Statements after an Arrest under the Immorality Act* and *A Lesson from Aloes* go one step further. They suggest that the social pressure in apartheid society not only hinders the development and duration of healthy interracial relationships, but that subsequent state intervention leads to the disintegration of the individuals' personal identities. The regime's strict racial categorisation of society and the creation of stereotypical versions of individuals from the various racial groups lead to distrust, fear and suspicion amongst members of different groups in society and hinder cross-racial friendships. For example, *Aloes*' Afrikaner character Piet suffers from social isolation. Although he sincerely supported the coloured struggle, he was wrongly stigmatised by the comrades as the traitor, once an informer was caught by the police. This break-down of cross-racial solidarity can again be evaluated as a success of apartheid's firm grip on society and its strict norms and lack of freedom to shape role identities.

All three plays by Athol Fugard show that the protagonists are not able to interact with other members of society in a healthy way. It is not possible to personally engage in role behaviour and shape this behaviour according to one's personal needs. Following Dreitzel this is a clear sign for the oppressive and totalitarian nature of apartheid society's norms and rules. The plays themselves are obviously critical of the inhumanity of the apartheid system, but the characters presented on stage have no way of escaping the firm grip that apartheid has in its subjects. Unlike Morrie and Zach, who can at least withdraw into their world of games to renegotiate their identity, the characters in the plays written in the 1970s, *Statements* and *Aloes*, are no longer capable of resisting apartheid-imposed definitions of identity. Their disintegration and isolation must be read as a sign for the fact that the power of apartheid over society is felt more and more as a threat to human existence, both to black and white groups of society.

Athol Fugard's collaboration with the actors John Kani and Winston Ntshona in the early 1970s led to an intensification of the theme of role-play in South African theatre of the time. The characters of *Sizwe Bansi is Dead* and *The Island* are clearly all prisoners of apartheid rules and regulations. However, in contrast to Piet, Morrie and Zach, they do not retreat into mental isolation. Their recipe for survival does not rely on role-play as an end in itself or personal isolation to escape from society, but they play with apartheid's norms and rules in an attempt to beat the system with its own weapons. The characters on stage take on different roles in their daily lives in order to condemn the status-quo and rebel against the situation of powerlessness imposed by apartheid. They are able to manifest, with their social theatricality, that they can gain strength through resistance and that this strength can bring about a shift in the power structure. Although the plays does not propagate an end to apartheid, they at least show how apartheid's degradation of blacks can be subverted. Sizwe Bansi is prepared to adopt Robert Zwelinzima's identity in public so that he can survive under the repressive regime. And *The Island*'s Winston gains strength from his and John's defiant interpretation of *Antigone* and their staging of this play at the prison concert. These actions challenge the system of domination and give proof of the characters' vitality and humanity as well as their will to live and be recognised as full and equal human beings. Although both Sizwe and Winston cannot change their physical situation in the long run, they at least fight for their rights and manifest their mental strength. The individuals in these plays distinguish themselves by their successful personal engagement in role-play. Their attempts to redefine the roles they are allowed to play may not lead to a revolution of society, but at least their overt role-play points to the gaps in apartheid's norm and rule system. These plays then suggest that a careful analysis of apartheid's definition of society may be the answer to a more tolerable existence.

The next group of black (consciousness) plays discussed here also stress the confinement of life under apartheid with the help of prison and mine metaphors. *Survival* by Workshop '71, *Egoli – City of Gold* by Matsemela Manaka and *Bopha!* by Percy Mtwa all show how blacks suffering from the domination by whites is perceived in the 1970s. The black characters find themselves in situations in the public world of apartheid in which they receive no help or solidarity from their brothers in times of trouble. Ironically, it is only in the confining gold mines where they find work under inhuman conditions or in the brutal South African gaols that the characters are able to create among each other a world of their own based on respect, support and understanding. These private worlds represent the counter-image of a microcosm of apartheid. These spaces allow mentor figures to create a healthy definition of their own identity outside of apartheid society and to convey this identity to their brothers. These mentors exhibit a strong personality that allows them to act in the face of role degeneration. These characters are important because they succeed in constructing an identity which, to a large extent, evades apartheid's definition of black existence. The teachers construct their identity by negating and inverting white norms and rules. While this act of creating a new identity shows that, on the one side, the characters have retained the faculty of personally engaging in the shaping of their role identities, it also implies that this process is only possible in a world in which the laws of apartheid can momentarily be cancelled out, at least in one's mind. This fact suggests that the pressure emanating from apartheid discourse has become so strong and paralysing that spontaneous resistance in daily behaviour is not possible and that, instead, a phase of conscientisation is necessary if resistance is to be successful. The idea that personal engagement in the shaping of one's roles and behaviour, a faculty that Dreitzel describes as automatic and unconscious in a healthy society, must happen consciously in apartheid society, shows that this society manipulates and oppresses its subjects. Healthy behaviour is doomed to fail because the society in which it takes place is pathological. Only if the apartheid regime is overthrown can a new organisation of South African society be possible. While black (consciousness) plays are often interpreted on the political level as militant calls for revolution, an analysis from the perspective of role-theory shows that radical change of the norms, rules and value structure of society is imperative for the creation of a healthy social structure.

In the 1980s multi-racial workshop productions focused on possibilities of co-existence in apartheid South Africa. *Born in the RSA* by Barney Simon and the cast as well as *Sophiatown* by Junction Avenue Theatre Company demonstrate that to a large extent the individual's identity is shaped according to society's predominant interests, attitudes and norms. The plays feature personalities who strive to break out of their socially confined lives with the help of individual, non-conform behaviour. Although the characters manage to redefine their identity for themselves, they must come to realise that socially accepted identity and role behaviour can never be defined by the individual alone but always require acceptance by other members of society.

Although *Sophiatown* stages characters who refuse to accept the state-imposed separation of the races, the play reveals that the pressure emanating from an inflexible and racially divided society prevents the characters from bridging the gap across the colour bar. Interracial co-habitation seems possible, yet appearances are deceptive. In the end, Ruth's stay in Sophiatown demonstrates that racial differences, successfully institutionalised by the apartheid state, cannot be overcome. The final farewell between the white woman Ruth and the black man Jakes signifies their surrender to they system. The characters are unable to integrate their personal attitudes and beliefs into the roles they play which proves that society is perceived as strongly repressive. Suffering from one's roles in Dreitzel's sense of the term is the inevitable consequence.

The story of Glen, the white police informer in *Born in the RSA*, suggests that the social opinion is so powerful that his failure to achieve public recognition of his identity eventually isolates him and forces him to the periphery of society. The stories of the black and white activists that he betrays, Thenjiwe and Susan, imply that a strong personal identity can prevail in the face of adversity but that this requires a psychological triumph over the refusal by others to recognise one's identity.

Thenjiwe's and Susan's narratives show two important aspects about apartheid society and possibilities for change. Firstly, resistance to the regime is possible if it is supported by a group large enough to imbue the individuals with the feeling that they are being socially recognised as activists. Secondly, if the support by one group is large enough, the activists will have the mental strength to fight for their beliefs and directly challenge the opposing group. In contrast to ideas that a revolution can only be successful by means of militant force, *Born in the RSA* suggests in a much stronger manner than the black (consciousness) plays that change can be brought about by re-evaluating social identities.

The last groups of plays under review, focus on the reality of women's lives in the patriarchal South African world. *You Strike the Woman, You Strike the Rock* by the Vusisizwe Players with Phyllis Klotz proceeds in a fashion similar to the black (consciousness) plays which focus on the conscientisation of the oppressed and the call for an armed struggle against the regime. However, the aim of the play is two-fold. Not only do the female protagonists learn to resist their oppression as blacks, but also as women. This means that the protagonists must learn to overcome their lack of self-confidence and insecurity to which they have been socially conditioned. They learn to construct a new and empowering identity for themselves that challenges both white and male norms and role expectations.

In *Have You Seen Zandile?* Gcina Mhlophe offers a different approach to the topic of female empowerment. This play focuses on the coming of age of Zandile, a girl whose development is influenced by women who have each gained their own experiences through oppression and embody different outlooks on life, from traditional to modern. Because Zandile is forced to negotiate very different approaches to life, she actually stands a chance of constructing her own identity and shaping her role set. Influenced by her progressive grandmother, her traditional mother and her modern best friend, three very different, personalities, Zandile cannot simply fall into a fixed set of roles. She must learn to find her place in society by challenging the existing, culturally and politically shaped definitions of identity. Mhlophe suggests that South African society is multi-faceted, not just based on racial criteria. Gender, ethnic and social elements also shape identity. This play then suggests that an escape from a fixed apartheid society is possible if the individuals succeed in defining their role identities according to all aspects of social life. A new norm and value structure would then arise and it seems that such a strategy would eventually diminish the importance of race and achieve a remodelling of society.

The final play discussed in this study, *Curl Up and Dye* by Susan Pam-Grant warns us that not all parts of society are prepared for the country's transition to a democratic state. The poor, working-class white population, supported by apartheid's racist labour laws, now finds itself threatened by a black working-class and an educated black middle-class motivated by the prospect of the upcoming abolition of legalised race discrimination. The existence of the white working-class is based entirely on passionate belief in the apartheid world-view. The white hairdresser Rolene has become a prisoner of this set of norms and values which is based on deception. She not only relies on the apartheid definition for human identity for her public life, but even her private world revolves around lies and denial. Rolene is caught up in apartheid's definition of reality. She cannot accept an educated black woman's help to escape her marital problems and develop a new identity for herself, but remains trapped in the set of roles defined by a racist, patriarchal system.

The majority of the plays under review present us with an optimistic strategy for subverting apartheid society from within. This is the conclusion that we arrive at if we analyse these plays with the help of role theory. The plays suggest that the individuals living under apartheid rule can develop enough counter-images of human identity and healthy interaction that the system of institutionalised racial discrimination can be challenged successfully. By reflecting on elements as diverse as their heritage, their economic needs and their personal, human desires, the protagonists develop models of human identity that can lead the way out of the inhuman system of apartheid. Although the protagonists experience their life under apartheid rule as confining, the plays make clear that the characters find gaps in the state-prescribed norm and rule system that make personal involvement in role behaviour possible. Apartheid's strict definition of identity and human value on the basis of racial superiority would seem to make individuals lose the role distance necessary to engage in healthy role behaviour and shape roles according to personal needs. However, the protagonists do not fall into apartheid's trap but reclaim their humanity by personally engaging in the negotiation of their identity.

Bibliography

Primary Literature[1]

Black, Stephen. *Helena's Hope, Ltd* [1910]. In *Three Plays*. Ed. & intro. Stephen Gray. Johannesburg: Ad Donker, 1984, 127-82.

--------. *Love and the Hyphen* [1908]. In *Three Plays*. Ed. & intro. Stephen Gray. Johannesburg: Ad Donker, 1984, 43-125.

Conrad, Joseph. *Heart of Darkness with The Congo Diary* [1899 & 1925]. Ed., intro. & notes Robert Hampson. London et al.: Penguin, 1995.

Dike, Fatima. *The Sacrifice of Kreli* [1976]. In *Theatre One: New South African Drama*. Ed. Stephen Gray. Johannesburg & London: Ad Donker, 1978, 33-79.

--------. *So What's New?* [1991]. In *Black South African Women: An Anthology of Plays*. Ed. Kathy A. Perkins. London and New York: Routledge, 1998, 26-46.

Fugard, Athol. *Blood Knot* [1985]. In *Selected Plays*. Ed. & intro. Dennis Walder. Oxford & Cape Town: Oxford UP, 1987, 51-123.

--------. *The Blood Knot* [1961]. Johannesburg: Simondium, 1963.

--------. *Boesman and Lena* [1969]. In *Selected Plays*. Ed. & intro. Dennis Walder. Oxford & Cape Town: Oxford UP, 1987, 191-247.

--------. *Hello and Goodbye* [1965]. In *Selected Plays*. Ed. & intro. Dennis Walder. Oxford & Cape Town: Oxford UP, 1987, 125-89.

--------. *A Lesson from Aloes* [1980]. New York: Theatre Communications Group, 1981.

--------. *'Master Harold' ... and the boys* [1982]. In *Selected Plays*. Ed. & intro. Dennis Walder. Oxford & Cape Town: Oxford UP, 1987, 1-49.

--------. *My Children! My Africa!* [1989]. In *Athol Fugard: Plays One*. Ed. & intro. *idem*. London & Boston: Faber & Faber, 1998, 149-238.

--------. *No-Good Friday* [1958]. In *The Township Plays*. Ed. & intro. Dennis Walder. Oxford & Cape Town: Oxford UP, 1993, 1-54.

--------. *Playland* [1992]. In *Athol Fugard: Plays One*. Ed. & intro. *idem*. London & Boston: Faber & Faber, 1998, 239-99.

--------. *People are Living There* [1968]. *Interior Plays*. Ed. & intro. Dennis Walder. Preface Athol Fugard. Oxford: Oxford UP, 2000, 1-74.

[1] Dates in brackets refer to the play's premiere or to the novel's first publication.

Fugard, Athol. *The Road to Mecca* [1985]. In *Athol Fugard: Plays One*. Ed. & intro. *idem*. London & Boston: Faber & Faber, 1998, 1-91.

--------. *Statements After an Arrest Under the Immorality Act* [1974]. In *Statements*. Athol Fugard, John Kani & Winston Ntshona. Intro. Athol Fugard. New York: Theatre Communications Group, 1986, 79-108.

--------. *Valley Song* [1996]. New York: Theatre Communications Group, 1996.

Fugard, Athol, John Kani & Winston Ntshona. *Sizwe Bansi is Dead* [1972]. In *Statements*. *Idem*. Intro. Athol Fugard. New York: Theatre Communications Group, 1986, 1-44.

--------. *The Island* [1973]. In *Statements*. *Idem*. Intro. Athol Fugard. New York: Theatre Communications Group, 1986, 45-77.

Gordimer, Nadine. *Burger's Daughter* [1979]. London et al.: Penguin, 1980.

Junction Avenue Theatre Company. *The Fantastical History of a Useless Man* [1976]. In *At the Junction: Four Plays by the Junction Avenue Theatre Company*. Ed & intro. Martin Orkin. Johannesburg: Witwatersrand UP, 1995, 14-68.

--------. *Randlords and Rotgut* [1978]. In *At the Junction: Four Plays by the Junction Avenue Theatre Company*. Ed & intro. Martin Orkin. Johannesburg: Witwatersrand UP, 1995, 70-130.

Junction Avenue Theatre Company. *Sophiatown* [1986]. Eds. Malcolm Purkey & Pippa Stein. Intro. Malcolm Purkey. Johannesburg: Witwatersrand UP, 1993.

Klotz, Phyllis, Thobeka Maqhutyana, Monvula Qosha, Xolani September, Poppy Tsira & Itumeleng Wa-Lehulere. *You Strike the Woman, You Strike the Rock (Wathint' Abafazi, Wathint' Imbokotho)* [1986]. In *More Market Plays*. Selection & intro. John Kani. Parklands: Ad Donker, 1994, 162-204.

Manaka, Matsemela. *Children of Asazi* [1986]. In *Beyond the Echoes of Soweto: Five Plays by Matsemela Manaka*. Ed. & intro. Geoffrey V. Davis. Amsterdam: Harwood Academic, 1997, 121-51.

--------. *Egoli* [1978]. In *Beyond the Echoes of Soweto: Five Plays by Matsemela Manaka*. Ed. & intro. Geoffrey V. Davis. Amsterdam: Harwood Academic, 1997, 49-71.

Maponya, Maishe. *The Hungry Earth* [1979]. In *Doing Plays for a Change*. Intro. Ian Steadman. Johannesburg: Witwatersrand UP, 1995, 1-24.

Mhlope, Gcina, Maralyn van Reenen & Thembi Mtshali. *Have You Seen Zandile? A Play originated by Gcina Mhlophe based on her Childhood* [1986]. In *Black South African Women: An Anthology of Plays*. Ed. Kathy A. Perkins. London & New York: Routledge, 1998, 83-101.

Mutwa, Credo V. *uNosilimela* [1974]. In *South African People's Plays. Ons Phola Hi. Plays by Gibson Kente, Credo V. Mutwa, Mthuli Shezi and Workshop '71.* Selection & intro. Robert Mshengu (McLaren) Kavanagh. London: Heinemann; Nairobi: Ibadan, 1981, 1-61.

Mtwa, Percy. *Bohpa!* [1986]. In *Woza Afrika!: An Anthology of South African Plays*. Ed. Duma Ndlovu. Foreword Wole Soyinka. Preface Amiri Baraka. New York: George Braziller, 1986, 225-57.

Mtwa, Percy, Mbongeni Ngema, Barney Simon. *Woza Albert!* [1982]. London: Methuen, 1983.

Ngema, Mbongeni. *Sarafina!* [1985]. In *The Best of Mbongeni Ngema: The Man and His Music*. Foreword & intro. *idem*. Braamfontein: Skotaville; Pretoria: Via Afrika, 1995, 55-125.

Orwell, George. *Nineteen Eighty-Four* [1949]. Harmondsworth: Penguin, 1966.

Pam-Grant, Susan. *Curl Up and Dye* [1988]. In *South Africa Plays.* Ed. Stephen Gray. London: Nick Hern, 1993, 81-140.

Shakespeare, William. *As You Like It* [1599/1623]. Ed. & intro. Alan Brissenden. Oxford: Clarendon, 1992.

Shezi, Mthuli. *Shanti* [1973]. In *South African People's Plays. Ons Phola Hi. Plays By Gibson Kente, Credo V. Mutwa, Mthuli Shezi and Workshop '71.* Selection & intro. Robert Mshengu (McLaren) Kavanagh. London: Heinemann; Nairobi: Ibadan, 1981, 63-84.

Simon, Barney with Vanessa Cooke, Timmy Kwebulana, Neil McCarthy, Gcina Mhlophe, Terry Norton, Thoko Ntshinga & Fiona Ramsey. *Born in the RSA* [1986]. In *Born in the RSA: Four Workshopped Plays.* Ed. Barney Simon. Intro. Pat Schwartz. Johannesburg: Witwatersrand UP, 1997, 91-127.

Stevenson, Robert Louis. *The Strange Case of Dr Jekyll and Mr Hyde* [1886]. London et al.: Penguin, 1994.

Taylor, Jane, William Kentridge & The Handspring Puppet Company. *Ubu and the Truth Commission* [1997]. Written by Jane Taylor, from the Production by William Kentridge & The Handspring Puppet Company. Cape Town: U of Cape Town P, 1998.

Workshop '71. *Survival* [1976]. In *South African People's Plays. Ons Phola Hi. Plays by Gibson Kente, Credo V. Mutwa, Mthuli Shezi and Workshop '71.* Selection & intro. Robert Mshengu (McLaren) Kavanagh. London: Heinemann; Nairobi: Ibadan, 1981, 125-71.

Secondary Literature

Abrahamse, Fred et al. 2000. "Stagings." Interview with Ashraf Jamal. *Senses of Culture: South African Culture Studies.* Eds. Sarah Nuttall & Cheryl-Ann Michael. Oxford: Oxford UP, 197-211.

Adam, Heribert. 1973. "The Rise of Black Consciousness in South Africa." *Race* 15.2: 149-65.

Akerman, Anthony. 1977/78. "Why Must These Shows Go On? A Critique of Black Musicals Made for White Audiences." *Theatre Quarterly* 28: 67-69.

Amankulor, J. Ndukaku. 1993. "English-Language Drama and Theater." *A History of Twentieth-Century African Literatures*. Ed. Oyekan Owomoyela. Lincoln & London: U of Nebraska P, 138-72.

Anderson, Lauri. 1986. "The Audience as Judge in Athol Fugard's *The Island*." *Notes on Contemporary Literature* 16.1: 5.

Angove, Coleen. 1989. "Afrikaner Stereotypes and Mavericks in Selected Fugard Plays." *South African Theatre Journal* 3.1: 55-68.

Anon. 1978. "Barney Began Where We All Began..." *Wits Student* [Johannesburg] 29 May: 8-9.

Anon. N.d. "Mail & Guardian Television: Completed Projects." *Electronic Mail & Guardian*. Accessed 20 Apr. 2002. <http://www.mg.co.za/mg/mgtv/mgtv-complete.htm>.

Arndt, Susan. 2000. *Feminismus im Widerstreit. Afrikanischer Feminismus in Gesellschaft und Literatur*. Münster: Unrast.

Ashcroft, Bill, Gareth Griffiths & Helen Tiffin. 1989. *The Empire Writes Back: Theory and Practice in Post-Colonial Literatures.* London & New York: Routledge.

Ashcroft, Bill. 1996. "On the Hyphen in Post-Colonial." *New Literatures Review* 32: 23-32.

Assman, Aleida & Jan Assman. 1988. "Schrift, Tradition und Kultur." *Zwischen Festtag und Alltag.* Ed. Wolfgang Raible. Tübingen: Narr, 25-51.

Aston, Elaine. 1995: *An Introduction to Feminism and Theatre*. London & New York: Routledge.

August, Tyrone. 1985. "Give us More than Just the Same." *City Press* [Johannesburg] 20 Oct.: 6.

--------. 1986. "Pass the Popcorn – *Bopha*'s Back." *City Press* [Johannesburg] 16 Mar.: 7.

Auslander, Philip. 1988. "Embodiment: The Politics of Postmodern Dance." *The Drama Review: TDR* 32.4: 7-23.

Baker-White, Robert. 1992. "Authority and 'Jouissance' in Fugard's *Statements After an Arrest Under the Immorality Act*." *Text and Performance Quarterly* 12: 228-44.

Bakhtin, Mikhail. 1968. *Rabelais and his World*. Trans. Helene Iswlosky. Cambridge, MA & London: MIT P.

Balme, Christopher. 1995. *Theater im postkolonialen Zeitalter: Studien zum Theatersynkretismus im englischsprachigen Raum*. Tübingen: Narr.

--------. 1996. "The Performance Aesthetics of Township Theatre: Frames and Codes." *Theatre and Change in South Africa*. Eds. Geoffrey V. Davis & Anne Fuchs. Amsterdam: Harwood Academic, 65-84.

--------. 1999. *Decolonizing the Stage: Theatrical Syncretism and Post-Colonial Theatre*. Oxford: Clarendon.

Banham, Martin & Jane Plastow. 1999. "Introduction." *Contemporary African Plays*. Eds. *idem*. London: Methuen, vii-xxvii.

Banning, Yvonne. 1989a. "Ghosts with Ears: The WESSA in Contemporary Drama." *English Academy Review* 6: 19-27.

--------. 1989b. "Junction Avenue Theatre Company: *Sophiatown*." Rev. of *Sophiatown*, by Junction Avenue Theatre Company. *South African Theatre Journal* 3.1: 95-102.

--------. 1990. "Language in the Theatre: Mediating Realities in an Audience." *South African Theatre Journal* 4.1: 12-37.

Baraka, Amiri. 1989. "Foreword." *Visions of a Liberated Future: Black Arts Movement Writings*. Larry Neal. Commentary by Amiri Baraka, Stanley Crouch, Charles Fuller and Jayne Cortez. Ed. Michael Schwartz. New York: Thunder Mouth, ix-xix.

Barber, James. 1999. *South Africa in the Twentieth Century*. Oxford & Malden: Blackwell.

Barker, Julie. 1997. "The SIBIKWA Community Project." *Vuka* 2.6: 44-5.

Barrell, Howard. 1997 [1979]. "Underground Gold." *South African Financial Mail* 28 Dec. 1979. Rpt. in *Beyond the Echoes of Soweto: Five Plays by Matsemela Manaka*. Ed. Geoffrey V. Davis. Amsterdam: Harwood Academic, 201-2.

Beinart, William & Saul Dubow. 1995. "Introduction: The Historiography of Segregation and Apartheid." *Segregation and Apartheid in Twentieth-Century South Africa*. Eds. *idem*. London & New York: Routledge, 1-24.

Beinart, William. 1995. "Chieftaincy and the Concept of Articulation: South Africa circa 1900-50." *Idem*. & Dubow 176-88.

Bender, John. 1987. *Imagining the Penitentiary*. Chicago: U of Chicago P.

Benson, Mary. 1973. "Athol Fugard and 'One Little Corner of the World'." *Yale/theatre* 4: 55-63.

--------. 1997. *Athol Fugard and Barney Simon: Bare Stage, a few Props, Great Theatre*. Randsburg: Ravan.

Bhabha, Homi. 1994. *The Location of Culture*. London & New York: Routledge.

Bigsby, C.W.E. 1982. *A Critical Introduction to Twentieth-Century American Drama. Vol. I: 1900-1940.* Cambridge et al.: Cambridge UP.

Biko, Steve. 1978. *I Write What I Like.* Ed. Aelred Stubbs C.R.. San Francisco et al.: Harper & Row.

Black Review. 1972. Ed. B.A. Khoapa (Durban 1973).

Black Review. 1973. Ed. M. Pascal Gwala (Durban 1974).

Blumberg, Marcia. 1993. "Performing Marginalities in the South African Interrgenum [*sic*]: Fatima Dike's *So What's New* and Susan Pam-Grant's *Curl Up and Dye*." *AUETSA Conference Papers.* Conference held at University of Port Elizabeth. Potchefstroom: Potchefstroom University for Christian Higher Education, 61-71.

--------. 1995. "Re-evaluating Otherness, Building for Difference: South African Theatre beyond the Interregnum." *South African Theatre Journal* 9.2: 27-37.

--------. 1999. "Revaluing Women's Storytelling in South African Theatre." *South African Theatre As/And Intervention.* Eds. *idem* & Dennis Walder. Amsterdam & Atlanta: Rodopi, 137-46.

Botha, Martin & Ari van Aswegen. 1992. *Images of South Africa: The Rise of the Alternative Film.* Pretoria: HSRC.

Botha, Martin & Johan Blignaut. 1992. *Movies – Moguls – Mavericks: South African Cinema 1979-1991.* Cape Town: Showdata.

Bourdieu, Pierre with Luc Boltanski et al. 1990. *Photography: A Middle-brow Art.* Trans. Shaun Whiteside. Stanford: Stanford UP.

Bozzoli, Belinda. 1995. "Marxism, Feminism and South African Studies." *Segregation and Apartheid in Twentieth-Century South Africa.* Eds. William Beinart & Saul Dubow. London & New York: Routledge, 118-44.

Breitinger, Eckhard. 2003[2]. "'...Satirising those Aspects of our Life we don't Approve of': A View of the 'Dark Comedies' from the Townships." *Theatre and Performance in Africa: Intercultural Perspectives*. Ed. *idem*. Bayreuth: Bayreuth African Studies, 136-60.

Brink, André. 1993. "'No Way Out': *Sizwe Bansi is Dead* and the Dilemma of Political Drama in South Africa." *Twentieth Century Literature* 39.4: 438-54.

Brink, André. 1997. "Challenge and Response: The Changing Face of Theater in South Africa." *Twentieth Century Literature* 43.2: 162-76.

--------. 1998. "Interrogating Silence: New Possibilities Faced by South African Literature." *Writing South Africa: Literature, Apartheid, and Democracy 1970-1995*. Eds. Derek Attridge & Rosemary Jolly. Cambridge: Cambridge UP, 14-28.

Brown, H. Douglas. 1986. "Learning a Second Language." *Culture Bound: Bridging the Cultural Gap in Language Teaching*. Ed. Joyce Merrill Valdes. Cambridge et al.: Cambridge UP, 33-48.

Brunkhorst. Martin. 1998. "Rituale der Grausamkeit – Traditionen des Widerstands: Antikenrezeption bei Ted Hughes, Wole Soyinka und Athol Fugard." *Antike Dramen – neu gelesen, neu gesehen.* Ed. Karl Hölz. Frankfurt am Main et al.: Peter Lang, 119-36.

Burns, Edward. 1990. *Character: Acting and Being on the Pre-Modern Stage.* London: Macmillan.

Byrne, Deirdre. 1994. "A Different Kind of Resistance: An Overview of South African Black Women's Writing." *Unisa English Studies* 32.1: 22-26.

Cameron, Trewhella, ed. & S. B. Spies, advisory ed. 1987. *An Illustrated History of South Africa.* Johannesburg: Jonathan Ball & Human & Rousseau.

Carmichael, Stockely & Charles Hamilton. 1967. *Black Power: The Politics of Liberation in America.* New York: Vintage.

Carusi, Annamaria. 1989. "Post, Post and Post. Or, Where is South African Literature in All This?" *ARIEL* 20.4: 79-95.

Case, Sue-Ellen. 1988. *Feminism and Theatre*. Houndmills & London: Macmillan.

Chapman, Michael. 1996. *Southern African Literatures*. London & New York: Longman.

Clark, VeVe A. 1981. "The Archeology of Black Theatre." *Critical Arts* 2.1: 34-50.

Coetzee, Ampie. 1997. "South African Literature and Discursive Formations. Land and the Farm Novel." *South African Literary History: Totality and, or Fragment*. Eds. Erhard Reckwitz, Karin Reitner & Lucia Vennarini. Essen: Blaue Eule, 95-110.

Coetzee, J.M. 1988. *White Writing: On the Culture of Letters in South Africa*. New Haven & London: Yale UP.

Coetzee, Yvette. 1998. "Visibly Invisible: How Shifting the Conventions of the Traditionally Invisible Puppeteer Allows for more Dimensions in both the Puppeteer-Puppet Relationship and the Creation of Theatrical Meaning in *Ubu & the Truth Commission*." *South African Theatre Journal* 12.1&2: 35-51.

Cohen, Derek. 1977. "A South African Drama: Athol Fugard's *The Blood Knot*." *Modern Language Studies* 7.1: 74-81.

--------. 1980. "Drama and the Police State: Athol Fugard's South Africa." *Canadian Drama* 9: 151-61.

Collins, Michael. 1983. "The Sabotage of Love: Athol Fugard's Recent Plays." *World Literature Today* 57: 369-71.

Combrink, Annette Louise. 1990. "Language as Barrier and Bridge: Aspects of the Language used by Selected South African Dramatists." *Space and Boundaries of Literature.* Eds. Roger Bauer et al. München: Iudicum, 63-68. Vol. 4 of Proceedings of the XIIth Congress of the International Comparative Literature Association. 5 vols.

Coplan, David. 1985. *In Township Tonight! South Africa's Black City Music and Theatre.* London: Longman.

--------. 1986. "Ideology and Tradition in South African Black Popular Theatre." *Journal of American Folklore* 99, 151-76.

--------. 1987. Retying the *Blood Knot*: Fugard on Broadway." *South African Theatre Journal* 1.1: 114-17.

--------. 2000. "Popular Culture in Southern Africa." *The Uncertain Promise of Southern Africa.* Eds. York W. Bradshaw & Stephen N. Ndegwa. Bloomington: Indiana UP, 215-30.

Coutu, Walter. 1951. "Role-playing vs. Role-taking: An Appeal for Clarification." *American Sociological Review* 16: 180-87.

Crow, Brian with Chris Banfield. 1996. "Athol Fugard and the South African 'Workshop' Play." *An Introduction to Post-Colonial Theatre.* Cambridge: Cambridge UP, 96-111.

Crow, Brian. 1992. "Athol Fugard." *Post-Colonial Drama: Commonwealth Drama since 1960.* Ed. Bruce King. New York: St Martin's P; London: Macmillan, 150-64.

--------. 1996. "'A Truly Living Moment': Acting and the Statements Plays." *Theatre and Change in South Africa.* Eds. Geoffrey V. Davis & Anne Fuchs. Amsterdam: Harwood Academic, 13-24.

Cujai, Nicole. 2001. *'And I too am not myself' – Konstruktionen weiblicher Identität in Werken der englischsprachigen Gegenwartsliteratur Südafrikas.* Peter Lang: Frankfurt am Main et al.

Cushman, Robert. 1982 [1974]. "'The Naked Truth': Review of *Statements After an Arrest under the Immorality Act*." *Observer* [London] 27 Jan. 1974. Rpt. in *Athol Fugard.* Ed. Stephen Gray. Johannesburg: McGraw-Hill, 87-88.

D.O.C.C. 1973. "The Mdali Black Arts Festival." *S'ketsh'* 43-44.

Dahrendorf, Ralf. 1974[14]. *Homo Sociologicus: Ein Versuch zur Geschichte, Bedeutung und Kritik der Kategorie der sozialen Rolle*. Opladen: Westdeutscher Verlag.

Darian-Smith, Kate, Liz Gunner & Sarah Nuttall, eds. 1996. *Text, Theory, Space: Land, Literature and History in South Africa and Australia.* London & New York: Routledge.

Davis, Geoffrey V. 1989. "Life on the Black Side of the Fence. Forced Removals and the Migrant Labour System in Recent Black South African Literature." *Current Themes in Contemporary South African Literature.* Eds. Elmar Lehmann & Erhard Reckwitz. Essen: Blaue Eule, 126-56.

--------. 1991. "'Repainting the Damaged Canvas': The Theatre of Matsemela Manaka." *Commonwealth: Essays and Studies* 14.1: 84-96.

--------. 1993. "'Born out of Flames': Matsemela Manaka's Theatre for Social Reconstruction." *Imagination and the Creative Impulse in the New Literatures in English*. Eds. M.-T. Bindella & *idem*. Amsterdam & Atlanta: Rodopi, 149-63.

--------. 1994a. "From Soweto to Gorée: A South African Writer in Search of the African Heritage." *South African Writing*. Ed. *idem*. Amsterdam: Rodopi, 25-37.

--------. 1997. "Introduction." *Beyond the Echoes of Soweto: Five Plays by Matsemela Manaka.* Ed. *idem.* Amsterdam: Harwood Academic, 1-31.

--------. 1999. "Of 'Undesirability': The Control of Theatre in South Africa during the Age of Apartheid." *New Theatre in Francophone and Anglophone Africa: A Selection of Papers held at a Conference in Mandelieu, 23-26 June, 1995.* Amsterdam & Atlanta: Rodopi, 183-208.

--------. 2000a. "Addressing the Silences of the Past: Truth and Reconciliation in Post-Apartheid Theatre." *South African Theatre Journal* 13.1&2 & *Bayreuth African Studies* 50: 59-72.

--------. 2000b. "'The Now is in Our Hands': Innovation and Reorientation in Post-Apartheid South African Drama." *Anglophonia/Caliban* 7: 165-77.

Dawson, Jeremy. 1989. "Amusing – But All Too Safe and Comfy." *Argus* 18 Sep.: 6.

Daymond, M.J. 1996 [1990]. "Feminism and Writing – Preface to Current Writing: Text and Reception in Southern Africa (1990)." *South African Feminisms: Writing, Theory, and Criticism, 1990-1994.* Ed. *idem*. New York & London: Garland, xlv-xlix. Rpt. of "Feminism and Writing." *Current Writing: Text and Reception in Southern Africa* 2.

--------. 1996. "Introduction." *South African Feminisms: Writing, Theory, and Criticism, 1990-1994.* Ed. *idem*. New York & London: Garland, xiii-xliii.

DeShazer, Mary K. 1994. *A Poetics of Resistance: Women Writing in El Salvador, South Africa, and the United States.* Ann Arbor: U of Michigan P.

Dreitzel, Hans Peter. 1980[3]. *Die gesellschaftlichen Leiden und das Leiden der Gesellschaft: Eine Pathologie des Alltags.* Rev. ed. Stuttgart: Enke.

Driver, Dorothy. 1990. "M'a-Ngoana O Tšoare Thipa Ka Bohaleng – The Child's Mother Grabs the Sharp End of the Knife: Women as Mothers, Women as Writers." *Rendering Things Visible: Essays on South African Literary Culture.* Ed. Martin Trump. Johannesburg: Ravan, 225-55.

--------. 1992. "Women and Nature, Women as Objects of Exchange. Towards a Feminist Analysis of South African Literature." *Perspectives on South African English Literature.* Eds. Michael Chapman, Colin Gardener & Es'kia Mphahlele. Parklands: Ad Donker, 454-74.

Du Bois, W.E.B. 1996. *The W.E.B. Du Bois Reader.* Ed. Eric J. Sundquist. New York & Oxford: Oxford UP.

Du Toit, André. 1976. "Ideological Change, Afrikaner Nationalism, and Pragmatic Racial Domination in South Africa." *Change in Contemporary South Africa.* Eds. Leonard Thompson & Jeffrey Butler. Berkeley & Los Angeles: U of California P, 19-50.

Dubow, Saul. 1987. "Race, Civilisation and Culture: The Elaboration of Segregationist Discourse in the Inter-War Years." *The Politics of Race, Class and Nationalism in Twentieth-Century South Africa.* Eds. Shula Marks & Stanley Trapido. London & New York: Longman, 71-94.

--------. 1995. "The Elaboration of Segregationist Ideology." *Segregation and Apartheid in Twentieth-Century South Africa.* Eds. William Beinart & *idem.* London & New York: Routledge, 145-75.

Durbach, Errol. 1989. "Surviving Xanadu: Athol Fugard's *Lesson from Aloes.*" *ARIEL* 20.1: 5-21.

--------. 1993. "Sophocles in South Africa: Athol Fugard's *The Island.*" *Drama and the Classical Heritage: Comparative and Critical Essays.* Eds. Clifford Davidson, Rand Johnson & John H. Stoupe. New York: AMS, 241-53.

Erikson, Erik H. 1979[5]. *Identität und Lebenszyklus: Drei Aufsätze.* Trans. Käte Hügel. Frankfurt am Main: Suhrkamp.

--------. 1974. *Identity: Youth and Crisis.* London: Faber & Faber.

Esslin, Martin. 1977. *An Anatomy of Drama.* New York: Hill & Wang.

Fairbairn, Jean. 1986. "Stress on Comedy Clouds Grim Political Message." *Argus* [Cape Town] 11 April: 9.

Fanon, Frantz. 1963. *The Wretched of the Earth.* Preface Jean-Paul Sartre. Trans. Constance Farrington. New York: Grove.

--------. 1967. *Black Skin, White Masks.* Trans. Charles Lam Karkmann. New York: Grove.

Fatton, Robert Jr. 1986. *Black Consciousness in South Africa: The Dialectics of Ideological Resistance to White Supremacy*. Albany: State U of New York P.

Flanagan, Hallie. 1973. "Introduction." *Federal Theatre Plays.* Ed. Pierre De Rohan. New York: Da Capo, vii-xii.

Fleischman, Mark. 1990. "Workshop Theatre as Oppositional Form." *South African Theatre Journal* 4.1: 88-118.

--------. 1991. *Workshop Theatre in South Africa in the 1980s: A Critical Examination with Specific Reference to Power, Orality and the Carnivalesque*. M.A. thesis, University of Cape Town.

--------. 1996. "Physical Images in the South African Theatre." *Theatre and Change in South Africa*. Eds. Geoffrey V. Davis & Anne Fuchs. Amsterdam: Harwood Academic, 173-82.

Flockemann, Miki. 1991. "Gcina Mhlohpe's *Have You Seen Zandile?*: English or english? The Situation of Drama in Literature and Language Developments in the Emergent Post-Apartheid South Africa." *South African Theatre Journal* 5.2: 40-54.

Fludernik, Monika. 1998a. "The Constitution of Hybridity: Postcolonial Interventions." *Hybridity and Postcolonialism. Twentieth-Century Indian Literature*. Ed. *idem*. Tübingen: Stauffenburg, 19-53.

--------. 1998b. "Introduction." *Hybridity and Postcolonialism. Twentieth-Century Indian Literature*. Ed. *idem*. Tübingen: Stauffenburg, 9-18.

Foley, Andrew. 1991. "The White English-Speaking South Africans: 'Bastards', 'Wimps', 'Ghosts with Ears', or Something Else Again?" *English Academy Review* 8: 15-29.

Forster, Deborah D. 1977. "*The Blood-Knot* and *The Island* as Anti-Tragedy." Occasional Paper, African Studies Programme, University of Wisconsin, Madison.

Foucault, Michel. 1965. *Madness and Civilization: A History of Insanity in the Age of Reason.* Trans. Richard Howard. New York: Pantheon.

--------. 1981a. "The Order of Discourse." *Untying the Text: A Post-Structuralist Reader*. Ed. Robert Young. Boston, London & Henley: Routledge & Paul Kegan, 48-78.

--------. 1981b. *Überwachen und Strafen: Die Geburt des Gefängnisses*. Trans. Walter Seitter. Frankfurt am Main: Suhrkamp.

--------. 1990. *The History of Sexuality. Volume I: An Introduction.* Trans. Robert Hurley. New York: Vintage.

France, Anna Kay & P.J. Corso, eds. 1993. *International Women Playwrights. Voices of Identity and Transformation – Proceedings of the First International Women Playwrights Conference, October 18-23, 1998.* Metchuen, NJ & London: Scarecrow P.

Frank, Haike. 2003. "'That's all out of Shape': Language and Racism in South African Drama." *The Politics of English as a World Language: New Horizons in Postcolonial Cultural Studies.* Ed. Christian Mair. Amsterdam & New York: Rodopi, 305-14.

Friedman, Hazel. 1987. "After the Play, the Women Strike Anew." *Weekly Mail* [Johannesburg] 9-15 Jan.: 23.

--------. 1997. "In Horror, Hope." *Mail & Guardian* Supplement 'Standard Bank National Arts Festival' [Johannesburg] July: 2.

Fuchs, Anne. 1985. "The Theatre, the Artist and Soweto." *Commonwealth Essays & Studies* 7.2: 55-62.

--------. 1987. "Re-Creation: One Aspect of Oral Tradition and the Theatre in South Africa." *Commonwealth* 9.2: 32-40.

--------. 1990. *Playing the Market: The Market Theatre Johannesburg 1976-1986.* Chur et al.: Harwood Academic.

--------. 1991. "Manipulating Puppets in the New South African Theatre." *Commonwealth Essays and Studies* 14.1: 78-83.

--------. 1992. "The New South African Theatre: Beyond Fugard". *Post-Colonial Drama: Commonwealth Drama since 1960.* Ed. Bruce King. New York: St Martin's; London: Macmillan, 165-80.

--------. 1999. "The Body of Change and the Changing Body in the Plays of Junction Avenue Theatre Company." *South African Theatre As/And Intervention.* Eds. Marcia Blumberg & Dennis Walder. Amsterdam & Atlanta: Rodopi, 137-46.

Fugard, Athol, John Kani & Winston Ntshona. 2000. "On *The Island.*" Interview with Esther Pan. *Newsweek* March 27: 32-33.

Fugard, Athol. 1973a. "Challenging the Silence." Interview with Michael Coveney. *Plays and Players* 21.2: 34-37.

--------. 1973b. "Interview with Athol Fugard." Interview with Jonathan Marks. *Yale/Theatre* 4: 64-72.

--------. 1977/78. "Keeping an Appointment with the Future: The Theatre of Athol Fugard." Interview with Mary Benson. *Theatre Quarterly* 28: 77-83.

--------. 1982 [1980]. "Notes on *A Lesson from Aloes*." *Theater* 11.2. Rpt. in Gray, ed., 65-67.

Fugard, Athol. 1982. "*Sizwe Bansi is Dead.*" *A Night at the Theatre.* Ed. Ronald Harwood. London: Methuen.

--------. 1983. *Notebooks 1960-1977.* Ed. Mary Benson. London: Faber & Faber.

--------. 1984. "An Interview." Interview with M.J. Daymond, J.U. Jacobs & Margaret Lenta. *Momentum: On Recent South African Writing*. Eds. *idem*. Pietermaritzburg: U of Natal P, 22-28.

--------. 1986. "Introduction." *Statements*. *Idem*, John Kani & Winston Ntshona. New York: Theatre Communications Group, n.p.

--------. 1993. "Some Problems of a Playwright from South Africa." *Twentieth Century Literature* 39.4: 381-93.

--------. 1998. "Foreword." *Athol Fugard: Plays One*. *The Road to Mecca, A Place with the Pigs, My Children! My Africa, Playland, Valley Song*. Ed. & intro. *idem*. London & Boston: Faber & Faber, vii-viii.

Gates, Jr., Henry Louis. 1988. *The Signifying Monkey: A Theory of Afro-American Literary Criticism.* New York & Oxford: Oxford UP.

Gerhart, Gail. 1978. *Black Power in South Africa: The Evolution of an Ideology*. Berkeley, Los Angeles & London: U of California P.

Gevisser, Mark. 1994/95. "Truth and Consequences in Post-Apartheid Theater." *Theater* 25.3: 9-18.

Gilbert, Helen & Joanne Tompkins. 1996. *Post-Colonial Drama: Theory, Practice, Politics*. London & New York: Routledge.

Gilbert, Helen. 1992. "The Dance as Text in Contemporary Australian Drama: Movement and Resistance Politics." *ARIEL* 23.1: 133-48.

--------. 1994. "De-Scribing Orality: Performance and the Recuperation of Voice." *De-Scribing Empire: Post-Colonialism and Textuality*. Eds. Chris Tiffin & Alan Lawson. London: Routledge, 98-111.

Giliomee, Hermann. 1995. "The Growth of Afrikaner Identity." *Segregation and Apartheid in Twentieth-Century South Africa.* Eds. William Beinart & Saul Dubow. London & New York: Routledge, 189-205.

Gilman, Sander L. 1985. *Difference and Pathology. Stereotypes of Sexuality, Race, and Madness*. Ithaca & London: Cornell UP.

Gilmore, Leigh. 2001. *The Limits of Autobiography: Trauma and Testimony*. Ithaca & London: Cornell UP.

Girvin, S.D. 1987. "Race and Race Classification." *Race and the Law in South Africa*. Ed. A. Rycroft et al. Cape Town: Wetton; Johannesburg: Juta: 1-10.

Glasser, Mona. 1960. "*King Kong*": *A Venture in the Theatre*. Cape Town: Norman Howell.

Goetsch, Paul. 1992[2]. *Bauformen des modernen englischen und amerikanischen Dramas*. Expanded ed. Darmstadt: Wissenschaftliche Buchgesellschaft.

--------. 1996. "Questioning Liberal Optimism: Athol Fugard's *Playland*." *Contemporary Drama in English* 3: 73-80.

--------. 1997. "Erziehung zu Toleranz: Das didaktische Drama Athol Fugards." *Erziehungsideale in englischsprachigen Literaturen: Heidelberger Symposium zum 70. Geburtstag von Kurt Otten*. Eds. Dieter Schulz & Thomas Kullmann. Frankfurt am Main: Peter Lang, 297-310.

Goffman, Erving. 1959. *The Presentation of Self in Everyday Life*. New York et al.: Anchor-Doubleday.

--------. 1961a. *Asylums: Essays on the Social Situation of Mental Patients and other Inmates*. Garden City, NY: Anchor.

--------. 1961b. *Encounters: Two Studies in the Sociology of Interaction.* Indianapolis: Bobbs-Merrill.

--------. 1963. *Stigma: Notes on the Management of Spoiled Identity*. New York et al.: Touchstone - Simon & Schuster.

Goldstein, Malcolm. 1974. *The Political Stage: American Drama and Theater of the Great Depression.* New York: Oxford UP.

Goodman, Lizbeth. 1993. *Contemporary Feminist Theatres: To Each Her Own.* London & New York: Routledge.

Goodman, Walter. 1988. "From Cape Town, a Mix of Humor and Pain." *New York Times* 24 June: C3.

Goody, Jack & Ian Watt. 1986. "Konsequenzen der Literalität." *Entstehung und Folgen der Schriftkultur*. Eds. *idem* & Kathleen Gough. Trans. Friedhelm Herborth. Frankfurt am Main: Suhrkamp, 63-122.

Gordimer, Nadine. 1990. "Who Writes? Who Reads? The Concept of a People's Literature." *Staffrider* 9.1: 36-41.

Govinden, Devarakshanam Betty. 1998. "'While She Watered the Morning Glories': Evaluating the Literary Achievement of Gcina Mhlophe." *Childhood in African Literature*. Eds. Eldred Durosimi Jones & Marjorie Jones. Oxford & Trenton: James Curry & Africa World P, 69-81.

Gray, Stephen. 1990. "Women in South African Theatre." *South African Theatre Journal* 4.1: 75-87.

--------. 1993a. Introduction to *Curl Up and Dye* by Susan-Pam Grant. *South Africa Plays*. London: Nick Hern, 81-82.

--------. 1993b. "Problems of Compiling a Collection of Plays of the 1980s." *South African Theatre Journal* 7.2: 63-76.

Gray, Stephen, ed. 1991. *File on Fugard.* London: Methuen.

Gready, Paul. 1990. "The Sophiatown Writers of the Fifties: The Unreal Reality of Their World." *Journal of Southern African Studies* 16.1: 139-64.

--------. 1994. "Political Autobiography in Search of Liberation: Working Class Theatre, Collaboration and the Construction of Identity." *Politics and Performance: Theatre, Poetry and Song in Southern Africa.* Ed. Liz Gunnar. Johannesburg: Witwatersrand UP, 162-98.

Green, Robert J. 1970. "South Africa's Plague: One View of *The Blood Knot.*" *Modern Drama* 12: 331-45.

--------. 1976. "Politics and Literature in Africa: The Drama of Athol Fugard." *Aspects of South African Literature.* Ed. Christopher Heywood. London: Heinemann, 163-73.

Greig, Robert. 1982 [1978]. "'The Drought in our Soul': Review of *A Lesson from Aloes.*" *Star* [Johannesburg] 1 Dec. 1978. Rpt. in *Athol Fugard.* Ed. Stephen Gray. Johannesburg: McGraw-Hill, 101-2.

--------. 1991. "Therapeutic Comedy Has Been Enhanced by Time." *Business Day* [Johannesburg] 15 Aug.: 6.

Gross, Neal, Ward S. Mason & Alexander W. McEachern. 1958. *Explorations in Role Analysis: Studies of the School Superintendency Role.* New York & London: John Wiley & Sons.

Grosz, Elizabeth. 1990. "Inscriptions and Body-maps: Representations of the Corporeal." *Feminine/Masculine and Representation.* Ed. Terry Threadgold. Sydney: Allen & Unwin, 62-74.

Grotowski, Jerzy. 1967. "Towards the Poor Theatre." Trans. T.K. Wiewiorowski. Ed. Kelly Morris. *Tulane Drama Review* 11.3: 60-65.

Gunnar, Elizabeth. 1989. "Songs of Innocence and Experience: Women as Composers and Performers of Izibongo, Zulu Praise Poetry." *Women and Writing in South Africa: A Critical Anthology.* Ed. Cherry Clayton. Marshalltown: Heinemann, 11-39.

Gwala, Mafika Pascal. 1973. "Towards a National Theatre." *South African Outlook* 131-33.

--------. 1984. "Writing as a Cultural Weapon." *Momentum: On Recent South African Writing.* Eds. M.J. Daymond, J.U. Jacobs, Margaret Lenta. Pietermaritzburg: U of Natal P, 37-53.

Hannerz, Ulf. 1994. "Sophiatown: The View from Afar." *Journal of Southern African Studies* 20.2: 181-93.

Hare, A. Paul. 1985. *Social Interaction as Drama: Applications from Conflict Resolution.* Beverly Hills, London & New Delhi: Sage.

Harlow, Barbara. 1987. *Resistance Literature*. New York & London: Methuen.

Hauptfleisch, Temple & Ian Steadman, eds. 1984. *South African Theatre: Four Plays and an Introduction.* Pretoria: HAUM.

Hauptfleisch, Temple. 1987. "Beyond Street Theatre and Festival: The Forms of South African Theatre." *Maske und Kothurn* 33: 175-88.

--------. 1990. "Multilingual Theatre and Apartheid Society (1970 – 1987)." *Space and Boundaries of Literature.* Eds. Roger Bauer et al. München: Iudicum, 103-9. Vol. 4 of Proceedings of the XIIth Congress of the International Comparative Literature Association. 5 vols.

--------. 1992. "Alternative Dreams. Recent South African Playwriting in English." *Perspectives on South African English Literature.* Eds. Michael Chapman, Colin Gardner & Es'kia Mphahlele. Parklands: Ad Donker, 403-21.

--------. 1996. "The (Re)Canonization of South African Theatre: Thoughts on Four Play Collections." *South African Theatre Journal* 10.1: 115-19.

--------. 1997. *Theatre and Society in South Africa*. Pretoria: Van Schaik.

Hayes, Diana L. 1996. *And Still We Rise: An Introduction to Black Liberation Theology*. New York & Mahwah, NJ: Paulist.

Hegel, Georg Wilhelm Friedrich. 1967. *The Phenomenology of Mind.* Trans., intro. & notes J. B. Baillie. New York: Harper & Row.

Henke, Suzette A. 1998. *Shattered Subjects: Trauma and Testimony in Women's Life-Writing.* Houndmills & London: Macmillan.

Herny, Tanu T. 2002. "Gumboots: South African Rhythms of Resistance." 9 May 2002. Accessed 25 June 2002. <http://www.africana.com/DailyArticles/index_20010109.htm>.

Hlongwane, Ali Khangela. 1994. "Reflections on a Cultural Day of Artists and Workers on 16 April 1989." *Politics and Performance: Theatre, Poetry and Song in Southern Africa.* Ed. Liz Gunnar. Johannesburg: Witwatersrand UP, 199-202.

Hodgson, Terry. 1992. *Modern Drama: From Ibsen to Fugard*. London: Batsford.

Hoijer, Harry. 1964. "Cultural Implications of Some Navaho Linguistic Categories." *Language in Culture and Society: A Reader in Linguistics and Anthropology*. Ed. Dell Hymes. New York, Evanston & London: Harper & Row, 142-53.

Holloway, Myles. 1993a. "Creative Co-operation: A Critical Survey of Workshop Theatre in South Africa." *South African Theatre Journal* 7.1: 17-31.

--------. 1993b. "*Playland*: Fugard's Liberalism." *Unisa-English Studies* 31: 36-42.

Horn, Andrew. 1986. "South African Theatre: Ideology and Rebellion." *Research in African Literatures* 17.2: 211-33.

Hutcheon, Linda. 1989. "'Circling the Downspout of Empire': Post-Colonialism and Postmodernism." *ARIEL* 20.4: 149-75.

Hutchison, Yvette. 1996. "'Access to Rather Than Ownership of': South African Theater History and Theory at a Crossroad." *South African Theatre Journal* 10.1: 35-47.

--------. 1999. "Present Trends in South African Theatre." *The Dancing Dwarf from the Land of Spirits*. Ed. Johannes A. Smit. Durban: CSSALL, 119-30.

International Defence and Aid Fund. 1977/78. "A New Wave of Cultural Energy: Black Theatre in South Africa." *Theatre Quarterly* 28: 57-63.

Jauss, Hans Robert. 1979. "Soziologischer und ästhetischer Rollenbegriff." *Identität*. Eds. Odo Marquard & Karlheinz Stierle. München: Fink, 599-607.

Jenkins, Ron. 1998. "South African Political Clowning: Laughter and Resistance to Apartheid." *Fools and Jesters in Literature, Art, and History: A Bio-Bibliographical Sourcebook*. Ed. Vicki K. Janik. Westport, CT & London: Greenwood: 419-27.

Jeyifo, Biodun. 1985. *The Truthful Lie: Essays in a Sociology of African Drama*. London: New Beacon.

Jones, Laura. 1994. *Nothing Except Ourselves: The Harsh Times and Bold Theater of South Africa's Mbongeni Ngema*. New York: Viking.

Jones, LeRoi. 1966. *Home: Social Essays*. New York: William Morrow & Co., 210-15.

Joubert, Elsa. 1982 [1972]. "'Immorality Drama': Review of *Statements After an Arrest under the Immorality Act*." *Rapport* [Johannesburg] 2 Apr. 1972. Trans. Josandra Janisch. Rpt. in *Athol Fugard*. Ed. Stephen Gray. Johannesburg: McGraw-Hill, 85-87.

K., R. 1974. "Sizwe Bansi is Alive and Struggling for Freedom." Letter to the Editor. *African Communist* 58: 122-28.

Kani, John & Winston Ntshona. 1976. "'Art is Life and Life is Art'." Interview with African Activist Association & Ufahamu. *Ufahamu* 6.2: 5-26.

Kani, John. 1988. "John Kani: Combatant from the Stage." Interview with Staffrider. *Staffrider* 7.1: 54-61.

--------. 1994. "Introduction." *More Market Plays*. Selected by *idem*. Parklands: Ad Donker, 7-9.

Kaufman, Michael W. 1980. "The Delicate World of Reprobation: A Note on the Black Revolutionary Theatre." *The Theater of Black Americans, Vol. 1:, Roots and Rituals: The Search for Identity, the Image Makers: Plays and Playwrights*.

A Collection of Critical Essays. Ed. Errol Hill. Englewood Cliffs, NJ: Prentice-Hall, 192-209.

Kavanagh, Robert Mshengu (McLaren), selection & intro. 1981. *South African People's Plays. Ons phola hi. Plays by Gibson Kente, Credo V. Mutwa, Mthuli Shezi and Workshop '71.* London et al.: Heinemann.

--------. 1985. *Theatre and Cultural Struggle in South Africa.* London: Zed Books.

Kennedy, Christina. 2000. "Phyllis takes Flight with new Rape Play." *Citizen* [Johannesburg] (Supplement Spotlight) June 20: 25.

Kerr David. 1996. "The Art of Writing Plays." *Southern African Review of Books* 48: 23.

--------. 1995. *African Popular Theatre: From Pre-Colonial Times to the Present Day.* London: James Currey.

Keysaar, Helene. 1984. *Feminist Theatre: An Introduction to Plays of Contemporary British and American Women.* Houndmills & London: Macmillan.

--------. 1996. "Introduction." *Feminist Theatre and Theory.* Ed. *idem.* Houndmills & London: Macmillan, 1-18.

King, Robert L. 1993. "The Rhetoric of Dramatic Technique in *Blood Knot.*" *South African Theatre Journal* 7.1: 40-49.

King, Woodie & Ron Milner, eds. 1972. *Black Drama Anthology.* New York & London: Columbia UP.

Krappmann, Lothar. 1982[6]. *Soziologische Dimensionen der Identität: Strukturelle Bedingungen für die Teilnahme an Interaktionsprozessen.* Stuttgart: Klett-Cotta.

Kristeva, Julia. 1980. *Pouvoirs de L'Horreur: Essai sur L'Abjection.* Paris: Seuil.

Kruger, Loren. 1991. "Apartheid on Display: South Africa Performs for New York." *Diaspora* 1.2: 191-208.

--------. 1995a. "'That Fluctuating Movement of National Consciousness': Protest, Publicity, and Postcolonial Theatre in South Africa" *Imperialism and Theatre: Essays on World Theatre, Drama and Performance.* Ed. J. Ellen Gainor. London & New York: Routledge, 148-63.

--------. 1995b. "So What's New? Women and Theatre in the 'New South Africa'." *Theater* 25.3: 46-54.

--------. 1995c. "The Uses of Nostalgia: Drama, History, and Liminal Moments in South Africa." *Modern Drama* 38: 60-70.

--------. 1997. "The Drama of Country and City: Tribalization, Urbanization and Theatre under Apartheid." *Journal of Southern African Studies* 23.4: 565-84.

Kruger, Loren. 1999. *The Drama of South Africa: Plays, Pageants and Publics since 1910.* London & New York: Routledge.

LaCapra, Dominick. 1983. *Rethinking Intellectual History: Texts, Contexts, Language.* Ithaca & London: Cornell UP.

Laing, R.D., H. Phillipson & A.R. Lee. 1978[4]. *Interpersonelle Wahrnehmung.* Trans. Hans-Dieter Teichman. Frankurt am Main: Suhrkamp.

Lapchick, Richard E. 1985. "The Role of Women in the Struggle Against Apartheid in South Africa." *The Black Woman Cross-Culturally.* Ed. Filomina Chioma Steady. Cambridge, MA: Schenkman, 231-61.

Larlham, Peter. 1985. *Black Theater, Dance, and Ritual in South Africa.* Ann Arbor, MI: UMI Research P.

--------. 1992. "The Impact of the Dismantling of Apartheid on Theatre in South Africa." *South African Theatre Journal* 6.2: 43-48.

Legassick, Martin. 1995. "British Hegemony and the Origins of Segregation in South Africa, 1901-14." *Segregation and Apartheid in Twentieth-Century South Africa.* Eds. William Beinart & Saul Dubow. London & New York: Routledge, 43-59.

Lehberger, Reiner. 1977. *Das sozialistische Theater in England 1934 bis zum Ausbruch des Zweiten Weltkriegs: Studien zur Geschichte und der Programmtätigkeiten des 'Left Theatre', 'Unity Theatre' und der 'Left Book Club Theatre Guild'.* Frankfurt am Main: Peter Lang.

Lenta, Margaret. 1989. "Intimate Knowledge and Wilful Ignorance: White Employers and Black Employees in South African Fiction." *Women and Writing in South Africa: A Critical Anthology.* Ed. Cherry Clayton. Marshalltown: Heinemann, 237-51.

Lewis, Desiree. 1992. "The Politics of Feminism in SA." *Staffrider* 10.3: 15-21.

Linton, Ralph. 1936. *The Study of Man: An Introduction.* Student's ed. New York : Appleton-Century-Crofts.

Lipman, Beata. 1984. *We Make Freedom: Women in South Africa.* London et al.: Pandora.

Lockett, Cecily. 1990. "Feminism(s) and Writing in English in South Africa." *Current Writing: Text and Reception in Southern Africa* 2.1: 1-21.

Lodge, Tom. 1981. "The Destruction of Sophiatown." *Journal of Modern African Studies* 19.1: 107-32.

--------. 1983. *Black Politics in South Africa since 1945.* London & New York: Longman.

Loots, Lliane. 1996. "'The Personal is Political' – Gender in the Context of Apartheid South Africa: A Look at Two Women Playwrights." *South African Theatre Journal* 10.1: 63-70.

--------. 1997. "Re-membering Protest Theatre in South Africa – a Gendered Review of the Historical and Cultural Production of Knowledge Around Two Plays; *The Hungry Earth* and *You Strike the Woman, You Strike the Rock*." *Critical Arts* 11.1&2: 142-52.

Lott, Tommy L. 1999. *The Invention of Race: Black Culture and the Politics of Representation.* Malden, MA & Oxford: Blackwell.

Luckmann, Thomas. 1979. "Persönliche Identität, Soziale Rolle und Rollendistanz." *Identität*. Eds. Odo Marquard & Karlheinz Stierle. München: Fink, 293-313.

MacDonald, Marianne. Forthcoming. *Space, Time, and Silence: The Craft of Athol Fugard.*

Mackay, E. Anne. 1989. "Fugard's *The Island* and Sophocles' *Antigone* within the Parameters of South African Protest Literature." *Literature and Revolution*. Ed. Davis Bevan. Amsterdam: Rodopi, 145-62.

MacKenzie, John M. 1987. "The Imperial Pioneer and Hunter and the British Masculine Stereotype in late Victorian and Edwardian Times." *Manliness and Morality: Middle-class Masculinity in Britain and America 1800-1940.* Eds. J. A. Mangan & James Walvin. Manchester: UP, 176-98.

MacLiam, Garalt. 1985. "New Play is a Call to the Conscience of All." *Star* [Johannesburg] 27 Sep.: 9.

--------. 1986. "*Bopha*: An Arresting Experience." *Star* [Johannesburg] 29 Mar.: 15.

--------. 1989. "This Play Will Open Your Eyes (Wide!) About SA." *Star Tonight* [Johannesburg] 26 June: 14.

Manaka, Matsemela. 1981. "The Balbaz People." *Staffrider* 4.3: 33-35.

--------. 1982. "Black Literature after Soweto: An Interview." Interview with Geoffrey V. Davis. *Englisch Amerikanische Studien* 4.4: 516-22.

--------. 1984. "Some Thoughts on Black Theatre." *English Academy Review* 2: 33-39.

--------. 1986. "Human Problems that Come from a Political Situation." Interview with T. Philemon Wakashe. *The Drama Review: TDR* 30.4: 48-50.

--------. 1987. *Echoes of African Art: A Century of Art in South Africa.* Foreword by Es'kia Mphahlele. Braamfontein: Skotaville.

--------. 1997a. "Theatre of the Dispossessed." *Beyond the Echoes of Soweto: Five Plays by Matsemela Manaka.* Ed. Geoffrey V. Davis. Afterword John Kani. Amsterdam: Harwood Academic, 33-48.

Manaka, Matsemela. 1997b. "Where There is Trouble There is Literature." Interview with Geoffrey V. Davis. *Beyond the Echoes of Soweto: Five Plays by Matsemela Manaka.* Ed. Geoffrey V. Davis. Afterword John Kani. Amsterdam: Harwood Academic, 97-113.

Manganyi, N.C. 1973. *Being-Black-in-the-World.* Johannesburg: Spro-Cas, Ravan.

Maqagi, Sisi. 1996 [1990]. "Who Theorizes?" *Current Writing: Text and Reception in Southern Africa* 2. Rpt. in *South African Feminisms: Writing, Theory, and Criticism, 1990-1994.* Ed. M.J. Daymond. New York & London: Garland: 27-30.

Maré, Gerhard & Georgina Hamilton. 1987. *An Appetite for Power: Buthelezi's Inkatha and South Africa.* Johannesburg : Ravan.

Maree, Cathy. 1995. "Truth and Reconciliation: Confronting the Past in *The Death and the Maiden* (Ariel Dorfman) and *Playland* (Athol Fugard)."*Literator* 16.2: 25-37.

--------. 1998. "Resistance and Remembrance: Theatre during and after Dictatorship and Apartheid." *South African Theatre Journal* 12.1&2: 11-33.

Marks, Shula & Stanley Trapido. 1987. "The Politics of Race, Class and Nationalism." *The Politics of Race, Class and Nationalism in Twentieth-Century South Africa.* Eds. *idem.* London & New York: Longman, 1-70.

Marks, Shula. 1995. "Natal, the Zulu Royal Family and the Ideology of Segregation." *Segregation and Apartheid in Twentieth-Century South Africa.* Eds. William Beinart & Saul Dubow. London & New York: Routledge, 91-117.

Marquard, Odo. 1979. "Identität: Schwundtelos und Mini-Essenz – Bemerkungen zur Genealogie einer aktuellen Diskussion. " *Identität.* Eds. *idem* & Karlheinz Stierle. München: Fink, 347-69.

Marx, Anthony. 1998. *Making Race and Nation: A Comparison of South Africa, the United States, and Brazil.* Cambridge: Cambridge UP.

Marx, Karl. 1977. "The Poverty of Philosophy." *Karl Marx Selected Writings.* Ed. David McLellan. Oxford: Oxford UP, 195-215.

Matlou, Rebecca. 1987. "The South African Woman Writer: In so Far as a Separate Entity." *Liberation and the Art of Writing: First Conference on South African English Literature, November 7-9, 1986* (Dokumente, Texte und Tendenzen 7). N.p.: Evangelische Akademie Bad Boll, 65-78.

McClintock, Anne. 1994. "The Angel of Progress: Pitfalls of the Term 'Postcolonialism'." *Colonial Discourse/Postcolonial Theory.* Eds. Francis Barker, Peter Hulme & Margaret Iversen. Manchester & New York: Manchester UP, 253-66.

McKay, Kim. 1987. "*The Blood Knot* Reborn in the Eighties: A Reflection of the Artist and his Times." *Modern Drama* 30.4: 496-504.

McLaren, Robert (Mshengu Kavanagh). 1996. "The Many Individual Wills": From *Crossroads* to *Survival*: The Work of Experimental Theatre Workshop '71." *Theatre and Change in South Africa*. Eds. Geoffrey V. Davis & Anne Fuchs. Amsterdam: Harwood Academic, 25-48.

McNaughton, Howard. 1994. "The Speaking Abject: The Impossible Possible World of Realized Empire." *De-Scribing Empire: Post-colonialism and Textuality*. London: Routledge, 218-29.

Mda, Zakes. 1993. *When People Play People: Development Communication through Theatre.* London & New Jersey: Zed; Johannesburg: Witwatersrand UP.

--------. 1994. "Maratholi Travelling Theatre: Towards an Alternative Perspective of Development." *Politics and Performance: Theatre, Poetry and Song in Southern Africa.* Ed. Liz Gunnar. Johannesburg: Witwatersrand UP, 203-10.

--------. 1996. "Politics and the Theatre: Current Trends in South Africa." *Theatre and Change in South Africa*. Eds. Geoffrey V. Davis & Anne Fuchs. Amsterdam: Harwood Academic, 192-217.

--------. 1998. "Current Trends in Theatre for Development in South Africa". *Writing South Africa: Literature, Apartheid, and Democracy, 1970-1995*. Eds. Derek Attridge & Rosemary Jolly. Cambridge: UP, 257-64.

--------. n.d. *Maratholi Travelling Theatre: The Theatre-for-Development Project of the National University of Lesotho*. Lesotho: Mazenod Institute.

Mead, George Herbert. 1957[15] *Mind, Self and Society: From the Standpoint of a Social Behaviorist*. Ed. Charles W. Morris. Chicago & London: U of Chicago P.

Meer, Shamim. 1997. "Introduction." *Women, Land and Authority: Perspectives from South Africa*. Ed. *idem*. Oxford: Oxfam; Claremont: David Philip, in association with the National Land Committee, Braamfontein, 1-14.

Meli, Francis. 1988. *South Africa Belongs to Us: A History of the ANC.* Harare: Zimbabwe Publishing House.

Mengel, Ewald. 1978. *Harold Pinters Dramen im Spiegel der soziologischen Rollentheorie.* Frankfurt am Main: Peter Lang.

Merton, Robert K. 1967. *Social Theory and Social Structure*. Rev. & enlarged ed. New York: Free P.

Mhlophe, Gcina. 1994. "Interview with Gcina Mhlophe." Interview with Tyrone August. *Politics and Performance: Theatre, Poetry and Song in Southern Africa.* Ed. Liz Gunnar. Johannesburg: Witwatersrand UP, 273-84.

Mhlophe, Gcina. 1996. "Gcina Mhlophe Interviewed on 7 December 1994." *Reflections: Perspectives on Writing in Post-Apartheid South Africa.* Eds. Rolf Solberg & Malcolm Hacksley. Grahamstown: NELM, 26-37.

--------. 1999a. Interview with Miki Flockemann and Thuli Mazibuko. "Between Women – An Interview with Gcina Mhlophe." *Contemporary Theatre Review* 9.1: 41-51.

--------. 1999b. Interview with Dennis Walder. "The Number of Girls is Growing – An Interview with Gcina Mhlophe." *Contemporary Theatre Review* 9.1: 27-39.

Miles, Robert. 1989. *Racism*. London: Routledge.

Minervini, Rina. 1987. "Sharing a Part of Someone's Life." *Sunday Star* [Johannesburg] 12 July: 15.

Minh-ha, Trinh T. 1989. *Women, Native, Other: Writing Postcoloniality and Feminism.* Bloomington & Indianapolis: Indiana UP.

Mishra, Vijay & Bob Hodge. 1994 [1991]. "What is Post(-)colonialism?" *Textual Practice* 5.3: 399-414. Rpt. in *Colonial Discourse and Post-Colonial Theory: A Reader.* Ed. & intro. Patrick Williams & Laura Chrisman. New York: Columbia UP, 276-90.

Mofokeng, Boitumelo, Nise Malange & Roseline Naapo. N.d. "Women Worker Writers: Breaking the Silence." *Buang Basadi, Khulumani Makhosikazi, Women Speak: Conference on Women and Writing.* Proceedings of the 1988 Conference on Women and Writing hosted by the Congress of South African Women Transvaal Region. N.p.: COSAW, 6-18.

Moodie, T. Dunbar. 1975. *The Rise of Afrikanerdom: Power, Apartheid, and the Afrikaner Civil Religion.* Berkeley, Los Angeles & London: U of California P.

Mooki, Bob. 1986. "Popular Theatre and Struggle." *Rixaca* 1: 4-7.

Moore, Basil, ed. 1973. *Black Theology: The South African Voice*. London: Hurst & Co.

Motanyane, Maud. 1986. "Hilarious but Full of Power." *Weekend Argus* [Cape Town] 5 Apr.: 4.

Mshengu (Robert McLaren Kavanagh). 1976. "South Africa: Where Mvelinqangi Still Limps: The Experimental Theatre of Workshop '71." *Yale/Theatre* 8.1: 38-48.

--------. 1977/78. "Tradition and Innovation in the Theatre of Workshop '71." *Theatre Quarterly* 28: 63-66.

--------. 1979. "After Soweto: People's Theatre and the Political Struggle in South Africa." *Theatre Quarterly* 33: 31-38.

--------. 1982. "Political Theatre in South Africa and the Work of Athol Fugard." *Theatrical Research International* 7.3: 160-79.

Mthoba, James & Themba Ntinga. 1973. "Seventy One in Seventy Three: Two Members of Workshop '71 Speak Out." *S'ketsh'* Summer: 46.

Mtwa, Percy. 1988. "'I've been an entertainer throughout my life...': An Interview with Percy Mtwa." Interview with Eckhard Breitinger. *Matatu* 3&4: 160-75.

Mudimbe, Valentine Y. 1988. *The Invention of Africa: Gnosis, Philosophy and the Order of Knowledge.* Bloomington & Indianapolis: Indiana UP.

Müller, Kurt. 1991. *Identität und Rolle bei Theodore Dreiser: Eine Untersuchung des Romanwerks unter rollentheoretischem Aspekt*. Paderborn et al.: Schönigh

Munro, Margaret. 1981. "The Fertility of Despair: Fugard's Bitter Aloes." *Meanjin* 40.4: 472-79.

Ndebele, Njabulo S. "The Rediscovery of the Ordinary: Some New Writings in South Africa." *South African Literature and Culture: Rediscovery of the Ordinary*. Intro. Graham Pechey. Manchester & New York: Manchester UP, 41-59.

Ndlovu, Duma, ed. 1986. *Woza Afrika! An Anthology of South African Plays*. Forewordby Wole Soyinka. Preface Amiri Baraka. New York: George Brazillier.

Neal, Larry. 1989. *Visions of a Liberated Future: Black Arts Movement Writings*. Commentary by Amiri Baraka, Stanley Crouch, Charles Fuller and Jayne Cortez. Ed. Michael Schwartz. New York: Thunder Mouth.

Nkosi, Lewis. 1983. *Home and Exile and Other Selections*. London & New York: Longman.

Nkululeko, Dabi. 1987. "The Right to Self-Determination in Research: Azania and Azanian Women." *Women in Southern Africa*. Ed. Christine Qunta. London & New York: Allison & Busby, 88-106.

Nnaemeka, Obioma, ed. 1997. "Introduction: Imag(in)ing Knowledge, Power, and Subversion in the Margins." *The Politics of (M)Othering: Womanhood, Identity, and Resistance in African Literature.* Ed. *idem*. London & New York: Routledge, 1-25.

O'Sheel, Patrick. 1978. "Athol Fugard's 'Poor Theatre'." *Journal of Commonwealth Literature* 12.3, 67-77.

Oberle, Martha. 1996. "'The More Things Change': Fourteenth-Century Yorkshire and Twentieth-Century South Africa." *Mittelalter-Rezeption V: Gesammelte Vorträge des V. Salzburger Symposiums.* Eds. Ulrich Müller & Kathleen Verduin. Göppingen: Kümmerle, 214-24.

Ojo-Ade, Femi. 1996. "Contemporary South African Theatre & the Complexities of Commitment." New Trends and Generations in African Literature. Eds. Eldred Durosimi Jones & Marjorie Jones. London: James Curry; Trenton, NJ: Africa World P, 120-34.

Okafor, C.G. 1989. "Of Spooks and Virile Men: Patterns of Response to Imperialism in *Sizwe Bansi is Dead* and *The Trial of Dedan Kimathi*." *Commonwealth Essays and Studies* 12: 87-94.

Oliphant, Andries. 1992. "*Isolate the Enemy*: Community and Conflict in Popular Theatre." *South African Theatre Journal* 6.2: 18-29.

O'Meara, Dan. 1983. *Volkskapitalisme: Class, Capital and Ideology in the Development of Afrikaner Nationalism, 1934-1948*. Cambridge: Cambridge UP.

Ong, Walter J. 1982. *Orality and Literacy : The Technologizing of the Word*. London & New York: Methuen.

Orkin, Martin. 1988. "Body and State in *Blood Knot/The Blood Knot*." *South African Theatre Journal* 2.1: 17-34.

--------. 1991. *Drama and the South African State*. Manchester: UP.

--------. 1996. "Whose Popular Theatre and Performance?" *Theatre and Change in South Africa*. Eds. Geoffrey V. Davis & Anne Fuchs. Amsterdam: Harwood Academic, 49-64.

--------. 2001. "General Introduction." *At the Junction*. Junction Avenue Theatre Company. Ed. & intro. Martin Orkin. Johannesburg: Witwatersrand UP, 1-12.

Parris-Bailey, Linda & Gcina Mhlophe. 1990. Interview with Patrick Kagan-Moore. "The Zandile Project. A Collaboration Between UT, Carpetbag Theatre, and South African Playwright Gcina Mhlophe." *The Drama Review: TDR* 34: 115-30.

Parsons, Talcott. 1967. *The Structure of Social Action: A Study in Social Theory with Specific Reference to a Group of Recent European Writers*. New York: Free Press; London: Collier-Macmillan.

Pechey, Graham. 1994. "Post-apartheid Narratives." *Colonial Discourse/Postcolonial Theory*. Eds. Francis Barker, Peter Hulme & Margaret Iversen. Manchester & New York: Manchester UP, 151-71.

Peck, Richard. 1997. *A Morbid Fascination: White Prose and Politics in Apartheid South Africa*. Westport, CT & London: Greenwood.

Pennycook, Alastair. 1998. *English and the Discourses of Colonialism*. London & New York: Routledge.

Perdekamp, Gabriele Grosse. 2003[2]. "Junction Avenue Theatre Company's *Tooth & Nail:* The State of 'Interregnum' and New Theatre Forms in South Africa." *Theatre and Performance in Africa: Intercultural Perspectives*. Ed. Eckard Breitinger. Bayreuth: Bayreuth African Studies, 161-65.

Peterson, Bhekizizwe. 1990. "Apartheid and the Political Imagination in Black South African Theatre." *Journal of Southern African Studies* 16.2: 229-45.

Peterson, Bhekizizwe. 1995. "'A Rain a Fall but the Dirt it Tough': Scholarship on African Theatre in South Africa." *Journal of Southern African Studies* 21.4: 573-84.

Pieterse, Cosmo. 1982 [1976]. "Notes on Athol Fugard." *Quarterly Journal of Africanist Opinion* 6.1. Rpt. in *Athol Fugard*. Ed. Stephen Gray. Johannesburg: McGraw-Hill, 198-201.

Pityana, Barney. 1972. "Power and Social Change in South Africa." *Student Perspectives on South Africa*. Eds. Hendrik van der Merwe & David Walsh. Cape Town: David Philip: 174-89.

Plessner, Helmuth. 1966. "Soziale Rolle und Menschliche Natur." *Diesseits der Utopie: Ausgewählte Beiträge zur Kultursoziologie*. Düsseldorf & Köln: Diedrichs, 23-35.

Posel, Deborah. 1991. *The Making of Apartheid 1948-1961: Conflict and Compromise*. Oxford: Clarendon.

--------. 1995. "The Meaning of Apartheid Before 1948: Conflicting Interests and Forces within the Afrikaner Nationalist Alliance." *Segregation and Apartheid in Twentieth-Century South Africa*. Eds. William Beinart & Saul Dubow. London & New York: Routledge, 206-30.

Post, Robert M. 1985. "Victims in the Writing of Athol Fugard." *ARIEL* 16.3: 3-17.

Purkey Malcom & Carol Steinberg. 2000. "Introduction." *Love, Crime and Johannesburg*. Junction Avenue Theatre Company. Witwatersrand UP, vii-xiv.

Purkey, Malcolm. 1984. "Drama in Education: - *Gandhi in South Africa: The Play*." *English Academy Review* 2: 61-67.

--------. 1993. "*Sophiatown* – The Play." *Sophiatown*. Junction Avenue Theatre Company. Eds. *idem* & Pippa Stein. Intro. Malcolm Purkey. Johannesburg: Witwatersrand UP, xi-xv.

--------. 1995. "En Souvenir de Sophiatown: Entretien avec Malcom Purkey." Interview with Denise Coussy. Trans. Pauline Baggio. *Notre Librairie: Revue Du Livre: Afrique, Caraïbes, Océan Indien* 123: 122-27.

--------. 1996. "*Tooth and Nail*: Rethinking Form for the South African Theatre." *Theatre and Change in South Africa*. Eds. Geoffrey V. Davis & Anne Fuchs. Amsterdam: Harwood Academic, 155-72.

Qunta, Christine. 1987. *Women in Southern Africa*. London & New York: Allison & Busby.

Rapp, Uri. 1973. *Handeln und Zuschauen: Untersuchungen über den theatersoziologischen Aspekt in der menschlichen Kommunikation*. Darmstadt & Neuwied: Luchterhand.

Rapp, Uri. 1993. *Rolle, Interaktion, Spiel: Eine Einführung in die Theatersoziologie*. Wien, Köln & Weimar: Böhlau.

Reckwitz, Erhard. 1996 [1995]. "Südafrikanische Literatur und the *Politics of the Other*." *Anglistik: Mitteilungen des Verbandes Deutscher Anglisten*. Ed. Rüdiger Ahrens. Heidelberg: Winter, 6.2: 35-50. Rpt. in *1985-1995: Ten Years of South African Literary Studies at Essen University; Selected Essays*. Eds. Elmar Lehmann, *idem* & Lucia Vennarini. Essen: Blaue Eule, 277-92.

Rich, Adrienne. 1997 [1977]. *Of Woman Born: Motherhood as Experience and Institution*. London: Virago.

Rich, Frank. 1986. "Stage: Tale of Apartheid, *Born in the R.S.A.*" *New York Times* 3 Oct.: C3.

Rivkin, Elizabeth Thaele. 1985. "The Black Woman in South Africa: An Azanian Profile." *The Black Woman Cross-Culturally*. Ed. Filomina Chioma Steady. Cambridge, MA: Schenkman, 215-29.

Roberts, Sheila. 1982. "'No Lessons Learnt': Reading the Texts of Fugard's *A Lesson from Aloes* and *Master Harold . . . and the Boys*." *English in Africa* 9.2: 27-33.

Robinson, Amy. 1994. "It Takes One to Know One: Passing and Communities of Common Interest." *Critical Inquiry* 20: 715-36.

Roux, Edward. 1964. *TimeLlonger than Rope: A History of the Black Man's Struggle for Freedom in South Africa.* Madison: U of Wisconsin P.

Rutherford, Anna. 1976. "Time, Space and Identity in Athol Fugard's *The Blood* Knot." *Neo-African Literature and Culture: Essays in Memory of Janheinz Jahn*. Eds. Bernth Lindfors & Ulla Schild. Wiesbaden: Heymann, 267-84.

Sachs, Albie. 1990. *Protecting Human rights in a New South Africa: Contemporary South African Debates.* Cape Town: OUP.

Said, Edward.1979. *Orientalism*. New York: Vintage.

Sanders, Leslie Catherine. 1988. *The Development of Black Theater in America: From Shadows to Selves.* Baton Rouge & London: Louisiana State UP.

SASO. 1971. "The Theatre and Black South Africa." SASO Newsletter (June).

Schechner, Richard. 1977. "Towards a Poetics of Performance." *Essays on Performance Theory 1970-1976*. New York: Drama Book Specialists, 108-39.

--------. 1988a. "Approaches." *Performance Theory*. Rev. & expanded ed. New York & London: Routledge, 1-34.

--------. 1988b. "Drama, Script, Theatre, and Performance." *Performance Theory*. Rev. & expanded ed. New York & London: Routledge, 68-105.

Schechner, Richard. 1988c. "Toward a Poetics of Performance." *Performance Theory*. Rev. & expanded ed. New York & London: Routledge, 153-86.

--------. 1988d. "Selective Inattention." *Performance Theory*. Rev. & expanded ed. New York & London: Routledge, 187-206.

Scheub, Harold. 1975. *The Xhosa Ntsomi*. Oxford: Claredon.

--------. 1977. "Body and Image in Oral Narrative Performance." *New Literary History* 8.3: 345-67.

Schwanitz, Dietrich.1977. *Die Wirklichkeit der Inszenierung und die Inszenierung der Wirklichkeit*. Meisenheim am Glan: Hain.

Schwartz, Pat. 1988: *The Best of Company: The Story of Johannesburg's Market Theatre*. Craighall: Ad Donker.

--------. 1989a. "Grey – It Comes Out in the Wash." *Weekly Mail* [Johannesburg] 23 June: 27.

--------. 1989b. "Humour, Tragedy in a Salon Mirror." *Weekly Mail* [Johannesburg] 30 June: 25.

--------. 1993. "Sophiatown – The Place." *Sophiatown*. Junction Avenue Theatre Company. Eds. Malcolm Purkey & Pippa Stein. Johannesburg: Witwatersrand UP, iv-x.

--------. 1997. "Introduction: Barney Simon." *Born in the RSA: Four Workshopped Plays*. Barney Simon. Johannesburg: Witwatersrand UP, xi-xxvi.

Seidenspinner, Margarete. 1986. *Exploring the Labyrinth: Athol Fugard's Approach to South African Drama*. Essen: Blaue Eule.

Sepamla, Sidney. 1973. "Sizwe Bansi." Review. *S'ketsh'*: 24.

Seymour, Hilary. 1980. "*Sizwe Bansi is Dead*: A Study of Artistic Ambivalence." *Race and Class* 21.3: 273-89.

Shava, Piniel Viriri. 1989. *A People's Voice: Black South African Writing in the Twentieth Century*. London: Zed; Athens: Ohio UP.

Sher, Emil. 1987. "Apartheid on Tour." *Canadian Theatre Review* 50: 59-62.

Sibikwa. n.d. *Sibikwa Community Theatre Project*. Benoni: n.p. [information brochure, 2001].

Sichel, Adrienne. 1984. "A 'Tender Shout' from Barney." *Star* [Johannesburg] 14 May: 10.

Simon, Barney. 1995a. "'One Point of Sanity': An Interview with Barney Simon." Interview with Joanne Tompkins. *South African Theatre Journal* 9.2: 83-96.

--------. 1995b. "This is Where the Life is: Impressions on the New South Africa." Interview with Anna Deavere Smith. *American Theatre* 12(5): 14-21, 67.

Simon, Barney. 1996. "'This Compost Heap of a Country.' An Interview with Barney Simon." An Interview with Geoffrey V. Davis & Anne Fuchs. *Theatre and Change in South Africa*. Eds. Geoffrey V. Davis & Anne Fuchs. Amsterdam: Harwood Academic, 225-241.

Sirayi, Mzo. 1996. "Oral African Drama in South Africa: The Xhosa Indigenous Drama Forms." *South African Theatre Journal* 10.1: 49-61.

Sitas, Ari. 1996a. "Description of a Struggle: South African Theatre Since 1970." *World Literature Today* 70.1: 83-7.

Sitas, Ari. 1996b. "The Worker's Theatre in Natal." *Theatre and Change in South Africa*. Eds. Geoffrey V. Davis & Anne Fuchs. Amsterdam: Harwood Academic, 132-39.

Six, Bernd. 1987. "Stereotype und Vorurteile im Kontext sozialpsychologischer Forschung." *Erstarrtes Denken: Studien zu Klischee, Stereotyp und Vorurteil in englischsprachiger Literatur*. Ed. Günther Blaicher. Tübingen: Narr, 41-54.

Slemon, Stephen. 1989. "Modernism's Last Post." *ARIEL* 20.4: 3-17.

Smiley, Sam. 1972. *The Drama of Attack: Didactic Plays of the American Depression*. Columbia: U of Missouri P.

Smit, Johannes A., Johan Van Wyk & Jean-Phillippe Wade. 1996. *Rethinking South African Literary History*. Durban: Y Press.

Snail, Mgebwi Lavin. 1993. *The Antecedens* [*sic*] *and the Emergence of the Black Consciousness Movement in South Africa – its Ideology and Organisat*ion. München: Akademischer Verlag.

Solberg, Rolf. 1999. *Alternative Theatre in South Africa: Talks with Prime Movers since the 1970s*. Scottsville: Hadeda.

Sole, Kelwyn. 1983. "Culture, Politics and the Black Writer: A Critical Look at Prevailing Assumptions." *English in Africa* 10: 37-84.

--------. 1984. "Black Literature and Performance: Some Notes on Class and Populism." *South African Labour Bulletin* 9.8: 54-76.

--------. 1987a. "Identities and Priorities in Recent Black Literature and Performance: A Preliminary Investigation." *South African Theatre Journal* 1.1: 45-113.

--------. 1987b. "Oral Performance and Social Struggle in Contemporary Black South African Literature." *TriQuarterly* 69 (special issue: *From South Africa: New Writing, Photographs and Art*. Eds. David Bunn & Jane Taylor with Reginald Gibbons & Sterling Plump. Evanston, Northwestern U), 254-71.

Sono, Themba. 1993. *Reflections on the Origins of Black Consciousness in South Africa*. Pretoria: HSRC.

Soule, Lesley Wade. 1998. "Performing Identities (Empowering Performers and Spectators)." *Theatre Praxis: Teaching Drama Through Practice*. Ed. Christopher McCullough. New York: St. Martin's P, 38-61.

Spacks, Patricia Meyer. 1986. *Gossip*. Chicago & London: U of Chicago P.

Spittler, Gerd. 1967. *Norm und Sanktion: Untersuchungen zum Sanktionsmechanismus*. Ed. Heinrich Popitz. Olten: Walter.

Spivak, Gayarti Chakravorty. 1988. "Can the Subaltern Speak?" *Marxism and the Interpretation of Culture*. Eds. Cary Nelson & Laurence Grossberg. Houndsmills: Macmillan, 271-313.

Stallybrass, Peter & Allon White. 1986. *The Politics and Poetics of Transgression*. London: Methuen.

Steadman, Ian. 1981. "Editorial: Culture and Context: Notes on Performance in South Africa." *Critical Arts* 2.1: 1-11.

--------. 1984a. "Alternative Politics, Alternative Performance: 1976 and Black South African Theatre." *Momentum: On Recent South African Writing*. Eds. M.J. Daymond, J.U. Jacobs, Margaret Lenta. Pietermaritzburg: U of Natal P, 215-32.

--------. 1984b. "Alternative Theatre: Fifty Years of Performance in Johannesburg." *Literature and Society in South Africa*. Eds. Landeg White & Tim Couzens. Burnt Mill, Harlow: Longman, 138-145.

--------. 1984c. "Black South African Theatre after Nationalism." *English Academy Review* 2: 9-18.

--------. 1985. *Drama and Social Consciousness: Themes in Black Theatre on the Witwatersrand until 1984*. Ph.D. thesis, University of the Witwatersrand, Johannesburg.

--------. 1986. *Popular Culture and Performance in South Africa*. Durban: University of Natal Contemporary Cultural Studies Unit.

--------. 1990a. "Collective Creativity: Theatre for a Post-Apartheid Society" *Rendering Things Visible: Essays on South African Literary Culture*. Ed. Martin Trump. Johannesburg: Ravan, 307-21.

--------. 1990b. "Towards Popular Theatre in South Africa." *Journal of Southern African Studies* 16.2: 208-28.

--------. 1991. "Theater Beyond Apartheid." *Research in African Literatures* 22: 77-90.

--------. 1992a. "Performance and Politics in Process: Practices of Representation in South African Theatre." *Theatre Survey* 33: 188-210.

--------. 1992b. "The Uses of Theatre." *South African Theatre Journal* 6.1: 33-45.

Steadman, Ian. 1994. "Black Theatre in South Africa." *Wasafiri* 19: 26-30.

--------. 1998. "Race Matters in South African Theatre." *Theatre Matters: Performance and Culture on the World Stage.* Eds. Richard Boon & Jane Plastow. Cambridge: Cambridge UP, 55-75.

Stein, Pippa & Ruth Jacobson. 1986. *Sophiatown Speaks. Father Trevor Huddleston, Don Mattera, Nadine Gordimer, Es'kia Mphahlele, Anthony Sampson, Arthur Maimane, Kort Boy, Phillip Stein, Jane Dakile Interviewed by Junction Avenue Theatre Company.* Johannesburg: Junction Avenue Press.

Steinberg, Carol. 1996 [1992]. "Now is the Time for Feminist Criticism: Reviewing *Asinamali*!" *Feminist Review* 41. Rpt. in *South African Feminisms: Writing, Theory, and Criticism, 1990-1994.* Ed. M.J. Daymond. New York & London: Garland, 313-26.

Swanson, Maynard W. 1995. "The Sanitation Syndrome: Bubonic Plague and Urban Native Policy in the Cape Colony, 1900-1909." *Segregation and Apartheid in Twentieth-Century South Africa.* Eds. William Beinart & Saul Dubow. London & New York: Routledge, 25-42.

Swiderski, Richard M. 1993. *Teaching Language, Learning Culture.* Westport, CT & London: Bergin & Garvey.

Szondi, Peter. 1965. *Theorie des modernen Dramas (1880-1950).* Frankfurt am Main: Suhrkamp.

Taylor, Jane. 1998. "Writer's Note." *Ubu and the Truth Commission.* Ed. *idem.* From the Production by William Kentridge and The Handspring Puppet Company. Cape Town: U of Cape Town P, ii-vii.

Thamm, Marianne. 1986. "Hacking at Illusion." *Cape Times* [Cape Town] 20 Mar.: 6.

--------. 1989. "Comic, Ultimately Sad Tale of Class Struggle." *Cape Times* [Cape Town] 16 Sep.: 22.

Thompson, Leonard Monteath. 1995. *A History of South Africa.* Rev. ed. New Haven: Yale UP.

Tiffin, Chris & Alan Lawson. 1994. "Introduction: The Textuality of Empire." *De-Scribing Empire: Post-Colonialism and Textuality.* Eds. *idem.* London & New York: Routledge, 1-11.

Tomaselli, Keyan G. & Johan Muller. 1987. "Class, Race and Oppression: Metaphor and Metonymy in 'Black' South African Theatre." *Critical Arts* 4.3: 40-58.

Tomaselli, Keyan G. 1980. "Black South African Theatre: Text & Context." *English in Africa* 8.1: 51-57.

Tomaselli, Keyan G. 1981a. “From the Laser to the Candle. Ilanga Le So Phonela Abasebanzi: an Example in the Devolution of Theatre.” *South African Labour Bulletin* 6(6): 64-70.

--------. 1981b. “The Semiotics of Alternative Theatre in South Africa.” *Critical Arts* 2.1: 14-33.

--------. 1982. “Theatre, Repression and the Working Class in South Africa.” *Kunapipi* 4.2: 139-45.

Tompkins, Joanne. 1995. “‘Spectacular Resistance’: Metatheatre in Post-Colonial Drama.” *Modern Drama* 38: 42-51.

Tompkins, Joanne. 1998. “Dressing Up/Dressing Down: Cultural Transvestism in Post-Colonial Drama.” *The Body in the Library*. Eds. Leigh Dale & Simon Ryan. Amsterdam & Atlanta: Rodopi: 185-94.

Tucker, Robert C., ed. 1978[2]. *The Marx-Engels Reader*. New York & London: Norton & Co.

Turner, Victor. 1974. *Dramas, Fields, and Metaphors: Symbolic Action in Human Society.* Ithaca & London. Cornell UP.

--------. 1986. *The Anthropology of Performance.* Preface by Richard Schechner. New York: PAJ Publications.

--------. 1990. “Are There Universals of Performance in Myth, Ritual, and Drama?” *By Means of Performance: Intercultural Studies of Theatre and Ritual.* Eds. Richard Schechner & Willa Appel. Cambridge et al.: UP, 8-18.

Valdes, Joyce Merrill, ed. 1986. *Culture Bound: Bridging the Cultural Gap in Language Teaching.* Cambridge et al.: Cambridge UP.

Van Deburg, William L. 1992. *New Day in Babylon: The Black Power Movement and American Culture, 1965-1975.* Chicago & London: U of Chicago P.

Van Rooyen, Brenda. 1989. “Susan Pam: Making her Play Work for Theatre.” *Pretoria News* 28 June: 8.

Van Zyl Slabbert, F. 1976. “Afrikaner Nationalism, White Politics, and Political Change in South Africa.” *Change in Contemporary South Africa*. Eds. Leonard Thompson & Jeffrey Butler. Berkeley & Los Angeles: U of California P, 3-18.

Vandenbroucke, Russell. 1976. “South African Blacksploitation” *Yale/Theatre* 8.1: 68-71.

--------. 1977/78. “Chiaroscuro: A Portrait of the South African Theatre.” *Theatre Quarterly* 28: 46-54.

--------. 1985. *Truths the Hand Can Touch – The Theatre of Athol Fugard.* New York: Theatre Communications Group.

Vandenbroucke, Russell. 1992. "Fugard and the Politics of Human Dignity: A Note on *Boesman and Lena* and *The Island*." *Perspectives on South African English Literature*. Eds. Michael Chapman, Colin Gardner & Es'kia Mphahlele. Parklands: Ad Donker, 301-13.

Von Kotze, Astrid. 1984. "Workshop Plays as Worker Education." South African Labour Bulletin 9.8: 92-111.

--------. 1988. *Organise and Act. The Natal Workers' Theatre Movement 1983-1987*. Durban: Culture and Working Life Publications.

Wakashe, T. Philemon. 1986. "*Pula*: An Example of Black Protest Theatre in South Africa." *The Drama Review: TDR* 30.4: 36-47.

Walder, Dennis. 1984. *Athol Fugard*. London: Macmillan.

--------. 1992. "Resituating Fugard: South African Drama as Witness." *New Theatre Quarterly* 8.32: 343-61.

--------. 1993a. "Crossing Boundaries: The Genesis of the Township Plays." *Twentieth Century Literature* 39.4: 409-22.

--------. 1993b. "Introduction." *The Township Plays*. Athol Fugard. Ed. & intro. Dennis Walder. Oxford & Cape Town: Oxford UP, ix-xxxiv.

--------. 1994. "South African Drama and Ideology: The Case of Athol Fugard." *Altered State? Writing and South Africa*. Eds. Elleke Boehmer, Laura Chrisman & Kenneth Parker. Dangaroo: Sydney et al., 121-33.

--------. 1998a. *Post-apartheid Literatures in English: History, Language, Theory*. Oxford: Blackwell.

--------. 1998b. "Spinning Out the Present: Narrative, Gender, and the Politics of South African Theatre." *Writing South Africa: Literature, Apartheid, and Democracy 1970-1995*. Eds. Derek Attridge & Rosemary Jolly. Cambridge: UP, 204-20.

Walker, Alice. 1984. *In Search of our Mothers' Gardens: Womanist Prose*. San Diego: Harcourt Brace Jovanovich.

Walker, Cherryl, ed. 1990. *Women and Gender in Southern Africa to 1945*. Cape Town: David Philip; London: James Curry.

Walker, Cherryl. 1982. *Women and Resistance in South Africa*. London: Onyx.

Warren, Allen. 1987. "Popular Manliness: Baden Powell, Scouting and the Development of Manly Character." *Manliness and Morality: Middle-class Masculinity in Britain and America 1800-1940*. Eds. J. A. Mangan & James Walvin. Manchester: Manchester UP, 199-219.

Weales, Gerald. 1993. "Fugard Masters the Code." *Twentieth Century Literature* 39.4: 503-16.

Weimann, Robert. 1981. "Society and the Individual in Shakespeare's Conception of Character." *Shakespeare Survey* 34: 23-31.

Wells, Ronald A., ed. 1987. *Writer and Region: Athol Fugard.* New York: Anson Phelps Stokes Institute for African, Afro-American, and American Indian Affairs.

Wertheim, Albert. 1988. "The Lacerations of Apartheid: *A Lesson from Aloes*." *Text & Presentation. The University of Florida Department of Classics Comparative Drama Conference Papers, Vol. VIII.* Lanham, MD & London: UP of America, 211-21.

--------. 1986. "Political Acting and Political Action: Athol Fugard's *The Island.*" *WLWE* 26.2: 245-52.

Wertheim, Albert. 1987. "The Prison as Theatre and the Theatre as Prison: Athol Fugard's *The Island.*" *Themes in Drama*. Ed. James Redmond. Cambridge: Cambridge UP, 229-37.

--------. 2000. *The Dramatic Art of Athol Fugard: From South Africa to the World.* Bloomington: Indiana UP.

Whisson, David. 1997. "Ubu Fails to Challenge." *Daily Dispatch* [East London] 15 July: 7.

Wicomb, Zoë. 1996 [1990]. "To Hear the Variety of Discourses." *Current Writing* 2 (1990): 35-44. Rpt. in *South African Feminisms: Writing, Theory, and Criticism, 1990-1994.* Ed. M.J. Daymond. New York & London: Garland: 45-55.

Williams, Jenny. 1990. "Can *Our Nig* Help *The Native Who Caused All the Trouble*? Some Thoughts on a Theory which Proposes that a Knowledge of American 'Black' Writing Can Provide Insights Which are Useful in the Study of South African 'Black' Writing." *AUETSA Conference Papers Vol. II: South African Autobiographical Writing.* Conference held at the Universtiy of Stellenbosch, 1990. Stellenbosch: University of Stellenbosch, n.p.

Williams, Mance. 1985. *Black Theatre in the 1960s and 1970s: A Historical-Critical Analysis of the Movement.* Westport, CT & London: Greenwood.

Wishire, Bruce. 1982. *Role Playing and Identity: The Limits of Theatre as Metaphor.* Bloomington: Indiana UP.

Wiswede, Günter. 1977. *Rollentheorie*. Stuttgart et al.: Kohlhammer.

Wolpe, Harold. 1970. "Industrialism and Race in South Africa." *Race and Racialism*. Ed. Sami Zubaida. London et al.: Tavistock, 151-79.

--------. 1995. "Capitalism and Cheap Labour Power in South Africa: From Segregation to Apartheid." *Segregation and Apartheid in Twentieth-Century South Africa.* Eds. William Beinart & Saul Dubow. London & New York: Routledge, 60-90.

Woods, Donald. 1987. *Biko*. London: Penguin.

Worden, Nigel. 1994. *The Making of Modern South Africa. Conquest, Segregation and Apartheid.* Oxford & Cambridge, MA: Blackwell.

Workshop '71 (Dannyboy Maredi, Themba Ntinga, Seth Sibanda, David Kekana and director Mshengu). 1977. "Jailbird's Eyeview." Interview with Shirley Pendlebury. *Quarry '77: New South African Writing.* Eds. Lionel Abrahams & Walter Saunders. Johannesburg: Ad Donker, 123-27.

Worrall, Denis J. 1972. "Afrikaner Nationalism: A Contemporary Analysis." *Southern Africa in Perspective: Essays in Regional Politics.* Eds. Christian P. Potholm & Richard Dale. New York: Free Press; London: Collier-Macmillan, 19-30.

Wortham, Chris. 1983. "A Sense of Place: Home and Homelessness in the Plays of Athol Fugard." *Olive Schreiner and After: Essays on South African Literature in Honour of Guy Butler*. Eds. Malvern van Wyk Smith & Don Maclennan. Cape Town: David Philip, 165-83.

Zenani, Nongenile Masithathu. 1992. *The World and the Word: Tales and Observations from the Xhosa Oral Tradition.* Ed. Harold Scheub. Madison: U of Wisconsin P.

Zijderveld, Anton C. 1987. "On the Nature and Function of Clichés." *Erstarrtes Denken: Studien zu Klischee, Stereotyp und Vorurteil in englischsprachiger Literatur*. Ed. Günther Blaicher. Tübingen: Narr, 26-40.

Index

What the critics say....

„Bayreuth African Studies produces a stream of texts on African cultural issues that few British or American publishers appear able to rival... I wish to applaud the result of the endeavour"
Jane Plastow in ***African Theatre Playwrights and Politics***

„une collection riche en publications de grande qualité" Abdourahman Waberi in ***Hommes & Migration***

On BASS 30: Anglophone Cameroon Writing
„an important landmark in the critical discourse of Cameroon literature as a whole"
Teddy Ako in ***Cameroon Post***

ON BASS 31: Breitinger: Theatre and Performance in Africa
„presents an excellent array of texts, good to pass on to students and colleagues"
Gaurav Desai in ***Research in African Literature*** (USA)
„an important resource for all concerned with African Theatre"
Martin Banham in ***TheatreResearch International*** (UK)

On BASS 32 Derek Wright: *The Novels of Nuruddin Farah.*
"a landmark in the criticism of the African novel"
Jaqueline Bardolph in ***Research in African Literature*** (USA*)*
„an admirable first book on Farah and indispensable reading"
Journal of Commonwealth Literature (UK)
„a most reliable critic, a rigourous scholar and yet a clearly a fan of the author"
Stewart Brown in ***African Affairs*** (UK)
„ an insightful introduction to Farah's work. Chris Dunton in ***West Africa*** (UK)
„Readers of Farah are in Wright's debt for his research"
R.W. Dasenbrock in ***World Literature Today*** (USA)
„un rapporto attivo ed intelligente..con pregio di nuovi stimolanti interrogativi"
Maria Guarducci in ***Africa*** (Italy)

On BASS 39 Breitinger. Uganda: The Cultural Landscape
„Breitinger has done Isis work..gathered and remembered the scattered fragments – a rediscovered Rosetta stone" Peter Nazareth in ***World Literature Today*** (USA)

On BASS 40 Obafemi: Contemporary Nigerian Theatre
„Obafemi knows his subject very well and his passion for theatre is in no doubt"
Osita Okagube in ***African Theatre*** (UK*)*

On BASS 42 Wright: Contemporary African Fiction
„Wright's distinguished scholarship guarantees that the contributions are so various, engaging and scholarly" Anne Collet in ***New Literature Review*** (Australia)
„the articles demonstrate the complexity with which African writers relate to changing national landscapes and offer enlightening close reading" Cecilia Moretti in ***Review Journal*** (Australia)

On BASS 43 Kerr: Dance, Media Entertainment & Popular Theatre
„Kerr is writing provocative and thoughtful good sense"
Jane Plastow in ***African Theatre:Writers and Politics*** (UK*)*

On BASS 48 Arndt: African Women's Literature

On BASS 49 Rohmer: Theatre and Performance in Zimbabwe
„another welcome nail in the coffin of library based criticism of African theatre"
Jane Plastow in ***African Theatre***: (UK)

On BASS 55 Simatei: The Novel and the Politics of Nation Building
„a brilliant book" Peter Nazareth in ***World Literature Today*** (USA)

Bayreuth African Studies

ECKHARD BREITINGER
New and forthcoming titles
2004

BASS 60
Onookome Okome: (ed) ***Writing the Homeland:The Poetry and Politics of Tanure Ojaide***, 285 pp; ISBN 3-927510-67-X, EUR 22.95;

BASS 63
Bode Omojola: ***Studies in African Pianism*** 125 pp; ISBN 3-927510-76-9; EUR 10.95;

BASS 64
Bode Omojola ***Three Yoruba Sacred Choral Works***, pp 84, ISBN 3-927510-77-7; EUR 10.95

BASS 65
Renè Philombe: ***Bedi-Ngula, L'Ancien Maquisard*** – *Un Roman,* pp 315, ISBN 3-927510-78-5; EUR 22.95

BASS 66
Wole Ogundele: ***Omoluabi Ulli Beier, Yoruba Society and Culture***, 288 pp. ISBN 3-927510-79-3; EUR 22.95;

BASS 67
Ambroise Kom (ed): ***Remember Mongo Beti***, pp 285, ISBN 3-927510-80-7; EUR 24.95;

BASS 68
Wotsuna Khamalwa: ***Identity, Power, and Culture: Imbalu Initiantion among the Bamasaba in Uganda,*** ca. 280 pp, ISBN 3-927510-81-5; ca EUR 22.99; (February 2004)

BASS 69
Alexi Tcheuyap (ed.): ***Cinema and Social Discourse in Cameroon***, ca pp 220, ISBN 3-927510-82-3 EUR 22.59; (May 2004)

BASS 70
Haike Frank: ***Role-Play in South African Theatre***, ca 325 pp; ISBN 3-927510-83-1 ca. EUR 24.95; (February 2004)

BASS 71
Akintune Akinyemi: ***Yoruba Royal Poetry***, ca 410pp ISBN 3-927510-84-X, ca EUR 30.95 (April 2004)

Derek Wright ***The Novels of Nuruddin Farah*** now available in a revised, updated, enlarged edition with new chapters on *Secrets* and Farah's Non-fiction book. (ISBN 3-927510-85-8,EUR 18.95). When it first appeared, this study was praised as „a landmark" in criticism of postcolonial writers.
Revised, enlarged edition of Eckhard Breitinger (ed.)***Theatre and Performance in Africa*** (236 pp, ISBN 3-927510-73-4, EUR 23.95) with new article on Soyinka's *Area Boy*. „ An important source for African Theatre" – Martin Banham

orders to Bayreuth African Studies / Eckhard Breitinger
eckhard.breitinger@uni-bayreuth.de or
Fax: 49-921- 55 3627 or 49-921-30728.
University of Bayreuth D 95440 BAYREUTH
www.breitinger.org

e-mail: eckhard.breitinger@uni-bayreuth.de